Cold War and Decolonization in Guinea, 1946–1958

ELIZABETH SCHMIDT

Ohio University Press

ATHENS

I am indebted to Cambridge University Press for permission to reproduce
extracts from my article "Cold War in Guinea: The Rassemblement
Démocratique Africain and the Struggle over Communism, 1950–1958,"
Journal of African History 48, no. 1 (March 2007): 95–121.

Ohio University Press, Athens, Ohio 45701
www.ohio.edu/oupress
© 2007 by Ohio University Press

14 13 12 11 10 09 08 07   5 4 3 2 1

Library of Congress Cataloging-in-Publication Data

Schmidt, Elizabeth, 1955–
Cold War and decolonization in Guinea, 1946–1958 / Elizabeth Schmidt.
     p. cm. — (Western African studies)
  Includes bibliographical references and index.
  ISBN-13: 978-0-8214-1763-8 (hc : alk. paper)
  ISBN-10: 0-8214-1763-0 (hc : alk. paper)
  ISBN-13: 978-0-8214-1764-5 (pb : alk. paper)
  ISBN-10: 0-8214-1764-9 (pb : alk. paper)
  1. Decolonization—Guinea. 2. Guinea—History—Autonomy and
independence movements. 3. Rassemblement démocratique africain.
4. Guinea—Politics and government. I. Title.
DT543.75.S35 2007
966.52'03—dc22

                    2007030265

For my son
Jann Albert Grovogui,
who made this book a labor of love

Contents

Illustrations

The nature of the photographs in this collection requires an explanation. Although the book focuses on grassroots mobilization in the Guinean nationalist movement, few of the photographs are of local activists. Rather, most are of African political leaders, who were almost exclusively male elites, or of French men and women engaged in activities that had ramifications in Guinea. A number of factors coalesced to produce this ironic situation. In the 1950s, few photographs were taken of local activists in Guinea. Of those that were created, few survived. The French burned the government archives when they left Guinea in 1958, and the Guinean military demolished the party archives after the coup in 1984. Moisture, insects, rodents, and mold contributed to the damage as well. Documents and photographs that were not lost or destroyed often migrated into private collections. Photographs of party leaders, in contrast, were safely stored in French government and foreign newspaper archives outside of Guinea. Finally, photographs once housed in the privately run Centre de Recherche et de Documentation Africaine (CRDA) in Paris, which served as the RDA's unofficial archive, are no longer publicly accessible. The CRDA closed in the 1990s, and its document and photograph collection was shipped to the Ivory Coast, where it remains in storage.

Abbreviations

AERDA	Association des Étudiants RDA
AOF	Afrique Occidentale Française
BAG	Bloc Africain de Guinée
CATC	Confédération Africaine des Travailleurs Croyants
CGT	Confédération Générale du Travail
CGTA	Confédération Générale des Travailleurs Africains
CJA	Conseil de la Jeunesse d'Afrique
DSG	Démocratie Socialiste de Guinée
FEANF	Fédération des Étudiants d'Afrique Noire en France
FIDES	Fond d'Investissement pour le Développement Économique et Sociale des Territoires d'Outre-Mer
FLN	Front de Libération Nationale
FOM	France Outre-Mer
GEC	Groupe d'Études Communistes
IOM	Indépendants d'Outre-Mer
MRP	Mouvement Républicain Populaire
MSA	Mouvement Socialiste Africain
PCF	Parti Communiste Français
PDG	Parti Démocratique de Guinée
PPG	Parti Progressiste de Guinée
PRA	Parti du Regroupement Africain
PTT	Postal, Telegraph, and Telephone
RDA	Rassemblement Démocratique Africain
RJDA	Rassemblement de la Jeunesse Démocratique Africaine
RPF	Rassemblement du Peuple Français
SAA	Syndicat Agricole Africain
SDECE	Service de Documentation Extérieure et de Contre-Espionnage
SFIO	Section Française de l'Internationale Ouvrière
UDSR	Union Démocratique et Socialiste de la Résistance
UGEAO	Union Générale des Étudiants d'Afrique Occidentale
UGEEG	Union Générale des Étudiants et Élèves de Guinée
UGTAN	Union Générale des Travailleurs d'Afrique Noire
URR	Union des Républicains et Résistants

ARCHIVES

AG	Archives de Guinée
ANS	Archives Nationales du Sénégal
CAOM	Centre des Archives d'Outre-Mer, Archives Nationales de France
CARAN	Centre d'Accueil et de Recherche des Archives Nationales de France
CRDA	Centre de Recherche et de Documentation Africaine
IFAN	Institut Fondamental d'Afrique Noire

French Colonial Officials (1944–59)

Paul Béchard (Jan. 1948–May 1951)
Paul Chauvet (Acting, May 1951–Sept. 1952)
Bernard Cornut-Gentille (Sept. 1952–July 1956)
Gaston Cusin (July 1956–July 1958)
Pierre Messmer (July 1958–Dec. 1958)

GOVERNORS OF GUINEA (1944–58)

Jacques Fourneau (Acting, March 1944–April 1946)
Édouard Terrac (Acting, May 1946–Jan. 1948)
Roland Pré (Jan. 1948–Jan. 1951)
Paul-Henri Sirieux (Feb. 1951–Feb. 1953)
Xavier Antoine Torré (Feb. 1953–March 1953)
Jean Paul Parisot (Acting, April 1953 to Dec. 1953) (Confirmed, Dec. 1953–
    July 1955)
Charles-Henri Bonfils (Aug. 1955–Oct. 1956)
Jean Ramadier (Oct. 1956–Jan. 1958)
Jean Mauberna (Acting, Jan. 1958–Sept. 1958)

Note: The decree of May 4, 1946, changed the title "Governor General of French West Africa" to "High Commissioner of the Republic for French West Africa." The constitution of the Fourth Republic (October 1946) changed the title "Minister of Colonies" to "Minister of Overseas France."[1]

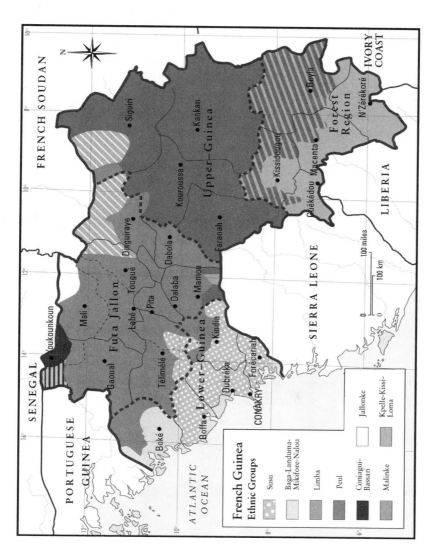

0.1 French Guinea. Cartographer, Malcolm Swanston. Reprinted by permission from *Mobilizing the Masses: Gender, Ethnicity, and Class in the Nationalist Movement in Guinea, 1939–1958*, by Elizabeth Schmidt. Copyright © 2005 by Elizabeth Schmidt. Published by Heinemann, a division of Reed Elsevier, Inc., Portsmouth NH. All rights reserved.

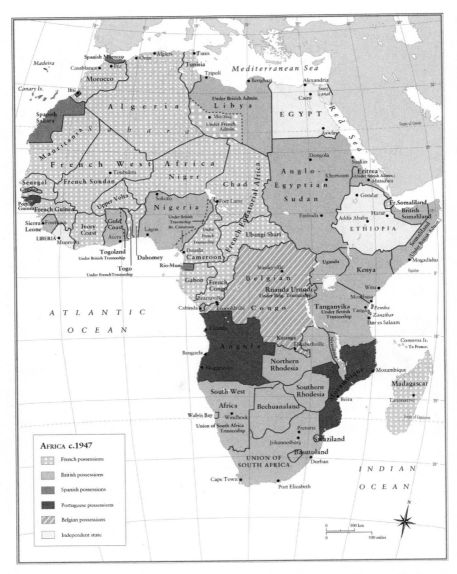

0.2 Africa, ca. 1947. Cartographer, Malcolm Swanston. Reprinted by permission from *Mobilizing the Masses: Gender, Ethnicity, and Class in the Nationalist Movement in Guinea, 1939–1958*, by Elizabeth Schmidt. Copyright © 2005 by Elizabeth Schmidt. Published by Heinemann, a division of Reed Elsevier, Inc., Portsmouth NH. All rights reserved.

Introduction

IN SEPTEMBER 1958, the French territory of Guinea claimed its independence. In a defiant "No" to France, the Guinean people, through a popular referendum, decisively rejected a constitution that would have relegated their country to junior partnership in a new French Community. Orchestrating the "No" vote was the Guinean branch of the Rassemblement Démocratique Africain (RDA), an interterritorial alliance of political parties with affiliates in most of the fourteen territories of French West Africa, French Equatorial Africa, and the United Nations trusts of Togo and Cameroon. In the whole of the French Empire, Guinea was the only territory to reject the constitution in favor of immediate independence.

Although Guinea's stance vis-à-vis the 1958 constitution has been recognized as unique, the historical roots of this phenomenon have not been adequately explained. Guinea's postwar political development can be understood only in the context of the Cold War, in which France was a key battleground. Deeply divided internally between communist and anticommunist forces, France was courted and pressured both by the United States and the Soviet Union.[1] Although neither superpower was involved in Guinea until the postindependence period, the "communist threat" was a major determinant of French colonial policy. In dire need of postwar economic aid, France was under enormous pressure from the United States to purge communists from its government, industry, and labor movement. France also was pushed to pursue domestic and foreign policies congruent with those of the United States—and in opposition to those of the Soviet Union.[2] France's choice of the West, and the ensuing crackdown on communists at home and their allies abroad, was the backdrop for the decolonization of Guinea and other territories throughout the French empire.

Guinea's vote for independence, and its break with the interterritorial RDA in this regard, were the culmination of a decade-long struggle between grassroots

1

activists and the party's territorial and interterritorial leadership for control of the political agenda. Since 1950, when RDA representatives in the French parliament severed their ties to the Parti Communiste Français (PCF), conservative elements had dominated the RDA. In Guinea, local cadres had opposed the break. Victimized by the administration and sidelined by their own leaders, they quietly rebuilt the party from the base. Their voices muted throughout most of the decade, leftist militants gained preeminence in 1958, when trade unionists, students, the party's women's and youth wings, and other grassroots actors pushed the Guinean RDA to endorse a "No" vote. Thus, Guinea's rejection of the proposed constitution in favor of immediate independence was not an isolated aberration. Rather, it was the outcome of years of political mobilization by grassroots militants who, despite Cold War repression, ultimately pushed the Guinean RDA to the Left.

THE SIGNIFICANCE OF THE PROJECT

As dozens of African colonies gained independence in the late 1950s and 1960s, scholars of Africa increasingly focused on the nationalist struggles that had led to this result. Most of the early studies paid little attention to the involvement of peasants, traders, and workers in the nationalist movements. Their subjects were primarily the Western-educated male elites who spearheaded the nationalist movements and assumed power after independence.[3] In the late 1960s, as social history gained prominence in the discipline, scholars of African nationalism began to shift their focus to "the role of ordinary . . . Africans."[4] They began to recognize that the success of the nationalist movements depended upon the ability of Western-educated elites to generate mass support, which they did by mobilizing around preexisting grievances and promising their resolution through the attainment of national independence.[5]

Most works on nationalism in French West Africa have focused on elite politics, with some reference to the key role played by the mass base.[6] Implicit in the majority of assessments is the erroneous assumption that the leaders called the shots and that the political positions taken by high-level nationalist leaders were mirrored in the views of their constituents. In the case of the RDA, many scholars have presumed that the accommodationist line promoted by Ivory Coast parliamentarian and interterritorial RDA president Félix Houphouët-Boigny was embraced by territorial branches and local sections, with the notable exception of Guinea in 1958.[7] These scholars generally have not recognized that the party line was the product of struggle, representing the domination of one point of view over others, accompanied by the silencing of opposing voices. An exception to this generalization are scholars who have noted the 1955 rift, when the Union Démocratique Nigérienne, Union Démocratique Sénégalaise, and Union des Populations du Cameroun were expelled from the RDA for refusing to sanction its break with the PCF.[8] While these scholars comment on disagreements within the highest echelons of the party, they fail to carry the discussion down to the grassroots, where the positions taken by territorial and interterritorial leaders were in dispute. Nor do they elaborate upon the long-term implications of the purge: By the time the 1958 constitutional referendum occurred, many of the RDA's most radical constituents already had been expunged.

In the case of Guinea, many scholars have assumed that the territorial RDA was radical from the outset, shaped by its charismatic secretary-general, Sékou Touré, who was supposed to have wielded absolute power over the party. For the most part, they have not understood that Sékou Touré was pushed to the Left by grassroots militants, particularly trade unionists, students, women, and youth—not the other way around. Deeply influenced by postindependence developments, Yves Person, Victor Du Bois, and Claude Rivière, for instance, conflate the Guinean RDA with the person of Sékou Touré, wrongly presupposing that he had autocratic power in the preindependence period and that he imposed his will on the party. They view Sékou Touré as a long-standing and unwavering leftist, rather than a pragmatic politician who responded to a progressive groundswell from the base.[9]

Other scholars, such as Ruth Schachter Morgenthau, Georges Chaffard, L. Gray Cowan, and Sylvain Soriba Camara, acknowledge that there was strife between rival RDA leaders, most notably Sékou Touré and Félix Houphouët-Boigny. However, they do not explore tensions between Guinean party leaders and the rank and file.[10] Ernest Milcent, Virginia Thompson and Richard Adloff, Thomas Hodgkin, and Tony Chafer allude to strains between the party base and leadership in Guinea, but they do not explore them in detail.[11] Although dedicated exclusively to Guinea, Sidiki Kobélé Kéïta's two-volume study and books by Jean Suret-Canale and 'Ladipo Adamolekun also fail to examine political fissures within the nationalist movement.[12] Most of my earlier work has considered gender, ethnic, and class divisions within the Guinean RDA, but not cleavages along the Left-Right political divide.[13] As a result of these omissions, none of the previously published work on Guinea permits us to assess adequately the implications of preindependence political divisions for postindependence nation-building.

This book stands received wisdom on its head and brings complexity to the often oversimplified Guinean case. Distinguishing between grassroots sentiments and leaders' pronouncements, it regards party positions as the product of struggle. The party's orientation was constantly challenged—from above, below, and outside. Rejecting the top-down approach inherent in the works cited above, I argue, first, that the positions taken by political leaders in Guinea were the result of pressure from the grassroots—not vice versa. Guinea's progressive politics emanated from the bottom, rather than the top. Second, although Sékou Touré had accumulated significant powers before independence, he did not monopolize decision-making. Local activists pushed Sékou Touré to the Left, even as he sought accommodation with both the interterritorial RDA and the colonial administration. Third, the Guinean RDA was not uniformly and consistently radical. Rather, its leftist tendency was the result of a protracted struggle. In the late 1940s and early 1950s, government repression—under the banner of anticommunism—wreaked havoc in the RDA. Claiming that moderation and accommodation were essential if the movement were to survive, conservative elements gained control of the party leadership. In most French West African territories, elite-run parties with shallow roots made peace with the colonial power. In Guinea, however, the RDA had built a solid grassroots organization. For nearly a decade, left-wing agitation continued at the local level. In September 1958, progressive activists finally won control of the political agenda.

In illuminating the Guinean case, this book will make a significant contribution to our understanding of both historical and contemporary Africa. It will help us to understand the difficulties encountered in postindependence nation-building, not only in Guinea, but in many parts of the developing world. If we are to understand contemporary Africa, with its strong antidemocratic tendencies and leadership crises, we must understand the dynamics of the independence process. We must reckon with the negative impact of the Cold War on democratic movements in Africa and elsewhere in the non-Western world. In many African territories, where local party structures were weak, party leaders invariably took matters into their own hands, unilaterally imposing their own agendas. Under severe pressure from colonial regimes, often sweetened by promises of privilege, many of these leaders collaborated in repressing the Left. Rewarded by colonial governments for their cooperation, these antidemocratic leaders frequently assumed the reins of power after independence.[14] In Guinea, where local party structures were strong, the antidemocratic actions of party leaders were effectively countered by mobilization at the grassroots. Although Guinea's democratic experiment failed after independence, it failed in spite of, not because of, the democratic character of the nationalist movement. Punitive policies by other nations, including coup attempts and an invasion, were part of the Cold War arsenal employed against the new Guinean government. Their impact on Sékou Touré's growing dictatorial tendencies is a subject that demands further scholarly investigation.[15]

The Organization of the Book

Viewing Guinea's postwar political scene through the Cold War lens, this book focuses on the period 1946–58. It assesses the local influence of the PCF, the impact of anti-RDA repression, the consequences of dissension within RDA ranks following the divorce from the PCF, and the phenomenon of grassroots party building as a prelude to the reemergence of the Left, which, by 1958, had become the dominant force in Guinean politics.

Focusing on the period 1946–50, with some reference to 1945, chapter 1 argues that France, humiliated and defeated during World War II, was determined to reassert its position as a great power in the war's aftermath. The maintenance of its empire was critical to the achievement of this status. However, French plans for greatness were threatened by African and Asian nationalist movements and by the emergence of the United States and the Soviet Union as the new world powers. The onset of the Cold War and the support of French communists and the Soviet Union for the anticolonial cause magnified French concerns. Under pressure in the colonies and in the international arena, France hoped to deter more radical solutions by reforming its empire. Examining Guinean politics in the Cold War context, this chapter considers the RDA-PCF alliance and the RDA's virtual destruction as a result of the government's "anticommunist" crackdown.

Covering the years 1950–53, chapter 2 explores the ways in which government persecution resulted in two contradictory reactions within the RDA. On the one hand, the repression of French communists and African RDA members seemed to underscore their common interests and substantiate the claim that only a communist government in France could lead to African emancipation. On the other hand, because the PCF was considered by the French government to be both dangerous and disloyal, the RDA was hurt rather than helped by its parliamentary alliance with the communists. Under duress, RDA parliamentarians severed their ties to the PCF and ordered their territorial branches to cut all remaining links to communist organizations. While the Guinean RDA ultimately complied with the parliamentarians' directive, its disavowal of the PCF alliance resulted in a rift between party leaders and more radical militants at the grass-roots.[16] The schism threatened to destroy the party. Doubtful of the RDA's sincerity, the government continued its campaign of repression.

Focusing on the years 1954–55, chapter 3 investigates the Guinean RDA's unsuccessful bid for a French National Assembly seat in June 1954 and the election's volatile aftermath. The legislative elections were widely believed to have been rigged. Chiefs, traditional elites, regional and ethnic associations, and government-supported parties benefitted from the electoral fraud. The years 1954–55 were marked by an upsurge in unrest as RDA supporters challenged chiefs, notables, and rival party members. Meanwhile, the government undertook a dual strategy of co-optation and repression, attempting to push the Guinean leadership to the Right while cracking down on local activists. The interterritorial RDA collaborated in the government's efforts, resulting in further disenchantment at the grassroots. Nonetheless, by 1955 it was evident that, despite repression and fraud, the Guinean RDA was far and away the most popular party in the territory. Even the governor was forced to conclude that the collaborationist parties had failed.

Chapters 4 examines the years 1956–57, when the French empire was under increasing pressure in both Africa and Asia. Once again, France hoped to salvage its empire by launching a program of imperial reform. In sub-Saharan Africa, France eased repression against nationalist movements and established a system of local self-government, according to the terms of *loi-cadre*. The Guinean RDA benefitted from the new policy of constructive collaboration, at least at the leadership level. In a wave of electoral victories, the RDA won two National Assembly seats, gained control of nearly all Guinea's major municipalities, and captured the vast majority of seats in the Territorial Assembly. The RDA dominated the local government established in 1957 under the reformed imperial system. However, accommodation with the administration and the assumption of power at the local level led to a rightward political shift. Bowing to pressures from an increasingly conservative RDA, most Guinean trade unions severed their ties to the French communist labor movement. A rift within the party again became evident as leftist militants openly expressed their discontent, denouncing the compromises of their leaders.

Chapter 5 examines the march toward independence in 1956–58, as grassroots militants, especially trade unionists, students, and other youths, condemned party leaders for accepting local self-government in lieu of complete independence. They criticized loi-cadre for undermining the French West and Equatorial

African federations, which in turn damaged Africans' prospects for meaningful independence. As rival parties attempted to win this disgruntled constituency by outflanking the RDA on the Left, the Guinean RDA leadership was forced to adopt an increasingly radical stance. In France, meanwhile, General de Gaulle returned to power and proposed a new constitution that further reduced federal powers and relegated overseas territories to perpetually inferior status in a new French Community. The Guinean Left pressed its leaders to reject this proposition and to champion immediate independence instead.

Chapter 6 explores the September 1958 constitutional referendum and its aftermath. Under tremendous pressure from the grassroots, Guinean RDA leaders adopted a proindependence position—but only in the eleventh hour. Of all the French territories participating in the referendum, Guinea alone rejected the 1958 constitution, opting instead for immediate independence. France quickly retaliated against the newly independent nation, sabotaging its economy and isolating it diplomatically. Although the Guinean government appealed to France and its NATO allies for aid and trade agreements, it was rebuffed by the West as a dangerous communist state. French warnings of Guinea's communist predilections became a reality when the new nation, in desperation, turned to the Eastern Bloc. Ironically, despite its overall success in the 1958 referendum, France proved unable to hold on to its empire. Most of its African territories had become independent by 1960. Guinea had led the way.

CHAPTER I

Reformed Imperialism and the Onset of the Cold War, 1945–50

FROM THE PEACE OF WESTPHALIA in 1648 to its defeat by Germany in 1940, France had taken its place among the world's great powers. When World War II ended, however, France's economy was in a shambles, its transportation system had been destroyed, and coal and food were in short supply. The country had been defeated, occupied, and humiliated during the war.[1] Yet it was still an imperial power, second only to Great Britain in the size of its colonial empire.[2] It was widely believed that because the empire had helped France to survive the war and allowed it to retain the illusion of grandeur, the empire would permit France once again to assume its position as a great power.[3]

French plans for greatness were threatened on several fronts. The imperial power's hold on its empire was endangered by African and Asian nationalist movements that flourished in the postwar period and by the emergence of the United States and the Soviet Union as the new world powers. Nationalist leaders argued that their people deserved increased political rights and economic compensation for their wartime sacrifices. The United States pressed for the breakup of colonial empires, in the name of free trade and, to a lesser extent, the self-determination of peoples. The onset of the Cold War and the support of French communists and the Soviet Union for the anticolonial cause magnified French concerns. Under pressure in the colonies and in the international arena, France adopted a two-pronged imperial strategy. On the one hand, it hoped to deter more radical solutions by reforming its empire.[4] On the other, it cracked down hard on emergent nationalist movements, particularly those with communist affiliations. In Guinea, the RDA was nearly destroyed during this period of intense repression.

WORLD WAR II AND THE NEW INTERNATIONAL ORDER

American pressure on the old imperial powers began during World War II. As an emerging industrial giant whose shores had not been devastated by war, the United States was in a strong bargaining position. Embattled Allies appealed to the United States for money, supplies, weaponry, and troops. In March 1941, the U.S. Congress passed the Lend-Lease Act, which authorized the president "to sell, transfer title to, exchange, lease, lend, or otherwise dispose of" war materials to any country whose defense was deemed necessary for U.S. security.[5] In exchange for wartime assistance, the United States sought access to European colonies in Africa and Asia for the purchase of raw materials, the exploitation of markets, and the establishment of military bases. Such access required a full-scale transformation of the old imperial order. In August 1941, American President Franklin Roosevelt and British Prime Minister Winston Churchill signed the Atlantic Charter, a document outlining the principles upon which the new order would be based.[6]

The Atlantic Charter championed a variety of liberal rights and liberties and addressed American economic concerns. It underscored the right of all nations to free trade and to "access, on equal terms, . . . to the raw materials of the world which are needed for their economic prosperity." It further declared "the right of all peoples to choose the form of government under which they will live" and the "wish to see sovereign rights and self-government restored to those who have been forcibly deprived of them."[7] These principles were endorsed by the United States, Great Britain, and twenty-four other nations on January 1, 1942, and subsequently by other countries, including France after its liberation by the Allies in 1944.[8] France's adherence to the principle of free trade was strengthened in February 1945, when it signed a lend-lease agreement with the United States that included a free-trade stipulation.[9]

Despite their endorsement of the Atlantic Charter principles, the imperial powers did not envision full-fledged decolonization. When France and Britain called for the restoration of "sovereign rights and self-government," they imagined European countries and their respective African and Asian empires, which had been overrun by the Axis powers. They protested the violation of European sovereignty, of which their empires were deemed an integral part. Americans, in contrast, were seeking an open door to world trade. They assumed that colonial states in Africa and Asia ultimately would give way to independent ones that would fly the banner of free trade. Eventually, under pressure from the British government, the United States conceded the notion of increased

1.1 General Charles de Gaulle, leader of the Free French, addressing the Brazzaville Conference, January 1944. ECPAD/Collection de la Documentation Française.

self-government within reformed European empires, as long as the reforms included free trade.[10]

When the Atlantic Charter was signed, France was under the authority of Germany and the collaborationist Vichy regime. Neither Germany nor Vichy had any interest in "enlightened" empire. Thus, it was left to Charles de Gaulle, leader of the Free French and later president of its provisional government, to devise a French response to the Atlantic Charter. De Gaulle hoped that the promise of future reforms would justify the intensified demands of the war effort in the colonies, inspire further sacrifice, undermine incipient communist and nationalist movements, satisfy American requirements for "modernized" colonial rule, and stave off American encroachments on the French domain. Reforms thus would guarantee France's continued hold on its empire and its tenuous claim to great power status in the postwar order. In order to rally support in the colonies, the Free French cause increasingly was described as one of democracy and republicanism opposing fascism and racism.[11]

It was in this context that de Gaulle convened the Brazzaville Conference in the French Congo on January 30, 1944.[12] The purpose of the conference was to propose a new African colonial policy, broadly outlining the political, economic, and social reforms that would be implemented at the war's end. In attendance were French colonial officials, including governors and governors-general, as well as leaders of transport, commerce, industry, and religious missions. Although their people's future was at stake, not a single African representative was invited.[13]

General de Gaulle opened the conference with a reiteration of France's historic "civilizing mission" in the colonies, reformulated for the new era that was about to begin. Stressing the importance of Africa in the war effort, he hinted at the postwar rewards that would result: "Up to the present, it has been largely an African war. . . . The absolute and relative importance of African resources, communications and contingents has become apparent in the harsh light of the theatres of operations." It was incumbent upon France, as part of its "civilizing mission," to raise up the people living under the French flag. France must help them "rise, stage by stage, to the level where they will be capable of participating, within their own country, in the management of their own affairs."[14] While de Gaulle included an escape clause, warning that "We do not close our eyes to the length of the successive stages," he had outlined a fundamental transformation in French colonial policy. Previous governments had denied the possibility of colonial subjects participating in "the management of their own affairs." Making this concession under pressure, de Gaulle and his colleagues firmly believed that any political activity by colonial subjects would take place under the tight control of the French government.[15] France would remain an imperial power, albeit under a revamped colonial system.

The final recommendations of the Brazzaville Conference made clear that "the management of their own affairs" was not synonymous with self-government. Nor was any future outside the French empire conceivable: "The purposes of the civilising work which France has accomplished in her colonies exclude any idea of autonomy, any possibility of evolution outside the French imperial bloc; the eventual establishment—at however remote a date—of 'self-governments' in the colonies must be ruled out."[16] However, there would be colonial representation in the Constituent Assembly, which was charged with drafting the new French constitution that would lay the basis of the Fourth Republic. That constitution would embrace both metropolitan France and the empire.[17]

1.2 General Charles de Gaulle walks through the streets of Bayeux after his triumphant return to France, June 18, 1944. © Bettmann/CORBIS.

If political developments in the empire were shaped by indigenous nationalist movements and American economic pressures, they also were influenced by the Cold War. In France, long-standing tensions between communist and noncommunist forces were sharpened by the divisions resulting from World War II. After the fall of France in June 1940, two-thirds of the country was occupied by Germany, while the collaborationist Vichy regime controlled the rest.[18] Although a minority of French citizens actively resisted Nazi occupation, the vast majority acquiesced to the harsh reality of German or Vichy rule. French communists were the driving force behind the internal resistance movement; the movement as a whole was deeply divided by ideological differences and party affiliations.[19]

After liberation in 1944, when enthusiasm for the Resistance reached its peak, the PCF enjoyed tremendous moral authority and a surge in membership. Boasting some 800,000 members in 1946, the PCF was by far the largest and best-organized political party in France, with bases in both industrial regions and the rural areas.[20] In the tripartite government of communists (PCF), socialists (Section Française de l'Internationale Ouvrière or SFIO), and Christian democrats (Mouvement Républicain Populaire or MRP) formed in November 1945, the PCF was the strongest of the governing parties and held important ministe-

1.3 Exuberant crowd welcoming General de Gaulle to a liberated Paris, August 26, 1944. © Ron Sachs/Consolidated News Photos/CORBIS.

rial portfolios.[21] The party press recorded a circulation of 10 million, accounting for 20–25 percent of the national total. The PCF was the dominant influence in the Confédération Générale du Travail (CGT), the country's largest trade union federation, and in a variety of women's, youth, and cultural organizations.[22]

The preeminence of the PCF was of great concern to anticommunist political forces in France and in the United States, which had become the most important benefactor in France's postwar reconstruction.[23] The U.S. government made it abundantly clear that, in return for critical economic aid, it expected communists to be eliminated from the French governing bureaucracy—from the lowest levels to the highest—from the armed forces, and from leadership positions in nationalized industries.[24]

THE PCF AND THE EMERGENCE OF GUINEAN NATIONALISM

If the United States was concerned about the PCF's influence on the French political economy, forces from across the French political spectrum worried that communists would weaken the nation's hold on its empire, already threatened by anticolonial movements in Africa and Asia. The PCF, more than any other metropolitan party, was identified with postwar African nationalism. The party made a concerted effort to develop the political analysis, organizing capabilities, and leadership skills of emerging African elites who subsequently led the postwar political movements.[25] Since the establishment of the Popular Front government (1936–38), French communists had taken positions in the colonial administration, working as teachers, technicians, and military officers throughout French West and Equatorial Africa. They had taught at École Normale William Ponty, the prestigious federal school in Senegal, and the upper-primary and vocational schools in Conakry and other important colonial cities.[26] Because their opposition to imperialism resonated strongly with African intellectuals, French communists had a tremendous influence on African elites educated during the 1930s and '40s.[27]

Communist influence in French West Africa diminished after the fall of the Popular Front government in 1938 and during Vichy's domination of the region (1940–42). However, in 1943, shortly after the French West African federation shifted its loyalty to the Free French, the PCF helped to establish the first Groupes d'Études Communistes (GECs) in French West Africa. These Marxist-Leninist study groups, along with other PCF-sponsored organizations, helped Western-educated Africans keep abreast of international events and the progress of anticolonial movements worldwide. Through PCF-sponsored courses, conferences, publications, and international travel, African intellectuals studied Marxist-Leninist theory and applied it to the social, economic, and political situations of their own territories.[28]

Elites in Guinea, like those in other French African territories, were extremely receptive to leftist ideology. A number of the most highly educated individuals had attended William Ponty when it was directed by Charles Béart, a Popular Front appointee.[29] Some were active in Guinea's first GEC, established in the capital city of Conakry in 1944.[30] Among the GEC's founding members were Joseph Montlouis and Sékou Touré, who cofounded the CGT's African postal, telegraph, and telephone (PTT) workers' union in 1945; Madéïra Kéïta, a technical assistant at the Institut Français d'Afrique Noire; and Léon Maka, a teacher. All of these men helped to establish the Guinean branch of the RDA in 1947.[31]

Leadership and organizational training also were provided by the PCF-associated trade union movement. Although the Popular Front government had recognized the right of Africans to form trade unions, the Vichy regime effectively terminated organized labor activity in French West Africa. In 1943, soon after the federation switched to the Free French, metropolitan unions, particularly the communist-affiliated CGT, initiated contacts with African workers. A government decree in August 1944 reiterated the right of African workers to organize.[32] In the postwar period, the CGT provided African unions with funds, organizational and leadership training, political experience, opportunities for international travel, and metropolitan allies in their labor struggles. Numerous RDA stalwarts possessed trade union backgrounds, which strongly influenced their organizing skills, strategies, and ideology.[33] Foremost among these was Sékou Touré, a founding member of the Guinean RDA, who became its secretary-general in 1952. In 1945, he had been elected secretary-general of the fledgling African PTT workers' union, a CGT affiliate. The following year, he organized and was elected secretary-general of the Union des Syndicats Confédérés de Guinée, which brought together all Guinean CGT affiliates.[34]

Constituent Assemblies and Constitution-Making

While a new generation of radicals was honing its skills in the GEC and trade union milieus, an older, more moderate generation benefitted from the Brazzaville political reforms. In keeping with promises made at Brazzaville, the French government permitted some colonial representation in the postwar Constituent Assembly, the body charged with drafting the constitution for the Fourth Republic. Elected in October 1945, the assembly was composed of 586 deputies, including 10 from French West Africa. Five of the latter represented the small first college electorate of French citizens, while an equal number represented the much larger second college population of qualified subjects.[35] Due to highly restrictive franchise requirements, Guinea, with a population of approximately 3,000 French citizens and 2.3 million African subjects, had a registered electorate of only 18,177. With 1,944 French citizens in the first college and 16,233 African subjects in the second, Guinea was allotted two deputies—one for each college.[36]

Under the old regime, Africans had not been permitted to organize political parties. Thus, most African candidates in the 1945 elections were sponsored by regional and ethnic associations. In Guinea, Yacine Diallo, a Ponty-educated teacher, was favored by the Peul aristocracy, wealthy Malinke merchants, government-appointed chiefs, and the colonial administration. Mamba Sano, another a Ponty-educated teacher, was the choice of Western-educated intellectuals of all ethnic groups, who were anxious to break the control of local chiefs and notables. The descendant of Malinke traders who had settled in the forest region, Sano was equally popular among Malinkes in Upper-Guinea and among the ethnically diverse peoples of the forest region.[37] Also vying for second college representation was a European circle commandant, Marcel Sammarcelli.[38]

The period immediately preceding the October 21 elections was marked by widespread popular unrest, revealing deep hostility toward the new political arrangement.[39] The protesters registered two key demands: first, they called for the augmentation of the noncitizen electorate through the expansion of voting rights; second, they insisted removing from second college candidacy the European circle commandant, Marcel Sammarcelli, who opposed the very notion of Africans representing Guinea. The protesters claimed that the second college was intended specifically for African representation and that only African candidates should be permitted to stand for election.[40]

The government's refusal to honor these requests sparked demonstrations in Conakry on October 16 through 18. On the morning of October 16, Peul and Malinke kettledrums began to beat in the neighborhoods of Boulbinet, Coronthie, and Sandervalia, calling the population to a public gathering. By 10 o'clock, 1,000 people had gathered before the police headquarters and in front of city hall. When Europeans and Lebano-Syrians fired from their balconies, at least eight demonstrators were killed and many more were injured. The crowd then stoned the police headquarters and sabotaged the central telegraph exchange, thereby obstructing communication.[41]

An all-night curfew was imposed. The following morning, the demonstrations resumed. Police fired on the crowd, killing more than fifteen and wounding dozens. Armed with hatchets, knives, machetes, clubs, rocks, and slingshots, the demonstrators randomly attacked Europeans and men wearing tarbooshes. The latter were assumed to be Lebano-Syrians, and thus colonial collaborators. Symbols of the colonial system were targeted: police headquarters, city hall, commercial establishments, and the railroads. In order to thwart the call for military and police reinforcements, the crowd attempted to cut telegraphic communications with the airport and to bar the route between Conakry and Kindia, where colonial troops were garrisoned. Reinforcements arrived nonetheless— police, soldiers, circle guards, even a European security force dispatched from Dakar. Many more Africans were killed and wounded.[42]

On October 19, two days before the elections, the administrator-mayor of Conakry issued a decree severely restricting movement in and out of the capital city. He also instituted a pass system to monitor movement within Conakry, and between Conakry and the nearby town of Dubréka, where, he alleged, the population had demonstrated its "hatred for France, saying that the French would be replaced by Blacks" up to the highest levels of government.[43]

Election day brought further unrest. The government was charged with ballot-box tampering and other irregularities. Demonstrations occurred in the capital city and in the coastal towns of Boké, Dubréka, and Forécariah. Protests in Upper-Guinea and the Futa Jallon were also marked by disobedience toward the canton chiefs—a phenomenon that would characterize the postwar era.[44]

For most Guineans, canton chiefs personified the evils of colonial rule. Appointed by the colonial administration, they served as intermediaries between the government and the rural population. As agents of the state, they collected taxes, recruited involuntary labor and military conscripts, and enforced the mandatory rendering of cash crops. They also transmitted the orders of European administrators to the local populace.[45] During the 1940s, peasants from all parts of Guinea had resisted the wartime exactions imposed by the canton chiefs. They had refused to pay taxes, carry out their unpaid labor obligations, and provide the requisite crops on demand. They had sold their crops on the black market and smuggled them across territorial boundaries.[46] After the war, rural resistance continued. As the main enforcers of government demands, canton chiefs bore the brunt of popular hostility.[47]

Despite the widespread protests, the October 1945 elections brought the anticipated results. Yacine Diallo, the government's choice, won the election by a slim margin—5,774 votes to Mamba Sano's 5,065. Diallo thus became Guinea's African representative to the Constituent Assembly. Free French General Paul Chevance-Bertin, a newcomer to Guinea, prominent Gaullist member of the noncommunist Resistance, and publisher of the pro-settler journal *Climats France et Outre-Mer,* was chosen to represent the territory's French citizens.[48] Chevance-Bertin belonged to a new socialist grouping, the Union Démocratique et Socialiste de la Résistance (UDSR), which had emerged from the noncommunist resistance movement and staunchly defended French interests in the colonies.[49]

African deputies to the Constituent Assembly were keenly aware of their minority status. In order to be heard, they had to forge alliances with sympathetic metropolitan parties, particularly those participating in the tripartite coalition government formed by Charles de Gaulle in November 1945. Together, the three governing parties represented three-quarters of the French electorate. The two parties on the Left made up a slim majority in the Constituent Assembly: the PCF, which had received 26.1 percent of the vote in the October elections, and the traditional French socialist party, the SFIO, which had won 24.6 percent.[50] The third governing party, the Christian democratic MRP, had received 25.6 percent of the vote. The MRP had been founded by Catholic resistance leaders who sympathized with French settler and colonial commercial interests and were vehemently anticommunist.[51] Yacine Diallo, Guinea's second college representative, allied himself with the SFIO.[52]

The alliance between African *évolués* and French progressives was a natural one, as both groups shared important values and goals. However, the alliance was weakened by disagreements within the French Left. African political leaders and French leftists concurred that Africans should transcend their subject status, acquiring citizenship and increased political rights. Both groups advocated the abolition of the discriminatory dual-college electoral system and found common ground in their promotion of assimilationist policies meant to transform Africans into "Black Frenchmen."[53] However, the support of the French Left for African emancipation was undermined by the mutual distrust and acrimony that characterized the relationship between the SFIO and the PCF. The hostility between these parties dated to 1920, when the SFIO's left wing seceded to form the PCF. While the communists generally disparaged the socialists as opportunists who were willing to ally with the Right, the socialists considered the communists to be dupes of Moscow and dangerous fomenters of revolution.[54] Fearing the growth of communist influence in France and overseas, SFIO deputies eventually undermined progressive components in the proposed constitution. The PCF, in contrast, was more steadfast in supporting African deputies' demands for political equality.[55]

Although French communists supported the notion of African emancipation, they defined the term rather narrowly. In the communist view, African emancipation could occur only within the framework of French governance. Like parties on the Right, the PCF believed that Africans were not ready for independence. From the communist perspective, Africans' lack of experience would make them easy prey to American imperialism and international capitalism. Hence, the PCF maintained, African emancipation could come about only when the communist party came to power in France and overhauled the economy and the state to benefit the French working class and all colonized peoples. In other words, the PCF, no less than parties on the Right, believed that Africans remained in need of French tutelage.[56] In the immediate postwar period, however, the communist view was no different from that of the African moderates represented in the Constituent Assembly. Like French progressives, African political leaders of the day did not imagine a future for Africans beyond local political autonomy. Independence, even in the future, simply was not on the agenda.[57]

Although Africans were demographically underrepresented in the Constituent Assembly, they played a prominent role in drafting the constitutional language pertaining to the colonies. Léopold Senghor (Senegal) wrote the colonial clauses for the Constitutional Committee. In the Committee on Overseas Territories, Lamine Guèye (Senegal), Gabriel d'Arboussier (Congo/Gabon), and Félix Houphouët-Boigny (Ivory Coast) helped to draft the colonial clauses, while d'Arboussier wrote the section on local assemblies.[58] Once again, the alliance between French progressives and African évolués was evident. Senghor and Guèye were affiliated with the SFIO, while d'Arboussier and Houphouët-Boigny were allied with the PCF.[59]

The Constituent Assembly met in Paris from November 1945 to May 1946.[60] In January 1946, following a bitter dispute over the extent of proposed presidential as opposed to parliamentary powers, de Gaulle resigned. Relinquishing his position as head of government, de Gaulle claimed that the PCF, the largest party in the Constituent Assembly and the one likely to dominate the new National Assembly, was maneuvering against him.[61] De Gaulle's departure strengthened the hand of French progressives. By April, the Assembly had drafted a constitution that clearly reflected the position of the French Left and was in keeping with the desires of African deputies. Its preamble included a declaration of political, economic, and social rights that were inspired by the 1789 French Revolution, the 1898 League of the Rights of Man, and recent resistance to Nazi occupation.[62] It extolled the principle that "all men are born and remain free and equal before the law." The people, rather than the nation, were deemed the source of sovereignty. The law, written by elected representatives of the people, was considered "the expression of the national will." A unicameral, popularly elected National Assembly would dominate a weak presidency. The right to resist oppression was guaranteed, and all citizens, male and female alike, were guaranteed education, vocational training, basic needs, the right of association, and the right to strike. The dual-college electoral system, which contravened the constitution's equality clause, would be abandoned in the colonies. The latter stipulation was among the African deputies' most urgent demands.[63]

According to the April constitution, the French empire would be transformed into the French Union. The Union would be composed of the "indivisible" French Republic, "associated states" such as Morocco, Tunisia, and the territories of Indochina, and the presumably less advanced "overseas territories"—i.e., the old colonies of French West and Equatorial Africa, Madagascar, and French Somaliland. Subjects of the old empire would become citizens of France, enjoying all the rights and freedoms that citizenship entailed. The franchise would be universal.

1.4 Sellers of the PCF newspaper *L'Humanité* advocating a "Yes" vote in the constitutional referendum, Aubervilliers, France, May 5, 1946. LAPI/Roger Viollet/Getty Images.

1.5 French citizens vote in the constitutional referendum of May 5, 1946, Paris, France. Ralph Morse/Time & Life Pictures/Getty Images.

The Union would be "freely consented to" by its members through ratification of the constitution. Thus, in contrast to pronouncements at Brazzaville, the door to eventual independence appeared open, should any members subsequently decide to withdraw their consent. In 1946, however, not even the PCF could imagine that overseas citizens would ever want to sever their ties to France.[64]

This relatively progressive constitution was not to be, however. The French citizenry rejected the draft in a referendum on May 5. Colonial subjects had not been permitted to vote.[65] In the *métropole,* fear of communism, rather than the terms of the French Union, was the major factor in the constitution's defeat. According to Gordon Wright, "The referendum, in the minds of many citizens, had turned into a plebiscite for or against the Communist party."[66] The MRP and other Center/Right parties had opposed the constitution, primarily because it strengthened the position of the PCF.[67] They warned of an imminent communist dictatorship—the inevitable result of a strong PCF-dominated parliamentary system. Right-wing fear-mongering also resulted in the defection of hundreds of thousands of socialists to the Right, where they joined other voters who opposed the constitution.[68]

If reformed imperialism was not a major concern in the métropole, it was critical to the constitution's defeat in the colonies. Throughout the empire, colonialists resisted the expansion of indigenous social and political rights, particularly the extension of citizenship. They worried that the communist-inspired constitution would be the death knell of the empire, already menaced by indigenous nationalist movements.[69] The UDSR, which championed French interests overseas and represented a significant number of first college voters, opposed the constitution because of the relatively liberal French Union provisions.[70] In territories where citizenship was restricted almost exclusively to white colonialists, the constitution was soundly defeated. Thus, it was rejected in Madagascar and all the territories of North Africa and sub-Saharan Africa—with the exception of Senegal. Only in Senegal, where Africans constituted the majority of citizens, was the constitution approved.[71]

Despite the failure of the April 1946 constitution, a number of laws and decrees were enacted during the Constituent Assembly sessions that realized some of the reforms proposed at Brazzaville. The Brazzaville Conference had urged the suppression, over a five-year period, of forced labor, and the gradual abolition of the *indigénat,* the harsh system of arbitrary justice applied to colonial subjects.[72] With the active support of African students in Paris, African deputies and the PCF pushed for legislation to enact these reforms immediately. On February 20, 1946, the indigénat was abolished by government decree. The Houphouët-Boigny Law of April 11, 1946, outlawed most forms of forced or obligatory labor.[73] On April 30, the native penal code, which imposed special penalties on African subjects, was suppressed; henceforth, Africans and Europeans would be held to the same legal standards.[74] Other decrees (March 13 and April 11) granted freedom of assembly and association in the colonies, effectively opening the way for the establishment of African political parties. Freedom of the press already had been conferred by an ordinance of September 13, 1945.[75]

The most significant reform was realized on May 7, 1946, when the Lamine Guèye Law abolished the category of subject and granted citizenship to all inhabitants of the French empire. The acquisition of citizenship did not, however, alter the former subjects' civil status for private matters.[76] The legal distinction between public law, which governed political affairs, and civil law, which dealt with private ones, resulted in another two-tiered legal system. Individuals of European ancestry were automatically *citoyens de statut français,* which meant that they were subject to French law in both public and private matters. Most Africans, in contrast, were *citoyens de statut local* and subject to African customary law for private affairs.[77] The retention of a dual legal system would have far-reaching ramifications for Africans' ability to exercise their newly acquired citizenship rights. Subsequent laws, which determined how the rights of citizenship were to be exercised, took advantage of the duality to discriminate against African citizens and to privilege citizens of European descent.[78]

It was in the context of these legal developments that elections for a second Constituent Assembly were held. The new Constituent Assembly, charged with redrafting the constitution, was elected on June 2, 1946. Alarmed by the reformist atmosphere in Paris and the liberal colonial provisions set forth in the April constitution, settler and commercial interests in the colonies had lobbied hard during the second electoral campaign.[79] While all of the deputies representing second college voters in French West Africa were reelected, only one of the four Europeans representing that region was returned to Paris—a strong indication of settler dissatisfaction with the April draft. In Guinea, Yacine Diallo was reelected by the second electoral college, while Jean-Baptiste Ferracci, a local businessman, replaced resistance leader Chevance-Bertin as the first college choice.[80] Gabriel d'Arboussier, who had represented first college voters in the Congo and Gabon (French Equatorial Africa), was removed from office for having championed African over settler interests.[81]

The second Constituent Assembly was far more conservative than the first. While communist support had remained relatively steady, the SFIO had lost ground both to the Left (the PCF) and the Right (the MRP). While some

SFIO defectors had abandoned their party for the communist Left, the majority shared the anticommunist concerns of the Center and Right. Worried about rising communist influence and the deteriorating situation in Indochina, the mainstream of the SFIO, led by Overseas Minister Marius Moutet, caved in to conservative pressures and realigned itself with the MRP. Thus, the MRP, which represented colonial interests and had opposed the April constitution, replaced the PCF as the party garnering the most votes. Despite earlier pledges to safeguard the rights incorporated into the April draft, in the second Constituent Assembly, the SFIO supported colonial alterations to the French Union provisions, leaving the PCF alone in support of African claims.[82]

During the second Constituent Assembly, France reasserted its authority over its empire. Provisions that had benefitted colonized populations in the first draft constitution were weakened or eliminated in the second.[83] For instance, although "all subjects of overseas territories" were now deemed citizens, at the behest of the settler lobby they were declared citizens of the French Union—not of the French Republic.[84] The constitution did not specify what this distinction meant in terms of citizenship rights; the conditions under which such rights would be exercised were left to the determination of "special laws" to be enacted at some future date.[85] Moreover, the Lamine Guèye Law, which distinguished between citizens based on their personal status, was incorporated into the constitution, entrenching differential treatment in a number of domains.[86]

The second draft constitution contained other disparities in rights that further distinguished overseas from metropolitan citizens. Suffrage for overseas citizens was highly restricted; only a tiny percentage of the adult population was eligible to vote. The representation of overseas territories in the French National Assembly was disproportionately small relative to their populations. While metropolitan France was allotted one deputy for every 75,000 people, overseas territories were granted one deputy for every 700,000 to 850,000 people. To the chagrin of African and PCF deputies, the constitution no longer referred to a Union "freely consented to." If the Union became untenable in the future, consent could not be withdrawn. Moreover, the new constitution made it clear that the overseas territories were deemed an integral part of the indivisible French Republic, rather than simply associated with it. Thus, any agitation for independence would be tantamount to secession—or treason.[87] When African deputies challenged the discriminatory nature of the new French Union provisions, only the PCF supported their demands for equal rights and treatment.[88]

As a result of pressure from African and PCF deputies, the April constitution and the electoral laws that followed it had eliminated the inequitable

1.6 Sellers of the PCF newspaper *L'Humanité* publicizing the second constitutional draft, Aubervilliers, France, September 29, 1946. LAPI/ Roger Viollet/Getty Images.

dual-college electoral system.[89] The electoral laws that followed the second draft constitution reinstated this discriminatory institution. The dual college would continue to prevail in some elections, with citizens of French civil status voting in the first college and a much greater number of Africans voting in the second.[90] French Equatorial Africa, Cameroon, and Madagascar would continue to utilize the dual college in National Assembly elections, while French West Africa and Togo would adopt a more equitable single-college system.[91] In all the territories except Senegal, where selective citizenship for Africans had been in effect since the nineteenth century, local advisory councils (general councils or territorial assemblies) would be elected according to the dual-college system. While the French government initially had agreed that the local councils would be elected by a single college, under pressure from settler interests, it had reneged on its pledge. The dual-college system, in which citizens of French civil status were disproportionately represented in the local councils, was thus entrenched in electoral law.[92]

Despite the obvious deficiencies, the second constitutional draft was the best that could be obtained under the circumstances. Thus, all of the French West and Equatorial African deputies ultimately voted for the revised constitution, although their feelings of anger and betrayal ran deep. The two-faced tactics of Overseas Minister Marius Moutet and the SFIO were particularly resented.[93] In the constitutional referendum of October 13, 1946, only individuals who had been citizens in October 1945 were permitted to vote. As a result, the compromise draft was approved by a referendum composed solely of first college citizens. On October 28, it was officially adopted as the constitution of the Fourth Republic.[94]

THE CONGRESS OF BAMAKO AND THE RASSEMBLEMENT DÉMOCRATIQUE AFRICAIN

On September 15, 1946, as the final provisions of the constitution were being debated, all of the African representatives to both Constituent Assemblies signed a manifesto written by Gabriel d'Arboussier and Félix Houphouët-Boigny. The manifesto called for equality of rights between peoples of the colonies and those of the métropole.[95] It was not a radical document asserting the right to independence. Rather, it expressed loyalty to the French Union and demanded constitutionally protected equal rights within it. These rights included political and social rights, the guarantee of individual and cultural liberties, and the right to establish popularly elected local assemblies that would legislate, rather than simply advise, on local matters. The manifesto reintroduced the notion of "a Union freely consented to," rather than one formed by right of French conquest, as the current constitutional draft implied. Finally, in order to protect the rights and liberties acquired since 1945 and to promote their extension, the document called for a congress of African parties and delegates, selected by the people of each territory, to be held in Bamako, the capital of the French Soudan. It invited representatives from each territory in French West and Equatorial Africa, French Somaliland, and Madagascar and other Indian Ocean islands, as well as from the United Nations trusts of Togo and Cameroon. Metropolitan parties also were invited to attend.[96]

Assisted by the local GEC and with the help of PCF funds, d'Arboussier and Houphouët-Boigny took the lead in organizing the Bamako Congress. The goal of the congress was to form an interterritorial movement to press for African political rights and liberties, as well as economic and social reforms.[97] Originally, the congress was scheduled to take place on October 11–13, simultaneous with the constitutional referendum. Since only a minuscule number of Africans were eligible to vote in the referendum, the congress would demonstrate the negative regard of the disenfranchised for the constitutional project.[98] However, numerous obstacles were placed in the path of the congress organizers, ultimately forcing the congress's postponement. The SFIO governor of the French Soudan was ordered to obstruct the congress, which, his superiors claimed, "answered to the Communists."[99] Colonial administrators in a number of territories prohibited the attendance of civil servants, threatening arbitrary transfer or job loss if they disobeyed. Transportation and financial difficulties posed other problems. While some delegates were able to fly at least part of the way, most went overland, traveling in convoys on rutted, unpaved roads. Some took boats and trains before transferring to trucks for the last leg of the journey. As a result of these hindrances, the Congress of Bamako did not open until October 18. An estimated 800 to 1,500 delegates and observers attended.[100]

Although all of the metropolitan parties had been invited to send representatives, only the PCF did so. The other parties, including the SFIO, considered the congress to be subversive and communist-inspired. Marius Moutet, the SFIO minister for Overseas France, intervened personally to persuade the metropolitan parties, as well as key African signatories of the manifesto, to boycott the congress. He instructed colonial administrators to discourage their subjects from attending. Under intense pressure, Lamine Guèye, Léopold Senghor, and Yacine Diallo stayed away. Jean-Félix Tchicaya (Congo/Gabon) was forced to remain at home when the French Equatorial African administration, in view of Moutet's instructions, confiscated the delegates' travel money. Fily Dabo Sissoko (French Soudan) attended, but only to denounce the congress as a "communist plot." Once again, Africans felt deeply betrayed by the SFIO and its allies.[101]

The Guinean delegation to the Bamako Congress included representatives from numerous bodies established since the Brazzaville Conference. Among these were members of the Parti Progressiste de Guinée (PPG), established in March 1946 as an outgrowth of the Conakry GEC; regional and ethnic associations; and trade unions, particularly those affiliated with the CGT.[102] The delegation was led by Madéïra Kéïta, a civil servant and GEC member who was secretary-general of the PPG, and included Sékou Touré, a member of both the GEC and the PPG as well as secretary-general of the Guinean CGT.[103]

The most significant event of the Bamako Congress was the founding of the RDA.[104] As a *rassemblement*, the RDA was intended to be a broad-based ethnic, class, and gender alliance whose constituents were brought together by their common struggle against capitalism and imperialism. Communist influence was evident from the outset, as the founders chose to call their movement a *rassemblement*, the term favored by the communists, rather than a *bloc*, which was preferred by the socialists.[105] Since the PCF was the only metropolitan party to attend the congress and to endorse the fledgling political movement, it gained considerable prestige in the African political arena. The SFIO, in contrast, was the victim of its own boycott and clearly "lost the battle of Bamako to the PCF."[106]

Although its detractors portrayed it as a radical organization, the RDA, like the PCF, was committed to working within the confines of the French Union. Within that framework, it strove to win greater political autonomy for the overseas territories, as well as equality of political, economic, and social rights for overseas and metropolitan peoples. Like the African and PCF deputies in the Constituent Assemblies, the RDA advocated increased local autonomy, rather than independence. However, it rejected the notion that African territories constituted an integral part of an "indivisible" French Republic. To be legitimate, the French Union had to be "freely consented to" by all its members. RDA documents made explicit reference to the United Nations Charter of June 26, 1945, which, building upon the Atlantic Charter of 1941, championed the right of all peoples to "equal rights and self-determination."[107]

While the RDA's vision was influenced by the liberties associated with the Enlightenment and the French Revolution, its structure and orientation bore the mark of the PCF. Even before the RDA's establishment, the PCF had encouraged transterritorial unity and action in the struggle against French imperialism. It had promoted the consolidation of diverse African organizations—ethnic, trade union, youth, and party—into a "single national anti-imperialist front."[108] Having emerged from the GEC/CGT milieu, RDA activists consciously modeled their party's pyramidal structure and political orientation on those of the PCF and associated workers' organizations, constructing chains of authority that linked each successive level of command.[109] While RDA branches eventually were established in most of the French West and Equatorial African territories, the extent to which party structures actually penetrated to the grassroots varied considerably from one territory to another.[110]

In Guinea, where the RDA was solidly rooted, the most basic party cells were village and neighborhood committees. Above these were canton committees, which had authority over all the villages of the canton. Above the canton committees were RDA subsections, established at the circle or subdivision level and incorporating all the base-level committees of the region. At the territorial level, the subsections were grouped together as the Guinean branch of the RDA. At the head of the territorial branch were the board of directors and executive committee, the supreme organs of the branch.[111] The strength of this structure at the grassroots was critical to the Guinean RDA's survival during the ensuing years of governmental repression.

THE POST-CONSTITUTIONAL ELECTIONS

The adoption of a new constitution and the establishment of the Fourth Republic were followed by a series of elections in rapid succession. All of these were held before the RDA was able to organize a Guinean branch. The first legislative elections took place on November 10, 1946, shortly after the conclusion of the Bamako congress. In Guinea, eight candidates vied for two National Assembly seats.[112] Yacine Diallo, the administration's favorite, won the first seat by a wide margin. Mamba Sano, Diallo's rival in the Constituent Assembly elections, won the second seat. Once again, Diallo's strength was greatest among the Peul aristocrats and officially sanctioned chiefs of the Futa Jallon, while Sano's support was heaviest among the Muslim Malinke of Upper-Guinea, the ethnically diverse forest population, and "modernizing" intellectuals of disparate backgrounds.[113]

Elections for the General Council were held on December 15, 1946, according to the old dual-college system. Guinea's new advisory body included sixteen councillors representing some 3,000 Europeans and twenty-four councillors representing approximately 2.3 million Africans.[114] It was heavily dominated by old-guard elites whose authority emanated from their collaboration with the colonial administration. According to a 1947 police report, the African councillors were mainly "canton chiefs or the sons of chiefs."[115]

On January 13, 1947, the General Council elected two councillors of the Republic, or senators, to represent Guinea in the Council of the Republic, the second—and much weaker—chamber of the French parliament. Jean-Baptiste Ferracci, previously elected to the Second Constituent Assembly, won the contest to represent Guinea's European citizens in the first electoral college. Fodé Mamadou Touré, a member of Yacine Diallo's party, was elected to represent second college citizens.[116] Like Diallo, Touré was a member of the Western-educated African elite. The sole African lawyer in Guinea between 1947 and the early 1950s, and one of a handful of Guineans with a French university degree, Touré had completed upper-primary school in Guinea, graduated from William Ponty in Senegal, and studied law in France. Touré also had strong "traditional" credentials. His father was a wealthy merchant of mixed Malinke-Susu descent, and one of his uncles was a canton chief.[117]

The election of so many chiefs, notables, and political moderates to the new councils and assemblies was largely due to the discriminatory nature of the franchise. Favoring the "traditional" and "modern" male elites, franchise laws were heavily weighted against the predominantly nonliterate rural population and against nearly all women. Those eligible to vote in 1946 included chiefs and other notables; individuals with primary school certificates and higher; members or former members of various local assemblies, cooperatives, professional associations, or unions; permanent (as opposed to contract) wage-earners in legally recognized establishments; religious officials; individuals decorated by France; military veterans; owners of registered property; and individuals possessing hunting or drivers' licenses. The Law of August 27, 1947, expanded the franchise to include adults who could "read and write in French or Arabic."[118] As a result of these limitations, the vast majority of Guinea's adult population was effectively barred from voting. In addition, the electoral system continued to discriminate against the inhabitants of overseas territories, requiring a far greater number of overseas as compared to metropolitan residents to elect one member to parliament.[119]

While conservative forces dominated the elections in Guinea, the Left experienced a resurgence in France. In the immediate postwar years, anticommunist elements in metropolitan France had to reckon with a strong communist party, its popularity bolstered by the leading role it had played in wartime resistance to Nazi occupation. Within the deeply divided population, the political pendulum swung from Left to Right and back again. The Left dominated the First Constituent Assembly. A sharp swing to the Right occurred between the drafting of the April and October 1946 constitutions.[120] In the November 1946 legislative elections, the Left again emerged victorious. The Center-Right MRP and the increasingly conservative SFIO lost more than two dozen National Assembly seats, their number declining from 161 to 158 (MRP) and 115 to 91 (SFIO). In the aftermath of the November elections, the PCF again became the largest single party in the French parliament, the number of communist seats having risen from 146 to 165.[121]

With only seven RDA deputies representing French West and Equatorial Africa in the National Assembly, the RDA was in desperate need of parliamentary allies. Faced with the hostility of the other metropolitan parties, the RDA turned to the PCF—the largest, "most consistently anti-imperialist" party in the French governing coalition. The PCF alone was willing to help the RDA promote its emancipatory program.[122] According to Madéïra Kéïta, the Guinean RDA's first secretary-general, the RDA-PCF alliance was the logical outcome of Africans' wartime and postwar experiences:

At the end of the war, men labeled "leftists," that is, those who were for immediate change, were the most numerous as a result of suffering endured in the zones occupied by the enemy and in the concentration camps. These were the Communists. The circumstances of the moment gave them the opportunity to be strong in the government. Our deputies of the period could work usefully for Africa only in cooperation with this party—whence came the affiliation of the R.D.A. with the Communist [parliamentary] Group.[123]

Houphouët-Boigny, the RDA's interterritorial president, elaborated on the political benefits of the affiliation: "Every time that we of the RDA defend a proposal we can count on the 183 votes of the Communist party."[124] Beyond its crucial support in the French parliament, the PCF was the only metropolitan party to provide money, equipment, and training to African political leaders during the immediate postwar period.[125]

THE ESTABLISHMENT OF THE GUINEAN RDA

While some territories had managed to elect RDA deputies to the National Assembly in November 1946, Guinea had not yet established a territorial branch. It was not until March 9, 1947, at a public meeting in Conakry, that plans for a Guinean branch were initiated. According to the police, some 300 people attended the meeting, "the great majority of whom were indigenous évolués." Also present were about a dozen Europeans, presumably PCF members or sympathizers.[126] The branch's constitution and charter were adopted on June 14, 1947, and the first board of directors was elected two days later. Madéïra Kéïta won the post of secretary-general. Since the PTT workers' strike in 1945–46, Sékou Touré had been under constant surveillance by the government and was considered too risky a choice.[127] The four under-secretaries included representatives from each of Guinea's major ethnic or regional associations: Union du Mandé (Malinke), Union de la Basse-Guinée (primarily Susu), Amicale Gilbert Vieillard (Peul), and Union Forestière (Kissi, Loma, Kpelle, and Malinke). A member of the Union des Métis held a lower-level position.[128] Several party leaders had been born in other French West African territories. The vast majority were civil servants—clerks in the government bureaucracy, African doctors, pharmacists, and teachers, low-level court employees—and trade unionists in the public sector. Others were employed in commercial enterprises. All were members of the Western-educated male elite.[129]

In the absence of political parties, regional and ethnic associations had been the dominant forces on the Guinean political scene. Once the RDA was established, the regional and ethnic associations rapidly gave way to the new nationally oriented organization. On June 16, the police noted that the Union du Mandé, Union Forestière, and Amicale Gilbert Vieillard had "practically fused with the RDA." Although the organizations continued to act independently in the social sphere, they "abandoned their prerogatives in political matters in favor of the RDA, to which their principal members belong." Reflecting the government's anticommunist fears, the police warned, "The R.D.A., which officially is supported by the Groupes d'Études Communistes, seems to be attempting to unite all the [ethnic groups]."[130]

In keeping with the communist ideal of a rassemblement, the RDA did, in fact, hope to unite all ethnic, regional, racial, and religious groups into a single national body. According to its statutes, the Guinean branch strove "to bring together and unite the inhabitants of this territory, in the view of realizing a program of democratization, of emancipation of the populations exploited by colonialism, and of the elevation of their standard of living."[131] Most chiefs opposed the RDA's emancipatory program, which challenged hierarchies of gender, age, and class, and which promoted young men, women, and people of low social status into leadership positions that historically had been the domain of elite senior men.[132] However, even the chiefs were welcomed into the RDA fold. Doudou Guèye elaborated in the local party paper: "The R.D.A. is the alliance of our young intellectuals—the products of French schools—of our cultivators from the bush, of fishermen, peasants, customary chiefs, their slaves of yesterday, their griots, wives, sorcerers—all of whom are slowly awakening in the cities to the modern world. It is an alliance of *all* socioeconomic strata in the exploited world. It is an alliance of those who want to break the chains of subjugation with the forces of democracy in the métropole—to assure the grandeur and future of the French community."[133]

The RDA, like the PCF, promoted national unity and international solidarity as the most effective means of achieving its objectives. Hence, in June 1947, RDA stalwarts from the Ivory Coast (Gabriel d'Arboussier), the French Soudan (Mamadou Konaté), and Upper Volta (Ouezzin Coulibaly), together with their Guinean counterparts, held a series of conferences in Guinea's major urban centers. Their purpose was to organize RDA subsections in Conakry and Kindia (Lower-Guinea); Mamou, Labé, Pita, and Dabola, (Futa Jallon); and Kankan, Bissikrima, and Kouroussa (Upper-Guinea). Most of the ethnic associations encouraged their members to join.[134] In July, the police reported that "[t]he civil servants, commercial employees, and the indigenous évolués ardently desire to create RDA subsections everywhere."[135]

In its gatherings and its membership, the RDA championed transethnic collaboration. When Gabriel d'Arboussier arrived in Kankan in June 1947, the police reported, "He was received at the entrance to the city by a large crowd of Africans," who joyously welcomed him with balafon music. An estimated 1,500 people of diverse ethnic groups attended a public meeting where he spoke.[136] In November 1947, Deputy Mamba Sano, who had joined the RDA after the National Assembly elections, urged Kankan residents at another large multiethnic gathering to unite across ethnic and national lines.[137] Similarly, party orators in Conakry exalted the RDA as the "grand party uniting all Africans (White and Black)."[138]

From August to December 1947, thousands of Guineans attended more than twenty informational meetings in Conakry, to learn about the RDA. The Conakry subsection soon boasted more than 5,000 members, while its counterpart in Kindia numbered some 600.[139] By the end of the year, the governor reported that, apart from two or three circles in Lower-Guinea, the RDA had established subsections in all the circles and important urban centers of the territory.[140] Even in the notoriously conservative Futa Jallon, Peul "modernizers" and members of other ethnic groups were rallying to the RDA. In Labé circle, the commandant reported that the RDA was the most active political party and was supported primarily by civil servants, commercial employees, and non-Peul residents.[141] In the Tougué subdivision of the circle, nearly all the civil servants had joined the RDA.[142] Similarly, most of the évolués in Mamou circle were also with the RDA—"in spirit or in fact." The subsection bureau included a teacher, an African doctor, and a clerk in the government service of health and pharmacy, as well as several commercial employees.[143]

In Guinea and elsewhere, the PCF was quick to help the fledgling party. The RDA press was a prime beneficiary of communist largesse. The PCF distributed its own publications throughout French Africa and helped to pay for the typewriters, mimeograph machines, and stencils that permitted the RDA to produce and circulate its own newspapers and pamphlets. *Réveil,* the official organ of the interterritorial RDA, originally had been a communist Resistance newspaper.[144]

Reluctant to rely exclusively on *Réveil,* which was published weekly in Dakar, the Guinean RDA established its own French-language newspaper in late September 1947. Under the direction of Mamadou Diallo, a former African doctor, *Le Phare de Guinée* was published biweekly. To ensure local coverage, each RDA subsection was expected to appoint a correspondent.[145] The party encouraged collective newspaper reading in order to minimize expenditures. To assist the non-French-speaking, nonliterate population, educated readers orally translated articles into indigenous languages.[146] However, because the paper was printed in Casablanca, there were long delays in circulation. Moreover, at ten francs per issue, it was expensive for most Africans.[147] As a result, despite the appearance of a local party paper, the more sophisticated and readily available *Réveil,* which sold for seven francs, continued to be widely read and discussed by the African elite, who were attracted to its spirited political commentary.[148]

The Demise of Coalition and the Onset of Repression

Even as the RDA gained strength in Guinea, the seeds of its destruction were being sown in France. In the aftermath of the November 1946 legislative elections, it was clear that the French governing coalition was doomed. Despite their large-party status, 165 communists could not successfully oppose 249 MRP/ SFIO deputies. Notorious for his anticommunist sentiments, General de Gaulle hastened the demise of the tripartite coalition with his provocative criticisms of both the April and October constitutions, which he had urged his compatriots to defeat. The April 1946 draft, he charged, granted too many liberties to colonial peoples—the overseas territories ought to be ruled by presidential decree. Moreover, de Gaulle claimed, both constitutional drafts provided for a National Assembly that was too strong and an executive that was too weak, providing an opening for communist domination.[149]

On May 5, 1947, following PCF dissent on government economic policy and criticisms of repression in Indochina and Madagascar, the communist ministers were dismissed from the tripartite government by the SFIO prime minister, Paul Ramadier. Ousted from power, the PCF entered into strong and systematic opposition.[150] As the dominant member of the governing coalition, the PCF had held that the emancipation of colonized peoples could best be achieved by working through the French government. Once its hopes of a progressive French government were dashed, the PCF began to champion greater colonial autonomy.[151] On the domestic front, the PCF supported massive CGT-led strikes in the autumn of 1947 that mobilized more than three million workers and paralyzed the French economy.[152] Claiming that the strikes were an attempt by the PCF to undermine the Marshall Plan, the government came down hard, brutally suppressing the strikes with the police, army, and national guard.[153] Many in France considered the communist position to be treasonous; those associated with it were deemed to be "anti-French."[154] Thus, within a few months of its establishment, the RDA found itself aligned with a much-maligned opposition party, rather than a member of the ruling coalition.

With its parliamentary ties to the PCF and its links to communist-affiliated trade unions and GECs, the RDA rapidly fell victim to the postwar anticommunist fervor.[155] Charging that the PCF was directed from Moscow, both the MRP and the SFIO were determined to rout its African allies.[156] In November 1947, the conservative government of SFIO Prime Minister Paul Ramadier was replaced by an even more right-wing MRP-dominated regime led by Robert Schuman. The ensuing cabinet reshuffle resulted in the ouster of Overseas Minister Marius Moutet (SFIO), who was replaced by Paul Coste-Floret, one of the MRP's most vociferous anticommunists. Coste-Floret immediately instigated a "tough" policy against the RDA in Africa.[157] The assault on communism at home and abroad had begun.

The official policy of repression in France was mirrored in sub-Saharan Africa, where colonial administrations cracked down on the RDA, encouraged its break with the PCF, and instigated a split in the CGT.[158] The French government's "anticommunist" crusade was aided and abetted by the Catholic church, which expressly forbade its members to associate with the RDA.[159] In Guinea, this edict was felt especially by the Catholic populations on the coast and in the forest region.

Between 1947 and 1951, the official policy toward the RDA in all the African territories was repression. In Guinea, the period of repression continued through 1955. Under Governor Roland Pré (1948–51), in particular, the colonial administration conducted an all-out campaign of harassment against RDA members.[160] During this period, RDA movements in Guinea were carefully monitored by the police. The party's organizational efforts were hampered by the inability to obtain meeting halls—the result of government pressure on private landlords and officials who controlled public spaces.[161] The colonial administration also took action against party newspapers, preventing their publication and burdening them with lawsuits and punitive damages that broke their budgets.[162] Arrests and imprisonment on trumped-up charges and suspension, dismissal, or transfer from their jobs were practices commonly employed against RDA members.[163]

With few private-sector opportunities, most of Guinea's Western-educated elites worked in government service, notably as teachers, clerks, and medical personnel. It was from these groups that much of the RDA leadership was drawn. Thus, the most effective weapon against the party was the arbitrary transfer of civil servants to remote areas far from their organizing bases. Some were sent to other territories. Most were sent to regions where their mother tongue was not spoken, further impeding their ability to mobilize the local population.[164]

The policy of arbitrary transfer and its purpose were clearly outlined in official documents. A May 1949 police report notes that "several very active members of the R.D.A. are among the African agents of administrative services in Conakry who recently have been transferred to the interior of the territory." Among these was a clerk, Baba Camara, who resigned from the relatively lucrative administrative service rather than accept his transfer to Gaoual in a remote corner of the Futa Jallon. After some hesitation, four other RDA activists accepted their new posts, which were tantamount to internal exile. The report concluded that the policy was achieving its objectives: "These transfers have produced a strong impression in the milieus of African administrative agents who have been involved in R.D.A. activities. . . . It is probable that the measures taken will bear fruit and contribute to braking the systematic attacks of certain African civil servants against the Government and the Administration."[165]

Because of his RDA, trade union, and GEC activities, Joseph Montlouis was an early and frequent victim of the arbitrary transfer policy. In the late 1940s and early 1950s, he was transferred so often that it was difficult for him to remember where he had lived during any given year. "I was transferred many times," he recalled, noting that he had done two stints each in Mamou (Futa Jallon), and Forécariah and Boffa (Lower-Guinea), and one each in Dubréka and Kindia (Lower-Guinea), and Macenta and N'Zérékoré (forest region).[166] In 1952, when Montlouis was manager of the Forécariah post office, the police reported that he was "*extremely dangerous* and is noted, in our archives, as having been one of the organizers of the Groupes d'Études Communistes. He is a *notorious anti-white* who can be considered as the perfect type of civil servant to 'keep in the bush.'" Arguing against his posting to Conakry, the police warned that his arrival in the capital would bring "new blood to the R.D.A. and to the trade unions."[167]

Léon Maka, another founder of the Guinean GEC and RDA, was considered by his colleagues to be among the party's "eminent leaders."[168] His experience was strikingly similar to Joseph Montlouis's. Between 1947 and 1952, Maka, a Ponty-trained teacher, was transferred from Mamou (Futa Jallon) to Guéckédou (forest region), to Télimélé (western Futa Jallon), and to Dabola (eastern Futa Jallon) as a result of his political activities.[169] Although Maka was recognized by the administration as one of the most effective teachers in the territory, the Dabola circle commandant rejected his appointment because of his RDA affiliation. Maka was ordered to return to Télimélé, but refused to go. His salary was immediately severed.[170] As the head of a large family, Maka was under enormous material pressure to halt his political activities.[171] However, as he asserted to an RDA gathering in Kankan, "To be R.D.A. implies the acceptance of all the sacrifices. [This is] the only means of bringing to fruition the program of the Party. . . . I remain R.D.A. and I am ready for everything. When Governor Sirieux came to Télimélé, he asked me what was my political position. I told him that I was R.D.A. and that, if I could, I would have these three letters engraved on my forehead so that everyone would know."[172]

Mamady Traoré, a clerk in the Bureau of Finances in Conakry, also was sentenced to internal exile. A fervent proponent of the RDA, Traoré was a depositary of the party newspapers, *Réveil, Action,* and *Coup de Bambou.* In June 1950, he was transferred to the Youkounkoun subdivision, in one of the most isolated parts of the Futa Jallon. RDA leaders in Conakry urged him not to despair; he would be the board of directors' link to that politically unexploited region, creating a subsection in Youkounkoun and distributing *Coup de Bambou* to the most insular areas.[173]

Like Traoré, Moricandian Savané was a clerk in the Bureau of Finances, but in Kankan circle, the most important urban center in Upper-Guinea. He was also the secretary of Kankan's RDA subsection.[174] In early December 1949, Savané described to an RDA audience the kinds of measures taken against RDA cadres by the government: "They intimidate us in threatening canton chiefs with dismissal, civil servants with transfers, merchants and traders with other difficulties in their businesses."[175] The following month, Savané himself fell victim to government reprisals. On January 26, 1950, dozens of people attending a meeting in the home of Lamine Camara, vice president of Kankan's RDA subsection, learned that Savané had been ordered to leave for the remote Futa subdivision of Mali that very evening. Paying tribute to Western-educated elites like Savané, and their leadership in the political arena, Lamine Camara declared, "Savané is among our children whom we sent to school to guide us. He has not shirked his duty!" However, it was Bah Kaba who gave expression to what, in the future, would become the administration's greatest concern: "There, where Savané has been sent, if there is no RDA subsection, he will create one!"[176]

While the administration attempted to destroy the RDA by transferring party leaders to remote locales, the policy largely backfired. Arbitrary transfers to the most isolated areas helped to spread the movement and its message to regions that otherwise would not have been reached as quickly. By the end of 1950, the government finally realized what Bah Kaba had seen so clearly months before. In early November, the police reported that the nurse, Mangane Sidibé, recently had arrived in Conakry to take up a new post. They kept a close tab on his movements because he had been one of Savané's assistants in Mali, where the latter had established an RDA subsection soon after his arrival.[177]

While some RDA leaders were subjected to internal exile, others were deported from the territory altogether. Mamadou Bela Doumbouya, a Ponty-trained civil servant and RDA activist, was transferred from one end of Guinea to the other before being expelled. In July 1947, he was working in the distant Futa outpost of Tougué, where he founded an RDA subsection. Three months later, he was summarily transferred to Kouroussa, a predominantly Maninka-speaking circle in Upper-Guinea. He remained there for a year before his transfer to the Ivory Coast and his effective exile from the Guinean political scene.[178] Doumbouya recalled the similar fate of other Guinean RDA leaders: "I was sent to the Ivory Coast with Moussa Diakité. . . . They sent all [civil servants] who were of the *cadre secondaire* to work in the other territories of French West Africa—systematically, outside of Guinea. There was Saïfoulaye [Diallo]; there was Ray Autra; there was Madéïra Kéïta, etc. I left like that and went to the Ivory Coast. I was absent [from Guinea] from 1949 to 1952."[179]

Like Doumbouya, Mamadou Traoré—more commonly known as Ray Autra—was targeted for exile.[180] A Ponty-trained teacher, journalist, and member of the Guinean RDA's board of directors, Autra founded and edited the journal *Servir l'Afrique,* which focused on social, economic, and cultural issues and was directed at Western-educated African elites.[181] In the early 1950s, Autra was transferred to Niger and subsequently to Dahomey "because of his subversive attitude."[182] Raising the specter of communism, the governor urged the high commissioner to prohibit Autra's to return to Guinea: "Mamadou Traoré called RAY AUTRA is in effect one of the most active representatives of the R.D.A. (marxist tendency) and has not missed the opportunity, since his arrival on vacation, to make numerous contacts with the local leaders of this party." The governor warned his superior that Autra's return "would gravely compromise" his attempts "to dislodge the veritable 'communist cell'" at the head of the RDA.[183]

The effort to smash the Guinean RDA's "communist cell" eventually resulted in the deportation of Madéïra Kéïta, the branch's secretary-general.[184] The police long had considered Kéïta to be a threat. In May 1949, the police reported, "It is certain that the departure from Conakry of Madéïra Kéïta and Sékou Touré . . . would result in the disappearance of the principal sources of agitation by which the R.D.A. constitutes a menace to public order in French Guinea."[185] In July 1950, Kéïta was transferred to Senegal. Rather than abandon his political activities in Guinea, he requested a leave of absence from the civil service.[186] In October of that year, the police reported that Madéïra Kéïta was still in Guinea, but without work. His situation was precarious due to his heavy family responsibilities, and trade unionists were actively seeking work for him in the private sector.[187] In 1952, Kéïta, who had returned to the civil service, was transferred to Dahomey.[188] Although he remained active in the interterritorial RDA, Madéïra Kéïta, the first secretary-general of the Guinean branch, had departed definitively from the Guinean political scene.

Sékou Touré, CGT leader and RDA activist, was also targeted for deportation. In September 1950, Touré, at that time an accountant at the Treasury, was transferred to Niger. After appealing unsuccessfully to the French overseas minister and requesting that Deputy Yacine Diallo intervene on his behalf, Sékou Touré simply refused to go. Having decided to dedicate himself full-time to trade union and political work, he resigned from his government position. His civil service status was definitively revoked by a governmental decree in January 1951.[189]

Arbitrary transfer and deportation were only two of the measures taken against RDA activists. The colonial administration also took action against RDA journals, obstructing their publication and encumbering them with litigation and penalties that drained their budgets. In April 1949, Madéïra Kéïta told an RDA rally in Conakry that the administration had brought nine judicial cases against *Réveil,* with the intent of exhausting its finances. In order to defeat the administration's plan, he said, RDA activists must sell subscriptions in offices and businesses, expanding the journal's readership and strengthening its financial position.[190] The same month, Mamadou Diallo, director of *Le Phare de Guinée,* resigned from the party. Formerly an African doctor, Diallo had been dismissed from his position as a result of his political activities. With no sure means of subsistence, the police reported, he desperately wished to be reintegrated into the civil service.[191] A few months later, Conakry police reported that *Le Phare de Guinée,* which had not appeared for nearly a year due to lack of funds, had effectively ceased publication. Under pressure from the government, no establishment would print it.[192]

On April 5, 1950, the locally produced, roneotyped *Coup de Bambou* replaced the defunct *Le Phare de Guinée.* Sold for only five francs per issue, the newspaper appeared every three weeks—when the roneo machine was in working order.[193] Like its predecessor, *Coup de Bambou* faced serious pressure from the government. It was plagued with libel trials in which heavy financial penalties were exacted.[194] In November 1950, the administration charged Madéïra Kéïta, the newspaper's publication director, with defaming the French ministers of national defense and of overseas France. Kéïta was found guilty and given a suspended sentence of six months in prison. He was also ordered to pay 100,000 francs in damages and interest. The governor pointedly noted that "[t]he convictions will, once again, seriously burden the budget of the [RDA]."[195] By the end of 1950, *Coup de Bambou* also had ceased publication.

Ray Autra, who eventually was deported for his RDA activities, was first targeted financially. In 1949, the police reported that Autra was forced to pay 35,000 francs in fines and damages for an article that was judged defamatory. The RDA took up a collection on his behalf, combing through the neighborhoods of Conakry, its suburbs, and as far afield as the coastal town of Coyah.[196] The following year, Autra and a colleague, Ibrahima Cissé, were convicted of swindling residents of the Upper-Guinea town of Siguiri, resulting in further penalties.[197]

The RDA's ability to mobilize was further obstructed by its failure to acquire sites for party meetings. Worried about government retaliation, few landlords or public officials were willing to accommodate the party. In June 1949, the Compagnie Française de l'Afrique Occidentale, which generally made land available for public meetings, refused to lend space to the RDA. The party then asked Conakry's mayor to permit the meeting at the public market. The request was denied.[198] In October 1949, the Conakry RDA subsection organized its first public meeting in five months. Unable to secure an indoor meeting place, it convened in the courtyard of the bar Boule Noire. Ray Autra told the assembly that the administration and the capitalist trusts were attempting to prevent RDA meetings by barring them from public meeting places. The police had tried to stop the circulation of handbills announcing the meeting, and *Guinée Française,* the organ of the local government, refused to publicize it.[199] Baba Camara declared, "If we can no longer get a room in Conakry, we will hold our meetings in [the suburb of] Kaporo, because the R.D.A. is everywhere. Even in the [Ivory Coast] prison of Grand-Bassam, there is an R.D.A. committee."[200]

MASS RESIGNATIONS AND THE TRIUMPH OF DIVISION

Administrative intimidation and reprisals took a heavy toll on the RDA. By the end of 1949, thousands of militants had abandoned the party as a result of governmental pressure, personal ambition, or economic distress. Most of the subsections had disintegrated; only those in Conakry, Kankan, and N'Zérékoré remained active. Police reports indicate that the RDA's financial situation was critical. The treasury had been depleted, but the campaign to renew membership cards had been halted due to the transfer of large numbers of RDA militants. In France, the Council of Ministers responded to unrest in various African territories by prohibiting all RDA meetings and demonstrations. As a result, cadres who remained loyal to the RDA were forced to operate clandestinely.[201]

One of the most serious blows to the RDA was the resignation of the regional and ethnic associations, which represented a large proportion of the party's constituents. The associations generally were led by civil servants and chiefs, who, as state employees, were particularly vulnerable to administrative coercion. They were under immense pressure from Governor Roland Pré, an anti-RDA hard-liner. Thus, it was under duress that the regional and ethnic associations first withdrew their representatives from the board of directors, then resigned from the RDA altogether.[202] The Union du Mandé was the first to abandon the party. In April 1948, it expelled all RDA members from its own board of directors. Then, in 1949, it broke with the RDA completely, as did the Union Forestière and Amicale Gilbert Vieillard. The Union de la Basse-Guinée split, with the anti-RDA minority establishing the Comité de Rénovation de la Basse-Guinée. In less than one year, most of the regional and ethnic associations that had helped to found the Guinean RDA had divorced themselves from it, shutting down a number of regional subsections and taking with them the bulk of the RDA membership.[203]

The government achieved a major coup when Mamba Sano, one of Guinea's two deputies in the National Assembly, resigned from the party.[204] A leader of the Union du Mandé and closely allied with the Union Forestière and Amicale Gilbert Vieillard, Sano had been elected to the Guinean RDA's first board of directors in 1947.[205] After his resignation, Sano disavowed the RDA's alliance with the PCF and the emancipatory program he previously had championed. In a rousing speech to a Kankan crowd he proclaimed, "My duty is always to prove that the population which I represent remains faithful to France and to its chiefs. . . . I want to bring you into only those movements that can develop the country within the French Union. I was R.D.A. But you all know that in 1948, I resigned from this party and that I invited all my supporters and the whole country to resign."[206]

Even more devastating than the wave of resignations was the new alliance between the regional and ethnic associations and the administration, and their all-out attack on the RDA. Amicale Gilbert Vieillard, which previously had catered to Peul "modernizers" and évolués by challenging progovernment chiefs and aristocrats, initiated a new policy of rapprochement with its erstwhile enemies.[207] The Union Forestière also aspired to a closer relationship with the colonial authorities. Announcing the reestablishment of a regional association independent of the RDA, one-time party stalwart Férébory Camara declared that such an organization would "achieve better collaboration with the administration."[208] In Lower-Guinea, economic as well as political interests came into play. The anti-RDA Comité de Rénovation de la Basse-Guinée included Nabi Youla, president of the Syndicat des Planteurs Africains, and many other African planters and chiefs, who profited from government favor.[209]

In opposing the RDA, the regional and ethnic associations were joined by two ethnically based political parties. The Union Franco-Guinéenne, founded in February 1947, was an RDA rival from the outset. It was essentially a Conakry-based coordinating committee of Yacine Diallo's various ethnic backers, and its strongest supporters included chiefs and notables from the Futa Jallon.[210] According to the Gaoual circle commandant, "M. Yacine vigorously insisted on the necessity of discipline, obedience to the chiefs and the presence of Europeans in the colony for a long time to come."[211] The second ethnically based party was the Comité d'Entente Guinéenne, founded by Mambo Sano in 1949. The Comité d'Entente was financed by several French trading concerns, including the three that dominated the Guinean market: Société Commerciale de l'Ouest Africain, Compagnie Française de l'Afrique Occidentale, and Compagnie du Niger Français. It was patronized by African chiefs, planters, and notables, as well as regional and ethnic associations such as the Comité de Rénovation de la Basse-Guinée.[212] Contemptuous of its rival's support base, the RDA derided the Comité d'Entente Guinéenne as "a party of the Administration."[213]

By late 1949, the RDA was in disarray everywhere but Conakry (Lower-Guinea), Kankan (Upper-Guinea), and N'Zérékoré (forest region). Employing a dual policy of repression and co-optation, the government was determined to destroy these last three RDA strongholds. While the Conakry subsection was able to survive the onslaught, those in Kankan and N'Zérékoré were decimated.

In Kankan, the administration enlisted the help of chiefs, notables, religious leaders, and members of the Union du Mandé to undermine the party's influence.[214] Particularly detrimental to the RDA was the co-optation of the *grand chérif* of Kankan, an influential Muslim teacher with disciples across vast stretches of West Africa. Although the grand chérif initially had tolerated the RDA, his beneficence had declined sharply under pressure. He forced two of his sons to resign from the party, after first rebuking them publicly.[215] During Friday prayers at the city's main mosque, he pronounced the RDA to be "anti-French," harmful to Africans, and the enemy of Islam. He urged all true believers to combat the enemy in their midst. After the grand chérif's diatribe, leaders of the Union du

Mandé recommended intense propaganda against the RDA. Kankan notables and chiefs exerted pressure. Under duress, Sidiki Dian Kaba, president of the local RDA subsection, resigned from the party. Large numbers of Kankan residents followed suit.[216]

By the end of 1950, the Kankan RDA subsection was in dire straits, its membership, morale, and finances in serious jeopardy. In November of that year, Lamine Camara, the new subsection president, was convicted of slander, sentenced to six months in prison, and forced to pay a fine of 2,000 francs, plus damages and interest of 25,000 francs.[217] The subsection's survival was in serious doubt.

Meanwhile, in the forest region, the RDA had continued to gain ground, largely because of its support for the ongoing campaign against the colonial chieftaincy.[218] Prior to conquest, forest chiefs, who had authority only at the village level, had been far less powerful than their counterparts in the Futa Jallon and Upper-Guinea. After conquest, the colonial administration established canton chieftaincies and installed officeholders with no inherent legitimacy. Unchecked by elders' councils, which had been abolished by the government, canton chiefs were granted unprecedented powers.[219] Without basis in traditional authority structures, the canton chieftaincy was relentlessly opposed by the forest population, with the backing of the RDA.[220] Under tremendous popular pressure, some of these chiefs ultimately endorsed the party.[221]

In 1949, as other subsections were struggling, the RDA recruited thousands of new members in N'Zérékoré. Focusing on issues of particular concern to the largely agrarian Kpelle population, the RDA agitated against the obligatory rendering of crops and labor to village and canton chiefs, high taxes, low wages, and low prices for raw materials produced in region.[222] Appealing to both Kpelle cultivators and Malinke traders, the RDA attempted to force price increases for various items sold in N'Zérékoré markets.[223] Transected by interterritorial routes to Liberia and the Ivory Coast, as well as internal routes to Macenta and Kankan, N'Zérékoré became a hotbed of political activity. Malinke traders, who were highly mobile and influenced by the cross-currents of new ideas, took the lead in establishing the RDA in the forest region.[224]

In the crackdown that followed, government employees, including the few sympathetic chiefs, were especially vulnerable. Plans were laid to sack the Lola canton chief because of his strong support for the RDA.[225] The chiefs of Dorota and N'Zao villages were targeted for dismissal because they had failed to forewarn the government of an RDA protest march on N'Zérékoré. The Dorota chief also was charged with harboring the protestors. Ali Soumaoro, who worked as a carpenter for the circle administration, was fired for leasing office space to the local RDA subsection. An African veterinarian in the government service was scheduled for transfer for fear that he would mobilize for the party in his wide-ranging work-related travels.[226] The official who recommended the reprisals stressed the sobering effect of the punishments: "We will give to the population and to our African collaborators the clear impression that we are firmly determined to act severely against the fomenters of disorder and their accomplices. Since the chiefs owe their position to us, if they desire to conserve it they will consider themselves warned."[227] In N'Zérékoré, as elsewhere, RDA members were well aware of the material consequences of their political activism. Thus, in December 1949, none of the subsection's executive committee were civil servants or employed by European-owned companies. Instead, all were self-employed.[228]

While specific individuals clearly were targeted for punishment, the anti-RDA crackdown was generalized throughout the N'Zérékoré region. In October 1949, the circle commandant prohibited all public meetings and sent guards to arrest those who contravened his orders. A military officer toured the circle, instructing village notables on the appropriate attitude toward the RDA. It was hoped that they would learn from "the dismissal of a few village chiefs and . . . the disgust of the majority of canton chiefs who understand that flirtation with the R.D.A. will bring them nothing but troubles."[229]

In conjunction with its crackdown on the RDA, the administration attempted to bolster the strength of the Union Forestière. In December 1949, government officials reported renewed regional association activity, principally in the realm of anti-RDA propaganda.[230] Together with chiefs and notables, Union Forestière leaders pressured local residents to renounce their RDA membership and to return their party cards. In December 1949, the police reported the rendering of 500 RDA cards, primarily by rural Kpelle who were easily subjected to pressures by chiefs and regional association leaders. In contrast, most of the urban-based Malinke traders and artisans remained faithful to the RDA and continued their political activities.[231]

Despite widespread local resistance, government repression eventually took its toll. After 1949, the spark in N'Zérékoré was snuffed out. In April 1950, the RDA offices in N'Zérékoré were burned to the ground.[232] In May, the N'Zérékoré subsection was dissolved by order of the governor, who claimed that it had been created illegally.[233]

CONCLUSION

During World War II and its aftermath, France experienced a dramatic change in its international status. A great power for some three hundred years, the nation was now under pressure on multiple fronts. African and Asian nationalist movements, the American and Soviet superpowers, and the rise to power of the French communist party all threatened the old order. In an attempt to salvage its empire, France employed a dual strategy. Initially, it implemented political reforms, both domestically and overseas. However, after PCF ministers were ousted from the tripartite government in 1947, repression against communists and their associates intensified. In French sub-Saharan Africa, the primary victims of this repression were RDA members, who were arrested, imprisoned, and arbitrarily transferred to remote locations. The party was temporarily stymied by these actions and by the mass resignations that followed.

CHAPTER 2
The Break with the PCF and Dissension within the Ranks, 1950–53

As the Cold War escalated in France and abroad, government repression against the RDA intensified. This persecution resulted in two contradictory conclusions by party members. On the one hand, the simultaneous crackdown on French communists and African RDA members seemed to reinforce their common interests and support the communist claim that only a government dominated by the PCF could bring about African emancipation. On the other hand, with the PCF out of power and cast as treasonous, the RDA was hindered rather than helped by its parliamentary alliance. In fact, during the repression of 1947–51, the National Assembly passed almost no Africa-related reforms. Based on knowledge gleaned from Parisian political circles, RDA parliamentarians increasingly believed that repression against the RDA was the result of the party's ties to French communists and that those ties had to be severed to save the movement.[1]

Hoping to salvage the organization, RDA parliamentarians urged the party to abandon its communist connections. While the Guinean RDA ultimately complied with the interterritorial directive, its break with the PCF caused serious dissension within the ranks. At the local level, rank-and-file militants repudiated the decision of the interterritorial and territorial leaders. Local leftists cried foul, and mass resignations ensued. The cleavage threatened to destroy the party. Skeptical of the Guinean RDA's avowedly centrist stance, the government continued its campaign against the party. This chapter explores the relationship of the PCF and the Guinean RDA during the tumultuous years 1950–53, as well as dissension within the RDA ranks.

THE DIVORCE OF THE RDA AND THE PCF

Government repression against the RDA had been justified largely by the RDA's communist affiliations. In 1950, after three years of official harassment, some party leaders argued that the RDA-PCF alliance should be abandoned, destroying the administration's main pretext for acting against the party. The RDA's interterritorial president, Ivory Coast Deputy Félix Houphouët-Boigny, was the primary proponent of this view. The strongest voice of opposition came from the interterritorial secretary-general, Gabriel d'Arboussier.[2] The split reflected both generational and class cleavages. The Houphouët-Boigny faction included most of the party's territorial leaders, who tended to be older and relatively well established in intellectual professions. In contrast, students, youths, and trade unionists—groups with overlapping constituencies—were deeply influenced by the anti-imperialism of the GECs; they tended to support the d'Arboussier faction.[3] In Guinea, grassroots activists generally were more radical than their territorial leaders, although many of the latter adhered to the d'Arboussier line—at least initially.

Houphouët-Boigny's position crystallized during the brutal crackdown on the RDA in the Ivory Coast. The campaign to reassert French colonial authority had begun on Houphouët-Boigny's home turf. If the government could shatter the RDA at its base, officials concluded, it could destroy communist influence throughout the rest of the continent.[4] In his campaign against "communism," Overseas Minister Coste-Floret had appointed as territorial governors several staunch opponents of the RDA. In February 1948, he instructed his new Ivory Coast appointee, "You are going there to suppress the RDA."[5] Between 1947 and 1950, hundreds of RDA cadres in the Ivory Coast and some of the leadership were injured or killed by the colonial government and its African collaborators. Thousands more were imprisoned. Houphouët-Boigny himself was forced to seek refuge in the forest among his Baule kin, and RDA meetings were temporarily outlawed.[6] According to Guinean RDA activist, Bocar Biro Barry, the interterritorial president wished to sever ties with the PCF before all the RDA cadres in French West Africa were liquidated.[7]

While Houphouët-Boigny clearly was concerned about the party's survival, his position also was influenced by the class base of the Ivorian RDA. In contrast to Guinea, where the RDA was led by civil servants and trade unionists, the Ivorian RDA was dominated by African planters and chiefs—powerful groups with intersecting memberships. Discriminatory policies in favor of French planters had prompted African cocoa and coffee producers to form the

2.1 Félix Houphouët-Boigny addressing members of the Syndicat Agricole Africain, the core of the future RDA, in Treichville, Ivory Coast, 1945. AFP/ Getty Images.

Syndicat Agricole Africain (SAA) in 1944. The SAA, in turn, served as the backbone of the Parti Démocratique de la Côte d'Ivoire, the Ivorian branch of the RDA. Houphouët-Boigny, a chief, planter, and Western-educated African doctor, was president of both bodies, as well as president of the interterritorial RDA.[8] With strong links to the colonial administration, and dependent upon it for the maintenance of their privileges, African chiefs and planters were eager to find common ground with the government.

Initially, Houphouët-Boigny's pleas for a break with the PCF fell on deaf ears. At the second interterritorial congress of the RDA, held in February 1949, the majority of territorial representatives rejected a motion to disaffiliate from the PCF.[9] Addressing a Conakry audience later that year, d'Arboussier elaborated on the merits of continued RDA-PCF solidarity: "It was in 1945–1946, when there were progressive elements, including the Communist Party, within the French government, that Africans obtained the right to vote, to have local governmental assemblies. It was then that forced labor was suppressed. Moreover, it has been since 1947, since the departure of these progressive elements from the government, that African rights have been contested."[10]

The conflict between the Houphouët and d'Arboussier factions intensified during 1950. Ultimately, it involved maneuvers of dubious legitimacy. According to RDA statutes, parliamentary representatives were subordinate to the RDA coordinating committee, which directed the movement. The head of the coordinating committee was the party's secretary-general—at that time, Gabriel d'Arboussier. In June 1950, the RDA parliamentarians, led by Houphouët-Boigny, asked d'Arboussier to resign in order to dissipate government actions against the RDA. Although he resigned in what he understood was a "tactical retreat," d'Arboussier later claimed that he had obtained an agreement permitting him to retain power unofficially. However, this situation did not come to pass; d'Arboussier had, in fact, been ousted from the interterritorial executive committee.[11]

With d'Arboussier silenced, RDA parliamentarians under Houphouët-Boigny's leadership were able to carry out their own agenda. On October 18, 1950, they severed all ties to the PCF and began to forge an alliance with the ruling coalition. The altered situation resulted in new language and policies, as the RDA prepared to collaborate with—rather than oppose—the French government.[12] *Réveil,* which was edited by d'Arboussier and which depended upon the Ivorian RDA for funding, suddenly ceased publication. All debate was stifled.[13]

The parliamentarians' unilateral action sowed serious division within the ranks. Because the coordinating committee alone had the power to take such action, and because they had failed to consult with RDA structures on the ground, the parliamentarians had violated party statutes. At the grassroots, there were strong feelings of confusion and betrayal. The Guinean RDA, which was concluding its second party congress on the day the parliamentarians announced the rupture, was in turmoil. Many regional leaders and local activists sharply disagreed with the parliamentarians' decision.[14]

The distinction between the parliamentarians' vote for disaffiliation and grassroots sentiment was not lost on the colonial administration. A state security official noted that local militants questioned the wisdom of the parliamentarians' action. In nearly all the territories, grassroots activists "have kept their old faith," rendering the territories "fertile ground for communist infiltration," he wrote. Local RDA activists were not prepared to declare common cause with their former political adversaries, and "Houphouët will have a hard time convincing them," he concluded. The official was certain that in Guinea, Sékou Touré, Madéïra Kéïta, and Ray Autra would follow d'Arboussier, rather than Houphouët-Boigny. Perhaps they even would separate from the RDA and establish an African communist party. If they did so, they would find willing cadres, he claimed: "They only will have to convince the crowds, and we have said frequently enough that a portion of African opinion is not a priori hostile to communist propaganda."[15]

Important segments of the Guinean RDA did indeed oppose the break with the PCF. On October 21, 1950, a few days after the rupture, a group of party stalwarts met at the Conakry home of Lamine Touré. Sékou Touré took the floor. According to the police, who had infiltrated the meeting, Sékou Touré "forcefully opposed the principle of disaffiliation advocated in Deputy Houphouët's last correspondence." Moreover, he noted that no new act of affiliation could be taken without the approval of the RDA boards of directors in all the territories, which alone were competent to act in this regard. Most worrisome, the police observed, "The other members of the local board of directors of the R.D.A. declared themselves to be of the same opinion as Sékou Touré."[16] Eventually, the Guinean RDA resolved to send a PCF-funded delegation to Paris to express "the discontent of the people of Guinea" with the new political line.[17]

While chaos brewed at the local level, RDA parliamentarians in Paris began to forge a new alliance with the parties in power.[18] They rejected an affiliation with the SFIO because of that party's profound involvement in the anti-RDA repression. At the urging of Overseas Minister François Mitterrand, they considered an association with the UDSR, which was desperately in search of parliamentary allies.[19] The UDSR had been severely weakened in 1947 when the Gaullist faction of the resistance movement broke from its noncommunist allies to form a separate right-wing party, the Rassemblement du Peuple Français (RPF). Most of the procolonialist UDSR members left with this contingent. Mitterrand hoped that their departure would facilitate the wooing of the RDA.[20]

For many RDA parliamentarians, an RDA-UDSR alliance was a reasonable proposition. The UDSR, led by René Pleven (prime minister, 1950–52) and Overseas Minister Mitterrand, was a party in power. It was Mitterrand who had convinced Houphouët-Boigny to sever the RDA's ties to the PCF, with the promise that collaboration with the government would result in a relaxation of pressure in Africa.[21] To provide an enticement, the overseas minister slightly eased constraints on the party just before the June 17, 1951, legislative elections. He removed some of the hard-line anti-RDA administrators from

2.2 François Mitterrand, minister of Overseas France, at the inauguration of the port of Abidjan, Ivory Coast, February 8, 1951. AFP/Getty Images.

French West Africa, including High Commissioner Paul Béchard and Guinea's governor, Roland Pré, replacing them with more conciliatory officials. The interterritorial RDA, in turn, sent missions throughout the federation, ordering local branches and sections to cooperate with the colonial administration.[22] The courtship was successful, and the RDA formally established an alliance with the UDSR in early 1952.[23]

The Legislative Elections of June 17, 1951

While RDA deputies in Paris negotiated a new parliamentary affiliation, territories throughout the French Union prepared for the Fourth Republic's second

round of legislative elections. On May 9, 1951, a new electoral law was enacted that was intended to forestall a communist victory and to swing the political balance further to the right. The new law permitted the formation of
pre-election alliances for the purpose of vote counting and seat distribution.
However, only the large, broadly based parties with lists in at least thirty constituencies were eligible for the vote-pooling benefit. In effect, the law allowed
the national parties of the Center-Left and Center-Right to acquire a major
portion of the redistributed votes. The big loser under the new system was the
PCF, which was both unwilling and unable to form electoral alliances.[24]

The new electoral system worked according to plan, seriously undermining communist strength and rendering the rabidly anticommunist RPF the
most powerful party in France.[25] In the June 1951 elections, the PCF received
nearly five million votes, more than any other single party. With 26 percent of
the vote, it was awarded 95 seats in the National Assembly. The RPF, which
came in second, received slightly more than four million votes (21.7 percent).
However, having benefitted from the new electoral law, it was allotted 106
seats in the National Assembly. Coming in third was the SFIO, which received
just under three million votes (15.3 percent). Profiting from vote pooling and
seat redistribution due to its pre-election alliances, the SFIO was awarded 95
seats—identical to the number granted the communists, with five million
votes.[26] The PCF's loss was even more significant when measured against its
previous strength. In the 1946 legislature, the PCF had occupied 165 seats, 70
more than in 1951. While the PCF's electorate had remained relatively stable,
the number of communist deputies had declined by 42 percent. In other words,
the PCF's losses, largely the result of a discriminatory electoral law, were dramatically disproportionate to the electorate's change of heart. [27]

In Guinea, the June 1951 elections initiated the RDA into electoral politics
on a major scale.[28] In April of that year, the French Commission on Universal Suffrage had augmented the number of overseas deputies in the National Assembly.
The number assigned to Guinea had risen from two to three. On May 23, overseas suffrage qualifications were broadened. The power of rural constituencies,
under the authority of colonial chiefs, was augmented at the expense of voters in
the urban areas, where progressive trade unionists and Western-educated elites
held sway.[29] As a result of the new franchise law, the number of Guineans registered to vote increased from 131,309 in November 1946 to 393,628 in June
1951.[30] Among the newly qualified voters were (male) family heads who had
paid their taxes, pensioners, and mothers of two children "vivants ou morts pour
la France."[31] The new law meant that mothers of at least two living children were

entitled to vote. Moreover, if a woman's children had died while serving in the French armed forces, they were counted as living for the purposes of the franchise. Given high birth and conscription rates, the number of African women eligible to vote increased dramatically.[32]

Although the parties had had only three and a half weeks to mobilize under the new franchise law, voter turnout in Guinea was significant. While 96,099 voters had cast their ballots in 1946, 224,182 electors, including many newly eligible voters, cast their ballots in 1951.[33] Yacine Diallo and Mamba Sano were returned to office, while Albert Liurette, an African doctor, became a first-time deputy in the French parliament.[34] Diallo and Liurette, sponsored by both the SFIO and the Union Franco-Guinéenne, were heavily supported by chiefs and notables from the Futa Jallon.[35] Mamba Sano ran on the tickets of both the Union Forestière and the Comité d'Entente Guinéenne, with its various ethnic backers. Like the Union Franco-Guinéenne, the Comité d'Entente supported the chieftaincy and campaigned against those who threatened law and order—notably, the RDA, which it derided as the "Rassemblement de Démagogues Africains."[36] Sékou Touré, who had been recruited by Guinean trade unionists to run on the RDA ticket, was soundly defeated.[37] The official election tally gave the RDA candidate only 32,000 votes—14 percent of the total.[38]

In fact, the election was marred by serious irregularities. Just as the May 9 election law had undermined the PCF in France, a decree of May 24, 1951, shattered any semblance of administrative neutrality in the overseas territories. The decree prescribed that polling station presidents, who were responsible for the stations' security, be appointed by the circle commandants. The administration claimed that, with the expansion of the franchise and the increase in the number of polling stations, it was difficult to find qualified and impartial individuals to preside over the stations, particularly in remote areas. By implication, civil servants, whose relatively advanced levels of instruction would have qualified them for these positions, were not chosen if they demonstrated sympathy for the RDA.[39]

In the course of the election campaign, the administration demonstrated its partiality in a number of ways. In an official letter of protest, the RDA claimed that the government had shown a clear preference for certain lists, particularly that of Yacine Diallo. It had openly pressured canton chiefs to encourage their subjects to vote for official favorites. It had stalled registration in regions that favored the RDA and accelerated the process in those where Yacine Diallo was strongest. It had manipulated the distribution of voter registration cards to the RDA's detriment. In Conakry, for instance, the cards had been given to employers, who had refused to distribute them. The result was that 4,680 voter registration cards had been unjustly withheld. In Siguiri (Upper-Guinea), registration cards had been handed out *after* election day. In Kissidougou (forest region), 2,669 of 4,674 residents had not been permitted to vote, even though they had registration cards, because the electoral lists had been "mislaid."[40] Other sources indicate that French commercial societies had subsidized the campaigns of anti-RDA candidates and that the results of the election had been falsified.[41] In total, the RDA claimed, Sékou Touré's candidacy had been deprived of approximately 30,000 votes, while Albert Liurette had won by only 1,700 votes.[42]

Charging that the election had been stolen from it, the Guinean RDA immediately contested the results. On June 26, party leaders meeting in Sékou Touré's home commissioned Madéïra Kéïta and Baba Camara to take the case to the National Assembly to reveal "the discontent of the people of Guinea." The PCF helped to finance the trip.[43] The RDA delegation urged the National Assembly to declare the elections invalid. Along with administrative partisanship and voter intimidation, the RDA provided evidence of official vote falsification that had seriously affected the election results. Despite solid proof supporting RDA claims of fraud, the National Assembly validated the election results by a vote of 237 to 45. The reseating of Yacine Diallo was a victory for the severely weakened SFIO, which had lost many supporters to the right-wing RPF.[44]

AFTERMATH OF THE LEGISLATIVE ELECTIONS: REBUILDING THE MASS BASE

Despite the RDA's divorce from the PCF, official opposition continued to block the party's electoral success. After the June 1951 elections, the Guinean RDA refocused its priorities. With access to high-level offices obstructed, it made no sense to expend huge amounts of time, energy, and resources on electoral campaigns alone. Moreover, the May 1951 franchise law gave a new importance to rural constituencies, home to 95 percent of the population, but where grassroots mobilization had just begun. Earlier laws had favored Western-educated elites in the urban areas. The government once had hoped that these *évolués* would become loyal government collaborators, but it was now clear that many—if not most—had cast their lot with the RDA. Apart from being bastions of the RDA, the urban areas also were centers of militant trade union activity. To counter these influences, the new law increased the power of older men in the populous rural areas, where canton and village chiefs held sway. The May 1951 franchise law thus compelled the party to reevaluate its urban orientation and to refocus its efforts on popular mobilization in the countryside.[45]

Although the franchise law stimulated the RDA's grassroots efforts, it was not the initial impetus. At its second party congress, held on October 15–18, 1950, the Guinean RDA had officially taken the name "Parti Démocratique de Guinée," or "PDG," reflecting the party's democratic, grassroots identity. However, Guineans generally continued to refer to their local branch as the "RDA."[46] After the congress, in the face of relentless government repression, the party had concentrated on the development of local party structures. Continuing to model their party on the PCF, RDA activists strove to create party cells in every village and urban center.[47] Specialized committees were formed: women's and youth committees were established at the village and neighborhood levels; enterprise committees were organized in businesses, in industries, and on construction sites; craft and trade-related committees were created to attract fishermen, tailors, masons, and traders.[48] In large urban centers, the RDA attempted to counter the influence of regional and ethnic associations by consciously mimicking their most appealing features; it instituted regional and ethnic committees that operated as mutual aid and social organizations.[49]

Within months of the second party congress, RDA activity in both the urban and rural areas had escalated markedly. During the first half of 1951, the governor reported, new neighborhood committees had been established in the capital city. In the rural areas, village and canton committees had been formed, exercising a significant influence over the local populations.[50] In October 1951, the police confirmed that "the Party appears to be organizing itself on a solid basis: village committees, canton committees, etc."[51] The following month, the police remarked that the RDA was "organizing methodically, creating branches and subsections in the bush, in the image of communist cells."[52] In its effort to establish a stronger rural base, the RDA increasingly abandoned the anticapitalist, anti-imperialist terminology associated with the GECs and the CGT. Instead, organizers increasingly referred to exploitation by local chiefs and made appeals to Muslim tradition.[53] The new party newspaper, La Liberté, underscored the commonalities between the RDA's emancipatory program and "the liberating principles of justice and hope in Islam."[54] Verses from the first chapter of the Qur'an (the fatiha) frequently were recited at RDA meetings.[55]

The Guinean RDA's ultimate triumph was linked to the success of the committee structure, which permitted the party to address local problems and adapt to local realities while carrying out territorial and interterritorial programs.[56] Village and neighborhood committees focused primarily on issues of grassroots concern—support for the building and maintenance of roads, schools, and clinics; and opposition to forced labor, mandatory crop requisitions, abuses by the chiefs, and excessive taxation.[57] Regular meetings at all levels were encouraged to ensure the rapid transmission of information and concerns—from top to bottom and bottom to top.[58] For example, the Guinean RDA's secretary-general reminded members of the N'Zérékoré subsection that its bureau should meet at least every two weeks, and whenever else deemed necessary. All decisions should be made democratically, after serious and frank discussion, at meetings of the subsection's bureau and in general assemblies of party members.[59]

Once again, support for the RDA spread rapidly through the forest region, where African traders and migrant laborers carried the message from Upper-Guinea and the Ivory Coast.[60] N'Zérékoré circle continued to be a hot spot. In early 1951, the governor reported that the RDA message had infiltrated into most of the circle's cantons.[61] In September, the military police reported that RDA activists were conducting "a strong activity in all the villages of the circle." In villages with more than ten RDA members, committees had been established and officers elected. The local RDA committees had begun to regulate all village disputes, forming a veritable shadow government. Colonial officials charged that RDA committees were usurping the functions of the chiefs, who were "complaining of having . . . difficulties in exercising their functions."[62] In October, the police reported that N'Zérékoré militants, especially PTT workers, were assuming such titles as "circle commandant," "canton chief," "village chief," and "block chief." The police official surmised that the RDA was creating these alternative posts in "preparation for pre-liberation."[63] Alarmed, the high commissioner's office charged that the Guinean RDA's usurpation of functions was tantamount to the assumption of "combat formation." Guinea in 1951 resembled the Ivory Coast in 1950, the official warned, implying that similar coercive measures might be necessary.[64]

Although repression against the RDA had lessened prior to the June 1951 legislative elections, it resumed with a vengeance in their aftermath. Circle commandants threatened RDA subsections with dissolution unless they submitted to a lengthy set of legal formalities. Declaring that their circle commandants opposed the party's presence, canton chiefs prohibited RDA leaders from entering their areas and their subjects from joining the movement. Civil servants who had supported RDA electoral lists in the June 1951 legislative elections were arbitrarily transferred to new locations.[65]

In an intercepted letter from Sékou Touré to Moussa Diakité, the police learned of further RDA grievances. Following the legislative elections, Sékou

Touré wrote, the governor of Guinea, heads of administrative services, and circle commandants had held regional conferences to plan repressive measures against the RDA. The crackdown was most severe in the circles of Kouroussa and Kankan in Upper-Guinea, and Beyla and N'Zérékoré in the forest region. Sékou Touré charged that government officials had violated the rights of RDA supporters by seizing their hunting guns, demanding payment for specially created licenses and taxes, and horse-whipping and arresting them without cause.[66] Despite the official policy of reconciliation in the aftermath of the RDA's break with the PCF, the targeting of RDA members continued. Anti-RDA activities were far too beneficial to chiefs and their associates to be terminated abruptly, and the government still considered the party to be a dangerous threat to political stability.[67]

Official hostility toward the RDA continued to take its toll on party membership. In the scattered settlements of the Futa Jallon, in particular, RDA cadres often had limited contacts with urban centers. It was difficult to mobilize and counter both government propaganda and the deeply rooted power of the chiefs. September 1951 brought the resignation of twelve RDA members in the remote Futa subdivision of Youkounkoun. Ibrahima Cissé, head of the RDA subsection in the Upper-Guinea town of Siguiri, also renounced his RDA membership.[68] In October, the Dalaba RDA subsection (Futa Jallon) collectively resigned. In N'Zérékoré circle (forest region), some 100 RDA members surrendered their membership cards to the circle commandant, publicly demonstrating their break with the party. At the same time, N'Zérékoré notables, loyal military veterans, and a few Malinke merchants reaffirmed their support of the chieftaincy.[69]

November 1951 brought the resignation of forty-eight members of the Guéckédou subsection in the forest region. Thirty-three of those who turned in their party cards were Malinke traders. Others included a handful of cultivators, two marabouts, and a military veteran. One resignation letter accused the party of "being nothing but an auxiliary of this Grand Communism of MOSCOW." Declaring victory, the Union Forestière applauded the resignations and called upon the government to transfer to another region the RDA militant and teacher, Jean Faragué Tounkara.[70]

IDEOLOGICAL DIVISIONS WITHIN THE GUINEAN RDA

Once again, the RDA was fighting for survival. The government claimed that the new rash of resignations was evidence of the rural population's deeply anticommunist, generally conservative nature. While this characterization may have been apt in some instances, intimidation rather than ideological orientation was responsible for many of the abdications. Moreover, at least some of the grassroots disenchantment with the RDA was due to the party's new collaborationist relationship with the government and its abandonment of its erstwhile allies.

The intraparty cleavage that had emerged in October 1950 continued to widen. An August 1951 police report referred to the deepening split between the RDA's interterritorial and territorial leadership. The report indicated that none of the Guinean leaders proclaimed, "We follow Houphouët." Although they continued to invoke the RDA president's name and publicly declare allegiance to his cause, they had not halted the stream of communist tracts and brochures flowing into the country, and they continued to broadcast their attachment to the CGT and the PCF.[71]

Skeptical about the veracity of the Guinean leadership's conversion, the police were even less certain that the new position would gain mass support.[72] Each month, large numbers of RDA militants continued to receive newspapers, brochures, and other publications of the PCF and the communist-linked CGT, World Federation of Trade Unions, and World Peace Council. These were rapidly diffused throughout the territory.[73] Communist publications, including *L'Humanité, Paix et Démocratie, France Nouvelle,* and *Cahiers du Communisme,* were especially sought after by civil servants.[74] Because of their influence over large numbers of people, African and European teachers were targeted for receipt of *L'École et la Nation,* the monthly organ of the CGT teachers' union.[75] Sékou Touré, Madéïra Kéïta, Moricandian Savané, and Sané Moussa Diallo were known to be major recipients and distributors of the subversive publications.[76]

In early November 1951, the police noted that one of Savané's correspondents in far-off Gaoual thanked him for having sent two (communist-inspired) books to that remote Futa outpost. The books in question were *Fils du Peuple,* the autobiography of PCF secretary-general Maurice Thorez, and *Volcans Coloniaux,* by the Martiniquan poet, essayist, and communist deputy to the French National Assembly Aimé Césaire.[77] Clearly agitated, the police observed, "This duplicity cannot continue much longer without being harmful to our interests."[78] Whatever the position of the interterritorial RDA, the police concluded, the Guinean branch "is firmly adhering to the line of the Communist Party."[79]

The growing gulf between the RDA's interterritorial and territorial leadership was evident in the position taken by Moricandian Savané, a member of the Guinean RDA's board of directors and secretary-general of the Union des Jeunesses

2.3 Maurice Thorez, secretary-general of the PCF, addressing French miners, December 5, 1947. Keystone/Getty Images.

Guinéennes. Local police reported that Savané, who had strongly opposed disaffiliation, continued to receive communist publications and to correspond with PCF members.[80] In a letter intercepted by the police, Savané wrote to Léon Maka, "The attitude of our R.D.A. parliamentarians is to be deplored. Houphouët and [Mamadou] Konaté [French Soudan] and all the others have betrayed the R.D.A. They have betrayed the will of the African masses." Urging adherence to the RDA's statutes, Savané pressed the coordinating committee to define the party's political line and to reclaim the powers usurped by RDA parliamentarians.[81]

Under growing pressure from both the interterritorial RDA and the colonial administration, the Guinean RDA rejected Savané's plea and instead bowed to the Houphouët line. On October 15, 1951, when the territorial board of directors met to clarify its position, Sékou Touré made an unanticipated about-face. Almost one year from the day he had denounced disaffiliation, he reversed his stance. Sékou Touré informed the Guinean leaders that the rupture with the PCF was real, not simply a tactical maneuver to trick the administration, as commonly had been assumed. Furthermore, Touré proclaimed, Houphouët-Boigny had not betrayed the principles of the 1946 Bamako Congress, as progressives had charged. Therefore, the Guinean RDA should follow his lead. The party's goals remained the same; only the means of achieving them had changed. After the speech, the Guinean board of directors voted. The pro-Houphouët faction, led by General Councillor Amara Soumah, won.[82] While the majority of the branch's board of directors now supported Houphouët's position, a vocal minority continued to oppose it.[83]

If the territorial board's new orientation caused dissension within the Guinean RDA, it was welcomed by Houphouët-Boigny and his supporters. The day after the vote, Sékou Touré received a letter from the interterritorial president indicating that he was sending 50,000 francs to the Guinean RDA. On October 17, Sékou Touré received a second letter from Houphouët-Boigny, urging him to continue working for the well-being of Guinea, with the support of the colonial administration and within the legal framework of the French Republic.[84] Houphouët-Boigny's mission seemed to have been accomplished. He had brought back into line one of the most recalcitrant branches of the RDA—at least in public, at the territorial leadership level.

By late 1951, both Sékou Touré and Madéïra Kéïta had publicly fallen into line behind Houphouët-Boigny. However, their private positions remained the subject of official debate. Madéïra Kéïta, the police noted, was in an extremely precarious financial situation. He had been suspended from his job and had to contend with serious domestic tensions as a result. He had been forced to go along with the board's majority, despite his own beliefs.[85] The police warned that Kéïta's and Touré's acquiescence, achieved only under duress, was merely a temporary tactical maneuver.[86]

Police suspicions were deepened by Sékou Touré's continued involvement in the PCF-linked French West African trade union movement. Since the departure of the communists from the French government in 1947, the administration's trade union policy had been marked by staunch anticommunism both in France and its overseas territories. The government had been implicated in the secession of the anticommunist Force Ouvrière from the CGT in 1948.[87] In French Africa, Force Ouvrière unions, supported by the colonial governments, were dominated by anticommunist European workers.[88] The following year, in an attempt to undermine the communist-linked World Federation of Trade Unions, with which the CGT was affiliated, the French government had helped to establish the rabidly anticommunist International Confederation of Free Trade Unions.[89]

Fearful of communist sway over the trade union movement, colonial security forces kept close tabs on Sékou Touré and other CGT activists. Official reports referred to Touré as a "notorious marxist," "fierce partisan of the Third International," and "star" of the French West African CGT. As secretary-general of Guinea's powerful CGT unions, Sékou Touré had achieved international prominence. He was known to have relationships with "eminent" people in Paris and "beyond the iron curtain." In 1950, he had become a councillor of the Warsaw-based World Peace Council. In November of that year, just after the interterritorial RDA's break from the PCF, he and d'Arboussier had attended the Warsaw Peace Conference. In 1951, Sékou Touré's trade union and political activities had taken him to Berlin and Prague, as well as Warsaw.[90]

Aware of Sékou Touré's nationalist inclinations and his personal political ambitions, the French government hoped to use Sékou Touré as a wedge to break apart the African trade union movement, severing it from its communist underpinnings. Police spies had noted that Sékou Touré was using his trade union base as a launching pad for political leadership. They had also reported on tensions between the French and African CGT leadership. African labor leaders were frustrated by the refusal of their metropolitan counterparts to give primacy to African concerns and to allow them a voice in policy-making. Given Sékou Touré's political ambitions and his recent—albeit reluctant—adherence to the Houphouët line, the government was convinced that he could be persuaded to lead an African secession from the CGT.[91]

The schism was expected to occur at the French West African CGT conference in Bamako on October 22–27, 1951. Sékou Touré was supposed to mount a coup, establishing an African trade union federation independent of the French communist-linked CGT. However, the Guinean leader made no such move, and the rupture did not occur.[92] In a letter to his superior in Paris, the French West African high commissioner expressed disappointment, noting that he had "nursed the hope for a moment that [Sékou Touré] would take the lead in a dissident movement."[93] If police records are accurate, Sékou Touré's delinquency was more than a disappointment. It was a betrayal. Touré actually had accepted government money to provoke a split within the CGT through the formation of an independent African federation. Not only had he failed to lead a dissident faction into secession, he had channeled the bribe money into his political organization, the Guinean branch of the RDA.[94] Sékou Touré had called the government's bluff.

Sékou Touré was taken to task for his inaction, not only by the government, but by the RDA's interterritorial president, Félix Houphouët-Boigny. After the Bamako conference, Houphouët-Boigny ordered Touré to Abidjan for a dressing-down. Many of the delegates to the conference were both CGT and RDA members. Most had ignored the interterritorial RDA president's orders that they break with the CGT, just as the RDA had broken with the PCF. Houphouët-Boigny was furious and held Sékou Touré accountable.[95] While Houphouët-Boigny subsequently forced Ivorian RDA members to choose "unequivocally between the C.G.T. and the R.D.A., with the threat of expulsion pure and simple from the party, in the case where the choice is for the C.G.T.," in other territories it was not so simple.[96] Sékou Touré carefully walked a fine line, bowing to the RDA's new collaborationist agenda in his political work, but adhering to the CGT's more militant stance in his trade union activities. He simply refused to disassociate himself completely from the PCF.[97] For the time being, the interterritorial RDA was forced to accept this anomaly.

While Houphouët-Boigny and his backers attacked Sékou Touré from the Right, in Guinea, the new party position was harshly criticized from the Left.[98] In November 1951, the police intercepted a letter from Ibrahima Diagne, head of the N'Zérékoré subsection, to Madéïra Kéïta, the territorial secretary-general. In the strongest of terms, Diagne denounced the fact that crucial decisions had been made by the territorial board of directors in the name of the party's rank and file without consulting the membership. He asserted that the party must convene a congress of all members, not just the board of directors, to study the new position and policies. "One does not decide on our behalf without consulting us," he declared. "Houphouët decided on our behalf without consulting us, and until now, we have not been informed of the real goal of this cynical decision. We demand rapid explanations." The police were convinced that Diagne's views represented those of a large number of Guinean militants.[99]

One week later, Moricandian Savané resigned from the RDA, announcing that he could not, in good conscience, follow the new party line.[100] His was the first of many resignations by disillusioned leftists. According to the police, "The epidemic of resignations is being carried out among the notorious R.D.A. members of Conakry and of the bush." A teacher and a nurse at the Conakry dispensary, both members of the board of directors and, according to the police, "communist diehards," were among those who recently had resigned. The police concluded that "[t]he leftists of the party are pulling back, not because they are abandoning their ideal, but more because the new orientation of the R.D.A. no longer corresponds to their ideas."[101] When Sékou Touré once again urged the Guinean RDA branch to sever its ties with the PCF and work with the colonial administration, he was roundly condemned by his colleagues, including Madéïra Kéïta.[102] The Guinean branch was at odds with Houphouët's new line, and Sékou Touré no longer represented his colleagues.[103]

The new cleavages highlighted stark differences between the experiences of the RDA leadership—especially the privileged parliamentarians—and the rank and file. Sané Moussa Diallo, an African pharmacist and a member of the Guinean RDA's board of directors, was among those who opposed the Houphouët line. At a November 21 RDA meeting, Diallo criticized both Houphouët-Boigny and Sékou Touré for practicing "ignoble maneuvers." He referred to the widespread discontent caused by Houphouët-Boigny's decision, blaming the interterritorial president and his supporters for the resignation of key militants. Unlike the Houphouëts, the partisans of the bush were not protected by parliamentary immunity, he charged. They bore the brunt of government repression: "These former comrades say that our leaders lack for nothing and that they are never bothered by the Administration, while, in contrast, simple militants are put in prison, suspended from their functions, dismissed from their jobs." Such cadres could never sanction collaboration with the oppressor.[104]

Once considered a paragon of the Left, Sékou Touré increasingly was viewed by Guinean partisans as a proponent of Houphouët-Boigny's right-wing politics of accommodation. As he gained power in both the political and trade union movements, Touré was criticized for opportunism and autocracy and for forgetting the movement at the base of his power. At an RDA meeting in December 1951, Moricandian Savané—who evidently had reconsidered his resignation—noted that Sékou Touré, like Houphouët-Boigny, had failed to consult his colleagues before taking action: "Yesterday, we decided to write collaboratively the text of the speech to be given at the meeting, during which Houphouët will speak, but I just learned that Sékou Touré is preparing the speech alone, without asking our opinions." Savané feared that Sékou Touré would not adequately represent the Guinean branch's disenchantment with Houphouët's new position and the selfish motivation behind it: "His change of course was solely the result of his fear of going to prison. He wanted to save his situation and his interests. For Houphouët and Sékou Touré interest takes first place; the suffering of others no longer interests them."[105] Although he opposed the RDA's new orientation, Madéïra Kéïta counseled private criticism—and public moderation. "In Guinea, we don't have the financial means to detach ourselves from Houphouët" and the mainstream of the RDA, he warned.[106]

The veracity of Kéïta's words was soon evident. On March 30, 1952, Guinea held elections for the Territorial Assembly (formerly the General Council).[107] As the governor's local advisory board, the Territorial Assembly lacked any real power. However, it could serve as a platform for delivery of the RDA message. The RDA contested seats in seven circles, including Conakry, Kankan, and N'Zérékoré—all RDA strongholds. General Council veteran Amara Soumah ran for the Conakry position; Moussa Diakité vied for Kankan; while Sékou Touré hoped to represent the forest region. Campaign funds were severely lacking. Sékou Touré requested assistance from the Ivorian RDA branch and from Houphouët-Boigny personally, but was met only with silence.[108]

The elections were catastrophic for the RDA and a victory for progovernment regional and ethnic associations. Once again, there were indications of electoral fraud. Diakité lost in Kankan. In N'Zérékoré, Sékou Touré lost to the Union Forestière candidate and N'Zérékoré canton chief Koly Kourouma. Amara Soumah, first elected to the General Council in 1946, won overwhelmingly in Conakry. However, after his victory, he honored a pre-election pledge to the Lower-Guinea regional association and abruptly resigned from the RDA.[109] His resignation was a severe blow to the party. Soumah had been one of the founding members of the Guinean RDA and had represented the Union de la Basse-Guinée on the Guinean RDA's first executive committee. In that capacity, he had attracted to the party a large number of young Bagas and Susus in the Conakry area.[110]

CRITICISM AND SELF-CRITICISM

A serious blow in and of itself, Soumah's resignation was also indicative of the deeper problems that plagued the party. In 1952, the RDA was in crisis, not only in Guinea but throughout the French African territories. Madéïra Kéïta and Sékou Touré, representing the Guinean RDA's board of directors, appealed to other territorial branches for cooperation. Their letter to the RDA branch in Niger was intercepted by the police. Despite recent electoral successes for the RDA in the Ivory Coast and the French Soudan, they wrote, "a veritable malaise persists." The leadership was divided. For a long time, there had been no effective link between the interterritorial coordinating committee and the individual territorial branches. In spite of the RDA's decision to collaborate with the government, the state-run radio and a segment of the colonial press continued to call for repression against the party. To save the movement, the Guinean board of directors called for an emergency meeting of the coordinating committee and a profound analysis of the RDA's past errors and of the current political situation. After penetrating self-criticism, they concluded, the coordinating committee should devise a general line around which a minimum program could be developed.[111]

The RDA parliamentary group, with Houphouët-Boigny at its head, was in no mood to compromise. Despite persistent appeals by d'Arboussier and his supporters, the interterritorial president refused to call a meeting of the party's coordinating committee.[112] Sensing victory, the parliamentarians hardened their stance. In July 1952, they ousted d'Arboussier from the RDA. The legality of this move, by a body officially subordinate to the coordinating committee, was highly questionable.[113] In October 1952, Houphouët-Boigny expelled from the party all Ivorian RDA members who remained affiliated with, or were suspected of being affiliated with, the PCF.[114] One by one, even the most militant of Guinea's territorial leaders fell into line behind Houphouët-Boigny—or left the party. In September 1952, the police reported that only Sané Moussa Diallo remained an unrepentant communist.[115] Having failed to co-opt him, the government hoped to expel him from the territory. In October 1952, the governor of Guinea broached this subject with his superior in Dakar: "It would be good, nevertheless, if the Territory definitively could be rid of the most dangerous elements, authentically communist, such as the pharmacist Sané Moussa Diallo, who requested his vacation and whom I formally have requested not to return to the Territory, and Ray Autra, the return of whom I already have given an unfavorable opinion."[116]

Other leaders had been co-opted successfully—or so the government hoped. In October 1952, Sékou Touré and Madéïra Kéïta convened a public meeting of the Guinean RDA, during which they reiterated the disaffiliation of the RDA from the PCF. Further, they announced their desire to collaborate with the administration in ameliorating the lives of the African population. *La Liberté,* which had not appeared for many months due to financial difficulties, suddenly found the resources to publish a special issue on these themes.[117]

Once again, the situation at the top did not reflect the reality on the ground. Grassroots activists continued to oppose the collaborationist line. The forest region, particularly N'Zérékoré and Macenta circles, remained a hotbed of militant activity. The governor lamented that the Western-educated elites and military veterans, who constituted the local party leadership, seemed unresponsive to the ideological fluctuations of the RDA's territorial board.[118] The steadfastness of militants in the forest region was due, in part, to their strong antagonism toward government-imposed chieftaincies and to their relatively egalitarian social structure, which resonated with the party program. It also was the result of the region's comparative inaccessibility from Conakry, which rendered forest activists less susceptible than others to pressures from territorial leaders in the capital.[119]

If the local population remained skeptical two years after the RDA-PCF divorce, the administration was equally so. The governor continued to worry that the leadership's public pronouncements were a ruse. "It seems infinitely probable that the Guinean R.D.A. actually is conducting a double cross," he fretted. He feared that while Guinean leaders publicly had supported Houphouët-Boigny, they had not burned their bridges to the PCF. The leadership's about-face was motivated not by a shift in ideology, he claimed, but rather by financial need. "The position officially adopted by Madéïra Kéïta and Sékou Touré is, without a doubt, influenced by the hope they nourish to see the President of the R.D.A. intercede with the Administration in their favor or to give them subsidies of which they always have great need."[120] As a precautionary measure, the government deported Madéïra Kéïta from Guinea in late 1952, hoping to capsize the rudderless boat.[121]

THE TERRITORIAL ELECTIONS OF AUGUST 2, 1953

Despite the setbacks of 1952, the Guinean RDA's persistent focus on grassroots organization began to bear fruit. On August 2, 1953, a special election was held to fill a Territorial Assembly vacancy left after the death of Paul Tétau, the territorial councillor for Beyla (forest region). Offering Sékou Touré as its candidate, the RDA campaigned on three basic themes: 1) ending the abuses by the circle commandants; 2) suppression of the mandatory government-run Société Indigène de Prévoyance and its replacement by voluntary peasant-run cooperatives; and 3) stricter control over the utilization of locally collected taxes.[122] In the face of continued government opposition, Sékou Touré won the election and became the Guinean RDA's sole representative in the Territorial Assembly.[123]

In the aftermath of the elections, even the governor acknowledged that the RDA had run an exemplary campaign:

> It must be recognized that the electoral campaign of Sékou Touré was extremely well-organized, with the support of Diagne Ibrahima, head of the subsection of N'Zérékoré, and that of Deputy Houphouët who sent him an

automobile, four R.D.A. delegates from the Ivory Coast as reinforcements, and a certain sum of money, it is said.

He also had the support of students on vacation, notably that of a certain Sékou Donzo (or Fofana), a student on the Faculty of Medicine in Dakar, who said at an electoral meeting in Kankan: "Touré Sékou favors the policies of Houphouët: to elect him runs no risks. I come from Dakar, and I want to let you know as well that Houphouët gets along well with the Governor General [High Commissioner] and with all the other superior authorities."

Sékou Touré's embrace of the new policy of conciliation and collaboration did not diminish the governor's concerns. He lamented that Sékou Touré's election "certainly will be interpreted as a victory for the R.D.A., and the echoes coming from N'Zérékoré confirm this impression."[124]

In contrast to the RDA, the regional and ethnic associations met with complete disaster. The Union du Mandé "lost in this electoral campaign the little prestige it still retained," the governor remarked. It had been unable to agree on its choice of candidates, which had worked to the benefit of the RDA. "Profiting from the disunity that reigned in the Union du Mandé," the governor continued, "Touré Sékou had the supreme cleverness to present himself as the candidate of this group, not exposing his game until a few days before the vote, when his name was followed by the notation, 'R.D.A.'" As for Mamba Sano, the Union Forestière candidate, "he lost in this unequal struggle his last illusions regarding the . . . feelings that his former electors now hold for him." For those who still harbored doubts, the governor concluded, the elections proved how badly torn the Union Forestière truly was. As for the Union de la Basse-Guinée and Amicale Gilbert Vieillard, these organizations had been totally inactive. The star of the Peul ethnic association had "paled at the same time as that of Deputy Yacine Diallo."[125]

CONCLUSION

The RDA's renewed strength in 1953 was a far cry from the situation a few years earlier, when the divided party had embarked on a downward spiral. In 1950, the escalation of Cold War repression and the brutal crackdown on the RDA had resulted in a decision by RDA parliamentarians to sever the party's ties to the French communist party. In Guinea, rank-and-file activists had denounced the decision, which was taken without proper consultation and authorization. While some grassroots militants ultimately accepted the new party line, many continued to defy the government.

If the period 1947–51 was characterized by government repression, the years 1951–53 were distinguished by uncertainty and malaise. The purging—or accommodation—of the radicals had not resolved the RDA's problems. The disaffiliation of the RDA from the PCF had disoriented and disillusioned many grassroots militants. Large numbers left the party in disgust. Yet accommodation had not put an end to government repression. The colonial administration continued to support "government parties," rig elections, and systematically persecute RDA partisans. Between 1951 and 1953, the Guinean RDA won only a single electoral competition—the seat accorded to Sékou Touré in the Territorial Assembly elections of August 1953.[126] Repression persisted, in part, because the government doubted the veracity of the RDA's transformation. Colonial officials charged that public disaffiliation masked unwavering private support for the PCF.[127] Faced with the disjuncture between the accommodation of the territorial leadership and the unyielding radicalism of grassroots militants, the government charged the party with deceit. What the government viewed as double-dealing was, in fact, a growing fissure between the leadership and the rank and file. In succeeding years, it would become evident that the popular revolt was beyond the leaders' control.

CHAPTER 3
The Fraudulent Elections of 1954 and the Resurgence of the RDA, 1954–55

INTENSE STATE REPRESSION in the early 1950s decimated the Guinean RDA's local structures. The crackdown on political organizing forced the party to shift tactics, driving some activists from overt political work to trade union activity. Taking advantage of the skills, organization, and momentum of the postwar labor unions, RDA militants attempted to build a mass political movement from the infrastructure laid down by the CGT.[1] The RDA–trade union alliance was cemented in 1952, when Sékou Touré, secretary-general of the Guinean CGT, assumed the leadership of the Guinean RDA.[2]

The highly politicized labor victory following the seventy-one-day general strike (September 21–December 1, 1953) provided a solid basis for RDA renewal.[3] Although the strike had taken place throughout the federation, it had lasted longer in Guinea than in any other territory.[4] Guinean trade union leaders, particularly, Sékou Touré, had been credited with the federation-wide 20 percent minimum hourly wage increase, an important outcome of the strike. Inspired by the strike's success, workers joined the labor movement in droves. The number of trade union members in Guinea skyrocketed from 4,600 at the beginning of 1953, to 20,000 in 1954, and to 44,000 in 1955.[5] Recognized throughout French West Africa for his organizing prowess, Sékou Touré was elected as one of three secretaries-general of the federal CGT in 1954.[6] As the most significant strike leader in the federation, Sékou Touré rapidly assumed an importance that extended from the labor into the political arena.[7]

In 1954, the same year that he acquired a key position in the federal CGT, Sékou Touré ran for an unexpected vacancy in the French National Assembly.

His loss at the polls was widely believed to have been the result of electoral fraud perpetrated by colonial officials and government-appointed chiefs. Widespread unrest followed Sékou Touré's defeat. The years 1954–55 were characterized by local challenges to chiefs, notables, and other government allies and to the political parties that supported them. Concerned that popular unrest in Guinea would undermine its precarious détente with the government, the interterritorial RDA rushed in to quell the rebellion. Despite all efforts to rein in the Guinean RDA, by 1955 it was clear that this party was by far the most popular in the territory.

CLASS ISSUES TO THE FORE: PRELUDE TO THE JUNE 1954 LEGISLATIVE ELECTIONS

In 1953, Sékou Touré was a newcomer to the ranks of officeholders. For several years, he had run unsuccessfully for office. His June 1951 candidacy for the National Assembly had gone down in defeat. In March 1952, he had run for a seat in Guinea's Territorial Assembly, but had been thwarted by the N'Zérékoré canton chief, Koly Kourouma, who had run on the list of the Union Forestière. When the councillor for Beyla died in 1953, Sékou Touré finally won a position in the Territorial Assembly.[8] However, he still aspired to office in the French parliament, where the real power lay.

Sékou Touré's opportunity came earlier than expected. In April 1954, Deputy Yacine Diallo died, two years short of completing his term. By-elections to replace him were scheduled for June 27.[9] The RDA selected Sékou Touré as its candidate. Most of the regional and ethnic associations supported Territorial Councillor Barry Diawadou, a Ponty-educated government clerk and the son of Almamy Barry Aguibou, a prominent canton chief. Barry Diawadou ran on the list of the Union Française pour une Action Sociale, which was financed by the French enterprises Compagnie Minière and L'Énergie Électrique de Guinée and supported by the colonial administration. The Union Française advertised itself as having a "*tendance* RPF"—that is, leaning toward the right-wing Gaullist party in the French parliament.[10] Seemingly overnight, Barry Diawadou was transformed from a champion of the Ponty-educated intellectuals and "modernizing" Peul elites in Amicale Gilbert Vieillard into a mouthpiece of Peul chiefs and traditionalists.[11]

Cleavages among the Peul had long strained the fabric of the ethnic association. For years, the association's "modernizers" had argued that education and merit, not lineage and traditional status, should determine an individual's position in society, while "traditionalists" supported the entrenched hierarchy of Peul aristocrats and chiefs. The RDA attack on the chieftaincy and its critique of ethnic politics now brought long-standing differences to the surface, splitting the ethnic association.[12] During the 1954 electoral campaign, some members rallied to Barry Diawadou. Others, including Amicale Gilbert Vieillard president Abdoulaye Diallo, along with Chaikhou Baldé and Ibrahima Barry ("Barry III"), founded a new socialist party, the Démocratie Socialiste de Guinée (DSG), which allied in parliament with the SFIO. A Ponty graduate and French-trained lawyer, Barry III became the new spokesman for Peul "modernizers" and stood as the DSG candidate in the 1954 legislative elections.[13]

Class issues came to the fore in 1954, trumping ethnicity as the most important voting determinant.[14] Barry Diawadou was supported by the privileged classes, particularly the old elite of chiefs, planters, and notables. Barry III was favored by many of Guinea's most highly educated, primarily Peul intellectuals, although some of this group remained loyal to Barry Diawadou. Sékou Touré, in contrast, garnered strong support among trade unionists and the urban poor of all ethnic groups.[15] While Sékou Touré's CGT unions included Western-educated civil servants, they were dominated numerically by nonliterate workers such as domestic servants, dock workers, and orderlies, who formed the base of the RDA's political organization.[16] The RDA also included large numbers of professionals from the bottom of the civil service hierarchy, who were products of lower state schools. Stymied by their lack of higher diplomas, these civil servants were unable to rise through the ranks. It was from this frustrated group that the Guinean RDA drew many of its local leaders.[17]

The higher echelons of the civil service, staffed primarily by Ponty graduates, tended to be hostile to the RDA.[18] The most privileged of the "modernizing" elites, Ponty alumni generally joined officially sanctioned parties and were dismissed as "valets of the administration" by RDA members.[19] Many Ponty graduates considered Sékou Touré to be beneath them, deriding him as an "illiterate," or at most, a man with "a sixth-grade education."[20] This erroneous assessment reflected the fact that, like most Guinean RDA leaders, Sékou Touré was not a Ponty graduate. However, compared to the majority of his compatriots, he was well educated, having attended lower-primary and vocational schools before continuing his studies by correspondence.[21]

Although Ponty-educated teachers had much in common with other Ponty alumni, they broke over the issue of the RDA, creating a schism among Guinea's most educated intellectuals. A number of sources indicate that the majority of teachers—perhaps as many as 90 percent—were RDA members.[22]

More than many other educated elites, teachers responded to the appeal of Marxism and its egalitarian, anti-imperialist orientation. A former RDA activist, teacher, and member of the African teachers' union, Bocar Biro Barry explained what many perceived to be the class differences between teachers and doctors, which resulted in divergent political perspectives:

> Doctors were considered to be the bourgeois class. Therefore, [the African doctors' union] was a bourgeois trade union. It was there only to take care of the doctors. . . . It wasn't concerned about domestic servants and teachers, because the doctors felt superior to us. In the political struggle that followed, the doctors' union played a minor role—because they had all the advantages. They were better paid. They were better treated. They had access to service vehicles. They had lodging—while the teachers had none of this. . . . We said to them, "You are bourgeois trade unionists. You cannot comprehend the situation of the poor, because you are rich. You have all the means. You cannot know the suffering of the people."[23]

The RDA's equalizing message resonated strongly among teachers from the forest region, where retrograde canton chieftaincies had been imposed on relatively egalitarian societies.[24] It struck a responsive chord among Peul teachers, many of whom were originally of low social status. While some Peul teachers were sons (and daughters) of the aristocracy, many were the descendants of slaves. The original intent of colonial education had been to educate the sons of chiefs in order to create an echelon of African intermediaries who could implement colonial policies. From the early days of empire, school attendance had been compulsory for these future chiefs.[25] However, during this period, chiefs often substituted slaves' sons for their own, refusing to subject aristocratic lineages to the deleterious influences of "infidel" Christian schools. Thus, in the Futa Jallon, the sons of Jallonke slaves (*captifs*), rather than the Peul aristocracy, formed the core of the first generation of "modernizing" elites, which included a large percentage of the first teachers.[26] This new class of elites, with deeper knowledge of European ways than the old ruling class, rapidly entered into fierce competition with the traditional aristocracy.[27]

While many teachers strove for a more egalitarian society, others aspired to the privilege associated with their rank. Some prominent members of the powerful Syndicat du Personnel Enseignant Africain de Guinée snubbed the RDA as an organization of illiterates.[28] Koumandian Kéïta, secretary-general of the African teachers' union at both the territorial and federal levels, was a case in point. A graduate of École Normale de Katibougou, the Ponty equivalent in the French Soudan, Kéïta shared with Sékou Touré a mutual antipathy that was both personal and political. Contemptuous of his RDA counterpart, whom he considered an ill-educated arriviste, Kéïta and his union had broken with the CGT in August 1953.[29] Although most members of the teachers' union were also RDA, they saw no conflict between their party membership and loyalty to their union leader, who vehemently opposed their party.[30]

The significance of class was starkly evident throughout the electoral campaign. In Upper-Guinea, Sékou Touré was opposed by influential religious leaders, canton chiefs, and other notables, who derided him as a low-level clerk and an "arriviste."[31] In Lower-Guinea, the Boké circle commandant noted,

> For the first time, the elections . . . were not exclusively ethnic in character. A whole proletariat became conscious of its force. . . . This political maturation reached all strata of the population. The *évolués* actively participated in the electoral campaign. Almost all the lower-level civil servants agitated for Sékou Touré; only the "high-level" African civil servants (African doctors, etc.) and the Peul civil servants supported Barry Diawadou. This group, which represents a significant minority . . . is reacting extremely badly to the rise of the R.D.A., and is worried about developments that could cost it its place as the ruling class.[32]

GOVERNMENT INTERFERENCE IN THE ELECTIONS

After its experience in the 1951 legislative elections, the RDA fully expected that the 1954 elections would be rigged. In spite of the official détente, the colonial government's primary objective remained the same—to thwart the RDA. Having selected Barry Diawadou as the best vehicle for these ends, the administration opposed any party that threatened to weaken his position. Thus, it objected strongly to the DSG.[33]

An unexpected change of government in Paris did nothing to alter the situation in Guinea. Prime Minister Joseph Laniel's government had collapsed on June 12, 1954, primarily as a result of the devastating French defeat at Dien Bien Phu the month before. The Laniel government had been noted for its "tough" anti-RDA stance. A new, more conciliatory government, led by Pierre Mendès France, was installed on June 18, only nine days before the legislative elections. However, in Guinea, Governor Jean Paul Parisot and his subordinates continued to implement the "tough" anti-RDA policies associated with the Laniel regime.[34]

According to the official tally, Barry Diawadou won the 1954 legislative elections by a wide margin. Out of 254,722 ballots cast, 145,497 (57.1 percent) were for Barry Diawadou; 85,808 (33.7 percent) were for Sékou Touré (RDA); 16,098 (6.3 percent) were for Barry III (DSG); and 7,319 (2.9 percent) were for various independent candidates.[35] The colonial government declared Barry Diawadou the victor. The RDA immediately charged that the results had been falsified.[36]

In the weeks and months that followed, the RDA persisted in its claim that Sékou Touré's loss was due to massive government interference and electoral fraud. Abundant evidence supports RDA contentions.[37] It was well known that Governor Parisot and his administration considered the party to be fundamentally subversive, because of both its nationalist agenda and its alleged communist inclinations.[38] Severely humiliated by the 1953 general strike, the governor blamed Sékou Touré and the RDA for this professional disaster. Thus, it came as no surprise when the governor instructed circle commandants and canton chiefs to ensure Barry Diawadou's victory.[39] Throughout the electoral campaign, administration officials publicly expressed their preference, pointedly noting that Barry Diawadou was the government's candidate. In the rural areas, circle commandants communicated their choice at gatherings of villagers and chiefs. Under threat of dismissal, chiefs were instructed to bring out the vote in their constituencies. Civil servants were threatened with job loss if they voted for another candidate. To further enhance Barry Diawadou's prospects, civil servants were granted leave from their jobs and accorded government transport to campaign for the administration's choice.[40]

If the colonial government violated the policy of official neutrality in local elections, it also broke a number of electoral laws. By law, voter registration cards were to be distributed by a commission that included representatives from each party. In fact, most registration cards were distributed by canton chiefs and RPF members, who simultaneously acted as Barry Diawadou's agents. Many electors also received Barry Diawadou's ballot attached to their voter registration cards.[41] In violation of the 1951 electoral law, illiterate government agents, who were incapable of recording accurate results or writing an official report, were placed in charge of polling stations. Circle commandants thus were able to cable arbitrary figures to the capital, where they were compiled under the governor's supervision.[42] In a number of circles, government agents, including canton chiefs, officiated at the polling stations. In Dabola, canton chief Almamy Barry Aguibou, the candidate's father, supervised the station. Secrecy of the ballot, although required by law, was nonexistent.[43] In many instances, RDA representatives were beaten with clubs and refused entry to polling stations. Without RDA representatives present, Barry Diawadou's agents had complete freedom of action.[44]

THE AFTERMATH OF THE JUNE 1954 ELECTIONS

The RDA's assessment of electoral fraud was corroborated by outside observers. Thus, the official pronouncement of Barry Diawadou as the winner fueled public anger against the state.[45] Popular demonstrations were staged throughout most of the territory.[46] News of the stolen election was transmitted through countless songs, the party's primary means of communication among its predominantly nonliterate constituency.[47] Former activist Fatou Diarra recalled that RDA women composed numerous songs about administrative complicity in the defeat of Sékou Touré and the RDA, both symbolized by the mighty elephant (or *syli* in Susu): "After the 1954 elections, women sang at the markets that the colonial authorities had rigged the elections. 'You women who go up, You women who go down. The other party has stolen our votes, Stolen the votes of Syli.' All the women sang this song, so by the time they heard the election results, they already knew that they had been cheated, that the elections had been rigged."[48]

Former RDA militant Aissatou N'Diaye remembered the intense local reaction to the official results:

> When it was said that Sékou had lost, there was a popular revolt. . . . Sékou was not in Conakry; he was campaigning in the interior. . . . We prepared songs for his return. We gathered at Fanta Camara's to prepare the songs. We asked the crowd to make up a song that would be sung. . . . He came at dusk or late afternoon. . . . By then the song was known to everyone in town, even to vagabonds. The song went like this:
>
> > The saboteurs said they were the leaders
> > Whereas Monsieur Touré said he is not the leader
> > But he gets to lead to the country
> > Look, people, at the RDA
> > Look, people, at the RDA
> > RDA women unite
> > Laugh with me, Touré
> > Laugh with me, Touré.[49]

Another song composed for the occasion, which was punctuated by mooing cows, derided Barry Diawadou's alleged victory as a fraud effected by inflated voter rolls. Vote rigging was deemed particularly notorious in the Futa Jallon, the candidate's home and bastion of the Peul aristocracy. Swaying and mooing like a cow, N'Diaye demonstrated how the people had sung:

> Look, people, at Barry Diawadou
> Look, people, at Barry Diawadou
> The cows have voted for you in the Futa
> "Mbu, mbe," we don't want you.[50]

When Sékou Touré arrived in Conakry, a crowd of some 30,000 supporters received him, crying, "Syli! Syli!" "Elephant! Elephant!" and singing:

> The elephant has entered the city
> Yes, the elephant has arrived
> The city is full
> Because the elephant has arrived.[51]

Women sang and danced all night in front of Sékou Touré's home, informing the world that despite the official results, Sékou Touré—the mighty elephant—was the people's choice.[52]

The following morning, before going to the market, the women went to Sékou Touré's home to greet him. They sang about Saliou Diallo (called "Salli Bobo"), an influential member of Barry Diawadou's entourage and a clerk at the Bureau of Finances:

> Those who go up, tell it
> Those who go down, tell it
> It is Salli Bobo who misappropriated the votes of Syli
> Oh yes, tell it, Salli Bobo stole the votes of Syli.[53]

In Conakry, Barry Diawadou required police protection in the face of teeming crowds that hailed Sékou Touré as "the real chief" and "the real deputy." RDA women sang to Sékou Touré,

> You are a new chief
> You are chosen as chief

The people [are] with you
You are a new chief
Lift up your head
Look at the sea of faces
That answers when you call.[54]

While most of the songs were composed anonymously by RDA women, some were the work of particular artists. One such composer/song leader was François Bonnet, who was fingered by the police as a prominent "griot of the RDA." According to a September 1954 police report, Bonnet had come to the fore during the three months following the legislative elections. He seemed to be at every demonstration in Conakry, leading the militants in song. Of El Hadji Alkaly Ibrahima Soumah, the government-appointed chief of the Coronthie neighborhood, who had helped to rig the elections, Bonnet sang,

Alkali Ibrahima, your name is ruined
Syli is ahead
You cheated for nothing
Your name is ruined
You are tiring yourself for nothing
Syli is ahead, always ahead

The chorus chanted,

Syli is ahead, always ahead
You have stolen the votes
But Syli is ahead
You can talk
Syli will always be ahead

Similarly, in parades throughout Conakry, Bonnet sang,

Barry Diawadou, Barry Diawadou
The thief of the [ballot]
The thief of the [ballot]
Sékou Touré is ahead of you
God will seek you out.[55]

For days, weeks, and months, the theme repeated itself. The colonial administration and its henchmen had stolen the elections from the RDA. The elections had been rigged, the vote-counting fraudulent, but in the end, justice would prevail. Allah was on the side of the RDA.

The ensuing year and a half were characterized by widespread and prolonged civil unrest, as violence erupted between Barry Diawadou's partisans and the RDA and tens of thousands of people demonstrated their support for Sékou Touré.[56] In the elections' immediate aftermath, the police reported violent incidents every few days. By October, such incidents were occurring several times a day.[57] In Conakry, the homes of Barry Diawadou's supporters and those of anti-RDA chiefs such as El Hadji Alkaly Ibrahima Soumah were attacked, while European-owned cars were stoned.[58] On the coast and in the forest region, people chased government-appointed chiefs from their towns and villages and declared Sékou Touré to be their elected representative.[59]

The RDA was caught in a bind. While party leaders hoped to raise the people's ire by relentlessly exposing the wrongdoing of the government and its African collaborators, they simultaneously appealed for calm and forbearance. Not surprisingly, the leadership could not have it both ways. Accompanied by male and female RDA leaders, Sékou Touré traversed the country, urging supporters to desist from violence.[60] He proclaimed that the RDA was a party of peace. "If they insult you, do not respond," he urged his followers. "If they insult your parents, do not respond. If they lay a hand on you, do not reply. Go to the police with your witnesses and file a complaint."[61] In Kindia, Sékou Touré and Ouezzin Coulibaly, the RDA's interterritorial political director, held a private meeting with the local party bureau and the neighborhood women's presidents. The two leaders urged party members to remain calm, respect administrative authorities, and pay their taxes.[62] Other RDA leaders also preached calm, warning that the administration was waiting for an opportunity to act against the party.[63]

As RDA leaders at both the territorial and interterritorial levels struggled to maintain discipline at the grassroots, the government debated the proper attitude toward the RDA. In Paris, the Mendès France government, which had quickly negotiated French withdrawal from Indochina in the wake of Dien Bien Phu, favored a more conciliatory policy. Robert Buron, the new overseas minister, hoped that such a policy would promote the RDA's closer collaboration with the colonial administration. The hard-line officials in Guinea were clearly out of step with the new government.[64] To calm the unrest and to set matters straight with the governor, Buron toured Guinea in October 1954.[65] During his sojourn in Conakry, the RDA organized an enormous reception in his honor, maintaining order and directing traffic as if it were the governing power.[66] Interpreting the ministerial visit as a disavowal of Governor Parisot's policies, RDA demonstrators waved placards with "Vive RDA" emblazoned on one side and "Vive le Ministre" on the other.[67] Certain that the new French government would reject the disputed election results, RDA militants taunted Barry Diawadou's supporters in song:

> The RDA is everywhere
> The saboteurs always said
> That they are the chiefs
> But a man is a chief
> If he is heard by the people
> Sékou says he is not a chief
> But today they wisely gave him power.[68]

During his Guinean tour, Buron promised that future elections would be honest. He subsequently wrote that the results of the June 1954 elections "had been shamefully falsified in order to provoke the elimination of Sékou Touré."[69]

RDA optimism had never been higher. In preparation for the next series of elections, the party again concentrated on strengthening its base. According to Mamadou Bela Doumbouya, "In the aftermath of the 1954 elections, the electoral committees, formed in the interior and around trade union sections, were transformed, purely and simply, into party committees."[70] Expanding from their urban base, party members systematically canvassed the markets, challenged the chiefs, courted the military veterans, and distributed party membership cards in the most remote corners of the territory.[71] In Lower-Guinea, Moricandian Savané claimed, there was not a city, village, or neighborhood without an RDA organization.[72] Even the governor admitted that the RDA's spectacular mobilization efforts had permitted the party to establish itself "in most of the circles of the territory, except the Futa"—the stronghold of the Peul aristocracy and the colonial chieftaincy.[73] Throughout the territory, Sékou Touré routinely was called "Governor," and his reputation extended to the most isolated rural villages, the governor reported.[74] Attributing the surge in grassroots support to "a judicious employment of the women's committees, whose adherence draws in its wake that of the men," the governor noted that if elections were held in December 1954, the RDA probably would double the number of votes it had received six months earlier.[75] By 1955, the RDA claimed that its membership rolls had reached 300,000.[76]

The RDA's political momentum was sustained by frequent meetings. In Lower-Guinea, political meetings were held nearly every night. "Everywhere meetings are organized during which orators, adroitly adapting themselves to local circumstances, take the floor," the governor observed. "Every occasion—a trial, a dispute, a controversy over land—is taken to prove to the peasants that they are mistreated by the rich notables and by the administration." Rallying the peasants against the rich was one of the most effective RDA strategies.[77] Once again, the specters of communism and class struggle reared their ugly heads.

Evidence of the party's strong grassroots organization was everywhere. Hundreds, even thousands, of disciplined, uniformed party members turned out to hear the party's leaders. When Sékou Touré arrived at the Kankan airport on November 8, more than 2,000 people awaited him. The women were grouped by neighborhood. Most of them wore the new blouse, "Sékou Touré," which was made of white percale, the sleeves and bottom bordered in blue. On their heads, they wore scarves of yellow or green. The men wore tarbooshes of white percale on which the letters "RDA" were embroidered or written. Crowd control was maintained by RDA guardians of public order, who wore white armbands emblazoned with the inscription "Service of Order" or "RDA Police."[78]

Increasingly, RDA militants instituted their own organs of authority and bypassed official structures. "In the villages, the party had committees that they practically substituted for the village chiefs," Doumbouya recalled.[79] Similarly, the governor remarked that the RDA had established "an administrative organization parallel to the legal administration," which included police, judges, chiefs, and tax collectors. These RDA structures gave "precedence to the party, its men and its slogans, over the legal authority and its representatives," the governor noted with concern.[80] In N'Zérékoré circle, the police claimed that such parallel administrative structures were organized in each and every village.[81]

In the elections' aftermath, the police recorded a growing list of the RDA's "usurpation of functions." In December 1954, in Dubréka circle (Lower-Guinea), RDA "troops" had forced the military police to release RDA members accused of attacking the canton chief's home.[82] The following month, in the Dubréka village of Tondon, four RDA "military police" were sent by their "commissioner" to arrest a man they accused of plotting the murder of Thierno Camara, the local RDA president. According to the attorney general for French West Africa, the RDA "military police" and "commissioner" were uniformed in either khaki or white shorts and jackets. They wore tricolor belts and cross-belts, shoes, and caps inscribed with the initials "RDA." The alleged murder plotter was brought to Tondon, interrogated by Thierno Camara and the RDA "commissioner," and detained. The colonial police issued warrants for the arrest of nine local RDA militants, including Thierno Camara, for usurpation of official functions.[83] Similar activities were reported in Macenta circle (forest region), where RDA "services of public order" had been established. The RDA "police" in Macenta wore distinctive party badges emblazoned with the French flag.[84]

The Emergence of the Bloc Africain de Guinée

The presence and effectiveness of the RDA were evident even to its opponents, most notably the two governors who served in Guinea in 1955. Governor Charles-Henri Bonfils (appointed August 1955) openly admired the RDA's efficacy and the principled positions adopted by its leaders, which he compared favorably to those of its adversaries. Most RDA leaders originally had been trade union militants, he wrote. With the trade union "imprint and formation," they demonstrated concern for detail and numbers, which prevented them from selling their people short. They consistently stood up and fought for their constituents. The party's exceptional efforts had gained it the adherence "of all the urban and rural elements who opposed the holders of traditional seats of power."[85]

Governor Parisot, who preceded Bonfils and was notorious for his anti-RDA policies, lamented the comparative weakness of RDA rivals. The regional and ethnic associations were no match for the highly organized, popular party. No matter how many advantages were bestowed upon them, he observed, the regional and ethnic associations squandered every opportunity and seemed "keenly gifted in making blunders." The numerous gaffes of these associations, plus cleavages within the Peul bloc, had contributed to the growth of the RDA, whose year-end strength in 1954 "surpassed even the RDA's own evaluations in May 1954."[86]

Parisot was equally scathing in his assessment of the chiefs, notables, and political incumbents who formed the core of these associations. In his view, these government allies were corrupt, inept, and incapable of building a mass organization. Temporarily united for the elections, they once again had fallen "prey to their particularist demons," their unity shattered by ethnic rivalries and personal ambition. Their postelection euphoria had turned to angst due to "the unsuspected amplitude of the RDA in the urban centers, in the countryside of Lower-Guinea, in the hamlets of the ex-slaves in the Futa."[87] To make matters worse, Sékou Touré had "succeeded perfectly in Conakry, in Kindia, even in Mamou," the fiefdom of the paramount chief of the Futa Jallon, where the people were solidly behind him.[88] According to the governor, the old guard elites suddenly realized, "with fear and anger, that the political security in which they had lived until now, was illusory and that the RDA movement was authentically a mass movement. The progress achieved by this movement, since the elections, has confirmed to them that they represented almost no one but themselves, except in the Futa, and that they were rich only as a result of the credit lent them by the Administration."[89] Determined to defend their material and moral interests, the chiefs and territorial councillors were demanding unconditional support from the population, without adapting their behavior to the new political exigencies.[90]

Colonial officials were not alone in recognizing the superior methods, structure, and organization of the RDA. The party's growing strength throughout the territory forced African rivals to reevaluate their own methods and organization. Determined to secure a mass base before the legislative elections of January 2, 1956, the more savvy of the RDA's opponents embarked on a new course.[91] On November 19, 1954, a meeting was convened in Conakry, bringing together representatives of the regional and ethnic associations that had supported Barry Diawadou. In contrast to the mass meetings of the RDA, only fifty-eight people attended. Presiding over the assembly, Barry Diawadou declared that the regional and ethnic associations were now obsolete. The RDA, with its mass transregional base, was the only true political party in the territory. Barry Diawadou warned his followers that to surpass the RDA, they must initiate a new party that was modeled on the RDA's strongest features.[92] Barry Diawadou's concerns were echoed in other quarters. Mamadi Baro, a member of both the Territorial Assembly and the Grand Council in Dakar, later warned the Union du Mandé, "No one is ignorant of the political situation in Guinea since the by-elections of 27 June. An evolution has occurred at the heart of the RDA, which has bypassed the strength of the ethnic groups."[93]

In subsequent discussions, Barry Diawadou's supporters concluded that the loosely coordinated regional and ethnic associations that had favored their candidate in the legislative elections were disorganized and ineffective. They thus proposed the creation of a well-organized party with a doctrine and a program.[94] Hence, in late 1954, the regional and ethnic associations united in a single territorial party, the Bloc Africain de Guinée (BAG). Essentially an outgrowth of Barry Diawadou's electoral committee, the BAG was supported by the traditional powers of the country, who considered RDA leaders to be inferior, pretentious, and a menace to the ideals of order, hierarchy, wisdom, and power that the old guard purported to represent. Understanding the key to the RDA's success, the new party vowed to mimic RDA tactics by organizing mass meetings, establishing neighborhood committees and women's and youth wings, and instituting party uniforms. For a short time, it published a newspaper, *La République.*[95] Within months of the party's founding, the governor observed that "the leaders of the B.A.G. claim to be animated with a new spirit and declare that they want to adopt the propaganda methods of the R.D.A. in order to relieve it of its clientele."[96]

Despite the BAG's promising claims, Governor Parisot was skeptical about the potential of the new party. "This party appeared very awkwardly," he informed the high commissioner. Its patrons—Deputy Barry Diawadou for the Peuls, and Territorial and French Union Councillor Karim Bangoura for the Susus—were old wine in new skins. Both were sons of canton chiefs.[97] In an attempt to move beyond its limited ethnic and class base, the BAG quickly brought new blood into its leadership. Koumandian Kéïta, secretary-general of the autonomous African teachers' union, was named president of the new party.[98]

It was an astute move. Koumandian Kéïta could potentially challenge his RDA rival on several fronts. Like Sékou Touré, Kéïta was both a trade union leader and a Malinke. As head of the African teachers' union, whose rank and file included Guinea's most influential intellectuals, Kéïta might weaken Sékou Touré's base in the colonial civil service. As a member of the Union du Mandé's board of directors, Kéïta had the means to undermine Sékou Touré's support in both Upper-Guinea and the forest region.[99]

The emergence of the new party lent even greater urgency to the RDA's campaign for respectability. Addressing a crowd of some 1,000 people in Mamou in January 1955, Sékou Touré proclaimed in French—for the benefit of the colonial administration—that the RDA was not antigovernment or disloyal. It was not a party of violence and disorder. Since its disaffiliation with the PCF, the RDA's fight with the government was over. The party was now linked to the UDSR, one of the ruling parties in the French government.[100] It was the RDA's hope that its new attitude would give greater weight to its claim of victory in the June 1954 elections.

Parliamentary Validation of the June 1954 Elections

During the six-month interval between the legislative elections and the official validation of the results, the RDA's primary objective had been to show evidence of massive popular support for the RDA and indignation concerning the electoral outcome. The party also had sought to win over parliamentary opinion, to persuade the National Assembly to reject as flawed the official election results. In the governor's estimation, the RDA nearly won on all fronts.[101]

In anticipation of the January 21, 1955, National Assembly vote, the RDA's interterritorial coordinating committee sent numerous telegrams to the French capital, urging that the results be rejected.[102] RDA claims of fraud were supported by outside observers and other political parties.[103] At its July 1954 congress, the SFIO—the parliamentary affiliate of the Guinean DSG—charged that during the electoral campaign, Guinea's governor had openly sided with Barry Diawadou. The SFIO decried the administration's failure to maintain neutrality.[104]

Ignoring popular protests and dismissing the claims of RDA deputies and their allies, the French National Assembly validated Barry Diawadou's election by a simple show of hands. The SFIO deputies, having gotten cold feet, abstained. Most members of the UDSR, the RDA's official ally, were conveniently absent from parliament during the vote. Only the RDA and the PCF voted against validation.[105]

Despite RDA leaders' pleas for calm, the period following the election validation was extremely turbulent. On January 30, 1955, Almamy Barry Aguibou, chief of the Dabola canton and father of Barry Diawadou, arrived in Conakry, which had voted massively for Sékou Touré.[106] The validation of the elections, compounded by the arrival of the chief in an RDA stronghold, sparked numerous incidents. RDA supporters sacked the home of El Hadji Alkaly Ibrahima Soumah, the Coronthie neighborhood chief who had helped to rig the elections. As the crowd burned his possessions, the chief fired upon it, wounding seven people. A melee ensued, in which more than forty people were injured, one of whom later died. Cars and houses were burned.[107] During the night of February 1, violence broke out in the Conakry suburb of Coléah, where one house and four shops were burned.[108] Violence also took root in the Lower-Guinea circles of Boffa and Dubréka, which, the government asserted, were in a "preinsurrectional state." In both circles, the RDA had openly organized its own administration and was running a shadow government, claiming that government officials, elected or otherwise, did not represent the will of the people.[109]

The violence brought to the fore a growing rift between the RDA leadership and the party's rank and file. While the territorial leadership decried vigilante justice, local militants, long subjected to abuses by the chiefs and notables, had no such compunction. The governor reported that Sékou Touré and other high-level RDA officials seemed sincere in their efforts to rein in overzealous local leaders and activists. However, they were overwhelmed by the tidal wave of popular discontent.[110] Former RDA militant Néné Diallo attributed the differing views on violence to generation. It was the young people, male and female, who were most prone to take matters into their own hands, she claimed:

> In those days, RDA women were so daring that even if you placed your fingers on their eyeballs they would not blink. They had nothing on their minds but the RDA. Our leader loved us for it, but . . . he never told anybody to fistfight. No leader gave us instructions to fight. . . . But young people liked to create havoc. That is all. They chased one another on all sides. . . . Sékou warned us against such things. He said, "Even if they should curse your mothers or fathers—whatever happens—do not play into their hands." . . . But no matter, there were two competing parties. Fights were only waiting to happen.[111]

As Guinea descended into violence, it became increasingly evident that the administration could no longer count on the loyalty of its own enforcers. A judicial inquiry revealed that the RDA had infiltrated the colonial police force; a majority of the African police in Lower-Guinea were RDA members. In an attempt to break the RDA's stranglehold, the administration had engaged in standard divide-and-rule tactics, transferring a large number of non-Susu police to Conakry and incorporating them into the local force. However, these efforts had been to no avail. During the recent wave of violence, the governor charged, the police had demonstrated "inadmissible passivity." Their inertia reinforced his conviction that African agents should never be stationed in their country of origin. Guinea's indigenous police and intelligence agents should be replaced with Africans from other territories, he noted. If internal ethnic differences were being transcended through political mobilization, a foreign police force, with less sympathy for the local population, was essential.[112]

The judicial inquiry also stressed the grassroots origins of the recent unrest. The incidents in Conakry and Coyah had been initiated by RDA village and neighborhood committees, rather than the territorial leadership. Demonstrating their growing sense of international solidarity, as well as their exuberance at the imperial power's recent defeat, local militants had established revealing code names for the various neighborhoods. "Little Tonkin" stood for Coyah and "Indochina" for the Conakry neighborhood of Sandervalia. Perhaps most salient was the sobriquet for El Hadji Alkaly Ibrahima Soumah's fiefdom of Coronthie. For that neighborhood, RDA militants selected the name "Dien Bien Phu."[113]

CHALLENGING THE CHIEFS

Although the unrest of 1954–55 had been sparked by the RDA's defeat in elections marked by fraud, other long-standing grievances quickly emerged. In the countryside, the furor over the validation of Barry Diawadou's election exacerbated preexisting tensions between the local population and government-appointed chiefs. Since the mid-1940s, when the burden of the war effort had fallen primarily on their shoulders, African peasants had resisted chiefly authority. They had refused to pay taxes or to engage in unpaid labor on the chiefs' behalf. They had deserted public works sites and avoided tax collectors and military recruiters by fleeing across interterritorial borders. Embracing the peasants' cause, the RDA had capitalized on their antichief sentiments. The chiefs had retaliated by targeting RDA activists and rigging elections to ensure the party's defeat. Since the party's ability to hold the populous rural areas depended upon undermining chiefly power, the antichief campaigns became central to the RDA's grassroots strategy.[114]

Following the election validation, the most serious incidents between the local population and government-appointed chiefs occurred in the village of Tondon, Dubréka circle, about 180 kilometers from Conakry. Tondon was the administrative seat of the Labaya canton, whose chief, Almamy David Sylla, was vehemently opposed to the RDA and equally determined to rout it from his domain.[115] It was widely believed that Sylla had helped to rig the June 1954 elections by confiscating the Tondon voting lists and augmenting the number of votes received by RDA opponents.[116]

It was in this atmosphere that the RDA had begun to build a shadow government in Tondon. In January 1955, Thierno Camara, a World War II veteran and the local RDA president, was arrested with eight other militants for usurpation of official functions.[117] One of the functions in question was the collection of local taxes. The RDA, following a practice initiated by military veterans, had begun to bypass the hated canton chiefs, sending tax revenues directly to the circle commandants.[118] This usurpation of functions both undermined chiefly power and threatened a major source of the chiefs' income.[119]

On February 8, 1955, Chief Sylla journeyed to the village of Bembaya, six kilometers from Tondon. His purported purpose was to collect taxes. However, the population claimed to have paid their taxes to the village chief, who had sent the money directly to the circle commandant. Furious that the Bembaya residents had bypassed his authority, Sylla demanded that they pay again, or be bound and beaten. Incensed, the village women surrounded and insulted him and seized his gun, horse, and drum, the insignia of his office. Showering him with insults and ridicule, they marched him back to Tondon and escorted him to the home of Thierno Camara. In accordance with RDA directives, Camara appealed for calm and urged the crowd to release the chief and permit him to return home.[120]

The following morning, a squadron of military police accompanied by forty auxiliaries arrived from Conakry to arrest the local RDA leaders, including Thierno Camara. In an attempt to thwart the arrests, a crowd of some 800 people pelted the squadron with rocks, trying to obstruct its entry into Tondon. The military police charged, throwing tear gas grenades. Armed with his saber and gun, Sylla struck out at the crowd. When the melee was over, thirty-seven villagers lay wounded, four of them seriously. Half of the wounded were women.[121]

After attacking the crowd, Sylla entered Thierno Camara's home, where he found Camara's twenty-six-year-old pregnant wife, M'Balia, an officer of the Tondon RDA women's committee. Sylla slashed open her belly with his saber.[122] According to Aissatou N'Diaye, one of the women present "took off her own wrapper and tied it on M'Balia's belly. . . . The [RDA] women brought more wrappers and knotted them around M'Balia's waist and chest in an attempt to stop the hemorrhage. M'Balia was taken to Ballay Hospital in Conakry. Mafory Bangoura and I were told to inform the women in the city that M'Balia had been hurt, that she was in a late stage of pregnancy, and that she was at the hospital. When we arrived at the hospital, the doctors would not allow us to enter."[123] On February 11, Camara's near-term fetus, wounded by the saber blows, was stillborn. Camara herself died a week later. Her husband, still imprisoned, was not permitted to attend the funeral.[124]

Outrage over the endless stream of abuses by the colonial chieftaincy coalesced in the furor over M'Balia Camara's death. In Conakry, the RDA distributed printed tracts, inviting all party members to the burial.[125] According to Aissatou N'Diaye,

> Almost all the RDA people came out. On the day of her funeral, Ballay Hospital was filled with people. . . . We all went on foot to the cemetery. . . . Sékou asked each person who attended the funeral to take along a small stone. Imagine the quantity with such a crowd! People obliged. The military police were sent in to intimidate the people. Sékou allayed people's fears and asked them to deposit the stones in one spot as they went by. In this way, the military police would know the number of people in attendance. The authorities soon gave up counting.[126]

Estimates of the number of people in the funeral cortege varied widely. While the police placed the figure at 1,500, the RDA and a sympathetic French journalist judged the crowd to be more than 10,000.[127]

For the Guinean RDA, the death of M'Balia Camara was a galvanizing event. Her contribution to the struggle rapidly assumed mythic proportions as she was transformed into a national heroine who had made the ultimate sacrifice. Women, especially, were exhorted to follow her example by standing up to colonial authorities, including the canton chiefs.[128] M'Balia Camara "was the sacrifice—for the women," explained Aissatou N'Diaye: "After the burial, Sékou held a meeting. He said, in the name of God and His Envoy, M'Balia had become the first heroine of the struggle in Guinea. He said that the day she was struck, February 9, 1955, would be commemorated from then on [in remembrance of women's role in the struggle]. Every year, February 9 would be commemorated throughout the land—in Upper-Guinea, Lower-Guinea, in the smallest town."[129] Songs, such as the following, were composed by RDA women in Camara's honor:

M'Balia, we will never forget your example
M'Balia, death spares no one in this world
M'Balia, may God The All-Powerful grant you his paradise
M'Balia, the Party weeps for you, M'Balia
M'Balia, we will never forget your example.[130]

After the funeral, the RDA immediately began planning a "Grand Day of Solidarity" for April 29. On that occasion, prayers would be offered for all RDA cadres who were prisoners or victims of colonial violence. The commemoration of M'Balia Camara would be central to the event. In anticipation of an embarrassing display, the government imposed a territory-wide ban on all large public meetings between April 29 and 30. Demonstrations on public roads were strictly prohibited. To carry out its plan, the RDA thus resorted to "prayer meetings" in mosques and private compounds.[131]

REINING IN THE GUINEAN RDA

If the growing militancy of the Guinean populace concerned the RDA's territorial leadership, it caused even greater consternation at the interterritorial level. Houphouët-Boigny and his followers were determined to reassert control over the Guinean RDA. To promote this objective, Houphouët-Boigny scheduled a coordinating committee congress for July 8–12, 1955, in Conakry. The purpose of the congress was to elaborate upon the RDA's new policy of collaboration and moderation. The choice of Conakry as the meeting's venue was deliberate; the campaign to bring the Guinean branch back into line would be launched at the congress.[132]

For several years, despite persistent appeals from d'Arboussier and his supporters, Houphouët-Boigny had refused to call a coordinating committee meeting. In fact, the party's supreme governing body had not met since 1948, two years before RDA parliamentarians broke with the PCF.[133] During its July 1955 congress, the coordinating committee retroactively confirmed the parliamentarians' decision to sever links with the PCF, finally rendering it binding. Moreover, it resolved to exclude from the party all dissident branches still operating with communist sympathies.[134] While the Union Démocratique Nigérienne, Union Démocratique Sénégalaise, and Union des Populations du Cameroun were expelled for refusing to toe the anticommunist line, the Guinean branch was spared.[135] It was hoped that the Guinean RDA, unlike the other branches, could be successfully wooed to the collaborationist position.

The co-optation of Sékou Touré was critical to the accomplishment of this goal. By the mid-1950s, a veritable personality cult had developed around the Guinean leader. A gifted speaker, Sékou Touré had an uncanny ability to appeal to the masses through culturally rooted images, anecdotes, and parables.[136] His popularity had been dramatically enhanced by his leadership of the successful 1953 general strike.[137] In addition, he had profited from the party's drive for women's emancipation.[138] The government was well aware of Sékou Touré's status. In March 1955, H. Pruvost, secretary of state for Overseas France, observed that Sékou Touré was an "excellent orator, knowing how to reach the crowds. . . . He is the beneficiary of an incontestable prestige and a large audience in Guinea." Pruvost concluded that Sékou Touré was the "idol of Lower-Guinea—especially of the women . . . and sufficiently popular in Upper-Guinea as in the forest region."[139] Likewise, the governor recognized Sékou Touré's tremendous hold over the local population, noting, "It is undeniable that Sékou Touré was able to show the degree of his personal ascendency over the mass of Guinean militants on the occasion of demonstrations cleverly carried out and magnificently orchestrated."[140] If the Guinean RDA were to be tamed, the leadership first had to be co-opted, and that meant Sékou Touré, first and foremost.

There had been previous attempts to corrupt Sékou Touré. In October 1951, the colonial government had hoped to produce a schism in the French West African trade union movement by enticing Sékou Touré to establish an African trade union federation independent of the PCF-linked CGT. Sékou Touré had not taken the bait.[141] By the mid-1950s, however, Sékou Touré had achieved even greater renown as a nationalist than as a workers' hero.[142] Having risen to prominence through the trade union movement, Sékou Touré had used the workers' struggle as a launching pad for the anticolonial cause. In 1955, with working-class issues securely subordinated to the broader nationalist program, Sékou Touré was prepared to break with his erstwhile allies in the CGT.

At the coordinating committee's Conakry congress, Sékou Touré completed his bow to the Houphouët line. Having endorsed the rift between the RDA and the PCF in October 1951, he now proposed the long-awaited break of African unions from the French CGT and the communist-dominated World Federation of Trade Unions, and the formation of a new labor federation under African control.[143] Sékou Touré, once denounced as a "notorious marxist" and a "fierce partisan of the Third International," now was regarded by the colonial administration as an *interlocuteur valable.*[144]

In the congress's aftermath, orders for moderation emanating from the territorial and interterritorial leadership were disseminated throughout Guinea.[145] Employing his personal prestige as interterritorial president, Houphouët-Boigny visited the local committees in Conakry to champion the new cause.[146] Ouezzin Coulibaly, who had spent most of 1955 touring Guinea with Sékou Touré, continued to campaign on behalf of the RDA and its new policy. According to Morgenthau, it was the involvement of these interterritorial leaders, especially Coulibaly, that laid the groundwork for the Guinean RDA's "shift from the tactics and vocabulary of total opposition to those of partial communication with French officials."[147]

Initially, it was not clear whether Guinea's local leaders and rank and file would accept the accommodationist stance or derail the new agenda. Activists from across Guinea had come to the capital in droves to attend the coordinating committee's congress. Some 5,000 people had participated in the public session on July 10.[148] Since 1950, local activists had proven to be far more radical than their territorial and interterritorial leaders. With grassroots militants looking over their shoulders, local leaders thus embraced the new policy only hesitantly.[149]

The Mamou subsection, long noted for its opposition to the Houphouët line, was a case in point. On the instructions of the RDA's territorial and interterritorial leaders, meetings were convened on July 15 and 25 to promulgate the new collaborationist policy.[150] On August 1, Pléah Koniba, an African doctor and head of the Mamou subsection, wrote an angry letter to the party's board of directors in Conakry. On behalf of the subsection's bureau, Koniba roundly criticized Sékou Touré's proposed break with the CGT. He accused Sékou Touré of leading a dictatorship within the party, fostering a personality cult, censoring the ideas of party members, holding numerous meetings with the high commissioner without witnesses, and using catastrophic management practices. Employing ideas and terminology emanating from the PCF/GEC milieu, Koniba demanded a return to collective leadership, the ideal of the party over the myth of the person, criticism and self-criticism within the party, and a trade union movement that was truly combative.[151]

A subsequent letter from Koniba and his colleagues raised similar concerns. It asserted that on August 9, Sékou Touré had sent a circular to the high commissioner without consulting anyone. Written communications between the party and the administration were not the domain of the secretary-general alone, but of the territorial board of directors as a whole, the Mamou officials noted. Furthermore, all physical contacts between party leaders and the administration were to include at least three members of the leadership, in order to thwart corruption and illicit deal-making. Yet Sékou Touré had made many solo trips to Paris and Dakar and had frequently used those occasions to meet with administration officials. In closing, the Mamou officials reiterated the need for collective leadership and democratic methods within the party.[152] For the next two years, the subsection's criticism of Sékou Touré and its refusal to accept the Houphouët line continued unabated. In November 1957, the Mamou subsection was expelled from the Guinean RDA for "Left deviationism" and general insubordination.[153] Although Mamou took the issue further than other subsections, its critique of Sékou Touré and the RDA's new orientation would resonate with other dissenting voices in the years that followed.

THE FAILURE OF THE BAG

The administration's determination that Sékou Touré was an interlocuteur valable, who could be used to push the Guinean RDA to the Right, marked an abrupt about-face. Throughout the previous year, the government's chosen vehicle for bolstering the chieftaincy and sustaining the status quo had been Barry Diawadou. Following the validation of his election, governing parties in France had lobbied hard for his allegiance, and the colonial administration hoped that it finally had found a dependable ally.[154] When the BAG held its first congress on August 4–7, 1955, the administration attempted to bolster the party's support by granting four days' leave to all civil servants who wished to attend. During the congress, the BAG voted unanimously to establish a parliamentary affiliation with the governing Parti Radical Socialiste, led by Prime Minister Edgar Faure. Further cementing its alliance with power, the BAG passed a motion condemning communism and affirming its attachment to a French Republic that was "one and indivisible."[155]

Despite these promising signs, the administration's hopes for a reliable ally were soon dashed. Concerns about the BAG had been percolating since January 1955, when the governor noted that the BAG had "only a small following from the forest, and an even smaller one from Upper-Guinea"—despite Koumandian Kéïta's presumed ethnic appeal in these regions.[156] The high commissioner drew an equally dismal picture. The regional and ethnic associations had fallen apart, he wrote, but the BAG, which was supposed to replace them, had absolutely no substance. The validation of the 1954 legislative elections had not begun to fix Guinea's problems. The territory's legal representatives—Barry Diawadou in the National Assembly and Karim Bangoura in the Assembly of the French Union— had been "outstripped by events" and did not have the necessary weight to command the situation.[157]

The government's concerns resonated among the regional and ethnic associations. In January 1955, Framoï Bérété, president of the Union du Mandé, warned his followers that, at present, the BAG existed only on paper.[158] In an effort to rally support among the Susu in Lower-Guinea, Territorial Assembly Councillors Karim Bangoura, Amara Soumah, Mamadou Sampil, and Fodé Mamadou Touré organized a tour of their cantons and pledged to unite their constituents in the new party. The police, however, disparaged their claims of popular support, remarking that the councillors would be lucky to gather enough adherents merely to conduct their meetings.[159] Prominent leaders clearly were no substitute for a mass base.

Indeed, Barry Diawadou's precarious position was evident from the outset. Shortly after his election was validated, the new deputy commenced his victory tour. He began in the capital city, an RDA stronghold. Arriving at the Conakry airport on March 23, he was greeted by fifty to sixty cars of supporters. The motorcade followed Barry Diawadou to his home, where another 500 people were assembled. According to the police, the BAG was attempting to demonstrate its authority by boldly parading in hostile territory. The Peul chiefs did not want their leader to hide fearfully, while the RDA held grandiose receptions at every opportunity.[160] Although the RDA could not command the same number of motor vehicles, RDA crowds regularly numbered in the thousands rather than the hundreds.

In May, Barry Diawadou began to tour the interior, long neglected by the BAG. Arriving in Kankan on May 23, he apologized to the crowd for not having visited since his election one year earlier.[161] In the interim, Sékou Touré had visited Kankan several times.[162] The next day, the BAG held a public meeting which, according to the police, attracted some 800 people, including most of Kankan's small-scale merchants and transporters, as well as the city's notables.[163]

Barry Diawadou soon learned that the warm reception in Kankan did not represent the norm. When the new deputy arrived in the forest region, he was greeted by angry protests. In Macenta, RDA demonstrators threw rocks, one of which struck the deputy on the head. One demonstrator was arrested. Several hundred people, including women and children, descended on the prison and administrative offices in the hope of forcing his release. Military reinforcements were sent from Kissidougou, Kankan, and Dakar.[164] Several local leaders, including the women's committee president, were arrested and charged with instigating the unrest.[165] Similar events transpired in Guéckédou, where the police were called in to disperse the crowd. Numerous arrests were made.[166]

In the months that followed, the situation did not improve. According to Governor Parisot, the BAG was "shaken" by the RDA's successful coordinating committee congress in Conakry.[167] In July and August, BAG activity diminished markedly. While the RDA was gearing up for the next round of elections, Governor Bonfils charged, the BAG was essentially dormant, having failed to establish a popular base. It had tried to implant itself in the rural areas "under the stimulus of a certain number of chiefs and territorial councillors attached to the cause of Barry Diawadou and his constituents." However, BAG leaders had shirked their duty to rally the population personally. Under the pretext of heavy professional responsibilities, they had chosen instead to send "people without influence" to campaign on their behalf. In a damning assessment, Bonfils concluded that the party favored by the administration was led by people who "lacked a fighting spirit" and "wasted their time in vain discussion and idle chatter."[168]

Unofficial sources were no more optimistic. In August, *Agence France-Presse* reported that the canton chiefs from all four geographic regions, as well as some African doctors, teachers, and other civil servants, had joined the BAG.[169] However, these gains among "traditional" and "modern" elites could not compensate for the fact that the BAG "had hardly any organized sections."[170]

Had BAG leaders possessed the requisite drive and organizational skills, it is still doubtful that they would have succeeded in establishing a mass base. In the 1950s, Guinea's population was predominantly rural, nonliterate, and poor. The BAG, in contrast, was a party of elites. With some insight, Governor Bonfils observed that "because the B.A.G. notables are in general people of means, some-times even rich," the RDA-BAG rivalry was essentially one of "the poor classes against the propertied class."[171] Moreover, he concluded, the "profound antago-nism" between the two parties was due largely to "the differentiation of social classes on which the parties are [based]: proletariat against the bourgeoisie, haves against have-nots, traditional notables and nouveaux-riches against the ambitious and plebeian." Far from winning the local population to their cause, BAG partisans demonstrated "the splendid arrogance of the rich for the poor." They were incensed by their adversaries' behavior, which they considered "the impertinence of valets."[172]

Throughout the remainder of the year, Governor Bonfils derided the party led by the government's protégés. While successive administrations had at-tempted to hand the territory to their client on a silver platter, the BAG had been too inept to take advantage of the opportunity. In his year-end report for 1955, the governor noted the party's "striking failure." The BAG had but a weak audience in the urban areas and almost no contact with the peasantry. It had demonstrated no interest in trade union or social questions. Barry Diawa-dou's speeches, unfortunately, had been geared toward the intellectuals, rather than the peasant masses, who most likely were unmoved by his claim that as an aristocrat he had the right to rule. The BAG's most active partisans were the colonial chiefs, who, throughout most of the territory, were rapidly losing strength. Even in the Futa Jallon, the last bastion of chiefly authority, the old order was beginning to crumble.[173]

Even more ominously, the governor concluded that the BAG's failure was due to its own errors, rather than RDA deceit. The BAG had no unifying vi-sion or set of principles. It was merely an ensemble of interests brought to-gether by a common adversary. At best, it represented a very limited constitu-ency of men greedy for honors and positions. Despite its claims to the contrary, the BAG had not learned the lessons of recent events and reformed its meth-ods. Rather, party leaders had devoted their energies to protecting their per-sonal interests. The chiefs and clerks who supported the party had little political sense, he wrote. They had virtually no influence on the masses. Other adherents, including prosperous Malinke merchants, were more interested in the perquisites they gained as party members than in the party program. Fi-nally, the governor concluded, the BAG had been completely negligent in es-tablishing a party organization. Its touted grassroots structures and rural mobilization campaign had come to naught. Believing itself to be assured of victory, due to the support of the chieftaincy and the administration, the BAG had failed to develop a mass base. In preparation for the January 1956 legislative elections, the BAG had conducted a truly "bourgeois campaign."[174]

Diminished by its elite focus, lack of dynamism, and poor organization, the BAG was further torn by dissension within the leadership. Party leaders disagreed sharply in their determination of the party's fundamental objectives and the means of achieving them. The major cleavage was between "modernizing" elites in Conakry and "traditional" elites in the interior of the country— that is, between young, Western-educated intellectuals and older chiefs and notables who had benefitted from their collaboration with the colonial regime. In Conakry, the BAG's board of directors had attempted to infuse new blood by ousting the old guard from positions of power. However, the elders had refused to step aside. Thus, the governor lamented, the masses inevitably saw the BAG as a government party, destined to support the chiefs and wealthy merchants. Because of the BAG's deficiencies, only the solidarity of Peul aristocrats— and the wealthy classes in general—could ensure that Barry Diawadou retained his seat in the January 1956 elections.[175]

THE FATE OF OTHER PARTIES AND ASSOCIATIONS

By 1955, only two parties—the RDA and, to a far lesser extent, the BAG— dominated the Guinean political scene. Other political parties and regional and ethnic associations had largely disappeared. The DSG remained a party of elites who regarded with contempt the less credentialed leaders of the RDA. It never managed to mobilize a mass base and was essentially a regional party that made little headway outside the Futa Jallon.[176] While Barry III had attempted to rally the followers of his socialist predecessor, Yacine Diallo, the DSG leader's virulent attacks against the chiefs, particularly those in the Futa, had alienated Diallo's most important base. With few exceptions, the chiefs had cast their lot with the BAG. According to Governor Bonfils, the DSG realized the match was over. With no chance of electoral success, the party "finally, more or less voluntarily, turned the game to the RDA in detaching from Barry Diawadou a certain number of Peuls, who believed in a less strictly regionalist and conservative conception of the political life of the Futa."[177]

The regional and ethnic associations were in even greater disarray. In a devastating critique, Governor Bonfils described the Union Forestière as divided, anarchic, and unable to define a program or find a candidate.[178] In his year-end report, he concluded that the Union Forestière "made a sorry figure in 1955.

Without doctrine, without response, without program, it constituted no more than a regional association, a consortium of people, rather than a true political party. Its influence in the forest circles has keenly diminished. Its congress in Macenta in October 1955 finished as a complete fiasco." The leadership, as well as the rank and file, were deserting the association. Some leaders were joining the BAG, others the RDA. Given the RDA's unity and organization, the governor lamented, that party would certainly profit from the internal divisions of its rivals, bringing it even greater success in the forest region.[179]

The governor's prediction proved true. By the end of 1955, the majority of the forest population had rallied to the RDA. In the forest region, as elsewhere, the governor wrote, the RDA had established a formidable organization, "covering the entire country with a tightly woven network of cells and implanting its leaders in even the most distant villages." Despite the relative poverty of its members, the RDA controlled significant financial resources and had considerable access to automobiles—thanks to Malinke traders and transporters, who were attracted by RDA demands for a reduction in customs fees between neighboring territories. Intellectuals also had joined the party in great numbers. Teachers used their vacations to promote the RDA. Nurses proved to be ideal recruiters, as they moved about the countryside implementing vaccination and sleeping sickness eradication campaigns. RDA militants "have won almost everyone to their cause," the governor concluded.[180]

CONCLUSION

The RDA's resurgence in 1955 was a remarkable achievement, particularly after the devastation of local party structures in the early 1950s. In the face of government repression, grassroots activists had carefully rebuilt the party from the base, establishing RDA committees in towns, villages, and hamlets throughout the territory. By 1955, it was clear that the Guinean RDA was by far the most popular party in the territory, despite the party's official defeat in the June 1954 legislative elections.

Because the RDA's popularity was not reflected in its political representation, protest continued at the grassroots. The years 1954–55 were characterized by local challenges to chiefs, notables, and other government allies, and to the political parties that supported them. Concerned that popular unrest in Guinea would undermine its precarious détente with the government, the interterritorial RDA rushed in to quell the rebellion. While some headway was made among territorial leaders, notably Sékou Touré, efforts to rein in the grassroots were to no avail.

Recognizing the need to collaborate with the only viable political party, the colonial administration embarked on a dual strategy of co-optation above and repression below. While courting the RDA leadership, it continued its campaign against radicals at the grassroots. In order to destroy the propaganda value of an anti-RDA governor and to secure the cooperation of the party leadership, the French government replaced Governor Parisot with Charles-Henri Bonfils on August 1, 1955.[181] Because Bonfils was considered a moderate, the RDA had anticipated a more constructive relationship with the local authorities. However, such predictions were soon proven wrong. In September, Governor Bonfils departed on a month-long vacation, leaving a subordinate in charge. The latter continued Parisot's "tough" anti-RDA policies. He immediately transferred a number of RDA civil servants, including the heads of the Labé, Pita, Tougué, and Guéckédou subsections. Five RDA leaders were transferred from Boké alone. Local activists continued to be arrested in large numbers. RDA peasants, artisans, and merchants were denied loans. Village chiefs sympathetic to the RDA were removed from their positions. To avoid arrest, many militants stopped sleeping at home. A number of leaders refused to appear publicly. Some party stalwarts resigned, while others declined to accept leadership positions.[182]

Despite the official policy of détente, little had altered on the ground. In 1955, government hostility toward the RDA continued unabated. In 1956 and 1957, however, the situation would change dramatically. Under increasing pressure throughout the empire, the government would be forced to embark on yet another program of imperial reform.

CHAPTER 4

The RDA's Rise to Power and Local Self-Government, 1956–57

FOR THE FRENCH GOVERNMENT, unrest in Guinea during 1954–55 was part of a larger, more troubling issue. By the mid-1950s, the French empire was under attack on several fronts, most notably in Indochina and North Africa. In Indochina, the Viet Minh, a broad-based national liberation movement led by the communist revolutionary Ho Chi Minh, defeated the French at Dien Bien Phu in May 1954. France withdrew from Indochina shortly thereafter. Within months of the French defeat at Dien Bien Phu, the Front de Libération Nationale (FLN) launched a war for independence in Algeria. Meanwhile, armed conflict escalated in Tunisia and Morocco, ultimately leading to their independence in 1956.[1]

Again, France embarked on a program of imperial reform in order to salvage what was left of the empire. Buffeted by the humiliating French defeat in Indochina, violent confrontations in Morocco and Tunisia, an escalating war in Algeria, and widespread grassroots mobilization elsewhere, the National Assembly recognized that more concessions were essential.[2] The result was a new legal framework or *loi-cadre,* enacted on June 23, 1956, which authorized the French government to implement a series of legal reforms that would lead to limited self-government in the overseas territories.[3] Defending the proposed system before parliament, Overseas Minister Gaston Defferre noted the need for reform before it was too late; limited self-government would forestall the move toward complete independence. Justice Minister François Mitterrand subsequently noted that loi-cadre was "the final fulfilment of the thirteen year old promises of Brazzaville."[4] As was the case with the Brazzaville reforms, Africans had little input into loi-cadre.[5] Neither the territorial assemblies nor the Grand Council in Dakar was consulted.[6] One of the few African deputies to influence the law's final text was Houphouët-Boigny. Appointed to the French cabinet as minister without portfolio in February 1956, Houphouët-Boigny was adamantly opposed to independence and favored the strengthening of territorial—at the expense of federal—powers. His views, more than any others, shaped the antifederal bias of loi-cadre.[7]

In Guinea, the year 1956 also marked a turning point in electoral politics. The colonial administration initiated a new policy of détente with the RDA, this time embracing the party from the highest echelons to the local level. Repression eased, and the hostile colonial chieftaincy was effectively neutralized. As a result, the RDA amassed significant victories at the polls. The party won two National Assembly seats in the legislative elections of January 1956 and gained control of nearly all the major municipalities in November 1956. In March 1957, the RDA swept away virtually all opposition in the Territorial Assembly. As a result, the new loi-cadre government, established in May 1957, was dominated by the RDA. However, the RDA's rise to power brought renewed dissension within the ranks. Accommodation with the colonial administration and the assumption of power, however limited, resulted in the RDA's rightward movement. Yielding to anticommunist pressures and the increasingly conservative RDA, most Guinean trade unions severed their ties to the French CGT. Another intraparty battle began to brew, as Guinean youths and other leftists publicly criticized their leaders' compromises.

THE LEGISLATIVE ELECTIONS OF JANUARY 2, 1956

The RDA's triumph in electoral politics commenced with the legislative elections of January 1956. The party's candidates were chosen at a conference of cadres held in Mamou on November 12–13, 1955; they subsequently were approved by all the subsections. The Mamou conference was the first major RDA conference to be held outside of Conakry. The choice of its location was carefully calculated. As the residence of the Grand Almamy—the paramount chief of the Futa Jallon—Mamou was in the heart of enemy territory. The convening of a major RDA meeting in that city was a taunt at chiefly authority.[8]

The site of the RDA conference was but the first strike. Recognizing its relative weakness among the Peul population, the RDA was determined to field a high-profile Peul candidate who would draw his brethren into the fold. The party first approached Barry III, leader of the severely weakened DSG, and in-

4.1 Sékou Touré (*center*) and Saïfoulaye Diallo (*right*), Conakry, October 2, 1958. AFP/Getty Images.

vited him to join Sékou Touré on the RDA ticket. When Barry III rejected the proposition, the party turned to Saïfoulaye Diallo. Diallo's early militance on behalf of the RDA, as well as his GEC membership, had attracted the attention of colonial authorities. As a result, he had been transferred from Guinea and posted successively in the French Soudan and Niger. Hence, in 1956, he was virtually unknown on the Guinean political scene. However, unlike most RDA leaders, Diallo had impeccable "traditional" as well as "modern" credentials. He was the son of Alpha Bocar Diallo, a canton chief in Labé circle and a senior member of the Futa chieftaincy. He was also a member of the Western-educated elite, having graduated first in his class at William Ponty.[9] Joining Saïfoulaye Diallo on the RDA ticket were Sékou Touré and Louis Lansana Béavogui. Together they vied for the three National Assembly seats allocated to Guinea.[10]

The political program for the January 1956 elections was defined by the interterritorial RDA during its 1955 coordinating committee congress. Foreshadowing the move toward local self-government, the party called for greater representation of Africans in political structures at all levels and the increased democratization of these structures. Among the most important demands were those advocating the democratization of the village and canton chieftaincies; the broadening of local assemblies' powers; increased representation of the territories in the Republic's various governing bodies; universal suffrage; abolition of the dual college for all elections; and the rapid expansion of the number of fully self-governing municipalities. The RDA also demanded intensified efforts against infant mortality, the extension of sanitary services, and the construction of more clinics, hospitals, and dispensaries. It called for a massive increase in student enrollment at all levels and the replacement of personal with indirect taxes. Finally, party leaders vowed that under RDA control, the much-hated Société Indigène de Prévoyance schemes would be transformed into producer-run cooperatives.[11] Although developed by an interterritorial body, the RDA's program had profound local appeal.

Critique of the chieftaincy was a central issue in the RDA campaign. Throughout much of the territory, the authority and prestige of the canton chiefs continued their precipitous decline, while that of RDA leaders rose accordingly.[12] Although the government had attempted to shore up the chiefs' waning authority through the reorganization of their administrations, these efforts had met with little success.[13] According to the governor, "For the mass of militants, worked up for many months, and again recently during the electoral campaign, against the exactions of the chiefs, the hostility to the chieftaincy constitutes the essential element of the [RDA's] action. . . . The propaganda centered on this theme strikes the imagination of the peasant masses in proposing to them the object and the cause of their frustrations and the daily difficulties of their existence."[14] RDA criticisms resonated strongly with the rural population, which had resisted chiefly authority since the war effort of the 1940s, when chiefs requisitioned increasing quantities of crops and labor. "It was in this regard that [the RDA's] campaign was very intelligently conducted," the governor concluded.[15] Capitalizing on popular disenchantment with the chiefs, the RDA effectively linked them to the rival party, campaigning under the slogan "To vote for the B.A.G. is to vote for the chiefs."[16]

The electoral campaign officially began on December 13, 1955.[17] Leaflets outlining the RDA program were widely distributed. All Guineans were urged to vote en masse for the RDA, which was described as a movement for African emancipation and for fraternity between the races and peoples.[18] Although it continued to envision a future in association with France, the RDA called for greater political autonomy and local management of internal affairs. As Sékou Touré put it, "We want to wear our own glasses."[19]

Apart from the widespread appeal of its program, the RDA had other comparative advantages. Its financial means were far superior to those of the BAG, despite the latter's support from chiefs, aristocrats, and other wealthy elites. According to the governor, "It is a fact that the RDA is very rich and very clever."[20] The party amassed a significant amount of money from a relatively impoverished constituency through membership dues and contributions. In its appeals, the RDA made much of its programs that, it promised, would bring a brighter future. There was some truth to the governor's claims that "the populations give all the more willingly, hoping that after its rise to power, the R.D.A. will considerably reduce the taxes. In giving today, the peasant calculates that he is buying tranquility and relief from taxes tomorrow."[21] As a result of its successful financial drive, the RDA had six million francs and more than fifteen vehicles at its disposal during the election campaign. Twelve of the vehicles had been newly purchased. Moreover, for some time before the elections, the RDA had bought up all the sound equipment and public address systems on the market, depriving its adversaries of an important means of communicating with the largely nonliterate population.[22]

The RDA also benefitted from a large number of newly registered voters. Despite continued limitations on the franchise, the period 1951–56 witnessed a dramatic increase in the number of registered voters in Guinea. Between the legislative elections of June 1951 and January 1956, the size of the electorate more than doubled. There were 393,628 registered voters in June 1951. By June 1954, that number had grown to 476,503. In January 1956, the electorate was 976,662 strong.[23] The vast majority of new recruits had been mobilized by the RDA.[24]

Having embarked on an enormous voter registration campaign, the RDA became deeply engaged in civic instruction.[25] "It seems that the masses, especially in the bush, are beginning to interest themselves in electoral problems," the governor observed in a classic understatement. "The flood of male and female voters, generally illiterate, understood the sense of the elections," he admitted, adding that "the education of the voting masses" was largely the work of the RDA.[26] The governor reported that RDA cadres, including students and teachers on Christmas vacation, carefully instructed their nonliterate constituencies in voting formalities. To those who could read, they distributed clear and comprehensive circulars describing voting regulations. They established evening courses for RDA officials who would be working at the polls. Finally, the party subsidized civil servants who had taken vacation without pay to mobilize for the RDA.[27]

The electoral campaign took shape primarily through the actions of RDA cells, rather than through mass meetings. It was the local committees that disseminated information and rallied the rural population to the cause.[28] Traders and transporters lent their vehicles to the RDA to facilitate their work in the rural areas. Local party officials provided food and lodging, as well as oil and gasoline, to large numbers of visiting cadres.[29] The RDA women's and youth wings played a prominent role, organizing dances and other social events, both to raise funds and to spread publicity for the party. Women as well as men explained the voting procedures and carried the party program to the villages, hamlets, and urban neighborhoods.[30] With the capital securely in their camp, Conakry-based cadres returned to their ancestral villages to campaign, mobilizing the populations of Lower-Guinea and the Futa Jallon.[31]

The administration's new policy of détente forced a change in official behavior. On December 12, the director of security services for French West Africa reminded his subordinates that the local police must maintain "strict neutrality" during the elections.[32] On the same day, the high commissioner requested that the territorial governors make "veritable efforts to separate the administration from all suspicion" and to instruct the circle commandants in this regard. In the hope of convincing the public of the government's new stance, the high commissioner addressed the populace by radio, explaining the principles of government neutrality. He requested that all governors do the same.[33] In Guinea, speeches by both the high commissioner and the governor were duly broadcast. They assured the population of the administration's absolute neutrality and appealed for calm during the electoral campaign.[34]

While the government freely employed the broadcast media to promote its own message, it refused to let the political parties do likewise. Claiming that their emissions were creating tensions, the high commissioner ordered the governors to stop all radio broadcasts by political parties from December 24 onward.[35] In territories like Guinea, with poor road systems and a largely nonliterate rural population, the parties were thus deprived of a critical means of communication.

Although the colonial administration pledged to remain neutral during the electoral campaign, such promises were met with general disbelief. With past experience as their guide, RDA leaders fully expected to be confronted with attempts at bribery and corruption, as well as fraud. Hence, they advised the rank and file: "If they offer you money, take it and give it to the party. If they offer you transport to the polls take it and vote for the [RDA]. . . . The money they give you cannot buy you. . . . It cannot buy a man; it cannot buy his thoughts; it cannot buy his faith. The money was stolen from you. Take it, it is yours. Use it not for yourself but for your brothers, for the [RDA]."[36] The RDA was particularly worried about the canton chiefs, who historically had been the primary perpetrators of electoral fraud. Although the chiefs were supposed to remain neutral during the January 1956 campaign, they used proxies to wage an active crusade on behalf of the BAG.[37]

Having learned a hard lesson from the June 1954 elections, the RDA was determined to oversee the election process. As a result of détente, the party was in a far better position to prevent fraud than in previous elections. It applied pressure to ensure that RDA representatives were included in all the commissions distributing voter registration cards, as well as in the 809 polling stations situated throughout the territory.[38] At the polls, RDA officials were instructed to follow intricate procedures to ensure that ballots had not been tampered with and that the election results were fair. According to the party's mimeographed instructions, RDA observers should verify that ballot envelopes and urns were empty when the voting began. They should confirm that the number of ballot envelopes matched the number of electors and that the urns did not contain false bottoms. The urns were to be fastened by two discrete locks, the key to each in the possession of a different election official. Further, party representatives were instructed to challenge the presence of all unauthorized people near the polls. Of particular concern were circle guards and chiefs who might exert pressure on the voters. The RDA officials should carefully observe the voting, opening of ballot envelopes, and ballot counting. They should record all observations, criticisms, and challenges. They must never vacate the polls without leaving a proxy in their place. They should refuse to respond to all provocations, which might be staged as a cover for the substitution of an electoral urn. They should carry a flashlight "in case the lights go out." Finally, all observations and results should be telegraphed to the RDA's political bureau in Conakry.[39]

ELECTION DAY

Peace prevailed on election day; only two incidents were reported in the whole of Guinea. The governor credited all sides, noting that party leaders had urged their followers to remain calm and disciplined, assuring them that this time the elections would be free of irregularities. They had explained that people could vote freely and would not be subject to pressure from the administration. An increase in the number and improvement in the accessibility of polling stations also helped to keep the peace.[40]

Aissatou N'Diaye clearly recalled election day in Conakry. She and Momo "Jo" were working at the polls as RDA representatives, she said. "We began early in the morning and stayed until midnight. We stayed to count the ballots. Then, suddenly, everybody got excited by the news that all was going our way—in Upper-Guinea, Lower-Guinea, the Futa Jallon. Everything was coming to the RDA."[41] Women quickly composed songs to commemorate the RDA victory:

We have carried away the victory
We have beaten the enemy
Sékou Touré is number one.

Employing some poetic license, they sang,

Comrades, oh yes comrades
Sékou Touré is also the governor of Conakry.[42]

Even the governor conceded that the election results were breathtaking, "over-turn[ing] all the predictions." The outcome "must mark an important turning point in the political life of the Territory," he concluded.[43] In the January 1956 elections, 346,716 electors (61.7 percent) voted for the RDA. The BAG, in contrast, obtained only 146,543 votes (26 percent). The DSG won 9.8 percent of the votes, and other parties, 2.5 percent.[44] These results diverged sharply from the official tally for the June 1954 elections, which gave the RDA only 85,808 votes (33.7 percent); Barry Diawadou, 145,497 votes (57.1 percent)—approximately the same number he received in 1956; the DSG, 6.3 percent; and other parties, 2.9 percent. Within the space of four and one-half years, the RDA's share of the vote had grown from 14 percent (June 1951) to 61.7 percent (January 1956). Due to this massive outpouring of popular support, the RDA won two of Guinea's three National Assembly seats. Sékou Touré and Saïfoulaye Diallo were newly elected, while Barry Diawadou retained his position.[45] The governor concluded that RDA "success has profoundly modified the political map of Guinea and it is likely that in the Territorial Assembly elections of 1957 important changes will occur."[46]

The transformation of Guinea's political map was indeed striking. From April 1952 to January 1956, the RDA had only a single representative in the Territorial Assembly: Sékou Touré, who had been elected to represent Beyla circle in August 1953. The party had no representatives in the National Assembly, the Council of the Republic, the Assembly of the French Union, the Grand Council in Dakar, or the municipal councils in Guinea.[47]

Writing to his superior in Dakar, the governor noted that the RDA's success had reversed all forecasts. The victory had taken the entire administration by surprise, for "even the most optimistic evaluations had predicted that [the party] would win only a single seat." The governor continued, "My prognostics were proven false in a manner that surpassed the normal margin of error for predictions of this genre. Those of the circle commandants, on which I relied, were also wrong and in identical if not greater proportions." The governor could not explain the reason for this dramatic intelligence failure. Suggesting gross negligence on the part of colonial officials, particularly circle commandants, he queried: How could government functionaries, who were supposedly living in contact with the population—some for as long as fifteen years—fail to see what was happening? How could a phenomenon that had become so evident in early January have gone unnoticed—even by those whose profession it was to observe? The veil torn away by the legislative elections revealed a Guinea that was quite different from the one they had imagined.[48]

The entrenchment of the RDA obviously had not occurred overnight, the governor continued. This process clearly had begun long before the January 1956 elections. The governor confessed that he now understood the popular upheavals of the previous eighteen months; they corresponded to the spirit of a majority that had had no legal way to express its voice. Finally, Guinea's legal representation was consistent with the popular will.[49]

Outside observers contend that the 1956 elections were conducted relatively honestly.[50] The RDA's success in neutralizing the chiefs and their agents had played an important role in its victory.[51] "Everywhere the chiefs [and] notables were shadowed by parallel [RDA] organizations, including military police, judges, and collectors of funds," the governor wrote. "The traditional cadres of African command" who long had functioned "as intermediaries between the circle commandant and the mass of the population are practically no longer existent."[52]

The governor's lengthy postmortem included grudging praise for the RDA. Referring to the RDA victory as a "dazzling triumph," he remarked that the party's extraordinary success was due "to its methodical organization, the sustained nature of its propaganda campaign, [and] the personal prestige of its leader."[53] The import of the RDA's grassroots structures was not lost on the governor. With undisguised admiration, he referred to "the perfection of the organization" that the party had established. Although undoubtedly communist-inspired, the organization was "adapted to the local milieu by utilizing the cadres of pre-existing village societies. Cells were constituted in even the most remote hamlets, and the transmission of slogans and information was done through a chain of party leaders from the circle seat to the villages and hamlets." Of particular importance was "the establishment of women's committees," whose "zeal and ardor" rapidly set the agenda "as a result of male indecision and tepidness." In the urban areas, the party made good use of its trade union base, which effectively had been merged into the party.[54]

REGIONAL BREAKDOWN OF THE ELECTION RESULTS

The regional breakdown of the election results provides further insight into the RDA's mobilizing strategies. The party experienced resounding victories in Lower-Guinea (87 percent) and Upper-Guinea (78 percent), took a large majority in the forest region (64 percent), and won by a small margin in the Futa Jallon. While the administration had expected the RDA to win in Lower- and Upper-Guinea, it was caught completely off guard by results in the forest region and the Futa Jallon.[55]

In the forest region, government forecasts had predicted that the RDA and BAG, deemed equally popular, would neutralize one another. Instead, the RDA garnered 64 percent of the votes, while only 29 percent went to the BAG.[56] Seeking to assign blame for the RDA success, the governor singled out the Union Forestière, which recently had abandoned its charter as a (purportedly) apolitical regional association and reconstituted itself as a political party. Prior to the elections, the governor had hoped that the Union would dissolve itself and throw its support to the BAG.[57] Instead, the party ran two candidates: Mamba Sano, the former deputy, who stood for both the Union Forestière and the BAG, and Farah Touré, a territorial councillor, who ran on a rival Union Forestière list. These competing lists split the vote, Touré's candidacy diverting votes from the BAG to the benefit of the RDA.[58]

Further surprises were in store in the Futa Jallon. All three parties had concentrated their efforts in the Futa, a densely populated region inhabited by approximately half the territory's electorate. For the RDA, focusing its principal efforts on a region considered deeply hostile to it was a risky proposition.[59]

Once again, the administration projected a BAG victory. However, even in that bastion of the colonial chieftaincy, the RDA "conquered . . . positions unanimously judged impregnable," the governor marveled.[60] "The R.D.A., to general astonishment, came in first," he noted, while the DSG did far better than had been expected.[61] Its success surpassing its wildest hopes, the RDA won 41 percent of the ballots cast, compared to 36.8 percent for the BAG and 19 percent for the DSG.[62] Barry Diawadou won a majority only in Pita and Mamou circles. According to the governor, "These figures highlight the very sharp regression of the B.A.G., the spectacular progress of the R.D.A. and the gains of the D.S.G. that were, in fact, very localized" in the Futa Jallon. While the DSG had taken votes from the RDA in 1954, in 1956 it gained at the expense of the BAG.[63]

In the "feudal citadel" of the Futa Jallon, the RDA won in both the urban and the rural areas.[64] Targeting the region's most important urban centers, Sékou Touré had focused on the towns of Labé, Mamou, Dalaba, and Pita, where he gave speeches on market days. Once they had mobilized the urban centers, Sékou Touré and other party militants worked their way into the interior. According to the governor, most of the hamlets and villages, including those of former slaves, ultimately were reached by the RDA.[65] It was the RDA's active opposition to slavery that permitted it to penetrate into Peul strongholds, the governor concluded. A large portion of the party's votes came from the former slave villages.[66]

Although slavery officially had been abolished in 1905, its enduring legacy was a powerful factor in regional politics.[67] In 1956, an estimated one-quarter of the Futa's population was of slave descent.[68] The majority of this population had descended from the original Jallonke inhabitants, agriculturalists who had been conquered by the Fulbe-Peul during the Islamic jihads of the eighteenth and nineteenth centuries, and from war captives imported into the region.[69] In the 1950s, the Peul aristocracy continued to dominate the region politically.

As the RDA penetrated this aristocratic Peul stronghold in 1955, class and status became the party's primary focus. People of slave descent were targeted by party organizers. At the bottom of the social hierarchy, members of this group had borne the brunt of colonial oppression. Their latent hostility to the colonial regime—and to the Peul aristocrats and chiefs who sustained it—was easily aroused. A number of factors contributed to their rancor. Individuals of slave descent were disproportionately recruited for involuntary labor and military service.[70] Although slavery had long been illegal, some former slaves and their descendants continued to serve their erstwhile masters without pay.[71] Social and economic discrimination against freed slaves and their descendants was rampant.[72]

The RDA's success in the Futa Jallon was due, once again, to its championing of issues identified by the local population. The party condemned class-based discrimination and denounced disparities between the rights of "free" Peuls and those of slave ancestry. It deplored the fact that the latter's rights to land and other property were less secure, and that, in contrast to earlier times, descendants of slaves had fewer opportunities for education and therefore less access to civil service positions. Finally, the party condemned the fact that men of slave descent suffered greater hardships in terms of military service. While "free" Peuls were conscripted in peacetime, men of slave descent were recruited in times of war.[73] The RDA's advocacy of equal rights appealed to a large segment of the Futa's population.

Although the RDA's foothold in the Futa was strongest among those of slave ancestry, other low-status populations eagerly joined the RDA as well. The RDA made significant inroads among the "bush" or "cow" Peul, a low-status but free people who herded cattle for the aristocratic minority.[74] The party did well among the Jakhanke, a Mande-speaking people who, like the Jallonke, had settled in the Futa prior to Peul arrival.[75] The RDA also met with success among the ethnically diverse peoples in low-status occupations, notably, traders, artisans, and *griots*.[76] Because blacksmiths, griots, slave descendants, and other people of caste lived in separate villages, apart from the Peul aristocracy, they could be mobilized in relative secrecy. The RDA used this residential segregation to its advantage.[77]

The RDA's success in the Futa Jallon was largely due to its appeal to the descendants of slaves and other low-status residents who harbored deep animosity toward the powerful Peul chiefs. The RDA's outspoken opposition to the chieftaincy and to the slave system that supported it, together with its promotion of an egalitarian social order, resonated strongly in the former slave villages. Although the ancestors of some residents had been sold into slavery by the nineteenth-century Malinke empire builder Samori Touré, and his agents, the RDA deflected potential hostility toward his descendant, Sékou Touré, by convincing them that "[i]f Samory Toure can make you slaves, Sekou Toure can make you free." During the legislative elections of 1951, 1954, and 1956, most of the RDA votes in the Futa Jallon came from the villages of former slaves and other low-status residents.[78]

The RDA's strong opposition to the chieftaincy was a factor that enhanced its status among a number of Futa populations. The party's position appealed to Western-educated elites as well as to people of low status. Like peasants and former slaves, "modernizing" elites despised the chiefs' unearned privileges and abuses of power. Such forward-looking *évolués,* particularly teachers and nurses of the trypanosomiasis service, constituted an important segment of RDA militants in the Futa Jallon.[79] During the elections, the governor wrote, the "stupendous rise of parties hostile to the chieftaincy" had shaken the institution to the core.[80] The chiefs were effectively neutralized by RDA cadres who blanketed the region with propaganda whose "efficacy was complete." This strategy proved that the RDA knew how "to do an election," the governor concluded.[81]

Even in the Futa Jallon, fissures in the colonial chieftaincy were emerging. During his pre-election tour of the rural areas, the governor had been struck by the "erosion and discredit" of the institution. The election results demonstrated that the situation was even more serious than he had imagined. "That such a rot [in the feudal structures] could have occurred without anyone revealing it is a repetition of the classic phenomenon of collective illusion and a lack of imagination of the people on the spot," he complained. If there had been an armed uprising against the tyrants, the feudal order could have remained for a long time, the governor contended. But the overthrow was done by secret, anonymous ballots in election urns. The incubation, like the crisis, had remained hidden.[82] "The people on the spot"—the circle commandants and the governor himself—had been taken in by their own myth of a passive, resigned, apolitical, and fatalistic rural population in the Futa Jallon, one that unquestioningly bowed down to feudal authorities.

By early 1956, the governor had begun to see what the RDA had long known: democracy and the feudal chieftaincy could not coexist.[83] Throughout all of French sub-Saharan Africa, "the inhabitants increasingly aspire to a regime of equality with the citizens of metropolitan France," the governor observed.[84] The quasidemocratic principles enshrined in the new postwar imperialism directly threatened the feudal chieftaincy. Only a miracle of political balancing would permit that anachronism to endure—and then, only temporarily. The contradictions inherent in the two systems would eventually result in the chieftaincy's collapse.[85]

If the chieftaincy was doomed, so was the party that supported it. Once again, the governor forcefully criticized the administration's long-favored party. The BAG, assured of the chiefs' support, had neglected to combat RDA propaganda and had failed to establish any organization capable of responding to it, he charged.[86] The BAG's dramatic loss was due to "the absence of a program, poor organization and the insufficient numbers of B.A.G. cadres against which were opposed the dynamism and efficacy of its adversaries."[87] In sharp contrast to the RDA, the BAG was inactive, except during the brief periods of the electoral campaigns.[88] While Sékou Touré and members of the RDA list spoke everywhere and constantly, their speeches peppered with poignant slogans, the BAG's efforts were only halfhearted.[89]

The governor was not alone in his assessment. After the elections, the BAG engaged in a striking exercise of self-criticism. Instead of advancing a specific program, its leaders admitted, the party had spoken in broad generalities. Its themes had been too theoretical to make an impression on the masses. While the RDA had focused on grievances against the chiefs and on concrete economic issues such as fees and taxes, the BAG had emphasized the need for public order and continued collaboration with France. In contrast to the RDA, the BAG had failed miserably in disseminating its message to the population in the interior. While some rural residents had managed to learn of the BAG program, even they had rejected it favor of the RDA.[90]

THE BREAK WITH THE CGT

While the BAG continued to tout a moderate program that included continued collaboration with France, by 1956 grassroots pressure for autonomy—from France and from French organizations—had become increasingly pronounced.[91] French and African political leaders manipulated the proautonomy sentiment to further distance African from French communist organizations. Once again, Sékou Touré was the target of both French and African lobbying.

Since 1950, Sékou Touré had been under considerable pressure from interterritorial RDA President Houphouët-Boigny to remove himself from communist influences and to sever all ties to the CGT. In 1955 and 1956, High Commissioner Bernard Cornut-Gentille expressed similar concerns about communist involvement in French West Africa and encouraged Sékou Touré to form an autonomous African trade union federation, thereby splitting the West African labor movement and weakening the CGT.[92] The compulsion to break all remaining links with French communist organizations intensified in February 1956, when Houphouët-Boigny was named minister without portfolio in the new French government.[93]

The notion of trade union autonomy had been broached in July 1955 at the interterritorial RDA's coordinating committee congress in Conakry. It was there that Sékou Touré had introduced the prospect of the African CGT's secession from its French parent body and the formation of a new federation under African

4.2 Abdoulaye Diallo, secretary-general of the French Soudanese CGT unions in the 1950s, was of Guinean origin. Photo, 1960. ECPAD/Collection de la Documentation Française.

control.[94] In November 1955, just prior to the legislative election campaign, the CGT's Senegalese-Mauritanian branch broke from the metropolitan body. In January 1956, shortly after the legislative elections, the Senegalese-Mauritanian unions joined Sékou Touré in forming the autonomous Confédération Générale des Travailleurs Africains (CGTA). Within months, Sékou Touré would become the CGTA's federal president.[95]

Once again, Sékou Touré altered his position when it worked to his political advantage. He made a clean break with the CGT—the springboard of the nationalist movement—only after the RDA's electoral sweep. As the undisputed leader of the Guinean RDA, whose position had been consolidated by his sensational electoral victory, Sékou Touré could now abandon his high-level appointments in both the French West African and Guinean CGT without jeopardizing his national stature or influence.[96] One month after the rupture, the coordinating committee of the French West African CGT acknowledged the new reality and expelled Sékou Touré from its ranks.[97] In Guinea, the CGT unions rapidly fell into line behind their erstwhile leader. When a Guinean branch of the CGTA was formed in May 1956, twenty-two of Guinea's twenty-seven CGT unions joined, and Sékou Touré was elected secretary-general.[98]

Other influential French West African CGT leaders, such as Niger's Bakary Djibo and the French Soudan's Abdoulaye Diallo, vigorously opposed the divorce of African unions from the French CGT.[99] They were supported by most of the leaders of the CGT's French West African territorial branches. The majority of branches remained loyal to the orthodox CGT until January 1957, when the CGT, the CGTA, and a number of autonomous unions merged to form the Union Générale des Travailleurs d'Afrique Noire (UGTAN). With the formation of UGTAN, more than two-thirds of all French West African trade unionists were united in a single, autonomous federation.[100]

LOI-CADRE AND LOCAL SELF-GOVERNMENT

The push for autonomy by African trade unions was followed by complementary action in the political sphere. Under the banner of self-government and political autonomy, a new legal framework, or loi-cadre, was enacted on June 23, 1956, authorizing the French government to implement a series of political reforms in the overseas territories.[101] Under the new system, the territories were retained within the framework of a unitary French Republic, continuing to fall under the jurisdiction of its constitution. However, the conduct of territorial affairs was decentralized and democratized. Significant powers previously exercised by the nonelected governor, high commissioner, and overseas minister, as well as the elected federal Grand Council, were transferred to elected governments in each territory.[102]

Before the implementation of loi-cadre, territorial assemblies were primarily consultative, rather than deliberative, bodies. They had few powers beyond financial and budgetary matters. Since the majority of expenditures were fixed, primarily administrative obligations, the assemblies had little room to maneuver. The new legal framework granted territorial assemblies much greater authority in running local affairs. They acquired legislative powers in a number of areas, including territorial services, public works, land, conservation, agriculture, fisheries, and most mineral rights. The territorial assemblies also gained responsibility for health, education, urbanization, cooperatives, and the codification of indigenous law.[103]

As well as augmenting the powers of the territorial assemblies, loi-cadre established elected cabinets, or councils of government, that served as territorial executive bodies. Each council of government included six to twelve ministers. Its workings were overseen by the governor, who was president of the council. A holdover from the old imperial system, the governor was, as before, a nonelected, usually European official appointed by the French government. The ministers were elected by—but not necessarily from—the territorial assembly. The chief minister was vice president of the council and oversaw its functioning in the governor's absence. In order to have legal effect, most of the council's decisions had to be ratified by the territorial assembly.[104]

Besides democratizing local governing structures, loi-cadre dramatically democratized the franchise. Articles #10–16 of the new legal framework instituted universal suffrage for adult citizens of both sexes within a single electoral college. The last vestiges of the discriminatory two-tiered electoral system were abolished. The single electoral college, already in place for National Assembly and municipal elections in French West Africa, was instituted for all bodies, including territorial assemblies, circle (district) councils, and the Council of the Republic.[105] The law of November 10, 1956, fixed the voting age at twenty-one years.[106]

Despite these advances, a number of nondemocratic features remained. As before, the chief executive of the territory was an appointed governor, who was subordinate to another appointed official, the high commissioner of the federation. Although some of his powers had been absorbed by the council of government, the governor still enjoyed substantial prerogatives. He continued to be in charge of foreign affairs, defense, the fiscal and monetary systems, and economic, social, and cultural development. He oversaw the council of government and could request that the territorial assembly reconsider its decisions and that the French government nullify decisions of both the territorial assembly and the council of government.[107]

If loi-cadre increased the powers of elected governments at the territorial level, it substantially reduced those of the French West and Equatorial African federations.[108] A number of matters previously under the jurisdiction of the Grand Councils in Dakar and Brazzaville were transferred to the French government in Paris or to the various territories.[109] Although many African representatives had lobbied for the creation of an elected federal executive, no such provision was included in the loi-cadre reforms. The appointed high commissioner retained complete control over federal services and the implementation of policies adopted by the Grand Councils.[110]

Despite the increased democratization and decentralization of powers, the loi-cadre system fell far short of independence. Metropolitan France preserved its dominant position in the overseas territories. The French parliament retained ultimate power over all legislation. In case of conflict, National Assembly laws overrode those of the territorial assemblies. Key services were defined as state public services, as opposed to territorial ones, and were financed and controlled by metropolitan France. The powerful circle commandants were included within the framework of state public services, and thus were not subject to territorial control. Finally, the French government retained the power to dissolve African assemblies and to nullify their decisions.[111]

The dispositions of loi-cadre were rendered immediately effective by decree #56–669 of July 7, 1956. This decree also authorized a massive revision of voters' lists between July 9 and September 30, 1956. The new lists, valid through March 31, 1957, would be effective for both the municipal and territorial elections. Every individual, male or female, who had reached the age of twenty-one before October 1, 1956, and had resided continuously for six months in the circle where he or she wished to register was henceforth eligible to vote.[112] The new electoral regime, including universal suffrage and a single electoral college, would be applied in the municipal elections of November 18, 1956, and the territorial elections of March 31, 1957.[113] In Guinea, the new suffrage provisions were widely publicized. The governor sent a communiqué to all circle commandants and to the local press, while the RDA embarked on a massive campaign to register all party militants, especially women, youths, and poor people in general, who had been barred from voting in the past.[114]

THE MUNICIPAL ELECTIONS OF NOVEMBER 18, 1956

The process of democratizing local government had begun piecemeal even before the enactment of loi-cadre. Some of the initial steps had taken place at the municipal level. Before November 1955, six Guinean municipalities—Conakry, Kankan, Kindia, Labé, Mamou, and Siguiri—were administered by mayors, who were assisted by local commissions. The mayors and the commissions were appointed by the governor. The French law of November 18, 1955, instituted partially self-governing and fully self-governing municipalities in French West and Equatorial Africa. These were called *communes de moyen exercice* and *communes de plein exercice,* respectively.[115] Nine Guinean municipalities were designated as partially self-governing: Beyla, Boké, Dalaba, Forécariah, Kissidougou, Kouroussa,

Labé, Macenta, and Siguiri. Five others were designated as fully self-governing: Conakry, Kankan, Kindia, Mamou, and N'Zérékoré.[116] In both types of municipalities, elected municipal councils replaced the appointed commissions. The councils were charged with some tasks previously under the authority of European officials, including control of the municipal budgets. In each partially self-governing municipality, the position of mayor was filled by the circle commandant, who was appointed by the governor. An assistant mayor, elected by the municipal council from among its members, was authorized to stand in for the mayor when absent. In each fully self-governing municipality, municipal councillors elected the mayor from within their ranks. In the aftermath of loi-cadre, the 1955 municipal council law was modified. The law of November 10, 1956, stipulated that municipal councillors were to be elected by direct, universal suffrage according to a system of proportional representation.[117]

The first elections under the new municipal council laws were scheduled for November 18, 1956. In Guinea, voter turnout was extremely high. As a result of the new universal suffrage law, there had been a tremendous growth in the number of people eligible to vote, and mobilization by the RDA had led to a massive increase in voter registration.[118] While 976,662 Guineans had been registered to vote in January 1956, that number had risen to 1,376,048 approximately one year later.[119] In the five fully self-governing municipalities, 70 percent of those registered voted. Of those who voted, 85 percent favored the RDA. In the nine partially self-governing municipalities, 66 percent of those registered cast their ballots, and the RDA received 63 percent of the votes.[120] According to the final tally, the RDA won 243 of 327 municipal council seats, the position of mayor in all five fully self-governing municipalities, and the position of assistant mayor in eight of the nine partially self-governing municipalities.[121] In Conakry, the RDA won 31 of 33 seats. Sékou Touré was elected mayor, defeating both Barry Diawadou and Barry III.[122]

In Mamou, the RDA's chief rival was the canton chief, Almamy Ibrahima Sory Dara, who headed the BAG list. Officially recognized as the paramount chief of the Futa Jallon, Dara led the region's traditionalist forces.[123] Despite the Almamy's obvious prestige, the RDA won 14 of Mamou's 23 council seats. The RDA's Saïfoulaye Diallo became mayor, and Pléah Koniba, his deputy.[124] Describing the RDA's "imposing" victory in Mamou, the police expressed surprise that support for the Almamy's list had not at least equaled that of the RDA.[125] The vanquishing of one of the Futa Jallon's most conservative spokesmen was the RDA's most precious victory, Sékou Touré said; it represented the defeat of feudalism. "When the head of the serpent is severed, the rest can be made into a belt," he asserted.[126] Even the police concurred that the RDA victory in Mamou, and the DSG's strong showing in Labé and Dalaba, were certain proof that "feudalism was crushed."[127]

If the RDA's electoral sweep threatened feudal interests, it also imperiled those of the party that represented them. The municipal council elections underscored the BAG's dramatic decline in the major urban centers. The RDA's rival received only 2 percent of the votes cast in Kankan, 3 percent in Conakry, and 11 percent in Kindia.[128] Barry Diawadou admitted that the party's weakness was especially marked in N'Zérékoré, where the BAG section had dwindled to practically nothing.[129]

Despite its precipitous descent, the BAG was not completely out of touch with Guinean realities. In late 1956, it still shared common ground with the victorious party's mainstream, as leaders of both parties continued to champion Franco-African unity. During the municipal council campaign, Koumandian Kéïta had warned the people of Mamou, "No one must tell you that France is worthless because we owe everything to it. It cannot transform stones into gold, but it can do a lot. We are here to work in the interest of Guinea and of France."[130] Themes emphasizing Guinea's French connection reverberated through both parties' postelection rallies. Former RDA activist Néné Diallo recalled that after Sékou Touré was elected mayor, he visited her neighborhood: "Before he arrived that day, our flag had 'Liberty, Equality, Fraternity' boldly written over it. We went with it wherever we pleased. . . . Then we named our neighborhood association 'Liberty.'"[131] On December 1, Sékou Touré declared to a Conakry crowd of 8,000 that he had greater pride in the thousands of men and women who had come to demonstrate their confidence in the RDA, in Guinea, and in the Franco-African union than in his post as mayor. After reiterating the RDA's plan for the construction of schools, hospitals, and adequate housing and for the provision of jobs and pensions, Sékou Touré led the crowd in crying, "Long Live Africa! Long live Franco-African Fraternity! Long live Guinea! Long live Conakry! and Long live the R.D.A.!"[132] Despite the RDA victory, the alliance with France still seemed secure. The majority party had chosen the path of collaboration.

New Calls for African Autonomy

Before 1957, independence, as opposed to local autonomy, was not on the mainstream African political agenda.[133] While segments of the student and youth movements had been agitating for immediate independence since 1956, the

RDA had merely used this pressure to extract more modest concessions.[134] As late as December 1956, Sékou Touré had extolled the virtues of the Franco-African union, declaring that the future of France was inseparable from that of the people overseas.[135] By early 1957, however, the movement for greater African control had intensified. In the campaigns leading up to the March 1957 territorial elections, there was little rallying to the Franco-African union. Instead, the twin themes of African unity and autonomy from France became the dominant cries. While African unity was necessary to effectively combat colonialism, African autonomy was desired in all domains, vis-à-vis French political parties, trade unions, youth organizations, culture, and government.[136]

Once again, trade unions were at the forefront. Having severed their ties to the French CGT and formed an independent African federation in January 1956, CGTA unions had achieved autonomy.[137] In July 1956, a much smaller group of unions took a similar step. French West African unions affiliated with the Confédération Française des Travailleurs Chrétiens ended their association with the French federation and reorganized themselves as the Confédération Africaine des Travailleurs Croyants (CATC). The French Equatorial African unions followed suit in early January 1957. Bowing to African realities, the new federation changed its name to embrace both Muslim and Christian members. However, it continued to be subsidized by the Catholic Church. In keeping with its conservative tendencies, the CATC affiliated with the anticommunist Confédération Internationale des Syndicats Chrétiens.[138]

With the majority of Guinean unions at least nominally independent of their French progenitors, trade union leaders prepared to make further advances toward African unity. Sékou Touré urged all Guinean unions to unite under the banner of the Guinean CGTA. He then took up the interterritorial CGTA's proposition that all trade unions in every French African territory come together in one pan-African confederation.[139]

In January 1957, this plan was largely realized. At a conference in Cotonou, Dahomey, the majority of rival African trade union bodies agreed to unite in a single interterritorial confederation, namely, UGTAN. Among those agreeing to unity were the CGT, the CGTA, and a number of autonomous unions such as those of teachers and railway workers. The CATC refused to affiliate with the new confederation, citing its political nature. Force Ouvrière had refused to participate in the conference altogether. Championing African autonomy—and under considerable pressure not to join the communist-linked World Federation of Trade Unions—UGTAN did not affiliate with any French or international trade union body.[140] According to the Cotonou agreement, a branch of UGTAN was to be created in each territory. In Guinea, this resulted in the establishment of the Union des Syndicats des Travailleurs de Guinée in March 1957.[141] With formation of UGTAN, the CGT's dominance of the French West African trade union movement was broken.[142] However, the victory for the moderates was far from complete. Many UGTAN leaders retained the radicalism of their CGT past, and in the future they would press the RDA from the Left.[143]

As African trade unions asserted their autonomy, to the detriment of their erstwhile communist allies, RDA activists in Guinea grew more militant in their speech. Increasingly, they made reference to French departure and the end of colonial rule. In an April 1956 march in Kindia, police reported that "a cortege of about a thousand people, the majority women, left the R.D.A. headquarters to congregate at the Residence square." Placards inscribed with provocative messages were prominently displayed. One read, "Down with colonialism. The people who were blind yesterday have found their sight."[144] Similarly, in March 1957, local RDA leaders told a crowd of 1,000 in Siguiri that, like the French, Guineans would acquire their liberty after a revolution. According to the police, the leaders declared, "We want to be independent. The French have done nothing for us. They are in Africa uniquely for their own interests—not for ours. As soon as we have [African] ministers, we will show the bad French the door and replace them with those who please us." El-Hadj Abdoulaye Touré, an African doctor from Kankan, told the people that they no longer should fear the circle commandant, the justice of the peace, or the military police, who would be chased from Africa after the territorial elections.[145] Oumar Diallo repeated Touré's claims a few days later, noting that since the November 1956 municipal elections, Siguiri belonged to the RDA, not to the European authorities. He added that the RDA was monitoring these authorities; at the first sign of irregularity, complaints would be lodged in Conkary, Dakar, and Paris.[146]

The radical stance of RDA partisans provoked a response from the BAG's Siguiri branch. At a rally behind the military police headquarters, BAG Territorial Councillor Bandiougou Magassouba warned the crowd: "The RDA wants to chase the French from Africa. What will we do without them? Because we are incapable of making even a *daba*. The Moroccans and the Tunisians sent the French away. Now they regret it. Let us not do as they did. We should reflect before it is too late." The griot Diessina Madi Diabaté then sang praises of the BAG and insisted on the necessity of French presence in Africa.[147] Meanwhile, in Deputy Barry Diawadou's hometown of Dabola, the BAG had received a new campaign truck emblazoned with the French flag and the BAG's star and crescent.[148]

THE TERRITORIAL ELECTIONS OF MARCH 31, 1957

Even as some local leaders and activists began to challenge the legitimacy of French presence, other leaders campaigned for their share of the self-government pie. Having swept the municipal council elections in November 1956, the RDA was now in charge of administering the largest cities and towns. The preservation of law and order in the urban areas had become the party's responsibility. If the RDA gained a strong majority in the next Territorial Assembly, its responsibilities would extend far beyond the urban centers; it would be charged with administering the whole territory. Hence, the RDA had an interest in maintaining the peace during the 1957 territorial election campaign.[149]

The March 31, 1957, Territorial Assembly elections—the first territory-wide elections under the universal suffrage law—served as the second major testing ground of loi-cadre.[150] With significant new powers to run local affairs, the Territorial Assembly was far more important than it previously had been. Moreover, the party winning the elections would dominate not only the legislative body, but also the Council of Government, the new territorial executive body, whose ministers would be elected by the Territorial Assembly.[151]

Since the first General Council elections in 1946, Guinea's local assembly had been enlarged from forty seats in 1946 to fifty seats ten years later. After the expansion, the first college, elected by metropolitan citizens, was composed of eighteen seats. The second college, reserved for citizens of the French Union, had thirty-two.[152] As was the case in 1946, racial representation remained highly disproportionate. Of a total population of just under 2.5 million people, some 3,000 were Europeans.[153] Thus, less than 1 percent of the population was represented by 36 percent of the councillors, while the remaining 99 plus percent was represented by 64 percent of the elected officials.

By 1957, further changes were in place. The National Assembly approved Deputy Barry Diawadou's proposal to revamp the territorial assemblies once more, resulting in the enlargement of Guinea's assembly to sixty seats.[154] The expansion was accompanied by the reallocation of a significant number of seats. Under the single-college system instituted by loi-cadre, the eighteen seats previously reserved for Europeans were redistributed to various circles on the basis of their population. Since ten of the eighteen first college seats had been held by residents of Lower-Guinea, the RDA hoped that these would be retained in the region, a bastion of the RDA.[155]

This was not to be. RDA strongholds were bypassed. Not even Conakry, a rapidly growing urban center whose population had swelled from 22,000 in

1946 to 40,000 in 1955, was allotted a single new seat.[156] The addition of ten new seats and the redistribution of eighteen primarily benefitted the region where Barry Diawadou was strongest, the densely populated Futa Jallon. Labé circle alone was allocated six seats in the Territorial Assembly, an arrangement that was hailed by both the BAG and the DSG.[157] With the protection of European privilege no longer an issue, the administration seemed to have gained a new respect for the principle of proportional representation.

Once again, the RDA overcame all obstacles and carried out a vigorous grass-roots campaign. The police reported that in mid-March, Sékou Touré campaigned in thirteen of the territory's twenty-six circles and subdivisions. On March 23, he made stops in Macenta, N'Zérékoré, and Beyla, with the objective of visiting the remaining districts before election day.[158] The RDA board of directors loaned a vehicle to the RDA candidate in the Youkounkoun subdivision of Gaoual circle so that he could visit even the most remote villages. On market days, the party organized large public meetings in many of the subdivision's towns.[159]

In contrast to the RDA, rival parties lagged behind, having only minimal contact with their constituents. The police reported that in Youkounkoun, the BAG had held only one meeting during the territorial election campaign.[160] In Kankan, BAG leader El-Hadj Sékou Sako had decried his party's feeble efforts during the municipal election drive, asserting that the BAG's position in the cantons was catastrophic. In October 1956, there was not a single functioning canton or village committee. Outside the city of Kankan, there was no party activity. He charged that this disastrous situation was largely the fault of Kankan's territorial councillors, who never bothered to go into the rural areas to talk with their constituents.[161] The BAG's record did not improve in the intervening months. Addressing an RDA rally in March 1957, Sékou Touré charged that rival parties did not trouble themselves to campaign in the interior and had no contact with the people. "Because you have no shoes, they take you for savages," he said. However, on election day, these parties would recoil before the strength of the RDA. "When they see that the administrators, the commissioners, and the military police are all under the orders of the RDA, they will stay home," he predicted. The RDA is very powerful, he concluded, but there was still one curtain left to fall—that of the Territorial Assembly.[162]

During the final days of the campaign, most of the RDA's board of directors were absent from Conakry, mobilizing in the interior. Sékou Touré returned to the capital on March 27 and addressed a rally of some 4,000 people. According to the police, the crowd was delirious. When Sékou Touré appeared, the shouts, acclamations, songs, and applause lasted for five minutes. The imam of the Coronthie mosque recited the *fatiha* with the prayer that on election day the RDA's adversaries would be crushed and that all sixty seats would be won by the RDA.[163] Meanwhile, the mission of voter education continued. On March 29, the RDA convened numerous neighborhood meetings in Conakry and its suburbs. Their purpose was to ensure that everyone had received their voter registration cards, understood how to vote, and could distinguish between the ballots of the various parties.[164]

Once again, the RDA victory was overwhelming. Prior to the March 1957 elections, the RDA had only one territorial councillor, Sékou Touré, who had represented Beyla circle since August 1953.[165] In the territorial elections of March 1957, the RDA won 75 percent of the vote and obtained fifty-six of the assembly's sixty seats.[166] Apart from Pita, where the DSG won all three seats, the RDA won 53 to 69 percent of the votes in the Futa Jallon. In the rest of the territory, the RDA garnered 62 to 96 percent of the ballots cast.[167] Commemorating the RDA victory and noting its significance in terms of things to come, the women sang:

> Brother Diawadou
> There is nothing more to do
> The [RDA] has won
> After the governor Ballay
> It is the [RDA] that will govern.[168]

Throughout the territory, administration sources reported that the DSG and the BAG were in crisis. After the RDA electoral sweep, rank-and-file members of both parties, as well as some of the DSG's top leaders, had resigned from their parties in large numbers and applied for RDA membership.[169]

With the Territorial Assembly firmly under RDA control, the first loi-cadre government was formed on May 14, 1957. Sékou Touré was elected vice president of the Council of Government. Saïfoulaye Diallo, the second-most-powerful RDA leader, was elected president of the Territorial Assembly. Although the governor was still Guinea's chief executive, the RDA had greater control over the organs of state than ever before.[170]

POSTELECTION DIVISIONS IN THE GUINEAN RDA

By the end of 1957, the RDA was ensconced in power. It occupied two of Guinea's three National Assembly seats and all five seats allocated to Guinea in the Grand Council. It controlled thirteen out of fourteen major municipal governments and commanded fifty-seven out of sixty seats in the Territorial Assembly, a member of the opposition having joined the RDA in September. All the ministers of the loi-cadre government were RDA.[171]

If the burdens of power weighed heavily on the newly elected RDA leaders, the rank and file continued to operate as underdogs oppressed by the machinery of state. Despite the pleas of their territorial leaders, RDA militants throughout the territory engaged in acts of political violence.[172] Lower-Guinea was especially hard hit. In the Forécariah village of Formoréah, RDA women organized a victory celebration in front of the home of BAG stalwart Youla Yansané. The men and women in the crowd mocked the defeated BAG and roughed up one of Yansané's wives. Yansané fired his hunting rifle into the mass of people, wounding about ten. In the course of these disturbances, the demonstrators pillaged and burned Yansané's home.[173] BAG partisans were not all innocent victims, however. On the outskirts of Coyah, BAG attacks on RDA homes provoked a cycle of violence. A mob of some one hundred people sacked an RDA house in the hamlet of Souroya. Another RDA house was ransacked some distance away. In retaliation, RDA militants attacked a BAG house. By the middle of April, the town of Coyah was embroiled in the unrest as numerous houses from both sides were plundered.[174]

Serious incidents also were reported in the forest region. Once again, the local party leadership demonstrated greater solidarity with their members' sentiments than with those of the territorial board in Conakry. Shortly after the elections, RDA women in the village of Pela, N'Zérékoré circle, organized a victory celebration. During the event, a dispute arose between RDA and DSG women. In the melee that followed, two RDA women were injured, at least one by a male DSG member. The local RDA committee then descended on his compound and destroyed seven buildings. After an investigation, six RDA women and four RDA men were arrested, along with two DSG members. Leaders of the RDA subsection organized a demonstration on April 18 to protest the arrests. With the mayor at their head, they rounded up some five hundred people to augment the size of the crowd. To add weight to the protest, women deserted the market and the offices of the city hall opened late. After the demonstrators threw rocks at the circle commandant, the police, unable to disperse the crowd, requested reinforcements.[175] The RDA board of directors sent instructions to the local leaders, pleading with them to be more conciliatory.[176]

Meanwhile, N'Zérékoré youths, led by nineteen-year-old Jean-Marie Gbla Doré, secretary-general of the local RDA youth wing, upped the ante. During the demonstration on April 18, Doré led a group of some ten chanting youths to the residence of the circle commandant, where Doré demanded that they be received. The circle authorities forced the group to vacate the premises. The authorities were assisted in this endeavor by Jean Faragué Tounkara, a teacher, RDA activist, and newly elected territorial councillor.[177]

In response to the unrest, the RDA board of directors issued a "Call to RDA Militants." The maintenance of order was indispensable to the realization of all constructive work, the appeal read. During the upcoming festival of Korité, which marked the end of Ramadan, all RDA militants, friends, and sympathizers were asked to obey the law. All democratic Muslims were invited to pray at their mosques, but to avoid all mass movements in the streets and to refrain from marching from one mosque to another. In reminding their followers that the festival should maintain a strictly religious character, the leaders abandoned the RDA's long-effective strategy of reinforcing politics with religion.[178]

Meanwhile, the disenchantment of RDA youths continued to escalate. Focused solely on its new responsibility of governing, the party was selecting personnel on the basis of their professional, rather than their political, credentials, the youths charged. On April 17, some fifty Conakry youths aired their grievances to Oumar Dramé, trade unionist, municipal councillor, and member of the RDA board of directors. Those who expressed the greatest anger were young men who had been imprisoned for RDA activities. They claimed that the party had been indifferent to their fate. Now that the RDA had become powerful—thanks to their sacrifices—it had forgotten them. While certain RDA youths had been unemployed for two years, the party had given positions to people who had never suffered for the cause.[179]

In early May, the Conakry youths held another meeting. This time, they decried the indiscriminate admittance of former BAG cadres into RDA ranks. Now that the party was in power, all and sundry were attempting to join. Scrambling onto the RDA bandwagon were conservative, and even reactionary, elements. While party elders had taken the position that all applicants should be accepted—no holds barred—the youths asserted that those who had fought the RDA should not be admitted unless they rectified their wrongs. The party had risen to its current position on the backs of the youths, who had borne the brunt of the suffering. The elders, who had endured few hardships, should not be the ones to grant immunity, they claimed. There were still many RDA partisans in detention, where conditions were abominable. The BAG had been responsible for their arrests. If former BAG members wanted to join the party, the youths concluded, they must begin by liberating RDA comrades from prison through the retraction of their charges.[180]

With a potential explosion on his hands, Oumar Dramé proposed the establishment of a political school in Conakry, where youths would be educated to be proper party cadres. While some RDA youths have been to school, they do not have political minds, he maintained. They must be instructed. If, in the struggle, there are violent incidents, injuries, and deaths, it is because of the lack of political maturity. "The whites mock us, and rightfully so," Dramé lamented. "We ask for our liberty, but do not know how to use it."[181] Some months later, the RDA committee of Conakry's Boulbinet neighborhood elaborated on Dramé's proposal. The school must teach RDA partisans the true nature of politics, the committee advised. "It is no longer about insults and brawls. We wish that, henceforth, all occurs in calm." Political courses should be taught in Susu, and women, as well as youths, should be asked to attend.[182] The militant mobilizing tactics of women and youths, long encouraged by the RDA, had outlived their usefulness for a party in power.

CONCLUSION

In 1946, France had reformed its empire in order to save it. A decade later, faced with armed liberation movements in Indochina and North Africa and unrest in other parts of the empire, France again attempted to liberalize colonial rule. The result was a new system of local government that allowed colonized peoples a greater voice. For some, these reforms were welcome. For many, they were too little too late.

In Guinea, the years 1956 and 1957 were tumultuous ones. They were marked by extraordinary victories at the polls for the RDA, resulting in RDA dominance of all elected bodies as well as the new local government established in May 1957. However, the acquisition of power resulted in further divisions within the nationalist movement, as the beneficiaries of the new system chose to collaborate, while those left outside criticized their erstwhile leaders for their accommodation. The rightward movement of Guinean territorial leaders had ramifications for the trade union movement, which was closely linked to the political party. Under increasing pressure from both the interterritorial and the territorial RDA, most Guinean unions severed their ties to the CGT in 1956. Meanwhile, grassroots leftists, sidelined since the RDA's split with the PCF in 1950, expressed growing disenchantment with their leaders' actions. This group would again take center stage during the waning years of colonial rule.

CHAPTER 5

The Renaissance of the Left: From Autonomy to Independence, 1956–58

WITH THE FORMATION of the *loi-cadre* government in May 1957, the old guard of the Guinean RDA rapidly consolidated its power. Although territorial leaders were criticized by the Left for their increasingly accommodationist stance, the RDA government did implement reforms that both benefitted its popular base and diminished the influence of chiefs and notables.[1] It replaced the hated Société Indigène de Prévoyance with peasant-run cooperatives and abolished the corrupt councils of notables in favor of district and village councils elected by universal suffrage.[2] Most significantly, in December 1957, the new government abolished the despised institution of the canton chieftaincy.[3]

Once again, party leaders had been propelled into action by a groundswell of opposition at the grassroots. While the RDA government had taken charge of the situation, the abolition of the chieftaincy was, in Suret-Canale's words, "the end result of a profound popular movement[,] . . . the legal consecration of a popular revolution."[4] The suppression of this institution, and its replacement by elected local councils that included low-status citizens, had tremendous political ramifications. Throughout the 1950s, the chiefs had used their significant coercive powers to manipulate elections to the RDA's detriment. Had they survived, the canton chiefs could have forced a very different outcome in the September 1958 referendum.[5]

Despite these reforms, grassroots militants—trade unionists, students, and other youths—claimed that loi-cadre was outmoded from the outset. While the acquisition of local self-government might have satisfied activists in 1946, a decade later, cries for independence increasingly drowned out those that championed local autonomy. Moreover, the loi-cadre system, which promoted individual territories at the expense of the French West and Equatorial African federations, undermined interterritorial solidarity and action. It balkanized French Africa into small, economically fragile territories that were less likely to seek independence on their own. Guinean leftists criticized their leaders' complicity in this dubious enterprise. At the same time, RDA rivals attempted to capture the party's disenchanted constituency. In 1958, the BAG and the DSG came together as the Guinean branch of the Parti du Regroupement Africain (PRA). Although the BAG once had been rooted in the territory's most conservative elements, it now joined other RDA rivals to challenge the governing party from the Left.

In France, meanwhile, a brewing crisis brought General de Gaulle back to power. Under his auspices, a new constitution was proposed that strengthened the power of the French president, further undermined the African federations, and sealed the fate of overseas territories as perpetual minors in the French empire (now called the French Community). In Guinea, grassroots activists condemned the constitution and demanded that the RDA advocate immediate independence instead.

CRITIQUE FROM THE LEFT

In 1958, the Guinean RDA increasingly was torn between radical elements of the party, who denounced the compromises of the loi-cadre government, and those who had acquired positions of power within it.[6] After the interterritorial RDA severed its ties to the PCF in 1950, the RDA's left wing had continued to promote the internationalist perspective associated with international communism. Trade unionists, students, and youths bypassed conservative party leaders and forged links with communist-affiliated organizations outside of Africa, in particular, the World Federation of Trade Unions, the International Union of Students, and the World Federation of Democratic Youth. Employing Marxist language, these organizations emphasized the common interests of working classes in industrialized countries and colonized peoples fighting imperialism.[7] As the RDA-dominated loi-cadre government moved toward a centrist policy of accommodation, dissident elements from these groups continued to press the party from the Left.[8] Trade unionists, particularly teachers and railway workers, as well as students and other youths, condemned both the new policy of "constructive collaboration" and the RDA leaders who promoted it.[9] They denounced loi-cadre for balkanizing Africa by weakening the federations and championing territorial over interterritorial powers and organizations.[10] Increasingly they called for political independence.[11]

The politics of position often coincided with generation, as younger elements reproached their elders for their complacency and collaboration.[12] Students and graduates, especially those with French university degrees, were less willing than their elders to compromise. While members of the older generation may have received primary school certificates in Guinea or diplomas from federal schools in Senegal, the Ivory Coast, or the French Soudan, these young men had earned university degrees from institutions in the *métropole*. Having been exposed to Marxist and Pan-African ideas in France, they had returned to Guinea as committed leftists.[13] They disparaged their elders, who accepted crumbs from the French table, and promoted radicalism among students who had remained in Africa. Young members of the teachers' union joined with students and other youths to push the party to a more radical stance.[14]

Shortly after the RDA broke from the PCF, African students in France, who had opposed disaffiliation, created a semiautonomous group within the RDA, the Association des Étudiants RDA (AERDA). Claiming loyalty to the 1946 Bamako Congress, the AERDA rejected the RDA's rightward shift and attacked conservative party leaders, as well as the colonial government.[15] AERDA members also joined the independent Fédération des Étudiants d'Afrique Noire en France (FEANF), which was founded in 1950 by Marxist intellectuals. The AERDA and the FEANF overlapped considerably in terms of philosophy and membership.[16] Both organizations were deeply influenced by the PCF and viewed the struggle against French colonialism as part of a wider war against Western imperialism.[17] By the mid-1950s, both had affiliated with the International Union of Students in Prague.[18]

African students in France were among the first proponents of radical nationalism, championing independence over local autonomy as early as 1952.[19] In 1956, the FEANF, under the leadership of Guinean medical student, Charles Diané, and his colleagues, adopted an avowedly proindependence position.[20] Decrying the antifederal bias of loi-cadre, as well as the severe limitations on the powers of the territorial governments, the FEANF portrayed loi-cadre as an African bound in chains.[21]

With the return of large numbers of African students from France in the mid-1950s, radical nationalism quickly spread to students and youths in French West Africa.[22] The Union Générale des Étudiants d'Afrique Occidentale (UGEAO), established in Dakar in 1954, worked closely with the FEANF.[23] Influenced by Marxist political thought, both the UGEAO and the FEANF were highly critical of the RDA's moderate line.[24] Like its counterpart in France, the French West African student movement was an early proponent of independence.[25] In 1956, police in Guinea reported that local students rejected limited self-government, as embodied in loi-cadre, and wanted "in a single leap, to jump over all stages leading to independence."[26] Barry Bassirou, the younger brother of BAG Deputy Barry Diawadou, told a large crowd in Dabola that African students in France ridiculed all of Guinea's political parties. In contrast to their elders, the students were nationalists, who demanded complete independence for their country. Tunisia and Morocco, which had achieved full independence that year, were their role models. Barry Diawadou had silenced his younger brother, saying, "Be quiet. Our country is not yet ripe for that."[27]

In contrast to the student movements, French West African youth movements tended to be led by young men who had been educated in their own territories, rather than abroad. As a result, these men tended to staff the lower echelons of the colonial bureaucracy. Many were involved in trade unions and political parties. Influenced by the anti-imperialism of the GECs, they opposed French wars in Indochina and Algeria and generally disagreed with the gradualist approach of party leaders who merely championed greater autonomy within the French Union. They frequently had more in common with youths in other parties than with the older leaders of their own parties. By the mid-1950s, youth movements, like their student counterparts, had denounced loi-cadre, opposed the balkanization of Africa, and called for immediate independence.[28] Within the RDA, youths were grouped in a semiautonomous wing, the Rassemblement de la Jeunesse Démocratique Africaine (RJDA), which was established in December 1954 and soon controlled all of Guinea's youth organizations.[29] In July 1955, all French West African youth organizations merged into a single interterritorial body, the Conseil Fédéral de la Jeunesse d'AOF, which in 1957 was renamed the Conseil de la Jeunesse d'Afrique (CJA). The CJA leadership was closely linked to the RDA's left wing.[30]

SILENCING THE PROINDEPENCE LEFT

As their opinions diverged from those of the RDA's territorial and interterritorial leadership, Guinean leftists complained that the party was attempting to sideline them. Teachers, who constituted a large proportion of the territory's intellectuals, were among the most vocal in this regard. An estimated 90 percent of Guinea's teachers were RDA members. Yet, in 1956, both the territorial and interterritorial congresses of the RDA were scheduled to take place after the beginning of the academic year, thus precluding teachers and students from participating. Many of the party's intellectuals concluded that the timing of the congresses was a conscious maneuver by Sékou Touré and Houphouët-Boigny to exclude teachers and students from policy discussions.[31]

Unable to attend the territorial congress, teachers addressed motions of protest to the Guinean RDA's board of directors, condemning the party's new orientation. They charged that Sékou Touré's plan to mold the Guinean RDA according to the collaborationist Houphouët line was both unprincipled and opportunistic. African teachers, like their students, claimed that loi-cadre was outmoded even before it was implemented. Rejecting the French Union compact, they called for the complete independence of all African territories. In light of these developments, the police observed, "The intellectuals of the [RDA], primarily teachers, are distancing themselves more and more from Sékou Touré, who has only a *certificat d'études.*"[32]

According to the police, the teachers' proindependence sentiments, sharply contrasting with those of the RDA board of directors, echoed the views of party leaders in the interior. Local leaders, in close proximity to the grassroots, tended to be more radical than those with territorial responsibility. Subsection leaders in the forest generally had adopted a proindependence position, as had Upper-Guinea leaders Lansana Diané, Moussa Diakité, and Moriba Magassouba. Again, the gulf between territorial and local leaders seemed to be widening. With students and other youths, teachers, and local leaders clamoring for independence, the police remarked that Houphouët-Boigny and Sékou Touré would need to be extremely clever in order to stem the tide.[33]

Within months of the establishment of the loi-cadre government, Guinean students, teachers, and railway workers—the nucleus of left-wing resistance to the RDA leadership—held their annual congresses. All were critical of loi-cadre and the compromises made by the RDA government. Charging that the leadership had become opportunistic and corrupt and had betrayed the people, they demanded immediate independence.[34] The teachers' and railway workers' unions, the great majority of whose members were RDA, criticized the party for attempting to quash independent trade unionism by bringing all labor unions under RDA control.[35]

Among the loi-cadre critics, Guinean students were the first to hold their congress. In July 1957, the Union Générale des Étudiants et Élèves de Guinée (UGEEG) convened its congress in Conakry. In the hope of winning the UGEEG's support, Sékou Touré invited the students to meet with the territorial councillors and members of the new government.[36] Once again, Barry Bassirou, who had been chastened by his brother when he called for independence, played a prominent role.[37] Confronting Sékou Touré, Barry Bassirou queried, "Have the elected leaders of the R.D.A. already posed the problem of independence to the masses?" Like BAG Deputy Barry Diawadou, Sékou Touré rejected the notion of independence. He replied, "No, the R.D.A. has never posed the problem of independence to the masses, and it will not pose it."[38]

To the general populace, party leaders portrayed the students as a privileged elite, unrepresentative of the majority of their compatriots.[39] The masses, it seemed, were willing to follow their leaders, at least for the time being. Dock workers, domestic servants, and market women had been mobilized by the RDA, as personified by Sékou Touré, not by the intellectual elite who had long disparaged them. In Conakry, local RDA committees organized a series of neighborhood meetings to denounce the "anti-mass" position of the students. In the neighborhood of Almamya, the meeting was attended by numerous elders, who clearly were irked by the youths' lack of respect for those more experienced and wiser than they. Papa N'Diaye and Momo Touré took the floor, charging, "The students accuse the RDA of being colonialist and francophile, because it has declared itself in favor of Franco-African collaboration. They demand the total divorce between the French and the Africans and immediate independence, without knowing where this adventure will take us." Displaying no sympathy for the students' position, the speakers charged that they were behaving like spoiled children. Having spent long years in France, they had lost touch with the masses and their struggles. The elders concluded,

> We are going to write and vote a motion that will be addressed to our Council of Government to ask it to reduce the scholarships for the métropole in order that the students henceforth do all their studies in [French West Africa], in Dakar or Conakry. In this way, they will better understand the difficulties in which we struggle to obtain the money that permits them to go to France and live like "princes." We do not understand why, instead of thanking their African brothers and France who give them this education, they spend their vacations trying to destroy our ten years of common labor.[40]

Piqued by the students' criticism, the RDA leadership was even more disenchanted by that of the teachers. The Syndicat du Personnel Enseignant Africain de Guinée held its congress in Mamou on August 6–10, 1957, during which it adopted a motion highly critical of loi-cadre.[41] The motion proclaimed that because the colonial regime should not exist in any form, the compromise package of self-government "constitutes a diversionary maneuver destined to distract us from our march toward independence." Moreover, the loi-cadre structures were intended to destroy the anticolonial movement's united front by weakening interterritorial governing structures and balkanizing the overseas territories. Finally, the motion deplored the failure of the RDA's elected representatives to demystify the institution of limited self-government and denounced party leaders as collaborators who perpetuated the divide-and-rule tactics of the colonial regime.[42] Beyond their devastating critique of loi-cadre, the teachers' union decried the annual transfer of its members, a technique that had long been used by the colonial government to silence its critics and that had continued under the loi-cadre system. To signal their opposition to such tactics, the teachers voted to strike in October 1957, at the beginning of academic year.[43] In the course of the congress, Koumandian Kéïta was reelected secretary-general of the teachers' union, a move that was harshly criticized by the RDA board of directors.[44]

Among the dissidents transferred by the RDA government was Ray Autra, a founding member of the Guinean RDA who was a militant, proindependence leftist and the press secretary of the teachers' union. Because Autra's position required that he be stationed near union headquarters in Conakry, the teachers charged that his transfer to Boffa was an attempt by the RDA government to disrupt the teachers' union. Although the teachers had struck in October 1957, they voted to strike again on November 19 to protest Autra's transfer, and again on December 9–10 if the November strike did not result in the cancellation of the transfer order.[45]

Sékou Touré used the controversy to generate popular discontent against the educated elite. Speaking to a crowd of some 2,500 people, he claimed that trade union and political activities were not independent of one another. Hence, the teachers' strike was aimed at the RDA. Appealing to their distrust of intellectuals, Sékou Touré warned nonelite parents that the teachers were using them and urged them not to attend the teachers' meetings. The teachers' subsequent attempt to garner the parents' support ended in failure when the Association des Parents d'Élèves passed a motion against them.[46]

While the conflict between the RDA and the teachers simmered, the railway workers' Syndicat des Cheminots Africains held its congress in Mamou (November 1–4, 1957). In attendance were representatives from all the Mamou trade unions, UGTAN, and the Union des Jeunes de Guinée, as well as Mamou's deputy mayor, Pléah Koniba.[47] The railway workers' union, like that of the teachers, was embroiled in conflict with the RDA. The union was led by Diéli Bakar Kouyaté, who recently had been expelled from the RDA for insubordination.[48]

After the trade union congress, Kouyaté urged railway workers to demonstrate solidarity with the teachers if the latter struck to protest Ray Autra's transfer. He spoke of serious dissension within the RDA and envisaged a preemptive alliance between the teachers' and railway workers' unions. According to the police, the railway workers' secretary-general was pleased "to lead the struggle so that trade unionism would not be dominated by the dictatorship of any political party."[49]

While political storms were brewing in Guinea, other battles were being fought at the interterrritorial level. In Guinea, Sékou Touré was associated with the collaborationist faction of the RDA. At the interterritorial level, however, he was linked with the party's progressive wing, supporting the federalist as opposed to the territorialist position. Federalists condemned loi-cadre for strengthening individual territories at the expense of the federation, thus undermining African political and economic viability. Territorialists, on the other hand, championed the integrity of individual territories and advocated the transfer of powers from the federal to the territorial levels. In July 1957, Sékou Touré embarked on a profederalist campaign in Guinea, resulting in a Territorial Assembly motion that called for the creation of a federal executive, a sentiment later echoed by Guinean youths and railway workers.[50] At the end of August, he helped to orchestrate a unanimous vote on a similar motion in the RDA-controlled Grand Council, despite the opposition of Houphouët-Boigny, who, a few months previously, had been elected Grand Council president. Sékou Touré collaborated in this endeavor with federalists in rival parties, and the motion was voted on in Houphouët-Boigny's absence, with Grand Council Vice President Gabriel d'Arboussier presiding.[51]

The federalist versus territorialist debate had much to do with the rivalry between Senegal and the Ivory Coast—and between Léopold Senghor and Houphouët-Boigny—for preeminence in French West Africa. Senegal had long dominated the federation, whose seat was in Dakar. Between 1947 and 1957, Senegal had essentially controlled the Grand Council. During the loi-cadre debates, the federalists, led by Senghor, had advocated more, rather than fewer, powers for the Grand Council. They had recommended that the Council be directly, rather than indirectly, elected and that an elected federal executive be created. During the course of these debates, it was Senghor who first had warned of the dangers of "balkanization," which would jeopardize African social, economic, cultural, and political development.[52]

The territorialists were led by Houphouët-Boigny, who had helped to craft the French policies that weakened federal powers and bolstered those of individual territories. Intent upon remaining in France's good graces and retaining the subsidies that resulted, the territorialists adamantly opposed independence in any form—and particularly at the federal level. Houphouët-Boigny's home territory, the Ivory Coast, had much to gain from this position. The Ivory Coast was the richest territory in the French West African federation. An entrenched African planting class, of which Houphouët-Boigny was the leader, resented the financial assistance the Ivory Coast was required to give to poorer territories through its subsidization of the federal budget. Far from the seat of the federation and the Grand Council, Houphouët-Boigny opposed any proposal that might strengthen the hand of his rivals, notably Senegal and Senghor. His election to the presidency of the Grand Council did not alter his position.[53]

Within the interterritorial RDA, federalists and territorialists prepared for a showdown that threatened to derail the movement. The gulf between RDA leaders was wider in 1957 than at any time since the party's divorce from the PCF seven years earlier. Propelled by the party's left wing, the issues of increased federal powers, the establishment of a federal executive, and the right to independence were placed on the agenda of the RDA's third interterritorial congress, held in Bamako on September 25–30, 1957.[54] At the Bamako congress, only the Ivory Coast supported the territorialist position. Thus, Sékou Touré spoke for the vast majority when he took a strong federalist position, advocating the establishment of elected federal governments in Dakar and Brazzaville.[55] As a sop to the Left, Sékou Touré and his supporters claimed that "the independence of peoples is an inalienable right." However, in keeping with his new stance of political moderation, he did not call for the immediate realization of that right. Instead, he inserted a clause in the congress's final political resolution that advocated the "realisation and reinforcement of a democratic and fraternal Franco-African Community based on equality."[56] Houphouët-Boigny would have had little argument with that position.

Despite the prevailing sentiment in favor of a stronger federation and the theoretical right to independence, Houphouët-Boigny remained adamant that there be no federal executive and no future independence for the territories. To prevent a schism within the party, the Bamako congress passed a compromise resolution in favor of democratizing the federal government, without specifically calling for the establishment of a federal executive. Although they opposed his territorialist position, the majority of delegates reelected Houphouët-Boigny as interterritorial president, in the hope of preserving party unity. However, they urged the president to use his position to promote the party's, rather than his own, views.[57] The RDA's announcement that it would continue to support the program of local self-government within the framework of the French Union was a profound disappointment for the Left, which had hoped that the RDA would adopt a position in favor of immediate independence. Outraged, Guinean youths declared that the party's solution "was no more than camouflaged colonialism."[58]

Hard-pressed from the Left, Guinea's RDA government became increasingly intolerant of criticism. Its attempt to silence its critics culminated in a crackdown on the Mamou RDA subsection, where many dissident elements had found a home. Mamou was the fiefdom of canton chief Almamy Ibrahima Sory Dara, the most powerful chief in the Futa Jallon. As such, it had been a bastion of anti-RDA activity in the early postwar years. From the late 1940s, the administration had systematically transferred troublesome RDA civil servants to Mamou to work under the Almamy's watchful eye. The plan had backfired, however. Rather than undermining the RDA, the administration's policy had helped the party to penetrate into the very heart of the Futa Jallon. The radical civil servants concentrated in Mamou developed one of the most progressive and energetic RDA subsections in the whole territory.[59]

The Mamou RDA leaders had a number of distinctive qualities. They were politically on the Left. Many had been early members of the GECs. Most had not sanctioned the rift between the RDA and the PCF and had rejected the collaborationist Houphouët line. As late as 1957, a number of Mamou leaders were involved in Marxist study groups. Because they had been transferred to Mamou, most of the leaders were not Peul. Therefore, they had no special reverence for the Almamy and his chiefly subordinates. Mamadou Bela Doumbouya was Malinke. Aboubakar Doukouré, a Soninke, had been transferred twenty-one times in the eighteen years prior to his arrival in Mamou. Some Mamou leaders were not even Guinean. Pléah Koniba and Samba Lamine Traoré were both Bambara from the French Soudan, although the latter was some generations removed. Léon Maka was of Gabonese descent, and Fatou Aribot was of mixed French and Guinean ancestry. Only Saïfoulaye Diallo was Peul, a renegade aristocrat whose family had supported his BAG opponent in the 1956 legislative elections.[60] Finally, several of the Mamou RDA leaders were Ponty alumni, and thus members of the tiny African elite with post-primary education. In contrast, the RDA leadership in Conakry was composed largely of lower-level civil servants and trade unionists, many with no more than primary school certificates. The territorial leaders were deeply suspicious of the Ponty graduates in Mamou.[61]

In November 1957, the Mamou RDA subsection was expelled from the party for insubordination and "Left deviationism." To the outrage of the RDA's loi-cadre government, the Mamou subsection had publicly associated itself with dissident organizations and their criticisms. It had taken up the refrain of students, teachers, and trade unionists, accusing RDA officials of styling themselves as a new colonial bourgeoisie; condemning the compromises of self-government; and demanding complete independence instead. Moreover, the Mamou subsection had been outspoken in its support of RDA dissident, Ray Autra.[62] Most of Mamou's expelled RDA members were teachers: Aboubakar Doukouré, who headed the Mamou subsection of the teachers' union; Samba Lamine Traoré, a teacher and territorial councillor; Fatou Aribot, a teacher and municipal councillor; and Léon Maka. Also expelled were Pléah Koniba, an African doctor and deputy mayor of Mamou, as well as Mamadou Bela Doumbouya, a civil servant in the economic sector, territorial councillor, and president of the Territorial Assembly's Permanent Commission. Doumbouya was deprived of his presidential post, and Koniba was forced to resign as deputy mayor. Demoralized, Koniba left Guinea soon thereafter.[63]

Outside of Mamou, Ray Autra and other teachers were also purged from the party. Activists in Labé were expelled for demonstrating solidarity with the Mamou dissidents. Other perceived enemies were arbitrarily transferred, a retaliatory method learned from the colonial regime. In the aftermath of the purge, a number of Mamou militants resigned from the territorial party to protest their leaders' treatment.[64]

Simultaneous with the crackdown on unrepentant leftists, the Guinean RDA, propelled by criticism from the grassroots, moved incrementally to a more progressive position. During the Guinean RDA's third party congress, held on January 23–26, 1958, party leaders proclaimed that loi-cadre was too limited and demanded complete internal autonomy. They proposed that the appointed governor be replaced with an elected African president of the Council of Government. Pressed by the Left to counter France's divide-and-rule strategies, party leaders warned against the dangers of balkanization and called for increased powers at the federal level. Rejecting the Houphouët line, they called for the creation of a federal executive that would be responsible to the Grand Council of French West Africa. The Grand Council, in turn, should be transformed into a federal legislature that would elect the executives in charge of all the interterritorial services. Finally, the appointed posts of high commissioner for both French West and Equatorial Africa should be abolished.[65] Continuing to value membership in the French Union, however, the Guinean RDA still refrained from demanding independence. It simply asserted that the relationship between France and the overseas territories should be reestablished on a more equitable basis.[66]

The Guinean party leadership also succumbed to pressures to democratize the internal structures of the Guinean RDA. The second party congress had been held more than seven years previously, in October 1950, and the Conakry leadership had consistently resisted appeals to convene a third one. Although Sékou Touré had assumed the position of secretary-general of the Guinean RDA in 1952, neither he nor the board of directors had been elected by a party congress. Internal critics of the Guinean RDA had long called for a territorial congress, in part to elect or reject the current leadership.[67] The third party congress revamped the Guinean RDA's governing structures. At the territorial level, the thirty-two-member board of directors and executive committee of five officers were replaced by a national political bureau of seventeen members, who would be elected at regular party congresses. As expected, Sékou Touré was confirmed in his position as secretary-general.[68] Henceforth, women would be represented in the national political bureau, in the bureau of Guinea's UGTAN branch, and in the bureaus of all the RDA subsections.[69] Like the women, RDA youths would be granted a greater official role in party affairs. Henceforth, they would be represented in the bureaus of all the subsections, and special youth committees would be created to work with those bureaus.[70]

If the Guinean RDA made some concessions to progressives at its third party congress, it also took steps to bring willful leftists back into line. The party determined that, in the future, all Guinean trade unions would join UGTAN's Guinean branch. The UGTAN branch, in turn, would become a specialized organ of the Guinean RDA. Through this maneuver, the labor movement would be subordinated to the party.[71]

RDA RIVALS UNITE

As the RDA struggled with internal conflict, dissension within its ranks provided an opportunity for rival parties to consolidate their power. In January 1957, the interterritorial Mouvement Socialiste Africain (MSA) was established at a congress in Conakry. Most of the congress delegates had been longtime leaders of the SFIO's African branches, and the MSA quickly established a parliamentary affiliation with the French socialist party. Like the RDA, the MSA was conceived to be an interterritorial party with branches throughout French West and Equatorial Africa. It was led by the Senegalese elder statesman and longtime SFIO leader Lamine Guèye (president), along with Barry III (secretary-general) and Bakary Djibo (deputy secretary-general). A militant trade unionist and one-time leader of the Nigerien RDA branch, Djibo and his party had been expelled from the interterritorial RDA in 1955 for refusing to sanction its breach with the PCF. Djibo also had opposed the disaffiliation of African trade unions from the French CGT. Thus, Bakary Djibo brought a left-leaning orientation to the MSA.[72]

The unity of anti-RDA forces was strengthened in March 1958 with the formation of the interterritorial PRA. The PRA brought together all political parties in French West Africa—with the exception of the RDA.[73] Forming a united front at both the interterritorial and territorial levels, the PRA took as its principal task the systematic critique of the interterritorial RDA, which continued to adhere to the Houphouët line.[74] Notably, the PRA called for strengthening the French West African federation through the creation of a federal executive.[75] The party's Guinean branch, the Union Progressiste Guinéenne, was formed in April 1958 as a union between the DSG-MSA and the BAG.[76] It was dominated by Western-educated Peul elites, including Barry III, Barry Diawadou, and Abdoulaye Diallo, an Amicale Gilbert Vieillard leader, lawyer, and councillor in the Assembly of the French Union.[77] Deprived of its chiefly base and rejected by the masses, the BAG had been all but defeated by the RDA. Although it had long supported Guinea's most conservative elements, the BAG saw the writing on the wall. With popular opinion more radical than the RDA leadership, the BAG qua PRA would attempt to outflank the RDA on the Left.

Political Crisis in France

While Guinea was coping with internal struggles, a crisis in France dramatically altered the political context in which the parties were operating. Since 1954, France had been engaged in a brutal war against the FLN and the civilian population in Algeria, where 1.5 million French people lived among 8 million Africans.[78] During the Battle of Algiers (January–October 1957), the French established tight control over the civilian population by recruiting informers, collaborators, and auxiliary forces and systematically using torture to discover and destroy rebel cells. By the end of the operation, all the local FLN leaders were either in prison or dead.[79]

In the spring of 1958, bloody battles along the Algerian-Tunisian border, which resulted in many civilian deaths, brought international opprobrium to France.[80] In France itself, the public was deeply divided over the Algerian question, resulting in tremendous political and economic instability.[81] The short-lived government of Prime Minister Félix Gaillard (Parti Radical Socialiste), installed on November 5, 1957, was brought down on April 15, 1958, buffeted from both Left and Right. Over the course of the next month, various political leaders attempted unsuccessfully to form a new government.[82]

Meanwhile, in Algeria, French citizens mobilized to keep Algeria French. Algerian-born French workers, artisans, shopkeepers, and low-level officials joined in antigovernment demonstrations led by right-wing veterans' associations.[83] On May 13, rioting broke out in Algiers, provoked by the nomination of Pierre Pflimlin (MRP) as prime minister. Outraged by Pflimlin's growing opposition to the Algerian war, a French mob took control of the central government building and urged the army to instigate a coup d'état.[84] To keep order, General Raoul Salan, commander in chief of the French armed forces in Algeria, was granted full powers of government. The result was a military dictatorship and a state of siege.[85]

On May 14, Pflimlin was invested as prime minister by the National Assembly. Indicative of the deep divisions in the French electorate, more deputies opposed the Pflimlin government or abstained from voting than supported it. Thus, the new government took office with only minority support.[86] A moderate on the Algerian question, Pflimlin steered between the old policy of continued intransigence and abandonment of the French cause. Instead, he proposed negotiations with the FLN. His proposals were satisfactory to no one.[87]

Meanwhile, General Charles de Gaulle prepared to step into the breach. Associated with French glory and patriotism, de Gaulle was popular among many segments of the French population. Between April and June 1958, numerous appeals had been made for his return from retirement.[88] In mid-May, as the crisis escalated, de Gaulle made it clear that he would assume the mantle of government only if granted substantial new powers.[89] On May 19, a coup d'état was narrowly averted. On May 24–25, dissident French paratroopers took control of Corsica. An invasion of the French mainland was expected on the night of May 27–28. In the course of these rapidly unfolding events, General de Gaulle suggested to the ineffectual prime minister that he step aside and make room for Charles de Gaulle.[90] On May 28, Pflimlin resigned and de Gaulle stepped into the power vacuum, demanding full powers and an immediate revision of the constitution.[91] A continuation of the present system would result in chaos, leading to civil war, he warned. Alternatively, he could lead France to salvation, if vested with the appropriate powers. His "national authority," he later wrote, would be "outside and above . . . the political regime of the moment." It would "immediately rally opinion, take over power and restore the state."[92]

The National Assembly took the bait. On May 29, Charles de Gaulle was formally designated prime minister. On June 1, the National Assembly

5.1 Minister Félix Houphouët-Boigny, after his appointment to de Gaulle's cabinet, arriving at Hôtel Matignon, Paris, France, June 1, 1958. Michael Rougier/Time Life Pictures/Getty Images.

voted 329 to 224 to invest his government. In opposition were all the communists, half the socialists, and a smattering of others.[93] Among de Gaulle's new ministers was Houphouët-Boigny, who was to advise him on matters relating to sub-Saharan Africa. Bernard Cornut-Gentille, high commissioner of French West Africa from 1952 to 1956, was designated minister of Overseas France.[94]

As the French desperately placed their hopes in him, de Gaulle sought to consolidate his powers. Cultivating a messiah image, he made it clear that he would brook no opposition. Reflecting on this period some years later, he wrote,

I therefore felt myself to be the chosen instrument of this fresh start, the obligation of which had fallen upon me in my retirement. On June 18, 1940, answering the call of the eternal fatherland bereft of any other alternative to save its honor and its soul, de Gaulle, alone and almost unknown, had had to assume the burden of France. In May 1958, on the eve of a disastrous tearing-apart of the nation and faced with the annihilation of the system which was allegedly in control, de Gaulle, now well-known, but with no other weapon save his legitimacy, must take destiny in his hands.[95]

It was with such a man, and his outsized ego, that African nationalists would soon have to contend.

On June 1, just prior to his government's investiture, de Gaulle warned the National Assembly that France was on the brink of civil war. He demanded full powers for his government for six months, the dissolution of parliament, and a new constitution to be drafted by his government and submitted to a popular referendum, subsequently scheduled for September 28, 1958. On June 3, the National Assembly and the Council of the Republic granted de Gaulle the emergency powers he had demanded.[96]

THE NEW CONSTITUTION AND THE FIFTH REPUBLIC

De Gaulle immediately began to work on the new constitution.[97] The final draft included components of the so-called Bayeux Constitution, which had been proposed by de Gaulle in June 1946 after a vehement attack on the draft constitution that had been defeated in the May 1946 referendum. At that time, de Gaulle had charged that the party-dominated parliament of the Third Republic was too strong and the executive too weak. Beholden to political parties, which had chosen the government ministers, the executive was incapable of governing. De Gaulle proposed instead a strong president, who would stand above the parties and preside over both the French Republic and the French Union. The president would have the right to consult the nation directly in times of crisis, through a popular referendum that circumvented parliament.[98]

The constitutional outline de Gaulle suggested at Bayeux lay dormant for twelve years. In 1958, it became the basis of the constitution that he proposed for the Fifth Republic. According to the new plan, the French Community would replace the French Union. The president of the French Republic would also serve as president of the French Community. The Community would be subordinate to the Republic, which would retain the most important powers. The Republic, primarily through the president, would determine common foreign, economic, and defense policies for the French Community. The Republic would also oversee justice, higher education, telecommunications, and transportation within the Community.[99]

Like the Bayeux Constitution, the 1958 draft proposed a strong president with little check on his executive powers. The Community's Senate and Executive Council would be merely consultative rather than deliberative bodies.[100] Compared to citizens of the Community, citizens of the Republic would be disproportionately represented. While the French territories in sub-Saharan Africa would have a total of 91 senators, metropolitan France would have 186.[101] Africans would no longer have representation in the National Assembly. The Council of the Republic and the Assembly of the French Union would disappear.[102] Thus, under the 1958 proposal, Africans would have an even smaller role in the making of common policies than they had had in 1946.

The 1958 proposal would disempower Africans in other ways. It would complete the work of loi-cadre in balkanizing the French African federations. Both French West Africa and French Equatorial Africa would be dissolved, and with them, the Grand Councils that brought together Africans from all the territories. The government hoped that the dissolution of the federations would forestall moves toward independence. With diverse resources and a population of more than twenty million people, French West Africa might well seek independence as a nation-state. However, the eight small territories that comprised the federation might be dissuaded from following such a course if they were forced to accede to independence as discrete entities with precarious, underdeveloped economies.[103]

Once again, the French government sought to use the staunchly territorialist Houphouët-Boigny to accomplish its aims. Houphouët-Boigny's willingness to collaborate, beginning with his break with the PCF, had a long history. In the aftermath of the January 1956 legislative elections, the new French government, dominated by the SFIO, recognized the RDA's growing strength. It was determined to mold Houphouët-Boigny into "the most devoted and effective support of the French government in Africa."[104] Thus, the SFIO prime minister, Guy Mollet, granted Houphouët-Boigny full ministerial status. He was the first African to achieve such a rank. Through the rise and fall of successive governments, Houphouët-Boigny remained a cabinet minister.[105] Aware of deep divisions within the RDA and the pull of radical elements at the local level, the government counted on Houphouët-Boigny to bring his followers into line. In return, it bestowed positions and prestige on the interterritorial president and like-minded RDA deputies.[106]

As a minister of state in the de Gaulle government, Houphouët-Boigny participated in both the ministerial committee that drafted the 1958 constitution and the consultative committee of thirty-nine parliamentarians and experts that considered the draft. Within the consultative committee, he was part of an ad hoc group that focused on the problem of the overseas territories. Besides Houphouët-Boigny, the ad hoc group included four other African parliamentarians: Léopold Senghor and Lamine Guèye (both PRA) of Senegal; Gabriel Lisette (RDA) of Chad; and Philibert Tsiranana of Madagascar.[107]

Wary of the growing strength of RDA federalists, Overseas Minister Bernard Cornut-Gentille hoped to flatter Sékou Touré into cooperation. He thus proposed Sékou Touré's appointment to the consultative committee. Houphouët-Boigny, however, was adamantly opposed to elevating his rival, and Sékou Touré was denied a committee seat.[108] As a result, Houphouët-Boigny's position, opposing both federalism and independence, rather than that of the majority of RDA members, was represented in the constitutional consultations.[109]

The African voice in the making of the 1958 constitution was extremely limited. As Sékou Touré noted in the June 17 issue of *La Presse de Guinée,* the constitution had been drafted without consulting the councils of government, territorial assemblies, and political movements in the various territories.[110] Millions of Africans would be permitted merely to vote "Yes" or "No" to a constitution that broke up the African federations and ruled out independence, now or in the future. Their choice was to accept the constitution or secede, submitting to all the ensuing consequences.[111]

If the Guinean RDA was concerned by the lack of transparency in the drafting process, it was even more troubled by the constitution's content. In June 1958, as the constitution was being written in Paris, the Guinean RDA convened its fourth party congress. The party resolutions, pushed through by young radicals, were a further indication of the growing cleavage between the Guinean RDA and the interterritorial leadership, as represented by Houphouët-Boigny. The Guinean RDA called for the strengthening of loi-cadre provisions that would result in the complete internal autonomy of the overseas territories. Further, all territories in French sub-Saharan Africa should be accorded the right to independence as part of the larger federations of French West and Equatorial Africa. A federal executive, elected by members of the Grand Council, should be established to oversee all interterritorial services. A federal state, responsible for foreign and economic affairs, defense, and higher education, would remove further powers from the French Republic.[112]

The question of independence, now or in the future, dominated all political discussions. At the PRA's interterritorial congress, held in Cotonou on July 25–27, 1958, the party's elder statesmen, like those of the RDA, were outflanked by young radicals. No longer satisfied with a principled right to independence, to be achieved at some future date, young leftists pushed through a resolution in favor of immediate independence—despite opposition from the PRA's president, Léopold Senghor. Among those who promoted the resolution were Bakary Djibo, the head of Niger's loi-cadre government, who was elected the PRA secretary-general at the Cotonou congress; Abdoulaye Ly, a former university student activist and Marxist intellectual from Senegal; and Abdoulaye Guèye, a Senegalese trade unionist and teacher.[113] In place of the constitutional proposals, the PRA's left wing demanded immediate independence on the basis of a united federation of French West Africa. Once sovereign and independent, the federation would decide whether or not to associate freely with France.[114]

Within both the PRA and the RDA, the wisdom, pace, and methods of the older generation were under attack. Impatient young men, inspired by burgeoning independence movements elsewhere in Africa and Asia, increasingly pressed for more radical and rapid change.[115] Youth, student, and trade union organizations such as the CJA, RJDA, AERDA, UGEAO, FEANF, and UGTAN—all led by young men—incessantly pushed the parties from the Left. By August 1958, these groups had formed a united front to fight for national independence.[116] While most leaders of the major political parties ultimately weighed in for a "Yes" vote, the parties' youth wings generally campaigned for a "No."[117]

The FEANF was among the most important student organizations to break with the interterritorial RDA's position. While the FEANF's founders and first leaders had been RDA members, by 1958, the organization had distanced itself from RDA parliamentarians, whom it considered too cozy with the French power structure. Decrying the RDA deputies' collaborationist stance, the FEANF increasingly leaned toward the positions taken by the PRA. In May 1958, a writer for the FEANF's *L'Étudiant d'Afrique Noire* denounced Sékou Touré for refusing to call for immediate independence. The following month, the FEANF's board of directors endorsed the principles of African unity and independence and declared their organization's support for any political party that favored those ends. Indicating hostility to the new French constitution, the board urged FEANF militants to campaign in favor of a "No" vote.[118] During the 1958 summer vacation, FEANF members returned to their homes to mobilize against the new constitution. They worked closely with the territorial affiliates of the UGEAO, CJA, RJDA, and UGTAN.[119]

Due to the small number of Guinean students in Senegal and France, the UGEAO and the FEANF were represented in Guinea by one local organization, the UGEEG.[120] In the aftermath of its sixth congress, held in Conakry on July 20–24, 1958, the UGEEG opened its campaign for a "No" vote. For the next two months, Guinean students crisscrossed the territory, speaking out against the proposed constitution.[121]

Pressed by students, trade unionists, and the party's youth wing, the Guinean RDA moved markedly to the Left. By July 1958, it was much closer to the PRA positions on federation and a federal executive than it was to the Houphouët line.[122] On July 25, 1958, as the PRA congress convened in Cotonou, the Guinean RDA published an editorial in *La Liberté* that demonstrated its conformity with the most important PRA positions. Like the PRA, the Guinean RDA affirmed the need for large political and economic ensembles such as French West and Equatorial Africa. These ensembles might form a union with France, but only "on the basis of free cooperation, absolute liberty and the right to independence."[123]

In the same issue, Sékou Touré moved cautiously toward a proindependence position, at least in theory. At the interterritorial level, Sékou Touré was considered to be a leftist and a young upstart. In the federalist versus territorialist debate, the thirty-six-year-old had defied Houphouët-Boigny, who was seventeen years his elder.[124] In Guinea, however, Sékou Touré was deemed old guard, too conservative for many of the younger generation. In July 1958, he continued to resist advocating immediate independence. He asserted in *La Liberté* that loi-cadre was obsolete and affirmed that all peoples had the "natural rights" of freedom of movement, self-determination, independence, and self-government. However, he envisaged continued association with France. The territories' "exercise of their right to self-determination" should not be confused "with any desire to separate themselves from France," Sékou Touré contended. To the contrary, the African people, their political organizations, and trade unions were all conscious of the role France could continue to play in the economic and cultural domains. Once the overseas territories had achieved political equality with their former colonial power, he asserted, they would enthusiastically form an association with the French Republic—but such equality was a prerequisite for any type of union. The constitution as it stood was not adequate. It did not provide for a "real association" or a "true community," because the one envisioned would not be established on the basis of mutual consent by politically equal, sovereign peoples. Any constitutional project that failed to recognize the right of overseas peoples to independence, and that did not affirm the principle of equality of peoples, would be unanimously and firmly rejected, Sékou Touré warned. However, he concluded, the constitution could still be revised in time for the referendum.[125] In July 1958, therefore, Sékou Touré's plea was for constitutional revision, not immediate independence. Under Sékou Touré's leadership, the Guinean RDA continued to hold out hope that France would accede to its demands for further concessions. Despite its disenchantment with the draft constitution, the party had not yet called for a "No" vote in the September referendum.

Despite deep divisions in the interterritorial RDA, Houphouët-Boigny refused to convene a meeting of the coordinating committee to determine a common position on the constitution.[126] Instead, he called a meeting of the secretaries-general of all the territorial branches. Because the meeting took place in Paris, it was most accessible to secretaries-general who were also parliamentarians, and thus likely to be under Houphouët-Boigny's influence. Indeed, at their August 3 meeting, the majority of territorial leaders supported Houphouët-Boigny's position on the constitution, which included opposition to the notion of immediate independence, opposition to the creation of a federal executive, and support for the abolition of the federations of French West and Equatorial Africa, along with their federal governments.[127]

The RDA's official position on the constitution was to be presented to Prime Minister de Gaulle on August 5. In yet another attempt to tie his hands, Sékou Touré was chosen to make the presentation. He duly presented the official position, avoiding all discussion of a federal executive and barely mentioning the possibility of independence. On August 7, Sékou Touré departed for Dakar, where he was scheduled to meet with UGTAN.[128] UGTAN leaders, still very much influenced by their CGT past, were as certain to push Sékou Touré to the Left as Houphouët-Boigny had pushed to the Right.[129]

With feedback on the constitutional draft from both the PRA and the RDA, de Gaulle addressed the consultative committee on August 8. Sidelining the PRA and the left wing of the RDA, de Gaulle posed two stark alternatives: adherence to the French Community through a "Yes" vote, or secession from France through a "No" vote.[130] Openly threatening those territories that were considering independence, de Gaulle declared, "It is well understood, and I understand it, one can desire secession. [Secession] imposes duties. It carries dangers. Independence has its burdens. The referendum will ascertain if the idea of secession carries the day. *But one cannot conceive of an independent territory and a France that continues to aid it. The [independent] government will bear the consequences, economic and otherwise, that are entailed in the manifestation of such a will.*"[131]

Thus, de Gaulle made it clear that any declaration of independence would be taken as a personal affront, with cause for retribution.

Safely out of Paris, Sékou Touré quickly backed away from the Houphouët line. On August 9, the official federal radio station, Radio-Dakar, broadcast an interview with Sékou Touré. If de Gaulle had thrown down the gauntlet with respect to independence, Sékou Touré was willing to pick it up. He told his audience: "Listening to General de Gaulle yesterday, frankly, I was shocked. My self-respect for the dignity of Africa was shocked. One tells us that we can opt for independence, but that it will be with all the consequences. All right, I respond that the consequences are not only African. They also can be French."[132]

Meanwhile, the French government, attempting to secure allegiances, acceded to one of the RDA's earlier demands. The Ordinance of July 26, 1958, revised loi-cadre by promoting African council of government vice presidents to the position of president.[133] Henceforth, appointed French governors would no longer preside over the ministerial cabinets. On August 12, Governor Jean Mauberna (appointed on January 29, 1958) stepped aside as president of Guinea's Council of Government, and Sékou Touré was duly installed in his place. Following his installation, Sékou Touré cried, "Long live Guinea! Long live United Africa and Long live France!"[134] There still appeared to be room for an accord with the imperial power.

DE GAULLE COMES TO AFRICA

During the month of August 1958, Prime Minister de Gaulle toured French West and Equatorial Africa to rally support for his constitutional project. Initially, Guinea was not on his itinerary.[135] According to former RDA activist, Bocar Biro Barry, de Gaulle had intended to avoid Guinea, believing that its leader was "boiling, hot, anti-French. So, he did not want to come to see himself insulted. Because, de Gaulle, you know, he had great pride. He was the great Frenchman. He did not want to be humiliated here. So, he was supposed to see all the countries except Guinea. He thought that Guinea was lost, the people were going to vote 'No.' They were a bunch of fools."[136] However, Bernard Cornut-Gentille, former high commissioner of French West Africa and de Gaulle's new minister of Overseas France, worried that if Sékou Touré decided to oppose the constitution, he would take all of Guinea with him.[137] Priding himself on "knowing" Sékou Touré, Cornut-Gentille believed that he could flatter the RDA leader into compliance. After Sékou Touré's Dakar radio address,

5.2 Prime Minister de Gaulle promoting the constitution in a suburb of Brazza-ville, French Congo, August 23, 1958. © Bettmann/CORBIS.

Cornut-Gentille inserted a Conakry stop in de Gaulle's Africa tour. Although Sékou Touré had been rebuffed from joining the consultative committee, Cornut-Gentille hoped that the prime minister's visit to Guinea would bolster his ego enough to prod him into supporting the constitutional project.[138]

De Gaulle was due to arrive in Conakry on August 25.[139] The day before his arrival, the prime minister made an important announcement in Brazzaville, the site of the historic conference that had laid the groundwork for the new postwar imperialism. On August 24, de Gaulle proclaimed that he had accepted two alterations to the proposed constitution. First, if a territory voted "Yes" in the referendum, choosing to join the French Community, it could still, at some future date, vote for independence "without risk or peril," provided that France and

5.3 Uniformed RDA women in Guinea with handmade poster featuring the party symbol. Centre de Recherche et de Documentation Africaine.

other members of the Community approved the decision. Such a vote, unlike a "No" vote in the referendum, would not be considered "secession," although upon attaining independence the state would cease to be a member of the Community. Second, territories would be permitted to join the Community individually or in groups. However, de Gaulle refused to accede to the demand that the territorial groupings be institutionalized in the constitution as, for instance, French West Africa or French Equatorial Africa. Their formation—or lack thereof—was left to the initiative of the various territorial assemblies. Moreover, there would be no federal executive.[140]

Given the concessions of August 24, Cornut-Gentille and Houphouët-Boigny anticipated a cordial reception for the prime minister in Guinea. Initially, all went according to plan. From the airport to the city center, Sékou Touré rode beside the general in the first car of the motorcade. The walls of Conakry's buildings were plastered with posters of the RDA elephant carrying de Gaulle's emblem, the *Croix de Lorraine*.[141] "We received him," Bocar Biro Barry recalled. "There had never been such a grandiose demonstration as the one that met de Gaulle upon his arrival in Conakry. Even the children were out in the streets."[142] With women on one side and men on the other, thousands of uniformed RDA members lined the road for fifteen kilometers, from the airport on the city's outskirts to the Territorial Assembly at its center. As the women danced, accompanied by tam-tams, coras, and balafons, the crowd greeted the motorcade, crying, "*Syli! Syli!*" and singing, "The elephant has entered the city!"[143] In his memoirs, de Gaulle recalled the sensation: "From the airport to the center of the town the crowd [was] evenly distributed in well-drilled battalions along both sides of the road. . . . The women were lined up in front in their hundreds, each group wearing dresses of the same cut and color, and all, as the procession passed by, jumping, dancing and singing to order."[144]

As the motorcade advanced, the crowds went wild—more for Sékou Touré, and his prominent position at de Gaulle's side, than for the French prime minister. De Gaulle, however, misunderstood the object of the crowd's enthusiasm. When the people cried, "Vive de Gaulle!" and "Syli!," the prime minister was told that "syli" meant elephant. Unaware that the elephant was the symbol of the Guinean RDA, and by extension of Sékou Touré personally, he believed that Africans were comparing him, Prime Minister de Gaulle, to the king of the savannah. His final error was his interpretation of the warm welcome as massive popular support for his constitutional project, rather than simple hospitality.[145]

RDA leaders had mandated that de Gaulle's reception be respectful, demonstrating the political maturity of the Guinean population.[146] Once again,

5.4 Prime Minister de Gaulle greeted by a crowd on his arrival in Conakry, August 25, 1958. AFP/Getty Images.

party elders had to work to keep the youth in line. Aissatou N'Diaye recalled, "The students were very active. . . . They made their views known on banners. They wrote many things, including insults. They hung some of the banners at the doorway of the Maison de la Jeunesse, so that when de Gaulle came in—he came in with Cornut-Gentille—[he would see them]. Sékou had heard about the banners and ordered them removed. He said he did not need anything inflammatory—no insults."[147]

In the afternoon, Sékou Touré was to receive the French prime minister officially and to address the Territorial Assembly, which had convened for that purpose. As requested, Sékou Touré provided an advance copy of his speech to the governor, who, in turn, showed the speech to the high commissioner and the overseas minister. At the suggestion of Gabriel d'Arboussier, who had replaced

Houphouët-Boigny as Grand Council president in early 1958, Sékou Touré already had made a few alterations. That morning, he had penned in reference to the concessions announced in de Gaulle's Brazzaville speech. Upon perusing the final version, Governor Mauberna, High Commissioner Messmer, and Overseas Minister Cornut-Gentille found nothing unusual. The speech was vintage Sékou Touré. A copy of the speech was given to Prime Minister de Gaulle.[148]

In his Territorial Assembly address, Sékou Touré called for further revisions in the proposed constitution. The Guinean people would not vote "Yes" unless the constitution proclaimed "the right to independence and the juridical equality of peoples associated [with France]," Sékou Touré asserted. The people must have the right to self-determination, to maintain the federation and its structures, and to dissolve the union with France if they so chose. Absent such rights, the Community would constitute an arbitrary construction forcibly imposed upon future generations.[149] Sékou Touré concluded with a flourish: "We will not renounce and we will never renounce our legitimate and natural right to independence. . . . We prefer poverty in liberty to riches in slavery. . . . We wish to be free citizens of our African states, members of the Franco-African Community. In effect, the French Republic, within the Franco-African association, will be an element, as all the African states equally will be elements, of this grand multinational community composed of free and equal states."[150]

For those who had listened to Sékou Touré during the previous few months, his message was not new. The governor, high commissioner, and overseas minister had heard such words many times before. Only de Gaulle, who apparently had not read his advance copy of the speech, appeared to be caught off guard. This time, Sékou Touré's message, pronounced in the prime minister's presence and in a tone of righteous anger, seemed particularly insolent. For de Gaulle it was a turning point. Thus, the speech became a historic event.[151]

De Gaulle refused to negotiate further. The constitution would stand as it was: Guinea could take it or leave it. Responding to the Guinean leader, de Gaulle declared: "France is proposing this Community; no one is bound to adhere to it. There has been talk of independence; I say more loudly here than elsewhere that independence is at Guinea's disposal. She can take it, she can take it on the 28th of September by saying 'No' to the proposition that has been made to her and in this case I guarantee that the métropole will create no obstacles. [The métropole] will, of course, draw inferences from it, but it will put up no obstacles."[152]

Upon exiting the Territorial Assembly hall, de Gaulle convened a meeting with the governor, high commissioner, and overseas minister.[153] Sékou Touré's behavior, which contrasted so starkly with the courteous, if not obsequious, demeanor of other African leaders, was intolerable. De Gaulle would have nothing further to do with him. "Messieurs," he informed the others, "Here is an individual with whom we will never be able to get along. We have nothing more to do here. Let us go, the thing is clear: the 29th of September in the morning, France will leave here. . . . Guinea, Messieurs, is not indispensable to France. Let her assume her responsibilities."[154]

Although de Gaulle presumed that the die was cast, it was not. He assumed that Sékou Touré's speech meant that he had called for a "No" vote in the referendum, and that an overwhelming Guinean vote against the constitution would result. He refused to listen to Governor Mauberna's plea that the text of Sékou Touré's speech did not point to a definitive position regarding the referendum, and that Touré's personal position was not necessarily that of the Guinean RDA. The Guinean RDA was due to hold a territorial congress on September 14, the governor told him. It was there that a final decision on the constitution would be made and the position for or against would be determined. Convinced that he had the answer in advance, de Gaulle did not wait for these niceties. On de Gaulle's orders, the high commissioner immediately began to prepare for France's departure from Guinea.[155]

Later that day, de Gaulle reiterated his position to Sékou Touré privately. If Guinea rejected the constitution, France immediately would withdraw all administrative, technical, and educational assistance. It would no longer subsidize Guinea's budget. In the future, Guinea would not receive any preferential treatment whatsoever.[156] En route to Dakar on August 26, Prime Minister de Gaulle informed Governor Mauberna that France indeed would sever its ties with Guinea: "Our decision has been made, Mr. Governor. Let it be known to the Guinean government." Opposing a rupture in relations, Mauberna suggested that Sékou Touré be given time to reflect. However, de Gaulle refused any further discussion.[157]

Scheduled to attend a political meeting in Dakar, Sékou Touré also planned to leave for Senegal on August 26. Before his departure, Sékou Touré addressed the Guinean people by radio. Although he had no authority to stake out an official position on the constitution before the territorial congress, he hinted at a personal one in his radio address. He was going to Dakar to consult with French West African political and trade union leaders, Sékou Touré said. He would explain Guinea's position on the constitution, which, he claimed, was the same as that of UGTAN, the youth, military veterans, and even elements of the PRA. Sékou Touré concluded,

We make a distinction between France, which we love, and a constitutional project. It is not just to say that to respond "No" to the constitution is to respond "No" to France. In effect, if the constitutional project submitted to us tends to brake African evolution, we will respond "Yes" to France and "No" to the constitutional project. . . .

We already have said that we are for association, but for an association that is a veritable community of free and equal peoples. If the dispositions of the constitution do not reflect this demand, Guinea will respond "No" and I would wish it to be the same in all the other territories.[158]

The Dakar meeting, convened on August 27, included RDA leaders from various French West African territories, as well as UGTAN's board of directors. At the conclusion of the meeting, the RDA laid out further conditions for acceptance of the constitution, while UGTAN's board of directors pronounced itself in favor of a "No" vote.[159] Because they were both scheduled to travel to Dakar on August 26, de Gaulle initially had offered to take Sékou Touré in his personal airplane. After Sékou Touré's speech, however, the offer had been abruptly withdrawn.[160] Temporarily stranded in Conakry, Sékou Touré arrived in Dakar only after the meeting was over. As a result, he did not participate in the discussions.[161]

Although Prime Minister de Gaulle wanted nothing further to do with him, other French officials continued to pursue the Guinean leader. Overseas Minister Cornut-Gentille sent an airplane to Conakry to bring Sékou Touré belatedly to Dakar. Throughout the night of August 27, Sékou Touré, bolstered by UGTAN's position, lobbied the overseas minister. The constitution must provide for a confederation of independent, equal states, rather than the inequitable association proposed by de Gaulle. Further, the constitution must create federal executives for both French West and Equatorial Africa. If these two changes were made, Sékou Touré asserted, Guinea would vote "Yes" in the upcoming referendum. When pressed on Guinea's position if the changes were not made, Sékou Touré refused a definitive answer.[162]

On August 28, in an address broadcast by Radio-Dakar and in a subsequent press communiqué, Sékou Touré took the same position. Guinea would not endorse a constitution that injured the dignity, liberty, or unity of Africa. If the French constitutional project denied Africans their right to self-determination and their demand for the maintenance of federal structures, the Guinean people would vote for independence on September 28. As a sovereign, independent nation, Guinea would seek a new relationship with France through contractual agreements. If France refused to enter into such accords, Guinea would reorient itself economically.[163] Convinced that the majority of African leaders would support his project, de Gaulle refused any further modifications of the constitutional text.[164]

In Guinea, the speeches of Sékou Touré and Charles de Gaulle were circulated widely. European residents, anticipating a "No" vote, made plans for their immediate departure from the territory.[165] Small business owners, fearing displacement by Africans, began wiring large amounts of capital to the métropole.[166] Upon his return to Conakry on August 28, Sékou Touré met with representatives of various European interests and attempted to reassure them. Guinea would vote "No" to the constitution as it presently was written, he told them, but this vote would not signify a desire to secede. Guinea wished to remain associated with France on other, more equitable bases.[167]

At Governor Mauberna's request, Sékou Touré addressed another European audience at the Chamber of Commerce on September 1. In attendance were more than two hundred representatives of Guinea's various economic sectors.[168] In a speech lasting more than two hours, Sékou Touré recapitulated the now familiar positions concerning independence, federation, and a Franco-African community of free and equal states. These positions had already been adopted by UGTAN and the French West African youth movements, Sékou Touré said. If the constitution were not modified to accommodate these demands, Guinea would vote "No" in referendum. However, this would not be a "No" to France, with which Guinea still wished to collaborate.[169] Africans had been warned that a "No" vote would be perceived as secession and would result in rupture with France and abandonment. There would be no more French economic assistance or investment. Technicians and civil servants would be recalled. Sékou Touré denounced these threats as unacceptable pressures on African voters.[170]

Sékou Touré's speeches did little to mollify European fears. Between September 1 and 21, the volume of money wired from Guinea to France increased markedly. By September 22, the figure had risen to 650 million francs CFA. Wage earners originally from the métropole sent their life's savings to France. Following instructions from their headquarters, large French-based commercial societies and enterprises transferred significant amounts of capital from Guinea to France, while others sent capital and merchandise to Dakar.[171]

Meanwhile, on August 31, the interterritorial RDA publicly distanced itself from Sékou Touré and criticized his actions as divisive. In Guinea, in contrast, the elusive quest for unity was finally meeting with some success. On the same day that the interterritorial RDA published its critique, Governor Mauberna learned that Barry Diawadou, on behalf of the PRA, had requested a meeting with Sékou Touré.[172] At the ensuing meeting, the PRA delegation, led by Deputy Barry Diawadou and French Union Councillors Abdoulaye Diallo and Karim Bangoura, was received by Sékou Touré, Minister of the Interior Fodéba Kéïta, and Senator Fodé Mamadou Touré—a former BAG stalwart who recently had joined the RDA. As the governor had feared, the PRA delegation proposed collaboration between the PRA and the RDA.[173]

Although the RDA was by far the dominant party, the alliance of the two parties was not exclusively on RDA terms. While the interterritorial PRA had called for immediate independence at the Cotonou congress in July, it had not taken an explicit position on the constitution.[174] During its congress on September 4–7, the Guinean PRA trumped the interterritorial body by unequivocally endorsing a "No" vote.[175] To prevent the PRA from capturing its disgruntled leftist constituency, the Guinean RDA was under enormous pressure to follow suit.

Meanwhile, Sékou Touré had been excluded from the interterritorial RDA's final deliberations on the draft constitution. The coordinating committee had been scheduled to meet in Ouagadougou, Upper Volta, on September 4 to engage in a collective study of the constitution. Sékou Touré had planned to attend this critical meeting.[176] However, at the last minute, the meeting was canceled. Ouezzin Coulibaly, the interterritorial political director, was gravely ill in Paris. (He would die on September 7.) Instead of a full coordinating committee meeting in Africa, a rump session was hastily convened on September 3 in Houphouët-Boigny's Paris home. Only those members of the RDA's coordinating committee who happened to be in Paris were able to attend. Sékou Touré, rallying RDA forces in Guinea, was absent. Without the assent of the full coordinating committee, a handful of RDA officials determined that the constitutional project satisfied the demands of the movement and should be adopted through a "Yes" vote in the referendum.[177] Once again, in a move reminiscent of 1950, a small group of RDA leaders had usurped the powers of the coordinating committee to impose their own agenda. On September 4, having won the interterritorial RDA's questionable endorsement, the French government published the definitive text of the constitution—only twenty-four days before the referendum.[178]

CONCLUSION

Guinea's RDA government, established in May 1957 under the loi-cadre system, had supporters and detractors on both Left and Right. Although it pushed through a number of progressive reforms, most notably, the democratization of local government and the abolition of the canton chieftaincy, opposition soon came from the Left. As the new governing elites consolidated their power and collaborated with the colonial administration, grassroots militants charged them with opportunism and corruption. They protested the balkanization inherent in the loi-cadre system and criticized their leaders for surrendering their future as a strong and united Africa. Demanding independence, rather than autonomy, the Guinean Left called for the establishment of elected governments based on the great African federations. Their criticisms were taken up by RDA rivals in the political arena, who, despite their past conservatism, attempted to win over the disenchanted Left. When the interterritorial RDA endorsed the proposed constitution for the Fifth Republic, leaders of the Guinean branch, like their counterparts elsewhere, were poised to follow suit. Resisting the pressures of the interterritorial party, grassroots militants in Guinea pushed their leaders to reject the constitution and demand immediate independence instead.

CHAPTER 6
Defiance and Retribution: The Referendum and Its Aftermath, 1958–60

IN 1958, IN ANOTHER ATTEMPT to save the French empire, the de Gaulle government proposed a new constitution that would provide the basis for the Fifth Republic. French citizens throughout the empire were to vote for or against the constitution in a referendum on September 28. In the weeks and months prior to the vote, grassroots activists in Guinea condemned the constitution as a formula for continued junior partnership in a French-dominated community and demanded that the RDA advocate immediate independence instead. The proindependence position adopted by the Guinean Left was contrary to the wishes of interterritorial RDA leaders, who attempted to impose their will on the party's constituent branches. Once again, the interterritorial party sent representatives to Conakry in an attempt to force the Guinean RDA back into line. However, this time the Guinean Left, led by students, teachers and other trade unionists, along with the party's women's and youth wings, won the day, forcing the Guinean leadership to endorse a "No" vote. In the September 1958 referendum, the people of Guinea overwhelmingly rejected the constitutional project that laid the groundwork for the Fifth French Republic, opting instead for immediate independence. In all the French empire, Guinea was the only territory to vote "No."

As previously threatened, France retaliated with a vengeance. Even before the vote, France began its withdrawal, sabotaging archives, infrastructure, and the economy. After the referendum, France attempted to isolate Guinea diplomatically, economically, and militarily. Its pleas for assistance rejected by France and that country's compliant NATO allies, Guinea was forced to seek new friends and partners in the East. Ironically, it was France that made its own worst nightmare

157

come true. It had forced Guinea into the communist camp. Meanwhile, the new constitution could not save the empire any more than earlier reforms. By 1960, most of French Africa was independent.

THE MOVE TOWARD INDEPENDENCE

Although the Guinean RDA had inched to the Left, it had not moved quickly enough. While the interterritorial RDA pushed for accommodation on French terms, students and other youths, trade unionists, and the Guinean PRA pushed Guinea in the other direction. By September 1958, all of these elements had endorsed a "No" vote.[1] Sékou Touré had met with university students in Paris who were extremely critical of the constitutional project.[2] In September, the FEANF sent two delegations to meet with Sékou Touré in Conakry, hoping to extract from him an unequivocal endorsement of the "No."[3] During its congress on September 4–7, the Guinean PRA officially weighed in against the constitution.[4] On September 10–11, the Guinean RDA's women's and youth wings paved the way for the territorial branch by calling for a "No" vote in the referendum.[5] Finally, UGTAN's board of directors had endorsed the "No" vote on August 27. Its position was ratified by a cadre conference on September 11 and publicly supported by Bakary Djibo, head of Niger's *loi-cadre* government and secretary-general of the PRA. Djibo's call for a "No" vote put considerable pressure on Sékou Touré.[6]

On September 14, the board of directors of the interterritorial PRA met in Niamey, Niger, to discuss the final version of the constitution. The Guinean PRA took the lead in condemning the project and urged its rejection in the upcoming referendum.[7] Dissension within the party, already evident at the Cotonou congress, ultimately forced the PRA to allow each territorial branch to determine its own position.[8] In the end, only the branches in Guinea and Niger supported a "No" vote, while those in Senegal, Dahomey, Upper Volta, and the French Soudan endorsed a "Yes."[9]

While the interterritorial PRA was meeting in Niamey, the Guinean RDA held a territorial congress in Conakry to determine its final position on the constitution. Although Sékou Touré's personal views were clear, the Guinean branch had not yet made an official pronouncement.[10] By September 14, all of the RDA's territorial branches, except Guinea and Senegal, had weighed in for a "Yes" vote. (Senegal endorsed the "Yes" on September 21.) Pressing the Guinean branch to toe the Houphouët line, the interterritorial RDA sent high-level representatives to the Conakry congress.[11]

6.1 Advocating the "No" vote in the September 1958 referendum campaign, Dakar, Senegal. ECPAD/Collection de la Documentation Française.

6.2 Advocating the "Yes" vote in the September 1958 referendum campaign, Dakar, Senegal. ECPAD/Collection de la Documentation Française.

Having awaited the publication of the definitive constitutional text before reaching a conclusion, the Guinean RDA was now ready to act. Thus, on September 14, some 680 RDA delegates, representing far-flung village and neighborhood committees, subsections, and the party's youth wing, converged on the capital to determine, through a democratic process, the party's final disposition.[12] Bocar Biro Barry remembered the September 14 congress, which was held in the Conakry neighborhood of Boulbinet.

> It was there that things were played out. That was the day fixed for the territorial congress to decide if one must vote "Yes" or "No." It was there that Houphouët sent a delegation—to plead with Sékou to vote "Yes." He wanted all the territories of the RDA—Conakry, Bamako, Niamey, Abidjan, Cotonou—to vote "Yes" to please General de Gaulle. Afterwards, one would see about independence.
>
> So, this delegation arrived here at the airport at 10 o'clock in the morning. They went to the Territorial Assembly building. The congress of Boulbinet was at the port of Boulbinet—there where the people fish. There was an old hangar there—a place where they smoked the fish. That is where they held the congress.

Then a young activist in the teachers' union as well as the left wing of the RDA, Barry remembered the surprising outcome of the interterritorial representatives' meeting with Sékou Touré:

> Sékou went into a meeting with Houphouët's delegation—from 10 o'clock until one o'clock. We were in the conference room. We waited for Sékou's order to vote "Yes"—to not follow the teachers, because we were teachers; to not follow the youth, to vote "Yes." He had accepted it. Until September 14, he was for the "Yes."
>
> He arrived at the territorial congress after the delegation's departure. We—the young people, the teachers' union—we were in the room, impatient. We said to ourselves, "The delegation of Houphouët is there. It is to corrupt Sékou. If he ever accepts to vote 'Yes,' we will liquidate him." That was whispered amongst ourselves in the conference room. All the secretaries-general were there—it was a territorial congress for which all the political leaders had been called to Conakry. All the subsections were led by teachers. There was an overwhelming majority of teachers, of young people. The youth of Guinea and the FEANF were there. We were there, side by side with the trade unions and the youth movements. All of us, we were for the "No."
>
> He arrived toward one o'clock. It was hot. Everyone was irritable. He arrived in the room. As soon as he entered, everyone cried, "No!" I still remember as if it were today. Everyone cried, "NO, NO, NO, NO, NO!" We were all sure that he had been led astray by Houphouët's delegation. He arrived. He sat down, calmly at first. The people continued to cry, "NO, NO, NO, NO, NO, NO!" He rose. He began to speak. The conference lasted five minutes. Because he was a great maneuverer, a great opportunist, he saw which way the wind was blowing, and he said to himself, "If I say the other thing, they are going to liquidate me." So, he said, "The 28th of September, we must vote. What will be the vote of the Parti Démocratique de Guinée?" The people cried, "NO, NO, NO, NO, NO, NO!" There we were. He saw that the atmosphere was for the "No." It was at this moment that he changed sides. . . . The teachers' union, the youth movement, and the students could have cast Sékou Touré aside for Koumandian Kéïta. It was that that frightened Sékou.[13]

Thus, it was not until September 14, two weeks before the referendum, that Sékou Touré came out definitively for a "No" vote. He reached this decision only after much debate, and under immense pressure from trade unions, students, and youths. The teachers' union, with its relatively young membership, the students' organizations, and the youth movement, whose membership overlapped with both teachers and students, were the driving force behind the "No" vote. According to Bocar Biro Barry, these groups had to push Sékou Touré to accept their position. "There were confrontations, meetings," he said, to move Sékou Touré away from the official position of the interterritorial RDA: "Many of the [RDA] subsection leaders were teachers. In Guéckédou, there was Sangaré Toumani; in Kissidougou, there was Tounkara Kissia; in Kankan, there was Fofana Khalil; in Siguiri, there was Doumbouya . . . ; in N'Zérékoré, there was Sagno Mamady. In practically all of Guinea, the subsections were led by teachers. It was they who were able to mobilize the masses, saying, 'The referendum is coming. You must vote "No!"'"[14] In his address to the territorial congress on September 14, Sékou Touré indeed made reference to the proindependence positions already taken by the PRA, UGTAN, CJA, and FEANF.[15]

Reporting on Sékou Touré's September 14 speech, *Agence France-Presse* observed that the Guinean leader had urged the populace to vote "No." He had argued that the proposed constitution would accord Africa neither freedom of action nor equality with France. Instead, it would create a great French state in which Africans would be dispossessed of the essential attributes of sovereignty. General de Gaulle had offered Africans a choice between claiming independence and joining a community that would be French, rather than multinational. The interests of its members would be subordinated to those of France. "Comrades," Sékou Touré had asserted, "We have declared unanimously to the Representative of France that we prefer poverty in liberty to riches in slavery. . . . We will vote 'No' to a community that is no more than the French Union rebaptized—the old merchandise with a new label. We will vote 'No' to inequality." A unanimous "No" vote would end French colonialism and permit independent African nations to create a truly egalitarian, fraternal association with France.[16]

On September 28 and in the weeks that followed, Sékou Touré had declared, the Guinean people should demonstrate their political maturity. They should ignore provocations and attempts at intimidation, corruption, division, and diversion. Instead, every man and woman should mobilize for African independence—in the cities, in the countryside, and in the military camps. They should mobilize "so that the victory is total, and the unity of Guinea is affirmed to the world." In this way they would demonstrate their fraternal rapport with the French people. They would constitute, together with the Europeans residing in Guinea, a society of men who were free and equal. "Long live France and African independence!" Sékou Touré had cried.[17]

On September 14, the Guinean RDA officially broke ranks with the party's interterritorial leadership and all the other territorial branches. That evening, the territorial congress unanimously approved Sékou Touré's political report and adopted a resolution in favor of independence and a "No" vote in the referendum. The resolution read: "Considering that there cannot be for a dependent people the slightest hesitation in choosing between Independence and the proposed Community, [the Guinean RDA] DECIDES TO CHOOSE INDEPENDENCE BY VOTING "NO" IN THE REFERENDUM OF 28 SEPTEMBER." The resolution decried the balkanization of Africa and the inequality of the future states inherent in the proposed constitution. Echoing its secretary-general, the party invited the Guinean people, including political and trade union organizations, youths, and students, to help the "No" vote triumph. To safeguard common interests, it cautioned that the goal should be accomplished in calm and dignity. In the hope of salvaging African unity, the Guinean political bureau would contact the interterritorial coordinating committee and other territorial branches and attempt to convince them to join in the vote for African independence. Even before it was put to a vote, the resolution received a standing ovation from those assembled for the territorial congress.[18]

On September 16, Guinea's Council of Government issued a communiqué announcing the formation of a broad front for national independence. United in this purpose were the two political parties—the RDA and the PRA—youth and military veterans' associations, and UGTAN. Echoing earlier proclamations by Sékou Touré, the Council of Government indicated that it had chosen independence, not to oppose Africans against Europeans or Guinea against France, but to lay the basis of frank and loyal collaboration between the two countries.[19] The following day, the Guinean branches of the RDA and the PRA met in Conakry and issued a joint communiqué inviting all militants—male and female, African and European—to campaign for a "No" vote in referendum.[20] The Guinean PRA then effectively dissolved itself, its members joining forces with the Guinean RDA, which now included forty-three subsections and 4,300 local committees.[21] The federal government in Dakar concluded that a "No" vote in Guinea was now certain.[22]

Fearing provocations and an excuse for a crackdown, the RDA did not organize public meetings after September 14.[23] Instead, RDA militants worked through local party cells and focused on getting-out-the-vote measures. RDA men and women from urban areas traveled to villages and hamlets, where they instructed nonliterate voters and distributed mauve-colored ballots signifying the "No" vote. In an attempt to keep the peace, slogans and directives were circulated

6.3 *La Liberté* promotes the "No" vote, September 1958 referendum campaign in Guinea. Centre de Recherche et de Documentation Africaine.

6.4 Local musicians perform during the September 1958 referendum campaign.
Centre de Recherche et de Documentation Africaine.

in all the local languages: "Failure to provocateurs!" "Stay calm!" "If people insult
you, say nothing. If they push you or hit you, don't react."[24]

Aissatou N'Diaye recalled the feverish activity that followed the Guinean
RDA congress. "We went all out. People were sent in all directions to campaign." They spread the message through word of mouth and song.[25] N'Diaye
remembered that women created new songs for the occasion, including,

> When de Gaulle came to Guinea
> He asked us to vote "Yes"
> Whereas President Sékou asked us to vote "No"
> No, No, No![26]

And,

> Guinea says "No"
> De Gaulle says "Yes"
> One must vote "No"
> Comarade Sékou Touré, one must choose the "No"
> Yes, one must choose the "No," Sékou Touré
> In any case, we have voted "No."[27]

French Retribution: Bearing the Consequences

As the Guinean RDA mobilized for a "No" vote, Sékou Touré continued to press the French government for accords to be concluded outside the framework offered by Prime Minister de Gaulle. After the referendum, Sékou Touré asserted, he would propose a formula of association with common currency, foreign, and defense policies. Guinea would remain in the franc zone and would reserve first place for France in its commercial relations.[28] Exasperated, the governor telegraphed the overseas minister. He noted that, despite the governor's statements to the contrary, Sékou Touré seemed certain that, following a negative vote in the referendum, he could negotiate a separate agreement of association with France as advantageous to Guinea as those offered to members of the French Community. The governor observed that these illusions were shared by nearly all political, trade union, and student leaders in Guinea. The French government must continue to reiterate that such an agreement could never be realized—as Prime Minister de Gaulle had so clearly stated in Conakry the previous month.[29]

Eleven days before the referendum, the governor began to make plans for a complete French evacuation from Guinea. In order "to demonstrate . . . the consequences of a negative vote," he urged the overseas minister to publish a communiqué enumerating the actions that would be taken against the presumed-to-be secessionist territory. He suggested that the minister issue the following command: "While waiting for a response from Guinea in the referendum, the relevant services are ordered to postpone the travel of members of the teaching corps due to return to this Territory." On the eve of the new academic year, the difficulties involved in replacing these teachers would be nearly insurmountable, the governor concluded. The prohibition against the teachers' return would be certain to have a profound psychological and moral effect. It would prove that France would carry through on its threats to terminate all aid to the rebel state.[30] The governor's suggestion was accepted, and teachers vacationing outside of Guinea were ordered not to return.[31]

The withholding of teachers would be the first in a long list of actions taken against the mutinous territory. In his September 17 telegram, the governor urged the overseas minister to prevent the return of all civil servants vacationing outside of Guinea. He noted that the government's overseas development fund, the Fond d'Investissement pour le Développement Économique et Sociale des Territoires d'Outre-Mer (FIDES), was scheduled to determine the new credits available for Guinea. The government must make it clear that FIDES would not be able to make such a determination until the results of the referendum were known. Communiqués outlining these measures should be diffused in two- to three-day intervals, the governor concluded. They surely would provoke a shock in both the European and African communities of Guinea, considerably augmenting local malaise.[32] The governor's suggestions were implemented both before and after the referendum.[33] In order to keep Sékou Touré's government in the dark, the governor prohibited the heads of state services from discussing the specifics of postreferendum plans with Guinean authorities.[34]

Local uneasiness was exacerbated by the continued flight of capital from Guinea. Again, the governor facilitated these moves. In mid-September, the radio broadcasting institute asked the governor for instructions concerning its liquid assets, worth four billion francs CFA, a quantity of money so large that it weighed several tons and was stored in three hundred to four hundred chests in the bank of French West Africa. Fearing that the money would be seized in the aftermath of independence, the high commissioner ordered the money transferred to Dakar. The governor, anxious to avoid a political incident, was uncertain how to transport such a large volume discreetly.[35] In response, the high commissioner sent a company of paratroopers to Guinea, charged with maintaining order and protecting the transfer to Dakar of the radio broadcasting institute's liquid assets. The high commissioner personally authorized the use of force, if necessary.[36]

Increasingly, Guinea was treated like a hostile territory. In the days before the referendum, the governor examined the possibility of naval maneuvers. He requested military reinforcements from other territories and authorization to form self-defense groups of metropolitan citizens to guard against "xenophobic movements."[37] The September 23 issue of *Le Monde* included a warning from Overseas Minister Cornut-Gentille: If Guinea voted "No" on September 28, at least it had been warned of the consequences. "General de Gaulle said unequivocally that a territory that wanted to separate itself from the Community would be free to do so, but, it is well understood, with risks and perils."[38]

The governor also cracked down on indiscipline in the ranks. A week be-fore the referendum, the director of the Conakry-Niger railway line informed the governor that the federal railway administration, a semiautonomous body not directly responsible to the colonial government, had determined its post-referendum policy. If Guinea voted "No" on September 28, the railway admin-istration would maintain the Conakry-Niger line until 1968. Furious, the governor informed the director that this policy was in absolute contradiction to the position taken by the French prime minister. The official position had been repeated many times in public and in private. There would be a total ces-sation of all aid of any kind from France to any overseas territory that voted "No" in the referendum.[39]

As the referendum approached, tensions escalated and the gulf between the two sides grew wider. On September 24, Sékou Touré asked the governor to inform the French government that Guinea hoped to send a delegation to Paris after the referendum to negotiate an agreement of association with the Community, as permitted by Article 88 of the constitutional project. The gov-ernor telegraphed this information to Paris, but received no response.[40] Two days before the referendum, Governor Mauberna was ordered to leave Guinea. Commercial transactions and credits were suspended. Cargo ships bound for Conakry were rerouted to Dakar or Abidjan. Flights leaving Conakry were packed with Europeans.[41] The era of French colonialism was drawing to a close. Independence was now imminent.

THE REFERENDUM AND ITS AFTERMATH

On September 28, 1958, citizens throughout the French *métropole* and empire went to the polls to vote for or against the constitution that would serve as the foundation of the Fifth Republic.[42] With the exception of Guinea and Niger, all the loi-cadre governments of French West and Equatorial Africa had pronounced themselves solidly in favor of the constitution.[43] In Guinea, with the canton chieftaincy eliminated and opposition parties effectively absorbed by the RDA, there was no counterauthority to the RDA in town or country. Victory for the RDA position was essentially assured.[44]

Referendum day brought no surprises. Eighty-five percent of Guinea's regis-tered voters went to the polls, where they rejected the constitution by an over-whelming majority. Of those who cast their ballots, 1,136,324 (94 percent) voted "No" and 56,981 (4.7 percent) voted "Yes."[45] Only in Guinea did the "No"

6.5 Woman voting in the referendum, Dakar, Senegal, September 28, 1958.
ECPAD/Collection de la Documentation Française.

prevail. In every other sub-Saharan African territory except Niger, the constitution was approved by an equally staggering majority. In Niger, the "Yes" vote was 75 percent.[46]

A number of factors account for Guinea's unique position. The Guinean RDA differed from other governing parties in French West Africa in the class base of its leadership, the strength of its organization at the grassroots, the degree of popular participation in party decisions, and the party's relationship to the colonial chieftaincy. While the dominant parties in some territories possessed some of the Guinean RDA's strengths, none had Guinea's winning combination. In every territory but Guinea and the French Soudan, varying amalgams of wealthy traders, planters, chiefs, and religious leaders dominated the parties' structures, although their conservative tendencies sometimes were mitigated by the more radical views of Western-educated elites.[47] In Guinea, the French Soudan, and Niger, radical trade unionists were among the parties' key leaders. In Niger, however, the trade unionists' influence was neutralized by that of conservative chiefs, who worked with the colonial administration to defeat the "No" vote.[48] The nature of the party leadership affected the degree of female mobilization. Women were mobilized in Guinea, and to a lesser extent in the French Soudan.[49] However, in Niger, conservative forces had successfully opposed women's political organization.[50]

In terms of a strong party organization down to the lowest levels, Guinea stood alone. Although the RDA in the French Soudan strove to create a local organization, in no territory but Guinea were party cells so well established in urban neighborhoods and rural villages.[51] Only in Guinea and the French Soudan were local cells actively involved in decision-making and leaders held accountable to their membership through regular party congresses and elections.[52] Guinea and the French Soudan parted ways, however, in their relationship to the colonial chieftaincy. In Guinea, the loi-cadre government had abolished the canton chieftaincy in December 1957, thus eliminating a long-standing obstacle to RDA success in the rural areas.[53] In every other French West African territory, the chiefs remained in place and continued to wield immense power in favor of the colonial administration—and in this case, the constitution.[54]

With the approval of the new constitution, the balkanization of French Africa was complete. In the referendum's aftermath, the federations of French West and Equatorial Africa were dissolved, and the interterritorial RDA disintegrated.[55] With Guinea effectively isolated, the French government wasted no time in demonstrating the consequences of a "No" vote. On the morning of September 29, Sékou Touré received an unsigned note from Overseas Minister Cornut-Gentille. Guinea had rejected the constitution, and thus membership in the French Community, the note read. Therefore, Guinea would no longer have representation in the Community or in metropolitan or African political organs. It would no longer receive French financial assistance or credits on equipment. Within two months, all French civil servants would be transferred out of Guinea.[56] However, even the two-month transition period proved illusory. Within forty-eight hours of the referendum, all French technical and administrative personnel were ordered to leave the territory. They were directed to take with them or destroy all materials and archives, including registers of vital statistics. Those who remained in Guinea would forfeit all job security.[57] Eighty teachers and technicians recruited for Guinea were forced to disembark in Dakar, on the pretext that their ranks and salaries could no longer be guaranteed. Intense pressure was applied to teachers vacationing outside of Guinea not to return to the territory after the referendum. Only a small number of contractual workers in the private sector and 150 French civil servants—including 110 teachers—remained in Guinea after independence. The civil servants who remained did so as volunteers.[58]

Local memory is strikingly similar to the official record. Former RDA activist Léon Maka recalled,

On Independence Day, the French government told all the French to leave Guinea. All the merchants, doctors, and teachers left. As a result, the economy was in complete disarray. However, the government forgot to convey similar orders to the circle commandants. They were stranded. Sékou Touré called all the circle commandants to Conakry and told them to leave the country; they were no longer needed. Almamy Barry Aguibou, the father of Barry Diawadou, had been canton chief of Dabola. He had been fired by the circle commandant when the chieftaincy was abolished. After independence, as the circle commandant left Dabola for Conakry, the old chief stood by the side of the road waiting for him. As the commandant's car drove by, the old chief yelled, "You, get out of here! Go home! I am in my home here!"[59]

Guinean women composed a good-bye song for the colonial civil servants:

Adieu, white man
Adieu, de Gaulle, adieu
We have not insulted you, nor beaten you
The return to the fatherland does not merit quarreling
Provided that you do not provoke us
Those who still want you are free to meet with you again
Adieu, de Gaulle, adieu
Those who want you can follow you.[60]

The French government was quick to carry out its threats. Immediately after the referendum, it severed most of its economic ties to Guinea, suspending all bank credits, development assistance, and cooperative endeavors—with one exception. Still on the books was the construction of a port for the export of alumina, which would benefit Société Fria, a bauxite mining and processing consortium dominated by American and French capital. However, plans to build a major dam on the Konkouré River, which would provide Guinea with a significant new source of hydroelectric power, were canceled. The construction of the dam was critical to the future on-site production of aluminum, a much more valuable export commodity than either bauxite or alumina.[61] Beyond these economic penalties, technical services were sabotaged and equipment destroyed. Telephone wires were cut, even in the main government building. Cranes at the port of Conakry disappeared. Military camps were stripped of their equipment, and hospitals of their medicines. Soldiers in Dalaba burned their barracks. In Sérédou, formulas for the production of quinine vanished. In Beyla, French doctors absconded with stocks of medicines from the hospitals and brand-new vehicles from the health center, all of which were sent to the Ivory Coast. Finally, in a gesture laden with pettiness and symbolism, state dishes were cracked.[62]

While important services were being disrupted, other measures were taken to deprive Guinea of vital goods. Convinced that France must act harshly toward Guinea or risk demoralizing the territories that had chosen the Community, High Commissioner Pierre Messmer detained in Dakar several boats bound for Conakry.[63] Ships filled with medicines and food, including rice, the dietary staple, were diverted from their course. Merchandise ordered by commercial establishments in Guinea was rerouted to other destinations. Businesses and private individuals continued to transfer large sums of money out of the country.[64] To prevent Guinea from using its CFA franc reserves for external purchases, the Bank of France canceled the old currency. Meanwhile, the French secret services peppered the country with counterfeit currency, creating widespread panic.[65]

By stimulating chaos in the economic and administrative sectors, the French government hoped to demonstrate Guinea's inability to assume the responsibilities of independence.[66] The denial of bank credit, deprivation of vital goods and services, and discouragement of private investment caused serious economic difficulties. These measures were explicitly designed to provoke economic panic, political discontent, and civil unrest.[67]

Undeterred by France's hostility, Sékou Touré continued to court the former colonial power. At a press conference two days after the referendum, he had proclaimed, "I hope that France will be the first nation to recognize independent Guinea, and equally, I hope that she will take charge of having us recognized by other governments and having us enter the UN."[68] These hopes were dashed as Guinea continued to be snubbed by its former ruler. On October 2, 1958, the French territory of Guinea officially became the independent Republic of Guinea. The Territorial Assembly was reconstituted as the National Constituent Assembly. The Council of Government was dissolved, and the Guinean RDA formed a government of national unity that included representatives from the diverse groups that had rallied to the RDA on the eve of the referendum. Barry Diawadou and Barry III were among the new government ministers. Not a single representative of France was present at the Independence Day ceremonies.[69]

If France devastated Guinea economically and rebuffed it diplomatically, the former imperial power also embarked on a campaign to isolate the new nation internationally.[70] Concerned that the Soviet Union would fill the void left by France, the United States had urged France to take the lead in recognizing the independent country so that its Western allies could follow suit. France

6.6 Sékou Touré, president of newly independent Guinea, October 6, 1958. AFP/Getty Images.

had refused and explicitly told the United States to refrain from recognizing Guinea on its own.[71] Out of deference to its NATO ally, and wishing to avert tension with the prickly French prime minister, the United States cautiously followed the French lead.[72] Thus, on October 2, the independent African nations of Ghana and Liberia became the first countries to recognize the sovereign state of Guinea. They were followed by various communist powers: the Soviet Union on October 5 and the People's Republic of China on October 6. Bulgaria and Czechoslovakia recognized Guinea shortly thereafter, while East Germany opened a trade mission. The Western powers, in contrast, spurned Guinea's overtures. France, West Germany, Great Britain, and the United States delayed recognition and stalled on offers of economic, technical, and military assistance.[73]

Even as France campaigned to isolate Guinea internationally, Sékou Touré continued his attempts to establish diplomatic and economic relations with the former colonial power. On Independence Day, Sékou Touré again proclaimed that the independent and sovereign nation of Guinea hoped to negotiate an association with the French Republic on the basis of Article 88 of the new constitution. That afternoon, he sent a telegram to Prime Minister de Gaulle spelling out these intentions. Subsequently, Sékou Touré indicated that Guinea wished to remain in the franc zone. These and numerous other overtures were ignored by the French government.[74] At a press conference in late October, de Gaulle reiterated his government's position:

> Guinea knew the consequences of its actions when it made its choice in the referendum. France put no obstacles in the way of its choice. If French citizens want to stay in Guinea, that is their business. . . . Naturally, this does not apply to civil servants and technicians that the French State furnished to Guinea under the loi-cadre system, or that of the Community, but that it cannot furnish under the system called "independence." As for the financial assistance that the French State brought to the development of Guinea, everyone understands why this assistance must cease.[75]

If de Gaulle was deaf to Sékou Touré's appeals, he also disregarded those of French businessmen in Guinea. Important business interests urged the French government to normalize economic relations with Guinea. The Péchiney-Ugine group, which had major investments in bauxite exploitation at Fria and counted on the alumina port and Konkouré dam projects, intervened several times with de Gaulle's economic adviser, but to no avail.[76] A delegation from Guinea's Chamber of Commerce, led by a French businessman, lobbied parliament and various government ministries. These bodies deferred to Prime Minister de Gaulle, who refused to meet with the delegation.[77]

Having repressed the RDA because of its communist connections, France now made its own worst nightmare a reality. By refusing to deal with Guinea after independence and by isolating it internationally, France pushed the new nation toward the Soviet Union and the Eastern Bloc.[78] Guinea eventually concluded loan, line of credit, and trade agreements with the Soviet Union, Czechoslovakia, East Germany, Poland, and China. When Guinea received no reply to its request for military assistance from the United States, it accepted Czech assistance instead.

6.7 Russians inspect the Patrice Lumumba printing plant in Conakry, built with Communist bloc aid, ca. 1962. Paul Fusco/*Look* Magazine/Magnum Photos.

French volunteers—especially PCF members—and teachers and technicians from Eastern Europe, North Vietnam, other parts of Africa, and the French Caribbean arrived to replace departing civil servants. Although the West had rejected its advances, Guinea's turn to the East was perceived by Western powers as a pernicious rallying to the communist camp, and retroactive justification for their policies.[79]

Despite his refusal to take positive preemptive action, Prime Minister de Gaulle shared Western concerns about Guinea's postindependence orientation. Determined to destroy the man he could not seduce, de Gaulle ordered the French secret services to bring down Sékou Touré's government. For the next twenty years, France engaged in successive plots to overthrow the Guinean president, sometimes with the assistance of espionage services from West Germany, Portugal, and the United States. Collaborators were sought in Guinea, and emissaries were sent into the Futa Jallon to convince conservative Muslims, former chiefs, and military veterans to engage in an armed uprising against the government. None of the coup attempts was successful.[80]

The anti-Guinea campaign was aided by Houphouët-Boigny, who pulled the interterritorial RDA in his wake. Furious at Sékou Touré's betrayal, Houphouët-Boigny insisted to High Commissioner Messmer that the Guinean leader had to be defeated. From September 29, 1958, he should be deprived of all French aid, and a vigorous propaganda campaign against him should be undertaken in Guinea.[81] On October 7–9, at the behest of Houphouët-Boigny and the French government, the coordinating committee of the interterritorial RDA expelled the Guinean branch from its ranks.[82] In a press interview on October 15, Houphouët-Boigny warned France that it must not give preference to territories that had seceded over those that had chosen the Community. Such a policy would send the wrong message to loyal territories.[83]

On October 19, as a result of the mounting campaign against it, the Guinean RDA embraced the name Parti Démocratique de Guinée and publicly disassociated itself from the interterritorial RDA.[84] Thus, it was necessity, as well as its long-standing Pan-African orientation, that led Guinea to seek allies outside its old cohort in francophone Africa. In late November, Sékou Touré made a state visit to Ghana, which had gained independence from Britain in 1957. Presidents Sékou Touré and Kwame Nkrumah subsequently established the Union of Guinea-Ghana, which they hoped would form the core of a future United States of West Africa.[85]

By the time Sékou Touré visited Ghana, more than thirty nations had recognized Guinea diplomatically. France was not among them. On November 22, Sékou Touré sent a message to de Gaulle from Ghana, this time requesting that France sponsor Guinea's application for admission to the United Nations. Again there was no response. Thus, it was without France's blessing that Iraq and Japan presented Guinea's candidacy on December 9.[86] Although the former colonial power attempted to delay consideration of the application, the United Nations General Assembly voted to admit the Republic of Guinea as a member on December 13. With one exception, all of the delegates approved the application. France alone abstained.[87]

It was not until January 2, 1960, that the French government accorded Guinea diplomatic recognition, shortly after acknowledging that the trend toward African independence was irreversible.[88] Having devised the means to maintain French dominance through economic and military agreements, France was ready to relinquish political control, and to unburden itself of the onus of colonial rule.[89] In the months that followed Guinea's official recognition, the French empire disintegrated rapidly. The United Nations trust territories of Cameroon and Togo claimed their independence on January 1 and April 27, 1960, respectively.[90] On June 4, 1960, the French parliament revised Article 86 of the constitution, which had made independence incompatible with membership in the French Community. Henceforth, a state could become independent, yet remain a member of the Renovated Community. A declaration of independence was no longer tantamount to secession.[91]

6.8 Four African leaders arrive at Casablanca airport for a summit of independent African states, January 1961. *Left to right:* Modibo Kéïta (Mali), Sékou Touré (Guinea), King Mohammed V (Morocco), Kwame Nkrumah (Ghana). AP/*New York World-Telegram & Sun.*

With the blessings of France, the other territories formerly constituting the federations of French West and Equatorial Africa, along with Madagascar, finally followed Guinea's lead. In June 1960, Senegal, the French Soudan, and Madagascar declared independence. They were followed in August by Dahomey, Niger, Upper Volta, the Ivory Coast, Chad, Oubangui-Chari, the French Congo, and Gabon. Finally, on November 28, 1960, Mauritania declared independence. Thus, by the end of 1960, virtually all French territories in sub-Saharan Africa had become sovereign, independent nations: the eight territories of the former French West African federation, the four territories previously constituting French Equatorial Africa, the two former United Nations trusts, and Madagascar. (The Algerian War ended with Algeria's independence in 1962. The Comoros islands and former French Somaliland became independent in 1975 and 1977, respectively.) None of the territories declaring independence in 1960 were subjected to the dire consequences imposed on Guinea two years previously.[92]

The French African territories were independent but weak. The 1958 constitution had sounded the death knell for internationalism in francophone Africa. The great federations had been destroyed. Balkanization had become a reality. By 1960, extragovernmental interterritorial bodies had met the same fate. All interterritorial structures—political parties, trade unions, youth organizations, the federal civil services, and the Grand Councils—had been dissolved. The former French territories joined the United Nations as separate states, most of them small and impoverished.[93] The old imperial power remained an important force in their economic and political realms, ushering in a new era of neocolonialism.

Conclusion

In the months before the September 1958 constitutional referendum, grassroots militants in Guinea mobilized for a "No" vote. They condemned the proposed constitution as a continuation of colonialism under a new name and demanded that the RDA champion immediate independence instead. The interterritorial RDA, however, was now established in the corridors of power. Its territorial branches controlled many of the local governments instituted under loi-cadre, and its leaders received significant benefits from the French political system. Once again, the interterritorial RDA felt compelled to rein in the rebellious Guinean branch. In contrast to 1955, however, Guinean leftists won the debate. On the eve of the referendum, Guinean students, teachers and other trade unionists, and the party's women's and youth wings forced the territorial leadership to call for a "No" vote. As a result, in the referendum that followed, the Guinean people overwhelmingly rejected the constitutional project and opted instead for immediate independence. Of all the French territories, Guinea alone voted "No."

France was quick to retaliate, withdrawing civil servants, severing aid, trade, and development agreements, absconding with government files, and sabotaging whatever the departing officials could not take with them. Guinea's pleas for assistance were rebuffed, not only by France, but by France's Western allies. As a result, Guinea looked to the East for allies and assistance. Guinea's relationship with communist powers was used retroactively to justify

French retribution. Meanwhile, in the words of British Prime Minister Harold Macmillan, "the wind of change" was blowing across the African continent.[94] Despite de Gaulle's hopes for the new constitution, it could not save France from the inevitable. The days of empire were numbered. By 1960, most of French Africa had become independent. However, many would argue that France still held the reins of power.

Conclusion and Postscript

FOR THE THREE CENTURIES preceding World War II, France had assumed its position among the world's great powers. At the war's end, however, France, wrecked and humiliated, was a mere shadow of its former self. Only its empire, unrivaled by none but Britain's, could salvage its great power status. French plans for a return to greatness were threatened by burgeoning African and Asian nationalist movements and by the emergence of the United States and the Soviet Union as the new world powers. The beginning of the Cold War, and the support of French communists and the Soviet Union for the anticolonial cause, intensified French concerns.

Under pressure in the colonies and in the international arena, France hoped to deter more radical solutions both by reforming its empire and by quashing incipient nationalist movements, especially those with communist affiliations. In Guinea, the RDA was nearly destroyed during the period of official repression (1947–51) and its aftermath (1951–55). Following the PCF's ouster from the French government in 1947, some RDA leaders argued that the party's survival was jeopardized by the RDA-PCF parliamentary alliance. In 1950, RDA parliamentarians severed their ties to the PCF and ordered all territorial branches to do likewise. While Guinean RDA leaders ultimately directed local militants to follow suit, the rupture with the PCF resulted in deep intraparty conflict. Grassroots activists denounced the break, and mass resignations ensued.

Despite the breach, state repression continued unabated, in part because the government doubted the veracity of the RDA's transformation. Noting the disjuncture between the territorial leadership's accommodation and the unyielding radicalism of the grassroots, colonial officials charged that public disaffiliation masked unwavering private support for the PCF. What the government viewed as double-dealing was, in fact, a growing fissure between the leadership and the rank and file—a rift that threatened to destroy the party.

If the period 1947–51 was marked by government repression, the years 1951–55 were characterized by doubt and discontent. The purging—or accommodation—of the Left had not put an end to the RDA's problems. The divorce of the RDA from the PCF had disillusioned many local militants. Large numbers left the party in disgust. Yet conciliation and collaboration had not halted government repression. The colonial administration continued to shore up "government parties," fix elections, and systematically persecute RDA militants. Between 1951 and 1953, the Guinean RDA won only a single election—Sékou Touré's seat in the Territorial Assembly.[1] In 1954, Sékou Touré ran unsuccessfully for the French parliament. His defeat, in an election marked by extensive fraud, resulted in widespread popular unrest. In both town and country, the years 1954–55 were distinguished by local resistance to chiefs, notables, and government-supported political parties. Despite its persistent electoral losses, it was clear by 1955 that the Guinean RDA was the most popular party in the territory. Both the interterritorial RDA and the colonial administration were determined to bring the Guinean party back into line.

For the French government, unrest in Guinea was part of a larger, more worrisome concern. By the mid-1950s, the viability of the French empire was again in doubt. The French defeat and subsequent withdrawal from Indochina, together with the widening war in Algeria and escalating unrest elsewhere in Africa, resulted in yet another program of imperial reform. The *loi-cadre* reforms of 1956, which led to limited self-government in the overseas territories in 1957, represented another attempt to thwart more radical moves toward complete independence.

The years 1956 and 1957 also marked a turning point in Guinean politics. As the administration attempted to co-opt the party it could not defeat, it eased repression and largely refrained from interfering in elections, which allowed the RDA to emerge victorious. After the January 1956 legislative elections, the RDA held two of Guinea's three National Assembly seats. After the municipal elections of November 1956, it controlled thirteen of Guinean's fourteen major municipalities. By 1957, it dominated the Territorial Assembly, holding fifty-seven of sixty seats, as well as the new Council of Government, whose ministers were all RDA.

The RDA's acquisition of power resulted in further discord within the party. While the party's territorial leaders were eager to benefit from the career opportunities implicit in running their "own affairs," regional and local leaders, under growing pressure from the grassroots, became more militant in their demands. As the RDA-led territorial government embraced a policy of accommodation with the administration, dissident elements continued to push from the Left, criticizing the new policy of "constructive collaboration" implicit in the loi-cadre system. Increasingly, students and other youths, teachers, railway workers, and other trade unionists called for the end of colonial rule. They demanded independence—not just territorial autonomy—on the basis of the French West and Equatorial African federations. Their proindependence sentiments were not the musings of an extremist fringe, but reflected the views of regional and local RDA leaders and grassroots militants in the interior. RDA rivals attempted to capitalize on grassroots discontent by outflanking the RDA on the Left.

In France, meanwhile, General de Gaulle had returned to power. In a final attempt to save the empire from collapse, de Gaulle proposed a new constitution that would lay the foundations for a fifth French republic. The 1958 constitution would enhance the power of the French president, abolish the African federations, and relegate the overseas territories to perpetual minor status in the renovated empire. In a referendum on September 28, French citizens throughout the empire were to vote for or against the constitution.

In Guinea, the constituency that had been silenced by Cold War repression in the early 1950s had emerged as the strongest faction by the decade's end. Students, trade unionists, and the Guinean RDA's women's and youth wings condemned the constitution and demanded that the RDA choose complete independence over moderate reforms. Rejecting the appeals of the interterritorial RDA, which tried to impose a "Yes" vote on its territorial branches, grassroots activists pushed the Guinean RDA to the Left, ultimately forcing it to endorse the "No."

In the September 1958 referendum, the people of Guinea overwhelmingly rejected the constitutional project that laid the groundwork for the Fifth Republic, opting instead for immediate independence. In all the French empire, it was the only territory to vote "No." Guinea's call for immediate independence, and its break with the interterritorial RDA over this issue, were the culmination of a decade-long struggle between local activists and the party's leadership for control of the political agenda. It was neither an aberration nor a fiat from on high, but the result of intensive mobilization by grassroots militants on the political Left, who had persevered in the face of Cold War repression.

France retaliated with a vengeance. It abruptly withdrew teachers, technicians, and medical personnel and sabotaged the Guinean economy. It moved to isolate Guinea in the international arena, pressuring its allies to withhold diplomatic recognition, trade agreements, and economic and military aid. With few alternatives, Guinea turned to the East, seeking assistance from communist countries that were eager to help. French retribution finally had forced Guinea into the communist camp.

Within two years of Guinea's independence, it was clear that the new constitution would not save the empire. By 1960, most of French Africa was independent. After years of division, African unity finally had been achieved—at least temporarily and on the single issue of independence. Leftists within the RDA had overcome years of marginalization to influence the political mainstream. Their position in favor of "Independence Now!" had become the dominant one. However, Guinea paid a heavy price. In the face of French economic retaliation, diplomatic isolation, and finally, political subversion, Sékou Touré's Guinea cracked down on most forms of opposition. This repression has come to dominate our mental associations with Guinea, rather than the extraordinary tale of a people who set themselves free.

POSTSCRIPT: REFLECTIONS ON THE POSTINDEPENDENCE PERIOD

By investigating the Guinean case, this book helps us to understand the dynamics of decolonization during the Cold War and foreshadows the difficulties encountered in postindependence nation-building throughout the developing world. Although the Guinean case was in some ways unique, its lessons can illuminate these processes elsewhere, if only by providing a counterexample. In preindependence Guinea, the RDA's local party structures were strong, and grassroots militants participated actively in the development of the party program. As a result, antidemocratic agendas could be, and often were, thwarted by popular mobilization. In numerous other colonies, in contrast, nationalist party structures were weak, and local elites collaborated with colonial governments in repressing progressive voices at the grassroots. Stepping into the authoritarian structures vacated by departing colonial officials, many of these elites acquired unchecked powers after independence. Countless new nations thus were ruled by military and civilian dictators—often bolstered by a single political party— who had been shaped by the colonial system.

Despite the democratic character of its nationalist movement, Guinea, like other former colonies, ultimately fell victim to the authoritarian trend. In a relatively short space of time, it too was governed by a single party that was intolerant of divergent views and run by bureaucrats beholden to an autocratic leader for the maintenance of their positions. Much scholarly attention has focused on Guinea during its first two and one-half decades of independence, when the democratic structures developed during the nationalist period increasingly were manipulated by the highest echelons of the party and repression of dissenting voices grew more brutal. In a marked departure from the past, mobilization for national development became a top-down affair, with only token input from the grassroots.[2] Presuming that Guinea's postindependence characteristics were simply a continuation of preindependence practices, few scholars felt the need to examine Guinea's actual preindependence political dynamics. Reflecting from the present to the past, many simply assumed that Sékou Touré had autocratic powers in the preindependence period and that the RDA program in Guinea represented his will.[3]

Rejecting this retrospective projection, this book has disputed the view that the Guinean RDA of the 1940s and '50s was controlled by Sékou Touré and that he possessed uncontested authority over it. It has shown instead that Guinea's progressive politics percolated upward from the grassroots. Local militants, empowered by a strong, unusually democratic party organization, forced party leaders to the Left, even as those leaders sought accommodation with the powers that be. Finally, it has argued, Guinea's radical position on the 1958 constitution was not a foregone conclusion, but the result of a long internal struggle that was won by the Left only in the final hour.

If these arguments are correct, there is a compelling need to explain Guinea's eventual decline. To date, no study has focused on the transitional period, accounting for the Guinean RDA's transformation from a highly democratic mass party to the ultimate source of power in a repressive authoritarian state. Until such a study is done, one can only speculate as to what went wrong and why.

Even in the realm of speculation, there is a logical place to begin. To fully understand Sékou Touré's Guinea, one must explore preindependence developments that presaged the possibility of postindependence authoritarianism. There is ample evidence that a personality cult was developing around Sékou Touré even before independence and that the latter had a tendency toward unilateral action.[4] Given the dearth of educated personnel, trade union and party leaders frequently accumulated multiple functions, concentrating considerable power in relatively few hands. When the September 1958 referendum occurred, Sékou Touré was the unofficial leader of Guinea's trade union movement and secretary-general of the Guinean RDA. He was a councillor in the Territorial Assembly, a deputy in the French National Assembly, mayor of Conakry, and president of Guinea's loi-cadre government.[5]

There is extensive evidence that after the establishment of the loi-cadre government in May 1957, the Guinean RDA leadership became increasingly intolerant of internal and external dissent. Within the party, students, teachers, and

Sékou Touré dwarfed by his own portrait, January 1, 1958. J. Cuinieres/Roger Viollet/Getty Images.

trade unionists were sanctioned—and the Mamou subsection was expelled—for disobedience and obstructionism. The interests of labor, long the mainstay of the RDA program, increasingly were subordinated to those of the nationalist movement.[6] Thus, the government crackdown on the teachers' union and other dissenting intellectuals in the early 1960s was foreshadowed by similar events prior to independence.[7] Nor was the emergence of a one-party state exclusively a postindependence phenomenon. The RDA's electoral sweeps in 1956 and 1957 had emptied Guinea's governing bodies of most RDA opponents, and in September 1958 the RDA's only rival party effectively dissolved itself, bringing to an end organized political opposition.[8] However, the real turning point came in the early years of independence, when France and its allies attempted to subvert Guinea politically, economically, and militarily. Threatened by diplomatic and economic isolation, multiple coup attempts, and finally a foreign invasion, Sékou Touré's government eventually clamped down on all forms of dissent, in the name of nation-building, national unity, and the struggle against imperialism.[9] It is the task of future historians to examine Guinea's transformation from popular democracy to authoritarian state—a phenomenon that again must be considered in the context of the Cold War.

Acknowledgments

THE ORIGIN OF THIS BOOK lies in the word "No"—Guinea's "No" to the 1958 French constitution and my editor's "No" to a 965-page manuscript. In the empire-wide referendum of September 1958, Guinea alone rejected the constitution and claimed immediate independence instead. Intrigued by Guinea's unique stance and determined to track its origins, I resolved to write a social history of Guinea's nationalist movement. My book would tell it all—gender and generation, ethnicity, race, and class. It would explore both local politics and the international context. It would be a total history. The result was a mammoth manuscript that left nothing out. Fortunately, my editor sent me back to the drawing board. Like the heartless mother in the Solomonic tale, I decided to divide my creation into two. The first book, *Mobilizing the Masses: Gender, Ethnicity, and Class in the Nationalist Movement in Guinea, 1939–1958,* was published in 2005. This volume explores the Guinean nationalist movement in the context of French politics and the Cold War.

This book and its predecessor were years in the making. Many people and institutions helped it along the way. Before I embarked on this journey, I had trained and conducted research in anglophone Southern Africa, focusing on colonial Zimbabwe and apartheid South Africa. Thus, I relied on the wisdom and experience of others as I retrained for research in francophone West Africa. Siba N'Zatioula Grovogui introduced me to Guinea and assisted in the oral aspects of the project. Using his extensive connections, he helped to locate former activists who agreed to share their memories of the anticolonial struggle. He also collaborated on interviews conducted in French, interpreted those in Susu and Maninka, and transcribed and translated the African-language tapes.

Sidiki Kobélé Kéïta shared his prodigious knowledge of nationalist history and rare copies of his published work. Kéïta, Fatou Aribot, and Hawa Fofana identified a number of key informants, while Hawa Fofana convinced many who were uncertain to speak with us. Ouessou "Körö" Nabé, a dedicated friend and supporter, introduced us to relatives with strong nationalist credentials and provided critical transport to interview sessions. Most important were the many informants who gave us their time and confidence and directed us to their colleagues in the nationalist struggle. Their names, too numerous to list here, are included in the bibliography.

The oral interviews were supplemented with archival and library research. For their willing assistance, I thank the staffs of the Archives de Guinée in Conakry; the Archives Nationales du Sénégal and the Institut Fondamental d'Afrique Noire in Dakar; and the Archives Nationales in France, including the Centre d'Accueil et de Recherche des Archives Nationales in Paris and the Centre des Archives d'Outre-Mer in Aix-en-Provence. At the Centre de Recherche et de Documentation Africaine in Paris, Vassiafa Touré went far beyond the call of duty. Besides invaluable professional help, he and his family graciously offered their friendship and welcomed us into their home. In the United States, Peggy Feild and the interlibrary loan staff of the Loyola Notre Dame Library faithfully responded to my numerous requests, obtaining even the most obscure publications in record time.

A number of scholars have both inspired me with their work and assisted me in my own endeavors. Frederick Cooper provided important information about archives in Senegal and France, and brought the CRDA's existence to my attention. Along with Steven Feierman, Allen Isaacman, and Susan Geiger, he wrote numerous funding letters on my behalf. Allen Isaacman, Jean Hay, Thaddeus Sunseri, and Joseph Miller critiqued earlier drafts of the manuscript, while Martin Klein and Nancy Lawler gave critical advice about the final version. Colleagues in the Loyola College History Department contributed insights through faculty colloquia, lectures, and works-in-progress seminars. Finally, at Ohio University Press, assistant director and senior editor Gillian Berchowitz and project editor John Morris persevered to make this book a reality. Working with them was truly a pleasure.

This project would not have come to fruition without external financial support. In 1989, Louise Bedicheck, then public affairs officer at the U.S. Embassy in Conakry, encouraged me to apply for a Fulbright grant. Since there was no senior Fulbright program in Guinea at the time, she helped to facilitate its establishment. During 1990–92, my research in the Republic of Guinea, Senegal, and France was supported by a Fulbright Senior Research and Lecturing Grant and funds from the Joint Committee on African Studies of the American Council of Learned Societies and the Social Science Research Council. From 1990 to the present, Loyola College in Maryland has supported this project, and its predecessor, in numerous ways. The college granted me a leave of absence in 1990–91 so that I could begin the research. In subsequent years, the college provided three sabbatical leaves and generous financial assistance that allowed me to draft and revise both manuscripts. Loyola's Center for the Humanities kindly paid for the costly maps and photographs.

Many friends and family members have offered their steadfast encouragement and moral support. In particular, I wish to thank my parents, Albert J. and Kathryn J. Schmidt, a historian and librarian respectively, who long ago inspired my love of history and research. They never wavered in their belief that I really could pull this off. I am eternally grateful to my partner, Mark Peyrot, whose unflagging enthusiasm urged me on even when I wanted to give up, and whose invaluable insights helped me to sharpen my arguments. Finally, I thank my son, Jann, who in his inimitable way always helped me to keep perspective. To acknowledge his contribution, he suggested the following dedication: "To Jann, who convinced his friends that it was more important that I work on my book than that they play games on the family computer." It brought much-needed laughter when he incessantly informed his impatient pals, "No, she's not done yet. She's writing a *book!*" So, I dedicate this book to Jann, who made it a labor of love, for it is a story of his people.

Notes

Research for this book was conducted at the Archives de Guinée (AG) in Conakry, the Archives Nationales du Sénégal (ANS) in Dakar, the Institut Fondamental d'Afrique Noire (IFAN) in Dakar, the Centre de Recherche et de Documentation Africaine (CRDA) in Paris, the Centre d'Accueil et de Recherche des Archives Nationales de France (CARAN) in Paris, and the Centre des Archives d'Outre-Mer, Archives Nationales de France (CAOM) in Aix-en-Provence. Unless otherwise indicated, I translated all French-language sources, and I conducted all interviews in collaboration with Siba N. Grovogui. In addition, I transcribed and translated all French-language interviews, while Siba N. Grovogui transcribed and translated those conducted in Susu and Maninka.

French Colonial Officials

1. The lists of French colonial officials and their dates of service have been compiled from Sidiki Kobélé Kéïta, *Le P.D.G.: Artisan de l'Indépendance Nationale en Guinée (1947–1958)* (Conakry: I.N.R.D.G., Bibliothèque Nationale, 1978), 1:127–29; Ruth Schachter Morgenthau, *Political Parties in French-Speaking West Africa* (Oxford: Clarendon Press, 1964), 61, 378; Edward Mortimer, *France and the Africans, 1944–1960: A Political History* (New York: Walker and Co., 1969), 103; D. Bruce Marshall, *The French Colonial Myth and Constitution-Making in the Fourth Republic* (New Haven: Yale University Press, 1973), 269, 280; Georges Chaffard, *Les Carnets Secrets de la Décolonisation* (Paris: Calmann-Lévy, 1967), 2:210; Rulers, "Guinea," http://rulers.org/rulg2.html#guinea; Rulers, "Senegal," http://rulers.org/ruls2.html; History and Flags of the Nations, "Senegal," http://www.ajaxbologna.it/Bandiere/Africa%5CSenegal.htm; Answers.com, "Minister of Overseas France," http://www.answers.com/topic/minister-of-overseas-france; Geoscopie, "Les Ministres de la Coopération," http://www.geoscopie.com/themes/t383fco2.html; André R. Lewin, "Les Ministres de la Coopération," http://www.geoscopie.com/themes/t383fco.html#_ftn3.

Introduction

1. Jean-Pierre Rioux, *The Fourth Republic, 1944–1958,* trans. Godfrey Rogers (New York: Cambridge University Press, 1987), 54, 59, 61, 76, 97–98, 102, 110, 125, 127,

130–31, 153, 164–66; Irwin M. Wall, *The United States and the Making of Postwar France, 1945–1954* (New York: Cambridge University Press, 1991), 63–69, 86, 211, 215; John W. Young, *France, the Cold War and the Western Alliance, 1944–49: French Foreign Policy and Post-war Europe* (New York: St. Martin's Press, 1990), 90, 97–114, 128, 134–54, 165; Frank Costigliola, *France and the United States: The Cold Alliance since World War II* (New York: Twayne, 1992), chaps. 1 and 2; Ronald Tiersky, *French Communism, 1920– 1972* (New York: Columbia University Press, 1972), 156–57; William I. Hitchcock, *France Restored: Cold War Diplomacy and the Quest for Leadership in Europe, 1944–1954* (Chapel Hill: University of North Carolina Press, 1998), 19; Georgette Elgey, *La République des Illusions, 1945–1951* (Paris: Fayard, 1965), 246–93.

2. Rioux, *Fourth Republic,* 84, 97–98, 112–15, 122, 131, 133–34, 156, 214; Wall, *United States and the Making of Postwar France,* 8, 11, 35–38, 42, 44–50, 53–56, 59, 64– 66, 68–69, 72–75, 81, 86–87, 93, 96–108, 128–29, 143, 149–50, 157, 159, 188, 213–14, 216–18; Young, *France, the Cold War and the Western Alliance,* 10, 18, 38–39, 64, 67, 97–99, 101–3, 114, 146–47, 149–51, 164–65, 167, 225; Costigliola, *France and the United States,* 9–13, 15, 22, 27, 29–31, 34, 42–48, 50–55, 58–61, 63, 65–68, 70, 73, 75, 78; Hitchcock, *France Restored,* 3–4, 42, 44, 62–63, 72–73, 83–84, 97–98, 227n36; Elgey, *République des Illusions,* 249; Edward Rice-Maximin, "The United States and the French Left, 1945–1949: The View from the State Department," *Journal of Contemporary History* 19, no. 4 (October 1984): 729–37, 739–40, 742; Melvyn P. Leffler, "The Cold War: What Do 'We Now Know'?" *American Historical Review* 104, no. 2 (April 1999): 520–21.

3. See, e.g., Thomas Hodgkin, *Nationalism in Colonial Africa* (New York: New York University Press, 1957); James S. Coleman, *Nigeria: Background to Nationalism* (Berkeley: University of California Press, 1958); David Apter, *Ghana in Transition* (Princeton: Princeton University Press, 1963); Robert I. Rotberg, *The Rise of Nationalism in Central Africa: The Making of Malawi and Zambia, 1873–1964* (Cambridge: Harvard University Press, 1965).

4. John Lonsdale, "Some Origins of Nationalism in East Africa," *Journal of African History* 9, no. 1 (1968): 146.

5. Lonsdale, "Origins of Nationalism in East Africa," 119–46; John Lonsdale, "The Emergence of African Nations: A Historiographical Analysis," *African Affairs* 67, no. 266 (1968): 11–28.

6. See, e.g., Ernest Milcent, *L'A.O.F. Entre en Scène* (Paris: Bibliothèque de l'Homme d'Action, 1958); André Blanchet, *L'Itinéraire des Partis Africains depuis Bamako* (Paris: Librarie Plon, 1958); Ruth Schachter Morgenthau, *Political Parties in French-Speaking West Africa* (Oxford: Clarendon Press, 1964); Georges Chaffard, *Les Carnets Secrets de la Décolonisation,* vol. 2 (Paris: Calmann-Lévy, 1967); Virginia Thompson and Richard Adloff, *French West Africa* (New York: Greenwood Press, 1969); Edward Mortimer, *France and the Africans, 1944–1960: A Political History* (New York: Walker and Co., 1969); Tony Chafer, *The End of Empire in French West Africa: France's Successful Decolonization?* (New York: Berg, 2002).

7. See, e.g., Immanuel Wallerstein, *The Road to Independence: Ghana and the Ivory Coast* (Paris: Mouton and Co., 1964); Virginia Thompson, "The Ivory Coast," in *African One-Party States,* ed. Gwendolen M. Carter (Ithaca: Cornell University Press, 1962),

237–324; Aristide R. Zolberg, "The Ivory Coast," in *Political Parties and National Integration in Tropical Africa,* ed. James S. Coleman and Carl G. Rosberg Jr. (Berkeley: University of California Press, 1964), 65–89; Frank Gregory Snyder, *One-Party Government in Mali: Transition toward Control* (New Haven: Yale University Press, 1965).

8. Morgenthau, *Political Parties in French-Speaking West Africa,* 157, 159, 307–9, 317; Milcent, *A.O.F. Entre en Scène,* 88–89; Mortimer, *France and the Africans,* 162, 176, 178, 200, 213, 219–20, 250–51; Thompson and Adloff, *French West Africa,* 94; Thomas Hodgkin, *African Political Parties: An Introductory Guide* (Gloucester, MA: Peter Smith, 1971), 71; Finn Fuglestad, "Djibo Bakary, the French, and the Referendum of 1958 in Niger," *Journal of African History* 14, no. 2 (1973): 315; Richard A. Joseph, *Radical Nationalism in Cameroun: Social Origins of the U.P.C. Rebellion* (Oxford: Oxford University Press, 1977), 172–73, 182, 290–92.

9. Yves Person, "French West Africa and Decolonization," in *The Transfer of Power in Africa: Decolonization, 1940–1960,* ed. Prosser Gifford and William Roger Louis (New Haven: Yale University Press, 1982), 141–72; Victor D. Du Bois, "Guinea," in Coleman and Rosberg, eds., *Political Parties and National Integration in Tropical Africa,* 186–215; Claude Rivière, *Guinea: The Mobilization of a People,* trans. Virginia Thompson and Richard Adloff (Ithaca: Cornell University Press, 1977).

10. Morgenthau, *Political Parties in French-Speaking West Africa;* Chaffard, *Carnets Secrets de la Décolonisation,* vol. 2; L. Gray Cowan, "Guinea," in Carter, ed., *African One-Party States,* 149–236; Sylvain Soriba Camara, *La Guinée sans la France* (Paris: Presses de la Fondation Nationale des Sciences Politiques, 1976). For a similar treatment of the RDA in Dahomey, see Patrick Manning, *Slavery, Colonialism and Economic Growth in Dahomey, 1640–1960* (New York: Cambridge University Press, 1982), 279.

11. See, e.g., Milcent, *A.O.F. Entre en Scène,* 54; Thompson and Adloff, *French West Africa;* Hodgkin, *African Political Parties;* Chafer, *End of Empire in French West Africa.*

Similarly, Aristide Zolberg briefly considers dissent within the Ivorian RDA. See Aristide R. Zolberg, *One-Party Government in the Ivory Coast* (Princeton: Princeton University Press, 1964), 154–55. For the French Soudan, see Thomas Hodgkin and Ruth Schachter Morgenthau, "Mali," in Coleman and Rosberg, eds., *Political Parties and National Integration in Tropical Africa,* 236.

12. Sidiki Kobélé Kéïta, *Le P.D.G.: Artisan de l'Indépendance Nationale en Guinée (1947–1958),* 2 vols. (Conakry: I.N.R.D.G., Bibliothèque Nationale, 1978); Jean Suret-Canale, *La République de Guinée* (Paris: Éditions Sociales, 1970); 'Ladipo Adamolekun, *Sékou Touré's Guinea: An Experiment in Nation Building* (London: Methuen, 1976); 'Ladipo Adamolekun, "The Road to Independence in French Tropical Africa," in *African Nationalism and Independence,* ed. Timothy K. Welliver (New York: Garland, 1993), 66–79.

13. See Elizabeth Schmidt, *Mobilizing the Masses: Gender, Ethnicity, and Class in the Nationalist Movement in Guinea, 1939–1958* (Portsmouth, NH: Heinemann, 2005); Elizabeth Schmidt, "Top Down or Bottom Up? Nationalist Mobilization Reconsidered, with Special Reference to Guinea (French West Africa)," *American Historical Review* 110, no. 4 (Oct. 2005): 975–1014; Elizabeth Schmidt, "'Emancipate Your Husbands!': Women and Nationalism in Guinea, 1953–1958," in *Women in African Colonial Histories,* ed. Jean Allman, Susan Geiger, and Nakanyike Musisi (Bloomington: Indiana University Press, 2002), 282–304.

An exception to this generalization is Elizabeth Schmidt, "Cold War in Guinea: The Rassemblement Démocratique Africain and the Struggle over Communism, 1950–1958," *Journal of African History* 48, no. 1 (March 2007): 95–121.

14. For repression against the Left and collaboration with the colonial government in Niger, see Chaffard, *Carnets Secrets de la Décolonisation,* 2:273, 275, 286, 294–98, 300–302, 306; Morgenthau, *Political Parties in French-Speaking West Africa,* 311–12, 317–18; Mortimer, *France and the Africans,* 266, 343–44, 351, 354, 363, 369; Fuglestad, "Djibo Bakary," 318, 326, 329–30; Finn Fuglestad, *A History of Niger, 1850–1960* (New York: Cambridge University Press, 1983), 184, 186; Virginia Thompson, "Niger," in *National Unity and Regionalism in Eight African States,* ed. Gwendolen M. Carter (Ithaca: Cornell University Press, 1966), 165–70, 176; Immanuel Wallerstein, "How Seven States Were Born in Former French West Africa," *Africa Report* (March 1961): 7.

For the Ivory Coast, see AG, 1E41, Côte d'Ivoire, Services de Police, Abidjan, "Renseignements A/S Position du R.D.A. après le Congrès Cégétiste de Bamako," 5 Nov. 1951, #5446/757/PS/BM/C; Morgenthau, *Political Parties in French-Speaking West Africa,* 184–85, 199, 200–202, 204–11, 214–15, 218, 339; Chafer, *End of Empire in French West Africa,* 123; Thompson and Adloff, *French West Africa,* 132; Thompson, "Ivory Coast," 241, 277; Wallerstein, *Road to Independence,* 54; Wallerstein, "How Seven States Were Born," 12; Immanuel Wallerstein, "Elites in French-Speaking West Africa: The Social Basis of Ideas," *Journal of Modern African Studies* 3, no. 1 (1965): 9–10; Zolberg, *One-Party Government in the Ivory Coast,* 3–4, 118–19, 143–44, 149–50, 152, 154, 184–86, 205–15, 238–39, 247, 297, 306–7; Zolberg, "Ivory Coast," 70–73, 79, 81, 84; Aristide R. Zolberg, "Political Development in the Ivory Coast since Independence," in *Ghana and the Ivory Coast: Perspectives on Modernization,* ed. Philip Foster and Aristide R. Zolberg (Chicago: University of Chicago Press, 1971), 13; Richard E. Stryker, "Political and Administrative Linkage in the Ivory Coast," in Foster and Zolberg, eds., *Ghana and the Ivory Coast,* 85–88; Martin Staniland, "Single-Party Regimes and Political Change: The P.D.C.I. and Ivory Coast Politics," in *Politics and Change in Developing Countries: Studies in the Theory and Practice of Development,* ed. Colin Leys (New York: Cambridge University Press, 1969), 152, 164; Frederick Cooper, *Decolonization and African Society: The Labor Question in French and British Africa* (New York: Cambridge University Press, 1996), 410.

15. For efforts to subvert Guinea's postindependence government, see Chaffard, *Carnets Secrets de la Décolonisation,* 2:218–19, 236–51, 259–61; Rivière, *Guinea,* 121–40; Mortimer, *France and the Africans,* 335; Cowan, "Guinea," 229; Roger Faligot and Pascal Krop, *La Piscine: Les Services Secrets Français, 1944–1984* (Paris: Éditions du Seuil, 1985), 217, 226, 245–49, 252, 335–37; Jacques Foccart, *Foccart Parle: Entretiens avec Philippe Gaillard* (Paris: Fayard/Jeune Afrique, 1995), 1:166, 175; Foccart, *Foccart Parle,* 2:193–94; R. W. Johnson, "Sekou Touré and the Guinean Revolution," *African Affairs* 69, no. 277 (Oct. 1970): 357–58; Bernard Charles, *La République de Guinée* (Paris: Éditions Berger-Levrault, 1972), 32; Lansiné Kaba, "Guinean Politics: A Critical Historical Overview," *Journal of Modern African Studies* 15, no. 1 (1977): 33.

16. Many local RDA leaders had emerged from the trade union milieu, specifically the PCF-linked Confédération Générale du Travail (CGT). In contravention of

interterritorial RDA orders, most Guinean RDA members did not sever their ties to the CGT until 1956. See chaps. 2 and 4.

CHAPTER ONE

1. John W. Young, *France, the Cold War and the Western Alliance, 1944–49: French Foreign Policy and Post-war Europe* (New York: St. Martin's Press, 1990), 18, 39; Irwin M. Wall, *The United States and the Making of Postwar France, 1945–1954* (New York: Cambridge University Press, 1991), 72; Frank Costigliola, *France and the United States: The Cold Alliance since World War II* (New York: Twayne, 1992), 13–16, 29, 44, 57, 66.

2. Young, *France, the Cold War and the Western Alliance,* 21.

3. Ibid., 2, 5, 21, 39, 52, 54, 56–57, 63–64, 79, 95, 125, 127, 218; Wall, *United States and the Making of Postwar France,* 189; Costigliola, *France and the United States,* 9–10, 24, 65; Jean-Pierre Rioux, *The Fourth Republic, 1944–1958,* trans. Godfrey Rogers (New York: Cambridge University Press, 1987), 81, 84–85; William I. Hitchcock, *France Restored: Cold War Diplomacy and the Quest for Leadership in Europe, 1944–1954* (Chapel Hill: University of North Carolina Press, 1998), 41–43; Edward Mortimer, *France and the Africans, 1944–1960: A Political History* (New York: Walker and Co., 1969), 27–28, 80; D. Bruce Marshall, *The French Colonial Myth and Constitution-Making in the Fourth Republic* (New Haven: Yale University Press, 1973), 93–94, 98–99, 143, 180, 191, 195, 206, 208–9, 235, 251, 262, 314; Tony Chafer, *The End of Empire in French West Africa: France's Successful Decolonization?* (New York: Berg, 2002), 226.

For the role of French West African territories in the war effort, see Myron Echenberg, *Colonial Conscripts: The Tirailleurs Sénégalais in French West Africa, 1857–1960* (Portsmouth, NH: Heinemann, 1991); Nancy Ellen Lawler, *Soldiers of Misfortune: Ivoirien Tirailleurs of World War II* (Athens: Ohio University Press, 1992); Elizabeth Schmidt, *Mobilizing the Masses: Gender, Ethnicity, and Class in the Nationalist Movement in Guinea, 1939–1958* (Portsmouth, NH: Heinemann, 2005), chap. 1.

4. For in-depth treatment of these issues, see Frederick Cooper, *Decolonization and African Society: The Labor Question in French and British Africa* (New York: Cambridge University Press, 1996); Echenberg, *Colonial Conscripts;* Lawler, *Soldiers of Misfortune;* Chafer, *End of Empire in French West Africa;* Schmidt, *Mobilizing the Masses.*

5. *Act of March 11, 1941 (Lend-Lease Act),* Public Law 11, 77th Congress. http://www.history.navy.mil/faqs/faq59-23.htm.

6. John D. Hargreaves, *Decolonization in Africa,* 2nd ed. (New York: Longman, 1996), 59–60.

7. "The Atlantic Charter, Joint Declaration by the President and the Prime Minister, Declaration of Principles, Known as the Atlantic Charter," 14 August 1941, U.S.-U.K., 55 Stat. app. 1603. http://www1.umn.edu/humanrts/education/FDRjointdec.html.

8. France endorsed the principles on December 26, 1944. "Declaration by United Nations," 1 January 1942, *FRUS* I, 25–26. http://www.ibiblio.org/pha/policy/1942/420101a.html.

9. Wall, *United States and the Making of Postwar France,* 38.

10. Mortimer, *France and the Africans*, 29–31; Costigliola, *France and the United States*, 9–10, 31, 43, 46, 54, 63, 65; Marshall, *French Colonial Myth and Constitution-Making*, 182; Hargreaves, *Decolonization in Africa*, 59–60, 68; Jean Suret-Canale, *La République de Guinée* (Paris: Éditions Sociales, 1970), 485; Thomas Hodgkin, *Nationalism in Colonial Africa* (New York: New York University Press, 1957), 19, 32–33, 142; James S. Coleman, *Nigeria: Background to Nationalism* (Berkeley: University of California Press, 1958), 231–33.

11. Marshall, *French Colonial Myth and Constitution-Making*, 180–83, 191, 208; Hargreaves, *Decolonization in Africa*, 68, 86–87; Costigliola, *France and the United States*, 23, 29; Jean Suret-Canale, *French Colonialism in Tropical Africa, 1900–1945*, trans. Till Gottheiner (New York: Pica Press, 1971), 484–86; Charles de Gaulle, *The War Memoirs of Charles de Gaulle: Unity, 1942–1944* (New York: Simon and Schuster, 1959), 205–9; Anthony D. Smith, *State and Nation in the Third World: The Western State and African Nationalism* (New York: St. Martin's Press, 1983), 48–49.

12. Suret-Canale, *French Colonialism in Tropical Africa*, 484–85; de Gaulle, *War Memoirs of Charles de Gaulle: Unity*, 207–9; Charles de Gaulle, *Memoirs of Hope: Renewal and Endeavor*, trans. Terence Kilmartin (New York: Simon and Schuster, 1971), 12; Patrick Manning, *Francophone Sub-Saharan Africa, 1880–1985* (New York: Cambridge University Press, 1988), 141.

13. Suret-Canale, *French Colonialism in Tropical Africa*, 486; Hargreaves, *Decolonization in Africa*, 69; Ruth Schachter Morgenthau, *Political Parties in French-Speaking West Africa* (Oxford: Clarendon Press, 1964), 37.

14. Quoted in Suret-Canale, *French Colonialism in Tropical Africa*, 485. See also de Gaulle, *War Memoirs of Charles de Gaulle: Unity*, 208.

15. Quoted in Suret-Canale, *French Colonialism in Tropical Africa*, 486. For a discussion of the self-conscious shift in French imperial policy, see Cooper, *Decolonization and African Society*.

16. "Recommendations Adopted by the Brazzaville Conference," in *Colonial Rule in Africa: Readings from Primary Sources*, ed. Bruce Fetter (Madison: University of Wisconsin Press, 1979), 169. See also Suret-Canale, *French Colonialism in Tropical Africa*, 487; Marshall, *French Colonial Myth and Constitution-Making*, 100.

17. "Recommendations Adopted by the Brazzaville Conference," 169; Morgenthau, *Political Parties in French-Speaking West Africa*, 38–40; Manning, *Francophone Sub-Saharan Africa*, 141.

18. Jean-Pierre Azema, *From Munich to the Liberation, 1938–1944*, trans. Janet Lloyd (New York: Cambridge University Press, 1984), 46–47; Ian Ousby, *Occupation: The Ordeal of France, 1940–1944* (New York: St. Martin's Press, 1997), 67–68.

In November 1942, German occupation was extended to the whole of metropolitan France. Costigliola, *France and the United States*, 29.

19. Young, *France, the Cold War and the Western Alliance*, 5–7; Costigliola, *France and the United States*, 11, 13, 29–30, 33.

Costigliola claims that before the Allied landing in Normandy in June 1944, only 2 percent of French adults were involved in the Resistance. Moreover, in 1943–44, approximately the same number of Frenchmen helped the German occupiers quell the Resistance as fought against the occupying forces. Costigliola, *France and the United States*, 28–30.

20. Young, *France, the Cold War and the Western Alliance*, 90; Rioux, *Fourth Republic*, 54, 59, 76, 97, 110; Hitchcock, *France Restored*, 19; Costigliola, *France and the United States*, 29, 33; Marshall, *French Colonial Myth and Constitution-Making*, 97, 144–45; Mortimer, *France and the Africans*, 31, 71.

21. Rioux, *Fourth Republic*, 59, 61, 98; Costigliola, *France and the United States*, 51, 53; Young, *France, the Cold War and the Western Alliance*, 90; Mortimer, *France and the Africans*, 71.

22. Rioux, *Fourth Republic*, 54.

23. Ibid., 112–13; Wall, *United States and the Making of Postwar France*, 44–48, 59, 67–68, 74–75, 188; Costigliola, *France and the United States*, 34, 43–45, 50, 52, 54–55, 58, 60–61, 63, 78; Hitchcock, *France Restored*, 44, 84, 227n36; Young, *France, the Cold War and the Western Alliance*, 147; Edward Rice-Maximin, "The United States and the French Left, 1945–1949: The View from the State Department," *Journal of Contemporary History* 19, no. 4 (Oct. 1984): 730–36.

24. Rice-Maximin, "United States and the French Left," 730–36; Wall, *United States and the Making of Postwar France*, 44–47; Costigliola, *France and the United States*, 48, 53, 65–66, 73; Young, *France, the Cold War and the Western Alliance*, 147.

25. Morgenthau, *Political Parties in French-Speaking West Africa*, 23–25, 27, 85; Hodgkin, *Nationalism in Colonial Africa*, 128; Schmidt, *Mobilizing the Masses*, 29, 32–34, 44, 51, 56, 58, 67–76, 159–60; Elizabeth Schmidt, "Top Down or Bottom Up? Nationalist Mobilization Reconsidered, with Special Reference to Guinea (French West Africa)," *American Historical Review* 110, no. 4 (Oct. 2005): 990, 1003–4; Elizabeth Schmidt, "Cold War in Guinea: The Rassemblement Démocratique Africain and the Struggle over Communism, 1950–1958," *Journal of African History* 48, no. 1 (March 2007): 98–101.

26. Morgenthau, *Political Parties in French-Speaking West Africa*, 14–15, 23, 36, 85; Thomas Hodgkin, *African Political Parties: An Introductory Guide* (Gloucester, MA: Peter Smith, 1971), 39–40.

27. ANS, 21G13, Guinée Française, Service de la Sûreté, "État d'Esprit de la Population," 1–15 Dec. 1950; Chafer, *End of Empire in French West Africa*, 146; Sidiki Kobélé Kéïta, *Le P.D.G.: Artisan de l'Indépendance Nationale en Guinée (1947–1958)* (Conakry: I.N.R.D.G., Bibliothèque Nationale, 1978), 1:233.

28. Morgenthau, *Political Parties in French-Speaking West Africa*, 23, 25–26; Hodgkin, *African Political Parties*, 43–44; Kéïta, *P.D.G.*, 1:169, 233; Cooper, *Decolonization and African Society*, 159.

29. Morgenthau, *Political Parties in French-Speaking West Africa*, 14, 19, 251–52.

30. Ibid., 23; Kéïta, *P.D.G.*, 1:169.

31. AG, 5B43, Guinée Française, Gouverneur, Conakry, à Gouverneur Général, Dakar, 3 March 1947, #42/C; 2Z27, "Syndicat Professionnel des Agents et Sous-Agents Indigènes du Service des Transmissions de la Guinée Française," Conakry, 18 March 1945; 5B47, Guinée Française, Gouverneur, Conakry, à Joseph Montlouis, Commis des P.T.T., Conakry, 13 June 1947, #390/C/P; Personal Archives of Joseph Montlouis, Letter from Joseph Montlouis, Conakry, to Jean Suret-Canale, Conakry, 5 April 1983; interviews in Conakry with Mamadou Bela Doumbouya, 26 Jan. 1991; Léon Maka, 20 Feb. 1991; Joseph Montlouis (assistant secretary-general, African PTT workers' union), 3 and 6 March 1991.

32. Morgenthau, *Political Parties in French-Speaking West Africa,* 28; Hodgkin, *Nationalism in Colonial Africa,* 129; Kéïta, *P.D.G.,* 1:175–76; Manning, *Francophone Sub-Saharan Africa,* 141; Cooper, *Decolonization and African Society,* 227–28; Frederick Cooper, "'Our Strike': Equality, Anticolonial Politics and the 1947–48 Railway Strike in French West Africa," *Journal of African History* 37, no. 1 (1996): 88–89.

33. ANS, 2G55/152, Guinée Française, Gouverneur, "Rapport Politique Annuel, 1955," #281/APA; 2G56/138, Guinée Française, Gouverneur, "Rapport Politique Mensuel, Mai 1956," 11 June 1956, #260/APA; CAOM, Carton 2199, dos. 3, Gouverneur, Guinée Française, Conakry, à Haut Commissaire, Dakar, "Revues Trimestrielles des Événements, 1er Trimestre 1956," 11 May 1956, #223/APA; Morgenthau, *Political Parties in French-Speaking West Africa,* 25, 227.

34. AG, 2Z27, "Syndicat Professionnel des Agents . . . Indigènes . . . ," 18 March 1945; 5B47, Gouverneur à Joseph Montlouis, 13 June 1947; interviews with Joseph Montlouis, 3 and 6 March 1991; Kéïta, *P.D.G.,* 1:176–77, 180, 186, 308; 'Ladipo Adamolekun, *Sékou Touré's Guinea: An Experiment in Nation Building* (London: Methuen, 1976), 11.

Henceforth, the Union des Syndicats Confédérés de Guinée will be referred to as the CGT.

35. Morgenthau, *Political Parties in French-Speaking West Africa,* 40; Hargreaves, *Decolonization in Africa,* 85–86; Mortimer, *France and the Africans,* 59; Manning, *Francophone Sub-Saharan Africa,* 142.

36. An ordinance of August 22, 1945 had extended voting rights to "veterans, those who had French decorations or distinctions, those who had school certificates higher than and including the primary school certificate, chiefs of ethnic groups, members of unions or professional groups and civil servants." A total of 1,418 votes were cast for Guinea's first college representative, and 12,829 for the second. Morgenthau, *Political Parties in French-Speaking West Africa,* 30, 396, 400; Kéïta, *P.D.G.,* 1:157, 182, 191; Mortimer, *France and the Africans,* 58; Hargreaves, *Decolonization in Africa,* 86; Virginia Thompson and Richard Adloff, *French West Africa* (New York: Greenwood Press, 1969), 555–56; CAOM, Carton 2181, dos. 6, "Note sur la Guinée," 6 May 1958.

37. AG, 2Z16, "Publication de Declaration d'Associations," Conakry, 18 Oct. 1946, #1439/APA; ANS, 17G573, Guinée Française, Service de Police, "Renseignements A/S Union Franco-Guinéenne–Touré Fodé Mamdou–Amicale Gilbert Vieillard," 8 Aug. 1948, #833/255/C; interview with Léon Maka, 20 Feb. 1991; Morgenthau, *Political Parties in French-Speaking West Africa,* 84, 90, 96, 222–24; Kéïta, *P.D.G.,* 1:190–91; Suret-Canale, *République de Guinée,* 144; Jean Suret-Canale, "La Fin de la Chefferie en Guinée," *Journal of African History* 7, no. 3 (1966): 477; Pierre Kipré, *Le Congrès de Bamako: Ou la Naissance du RDA en 1946* (Paris: Collection Afrique Contemporaine, 1989), 75.

38. Kéïta, *P.D.G.,* 1:160.

39. I am indebted to Sidiki Kobélé Kéïta for his account of the disturbances that preceded the October 1945 elections. Kéïta, *P.D.G.,* 159–68. See also ANS, 17G573, Guinée Française, Services de Police, "Renseignements A/S Soumah Amara, Conseiller R.D.A.," 26 April 1949, #378, C/PS; interview with Léon Maka, 20 Feb. 1991; Kipré, *Congrès de Bamako,* 75.

40. Kéïta, *P.D.G.,* 1:160.

41. Ibid., 1:161. I am indebted to Siba N. Grovogui for explaining the nature and purpose of *tabala* (kettledrums).

Between World War I and World War II, a significant number of traders and merchants from the French mandate of Syria-Lebanon settled in West Africa. Serving as commercial middlemen between French concerns and the local population, they often were considered by Africans to be exploiters and collaborators. See Thompson and Adloff, *French West Africa*, 429–31; Claude Rivière, *Guinea: The Mobilization of a People*, trans. Virginia Thompson and Richard Adloff (Ithaca: Cornell University Press, 1977), 47; Walter Rodney, "The Colonial Economy," in *Africa under Colonial Domination, 1880–1935*, ed. A. Adu Boahen, vol. 7 of *General History of Africa* (Berkeley: University of California Press, 1985), 344; M. H. Y. Kaniki, "The Colonial Economy: The Former British Zones," in Boahen, ed., *Africa under Colonial Domination*, 407; A. Adu Boahen, "Politics and Nationalism in West Africa, 1919–35," in Boahen, ed., *Africa under Colonial Domination*, 627; A. Adu Boahen, "Colonialism in Africa: Its Impact and Significance," in Boahen, ed., *Africa under Colonial Domination*, 799.

42. Kéïta, *P.D.G.*, 1:161–62.

43. Quoted in ibid., 1:163.

44. Ibid., 1:160, 164–65, 173.

45. ANS, 2G41/21, Guinée Française, Gouverneur, "Rapport Politique Annuel, 1941"; 2G42/22, Guinée Française, Gouverneur, "Rapport Politique Annuel, 1942"; 2G47/121, Guinée Française, Affaires Politiques et Administratives, "Revues Trimestrielles des Événements, 3ème Trimestre 1947," 5 Dec. 1947, #389 APA; AG, 5B47, Guinée Française, Gouverneur, Conakry, à Administrateurs de Cercle et Chefs de Subdivision, 3 July 1947, #442/APA; 5B49, Guinée Française, Gouverneur, Conakry, à Commandant de Cercle, Boffa, 5 June 1948, #322/APA; Kéïta, *P.D.G.*, 1:87–88, 99–102; Suret-Canale, *République de Guinée*, 95, 97, 137; Suret-Canale, *French Colonialism in Tropical Africa*, 80, 322–25, 341–42; Suret-Canale, "Fin de la Chefferie en Guinée," 462, 467, 470; Martin Klein, *Slavery and Colonial Rule in French West Africa* (New York: Cambridge University Press, 1998), 212–13; Mahmood Mamdani, *Citizen and Subject: Contemporary Africa and the Legacy of Late Colonialism* (Princeton: Princeton University Press, 1996), 22–23, 33, 39–61. For further discussion of the role of colonial chiefs and popular resistance to them, see Schmidt, *Mobilizing the Masses*, chap. 4.

46. During the war, the forest town of N'Zérékoré, for instance, was notorious for its smuggling operations into Liberia. Morgenthau, *Political Parties in French-Speaking West Africa*, 9.

47. See, e.g., ANS, 2G41/21, "Rapport Politique Annuel, 1941"; 2G46/22, Guinée Française, Gouverneur, "Rapport Politique Annuel, 1946," #284/APA; 2G47/121, Guinée Française, Affaires Politiques et Administratives, "Revues Trimestrielles des Événements, 1er Trimestre 1947," 17 June 1947, #143 APA; Suret-Canale, *République de Guinée*, 139.

48. Chevance-Bertin arrived in Guinea in 1945. Léon Maka observed that in May 1946, at the height of the constitutional debate, Chevance-Bertin's journal published an article that argued, in essence, "that black intellectuals wanted independence, and that they would conduct themselves like the tyrant, Samori Touré." Interview with Léon Maka, 20 Feb. 1991. See also Morgenthau, *Political Parties in*

French-Speaking West Africa, 221, 223, 396; Kéïta, *P.D.G.,* 1:182; Marshall, *French Colonial Myth and Constitution-Making,* 155; Charles de Gaulle, *The War Memoirs of Charles de Gaulle: Salvation, 1944–1946* (New York: Simon and Schuster, 1960), 18, 32.

49. Marshall, *French Colonial Myth and Constitution-Making,* 154–55; Mortimer, *France and the Africans,* 71; Gordon Wright, *The Reshaping of French Democracy* (New York: Howard Fertig, 1970), 77–78, 103–4.

50. Rioux, *Fourth Republic,* 59, 61, 97–98, 100; Kipré, *Congrès de Bamako,* 55, 68–79, 82; Morgenthau, *Political Parties in French-Speaking West Africa,* 40, 84, 225; Kéïta, *P.D.G.,* 1:182; de Gaulle, *War Memoirs of Charles de Gaulle: Salvation,* 306–7, 313–14; interview with Mamadou Bela Doumbouya, 26 Jan. 1991.

51. Rioux, *Fourth Republic,* 59, 97; Morgenthau, *Political Parties in French-Speaking West Africa,* 44–45; Mortimer, *France and the Africans,* 71.

52. Morgenthau, *Political Parties in French-Speaking West Africa,* 84.

53. Kipré, *Congrès de Bamako,* 56, 61–62; Hargreaves, *Decolonization in Africa,* 87.

54. The secessionist party initially was called the Section Française de l'Internationale Communiste. It became the PCF in October 1921. Chafer, *End of Empire in French West Africa,* 92; Ronald Tiersky, *French Communism, 1920–1972* (New York: Columbia University Press, 1972), 14–15; George Ross, *Workers and Communists in France: From Popular Front to Eurocommunism* (Berkeley: University of California Press, 1982), 4.

55. Kipré, *Congrès de Bamako,* 56; Mortimer, *France and the Africans,* 73. Marshall takes a more skeptical view of the communist position on African emancipation. See Marshall, *French Colonial Myth and Constitution-Making,* 240–43, 304–7.

56. Morgenthau, *Political Parties in French-Speaking West Africa,* 26–27, 36, 93–94; Marshall, *French Colonial Myth and Constitution-Making,* 188–89, 236–45, 271, 304–5; Mortimer, *France and the Africans,* 72, 80; Kipré, *Congrès de Bamako,* 56; Chafer, *End of Empire in French West Africa,* 93, 107.

57. AG, 1E41, Guinée Française, Services de Police, "Renseignements A/S Réunion Publique du R.D.A., tenue à Kankan, le 8 Avril 1952," 10 April 1952, #693/400/C/PS.2; Morgenthau, *Political Parties in French-Speaking West Africa,* 26–27, 36–37; Mortimer, *France and the Africans,* 80–81; Kipré, *Congrès de Bamako,* 61–62, 133, 138–39; Hargreaves, *Decolonization in Africa,* 87.

58. Of mixed African and European ancestry, Gabriel d'Arboussier would become a driving force in the postwar nationalist movement in French sub-Saharan Africa. His father, Henri d'Arboussier, hailed from an aristocratic French family and was a colonial administrator in the French Soudan. His mother's family was associated with the Tukulor politico-religious leader El-Hadj Umar b. Said Tall. As the recognized son of a well-to-do Frenchman, Gabriel d'Arboussier received an elite education, including a law degree in France. As a colonial administrator in the French Congo, d'Arboussier was elected to the 1945 Constituent Assembly by the first college voters of the Congo and Gabon. Marshall, *French Colonial Myth and Constitution-Making,* 165–69, 220–22, 265, Mortimer, *France and the Africans,* 68, 73–75, 77; Kipré, *Congrès de Bamako,* 76–77; Morgenthau, *Political Parties in French-Speaking West Africa,* 81n2; Georges Chaffard, *Les Carnets Secrets de la Décolonisation* (Paris: Calmann-Lévy, 1965), 1:103–4; Siba N. Grovogui, *Beyond Eurocentrism and Anarchy: Memories of International Order and Institutions* (New York: Palgrave Macmillan, 2006), 173–74; Klein, *Slavery and Colonial Rule,* 279n112 and n113,

302n50; Martin Klein, "Slavery and the French Colonial State." http://scholar.google. com/scholar?hl=en&lr=&q=cache:9eTKZB09Y20J:www.tekrur.org/publications/ AOFINTERNET.PDF/4S1CULTOK.PDF/04S1KLEIN.pdf+henri+d%27arboussier; Ibrahima Thioub, "Gabriel d'Arboussier et la Question de l'Unité Africaine, 1945–1965." http://scholar.google.com/scholar?hl=en&lr=&q=cache:UOIMwgIYHcMJ:www. tekrur.org/publications/AOF/2POLBALK.PDF/09P4TIUBAR.pdf+henri+ d%27arboussier.

59. Kipré, *Congrès de Bamako,* 68–69, 76–78; *Mortimer, France and the Africans,* 71.

Technically, d'Arboussier and Houphouët-Boigny joined the Union des Républicains et Résistants (URR), a parliamentary alliance that had grown out of the Communist Resistance group Mouvement Unifié de la Résistance Française. The URR worked closely with the PCF. However, URR members were not themselves communists. Morgenthau, *Political Parties in French-Speaking West Africa,* 79–80; Mortimer, *France and the Africans,* 71–72; Wright, *Reshaping of French Democracy,* 77, 103 ; Thioub, "Gabriel d'Arboussier."

60. Kipré, *Congrès de Bamako,* 82.

61. Rioux, *Fourth Republic,* 61–62; Marshall, *French Colonial Myth and Constitution-Making,* 148–49; Wall, *United States and the Making of Postwar France,* 42–43; Costigliola, *France and the United States,* 54.

62. De Gaulle, *War Memoirs of Charles de Gaulle: Unity,* 159–60, 164, 169–70, 186, 205, 286–87, 327, 357; de Gaulle, *War Memoirs of Charles de Gaulle: Salvation,* 10–11, 48, 113, 270–72, 307; Marshall, *French Colonial Myth and Constitution-Making,* 215, 220–21, 243–45; Rioux, *Fourth Republic,* 100–101. The relevant text of the April 1946 Constitution can be found in Morgenthau, *Political Parties in French-Speaking West Africa,* 379–81.

63. Marshall, *French Colonial Myth and Constitution-Making,* 149–50, 215–16, 242–43; Mortimer, *France and the Africans,* 78–79; Rioux, *Fourth Republic,* 100–101; Thompson and Adloff, *French West Africa,* 55–56; Morgenthau, *Political Parties in French-Speaking West Africa,* 43. See also de Gaulle, *War Memoirs of Charles de Gaulle: Salvation,* 319–20.

64. It was assumed that overseas territories would some day attain the status of associated states, with a greater degree of autonomy—but not independence from the French Union. Marshall, *French Colonial Myth and Constitution-Making,* 216–17, 243–44, 266, 271; Mortimer, *France and the Africans,* 80–81; Hargreaves, *Decolonization in Africa,* 86–87; Manning, *Francophone Sub-Saharan Africa,* 142; Morgenthau, *Political Parties in French-Speaking West Africa,* 41–43, 85, 379–81, 396–97. Relevant excerpts of the April 1946 Constitution can be found in Morgenthau, *Political Parties in French-Speaking West Africa,* 379–81.

65. Only individuals who were French citizens in October 1945 were allowed to vote in the referendum. Marshall, *French Colonial Myth and Constitution-Making,* 171, 227–28. Morgenthau, *Political Parties in French-Speaking West Africa,* 43–44, 396–98; Mortimer, *France and the Africans,* 81–82; Rioux, *Fourth Republic,* 101.

66. Wright, *Reshaping of French Democracy,* 179. See also Marshall, *French Colonial Myth and Constitution-Making,* 150; Mortimer, *France and the Africans,* 85; Rioux, *Fourth Republic,* 101–2.

67. Marshall, *French Colonial Myth and Constitution-Making*, 228; Mortimer, *France and the Africans*, 82, 85; Rioux, *Fourth Republic*, 101–2.

68. Marshall, *French Colonial Myth and Constitution-Making*, 149–50, 294; Wright, *Reshaping of French Democracy*, 178–84; Rioux, *Fourth Republic*, 99–103.

69. Wright, *Reshaping of French Democracy*, 179–80; Mortimer, *France and the Africans*, 85–86; Marshall, *French Colonial Myth and Constitution-Making*, 228.

70. One-third of the UDSR deputies in the Constituent Assembly represented first college voters overseas. Most were devoted supporters of Charles de Gaulle—and fervent anticommunists. Marshall, *French Colonial Myth and Constitution-Making*, 154–55, 228; Mortimer, *France and the Africans*, 71.

71. Morgenthau, *Political Parties in French-Speaking West Africa*, 127–29, 396; Mortimer, *France and the Africans*, 85–86; Wright, *Reshaping of French Democracy*, 179–80; Marshall, *French Colonial Myth and Constitution-Making*, 171–72.

Since the nineteenth century, Africans born in Senegal's four oldest communes—Dakar, Saint-Louis, Rufisqe, and Gorée—had automatically been French citizens. In 1945, there were 93,328 African and 17,529 European citizens in Senegal. Morgenthau, *Political Parties in French-Speaking West Africa*, 127–28.

72. "Recommendations Adopted by the Brazzaville Conference," 170–72.

73. ANS, 2G46/22, "Rapport Politique Annuel, 1946"; Thompson and Adloff, *French West Africa*, 33–34; Kipré, *Congrès de Bamako*, 53–54; Morgenthau, *Political Parties in French-Speaking West Africa*, 43; Marshall, *French Colonial Myth and Constitution-Making*, 222; Hodgkin, *Nationalism in Colonial Africa*, 36; Hargreaves, *Decolonization in Africa*, 69, 87.

74. Morgenthau, *Political Parties in French-Speaking West Africa*, 43; Mortimer, *France and the Africans*, 37; Thompson and Adloff, *French West Africa*, 34; Hodgkin, *Nationalism in Colonial Africa*, 36; Kipré, *Congrès de Bamako*, 53.

75. Morgenthau, *Political Parties in French-Speaking West Africa*, 43; Thompson and Adloff, *French West Africa*, 34; Hodgkin, *Nationalism in Colonial Africa*, 36; Kipré, *Congrès de Bamako*, 54.

76. ANS, 2G46/22, "Rapport Politique Annuel, 1946"; Morgenthau, *Political Parties in French-Speaking West Africa*, 43; Thompson and Adloff, *French West Africa*, 33–34; Hodgkin, *Nationalism in Colonial Africa*, 36; Mortimer, *France and the Africans*, 82; Marshall, *French Colonial Myth and Constitution-Making*, 222; Hargreaves, *Decolonization in Africa*, 69, 87; Kipré, *Congrès de Bamako*, 53–54.

77. Morgenthau, *Political Parties in French-Speaking West Africa*, 43, 49–50; Mortimer, *France and the Africans*, 39, 101–2; Marshall, *French Colonial Myth and Constitution-Making*, 210, 289; Kipré, *Congrès de Bamako*, 62.

78. Mortimer, *France and the Africans*, 82; Marshall, *French Colonial Myth and Constitution-Making*, 222.

By distinguishing between those who lived according to French civil and African customary law, France justified its policy of granting disparate political rights to those of French and African origin. See Catherine Coquery-Vidrovitch, "Nationalité et Citoyenneté en Afrique Occidentale Français[e]: Originaires et Citoyens dans le Sénégal Colonial," *Journal of African History* 42, no. 2 (2001): 285, 290–92, 296–97, 299–301, 303; Gary Wilder, *The French Imperial Nation-State: Negritude and Colonial Humanism between the Two World Wars* (Chicago: University of Chicago Press, 2005), chap. 5.

79. Morgenthau, *Political Parties in French-Speaking West Africa*, 46–47, 86; Mortimer, *France and the Africans*, 86, 93; Marshall, *French Colonial Myth and Constitution-Making*, 172–74, 228; Rioux, *Fourth Republic*, 101; Wright, *Reshaping of French Democracy*, 189; Kipré, *Congrès de Bamako*, 83.

80. Morgenthau, *Political Parties in French-Speaking West Africa*, 46, 86, 394; Mortimer, *France and the Africans*, 86, 93; Kéïta, *P.D.G.*, 1:182–83; Kipré, *Congrès de Bamako*, 75.

81. Kipré, *Congrès de Bamako*, 66, 68, 76–77. Mortimer, *France and the Africans*, 86; Thioub, "Gabriel d'Arboussier."

82. Mortimer, *France and the Africans*, 87–88; Marshall, *French Colonial Myth and Constitution-Making*, 150, 228; Rioux, *Fourth Republic*, 59, 102–3; Wright, *Reshaping of French Democracy*, 189; Kipré, *Congrès de Bamako*, 55, 83–84; Manning, *Francophone Sub-Saharan Africa*, 142; Morgenthau, *Political Parties in French-Speaking West Africa*, 43–48, 86–87. Relevant excerpts of what would become the October 1946 Constitution can be found in Morgenthau, *Political Parties in French-Speaking West Africa*, 382–85.

83. Morgenthau, *Political Parties in French-Speaking West Africa*, 44, 48, 87; Mortimer, *France and the Africans*, 88.

84. Articles 80 and 81, "Constitution of the French Republic of 28 October 1946," as quoted in Morgenthau, *Political Parties in French-Speaking West Africa*, 384–85. See also Morgenthau, *Political Parties in French-Speaking West Africa*, 46–47; Marshall, *French Colonial Myth and Constitution-Making*, 173–74, 246–47, 298; Mortimer, *France and the Africans*, 89, 93.

85. See Article 80, "Constitution of the French Republic of 28 October 1946," in Morgenthau, *Political Parties in French-Speaking West Africa*, 384. See also Marshall, *French Colonial Myth and Constitution-Making*, 297–98.

86. Morgenthau, *Political Parties in French-Speaking West Africa*, 43, 43n2, 49–50; Articles 80–82 of the "October Constitution," as quoted in Morgenthau, *Political Parties in French-Speaking West Africa*, 384–85; Mortimer, *France and the Africans*, 39, 92, 101–2; Marshall, *French Colonial Myth and Constitution-Making*, 293; Kipré, *Congrès de Bamako*, 62; Chafer, *End of Empire in French West Africa*, 64, 115n40.

87. The text of the October 1946 Constitution is included in Morgenthau, *Political Parties in French-Speaking West Africa*, 87, 382–85. See also Morgenthau, *Political Parties in French-Speaking West Africa*, 48–50, 53, 56; Mortimer, *France and the Africans*, 79–81, 100–101; Marshall, *French Colonial Myth and Constitution-Making*, 281; Kéïta, *P.D.G.*, 1:84; Kipré, *Congrès de Bamako*, 62–63.

88. Morgenthau, *Political Parties in French-Speaking West Africa*, 87; Marshall, *French Colonial Myth and Constitution-Making*, 289–90; Kéïta, *P.D.G.*, 1:233; Kipré, *Congrès de Bamako*, 85; Chafer, *End of Empire in French West Africa*, 104.

89. Morgenthau, *Political Parties in French-Speaking West Africa*, 43; Marshall, *French Colonial Myth and Constitution-Making*, 242–43; Thompson and Adloff, *French West Africa*, 55–56.

90. Morgenthau, *Political Parties in French-Speaking West Africa*, 50–52, 87; Marshall, *French Colonial Myth and Constitution-Making*, 248, 293–94, 299–300, 305, 312; Thompson and Adloff, *French West Africa*, 45–46, 54–56; Kenneth Robinson, "Senegal: The Elections to the Territorial Assembly, March 1957," in *Five Elections in Africa,*

ed. W. J. M. MacKenzie and Kenneth Robinson (Oxford: Oxford University Press, 1960), 291.

91. Morgenthau, *Political Parties in French-Speaking West Africa*, 50n5, 50–52, 396–97; Marshall, *French Colonial Myth and Constitution-Making*, 305; Hargreaves, *Decolonization in Africa*, 88.

92. Morgenthau, *Political Parties in French-Speaking West Africa*, 50–52, 127–28, 384–85; Marshall, *French Colonial Myth and Constitution-Making*, 248, 293–94, 298–300, 305, 312; Mortimer, *France and the Africans*, 173–74; Thompson and Adloff, *French West Africa*, 54–55; Robinson, "Senegal," 290–91.

According to the second draft constitution, French territorial governors would continue to operate with enormous executive powers. However, they would be advised by elected local assemblies, first called "general councils," and in 1952 renamed "territorial assemblies." Morgenthau, *Political Parties in French-Speaking West Africa*, 53–54, 56–57; Mortimer, *France and the Africans*, 173–74; Thompson and Adloff, *French West Africa*, 55; Hargreaves, *Decolonization in Africa*, 88.

93. The African deputies from Algeria and Madagascar abstained. Marshall, *French Colonial Myth and Constitution-Making*, 294, 302, 307–12; Morgenthau, *Political Parties in French-Speaking West Africa*, 87; Mortimer, *France and the Africans*, 105.

94. Morgenthau, *Political Parties in French-Speaking West Africa*, 382, 397–98; Marshall, *French Colonial Myth and Constitution-Making*, 294–95; Rioux, *Fourth Republic*, 106.

95. Kipré, *Congrès de Bamako*, 63, 65, 67, 76–77, 79, 82–83, 89–90; Mortimer, *France and the Africans*, 105; Manning, *Francophone Sub-Saharan Africa*, 142.

96. Kipré, *Congrès de Bamako*, 63, 65, 75–76, 79, 86–90, 93; Morgenthau, *Political Parties in French-Speaking West Africa*, 88; Mortimer, *France and the Africans*, 106; Marshall, *French Colonial Myth and Constitution-Making*, 272; Hargreaves, *Decolonization in Africa*, 99; Manning, *Francophone Sub-Saharan Africa*, 142.

97. Kipré, *Congrès de Bamako*, 87, 89–90, 108; Morgenthau, *Political Parties in French-Speaking West Africa*, 26, 88–89; Mortimer, *France and the Africans*, 105, 107.

98. Kipré, *Congrès de Bamako*, 79, 93, 110.

99. Quoted in Kipré, *Congrès de Bamako*, 92.

100. Kipré, *Congrès de Bamako*, 94, 110, 113–16, 119–21, 125; Mortimer, *France and the Africans*, 106–8; Kéïta, *P.D.G.*, 1:184–85; Morgenthau, *Political Parties in French-Speaking West Africa*, 88.

101. Morgenthau, *Political Parties in French-Speaking West Africa*, 26, 84, 88–89, 224–25, 275, 304–5; Kipré, *Congrès de Bamako*, 88–89, 93, 108, 123, 133; Mortimer, *France and the Africans*, 105–8; Kéïta, *P.D.G.*, 1:185, 233; Hargreaves, *Decolonization in Africa*, 99; Manning, *Francophone Sub-Saharan Africa*, 142; Chafer, *End of Empire in French West Africa*, 72, 104; Ernest Milcent, *L'A.O.F. Entre en Scène* (Paris: Bibliothèque de l'Homme d'Action, 1958), 37–38; L. Gray Cowan, "Guinea," in *African One-Party States*, ed. Gwendolen M. Carter (Ithaca: Cornell University Press, 1962), 158; interview with Mamadou Bela Doumbouya, 26 Jan. 1991.

102. Morgenthau, *Political Parties in French-Speaking West Africa*, 225, 418; Kéïta, *P.D.G.*, 1:169–72, 186.

103. AG, 1E41, Guinée Française, Services de Police, Conakry, "Renseignements A/S Réunion tenue sous l'Initiative du Comité du Rassemblement Démocratique Afri-

cain de Bamako," 15 Oct. 1946; ANS, 17G573, Section Locale du R.D.A. à Conakry, 9 July 1947; interview with Mamadou Bela Doumbouya, 26 Jan. 1991; interview with Joseph Montlouis, 6 March 1991; Kipré, *Congrès de Bamako*, 111; Kéïta, *P.D.G.*, 1:186; B. Ameillon, *La Guinée: Bilan d'une Indépendance* (Paris: François Maspero, 1964), 49, 51.

104. Kipré, *Congrès de Bamako*, 135.

105. Morgenthau, *Political Parties in French-Speaking West Africa*, 138, 225, 304–5; Mortimer, *France and the Africans*, 110, 142; Milcent, *A.O.F. Entre en Scène*, 44.

106. Kipré, *Congrès de Bamako*, 125. See also Morgenthau, *Political Parties in French-Speaking West Africa*, 89–90; Chafer, *End of Empire in French West Africa*, 72.

107. Kipré, *Congrès de Bamako*, 135–38, 160–62, 164–69; Hodgkin, *Nationalism in Colonial Africa*, 145–46; Mortimer, *France and the Africans*, 109–10; Marshall, *French Colonial Myth and Constitution-Making*, 182; Kéïta, *P.D.G.*, 1:187–88.

The UN Charter stresses that "relations among nations" will be "based on respect for the principle of equal rights and self-determination of peoples." The United Nations, as a body, will promote "universal respect for, and observance of, human rights and fundamental freedoms for all without distinction as to race, sex, language, or religion." Finally, colonial powers are obliged "to develop self-government, to take due account of the political aspirations of the peoples, and to assist them in the progressive development of their free political institutions." Chapter I, Article 1; Chapter IX, Article 55; and Chapter XI, Article 73 "Charter of the United Nations," San Francisco, 26 June 1945, 59 Stat. 1031, *Treaty Ser.* 993. http://www.un.org/aboutun/charter/chapter1.htm; http://www.un.org/aboutun/charter/chapter9.htm; http://www.un.org/aboutun/charter/chapt11.htm.

108. Quoted in Morgenthau, *Political Parties in French-Speaking West Africa*, 26.

109. ANS, 17G573, "Les Partis Politiques en Guinée, 1er Semestre 1951"; 17G573, Gendarmerie, AOF, "En Guinée Française," 12 Sept. 1951, #174/4; 17G573, Guinée Française, Services de Police, Conakry, "Rapport de Quinzaine du 1er au 15 Octobre 1951," #1847/1019, C/PS.2; 17G573, Guinée Française, Services de Police, "Revue Trimestrielle, 3ème Trimestre 1951," 24 Nov. 1951; 17G573, Comité Directeur, *P.D.G.*, "Analyse de la Situation Politique en Afrique Noire et des Méthodes du R.D.A. en Vue de Dégager un Programme d'Action," ca. 14 Jan. 1952; 17G573, Gouverneur, Guinée Française, Conakry, à Haut Commissaire, Dakar, 7 Oct. 1952, #444/APA; 2G56/138, "Rapport Politique Mensuel, Mai 1956"; CAOM, Carton 2199, dos. 3, "Revues Trimestrielles des Événements, 1er Trimestre 1956," 11 May 1956; Kéïta, *P.D.G.*, 1:241–42; Morgenthau, *Political Parties in French-Speaking West Africa*, 26, 98; Hodgkin, *Nationalism in Colonial Africa*, 147.

110. In French West Africa, Guinea and, to a lesser extent, the French Soudan were unique in having strong party organizations at the grassroots. See Morgenthau, *Political Parties in French-Speaking West Africa*, 291–93, 295–96, 339; Thomas Hodgkin and Ruth Schachter Morgenthau, "Mali," in *Political Parties and National Integration in Tropical Africa*, ed. James S. Coleman and Carl G. Rosberg Jr. (Berkeley: University of California Press, 1964), 223–25, 237; Aristide R. Zolberg, *Creating Political Order: The Party-States of West Africa* (Chicago: Rand McNally, 1966), 28, 32–34; Martin Staniland, "The Three-Party System in Dahomey: I, 1946–56," *Journal of African History* 14, no. 2 (1973): 291, 301, 303, 305–6, 312; Martin Staniland, "The Three-Party System in Dahomey: II, 1956–57," *Journal of African History* 14, no. 3 (1973): 495–99, 503.

111. ANS, 17G573, Gendarmerie, "En Guinée Française," 12 Sept. 1951; 17G573, "Les Partis Politiques en Guinée, 1er Semestre 1951"; 17G573, Police, "Rapport de Quinzaine du 1er au 15 Octobre 1951"; Kéïta, *P.D.G.*, 1:194–96, 241–42; Kéïta, *P.D.G.*, 2:179.

112. Morgenthau, *Political Parties in French-Speaking West Africa*, 224; Thompson and Adloff, *French West Africa*, 45; Kéïta, *P.D.G.*, 1:190–91.

113. AG, 2Z16, ". . . Declaration d'Associations," 18 Oct. 1946; interview with Léon Maka, 20 Feb. 1991; Morgenthau, *Political Parties in French-Speaking West Africa*, 96, 222, 224; Kéïta, *P.D.G.*, 1:190–91.

114. Thompson and Adloff, *French West Africa*, 56, 555–56; Morgenthau, *Political Parties in French-Speaking West Africa*, 400; Kéïta, *P.D.G.*, 1:191.

115. AG, 5B43, Guinée Française, Commissariat de Police, Kankan, "Retour à Kankan du 'Laministe' Mory-Oulin Caba," ca. 9 April 1947. See also ANS, 2G46/22, "Rapport Politique Annuel, 1946"; 2G47/121, "Revues Trimestrielles des Événements, 1er Trimestre 1947," 17 June 1947.

116. Kéïta, *P.D.G.*, 1:192–93; Rioux, *Fourth Republic*, 107; Thompson and Adloff, *French West Africa*, 45.

117. Interview with Fodé Mamadou Touré, Conakry, 13 March 1991; Morgenthau, *Political Parties in French-Speaking West Africa*, 222–23.

118. Morgenthau, *Political Parties in French-Speaking West Africa*, 55–56; Suret-Canale, *République de Guinée*, 30, 143; Thompson and Adloff, *French West Africa*, 47; Manning, *Francophone Sub-Saharan Africa*, 143.
Anyone who had served in the French armed forces, whether as conscript or career soldier, was considered to be a veteran. Although this book refers to such men as "military veterans," they were, in fact, all former soldiers, since all had been members of the colonial army, rather than a navy or an air force. Among military veterans, there were several distinctions. Former career soldiers (*anciens militaires*) generally had enlisted for fifteen to twenty-five years. Conscripts, in contrast, had served a three-year term, mandatory for all male subjects of the French Empire. Among these soldiers, only those who had served at the front for ninety consecutive days were given the title of *ancien combattant*. Echenberg, *Colonial Conscripts*, 51, 83–84, 128; Lawler, *Soldiers of Misfortune*, 24, 239–40.

119. Morgenthau, *Political Parties in French-Speaking West Africa*, 56.

120. Ibid., 43–46, 47–48, 86–87; Kipré, *Congrès de Bamako*, 55, 83–84; Manning, *Francophone Sub-Saharan Africa*, 142.

121. Rioux, *Fourth Republic*, 102, 110.

122. Chafer, *End of Empire in French West Africa*, 92, 104. See also Morgenthau, *Political Parties in French-Speaking West Africa*, 26–27, 88–90; Mortimer, *France and the Africans*, 142–43.

123. AG, 1E41, Police, "Renseignements A/S Réunion Publique . . . Kankan . . . ," 10 April 1952. See also Mortimer, *France and the Africans*, 142–43.
As was the case in the constituent assemblies, African deputies in the French parliament were affiliated to the PCF only indirectly. Technically, they were members of the URR parliamentary group, which in turn was associated with the PCF. The interests of the two groups were so closely identified that URR and PCF members almost

always voted together. Morgenthau, *Political Parties in French-Speaking West Africa*, 79–80, 93; Wright, *Reshaping of French Democracy*, 103.

124. Quoted in Marshall, *French Colonial Myth and Constitution-Making*, 167–68; Chaffard, *Carnets Secrets de la Décolonisation*, 1:102–3; Morgenthau, *Political Parties in French-Speaking West Africa*, 85.

There is some discrepancy concerning the number of seats the PCF won in the November 1946 legislative elections. Morgenthau puts the number at 183, while Rioux indicates that the figure was 165. Wright claims that the PCF won 168 seats, while the allied URR won 15. Thus, together, the communists and their allies held 183 seats. Morgenthau, *Political Parties in French-Speaking West Africa*, 395; Rioux, *Fourth Republic*, 110; Wright, *Reshaping of French Democracy*, 261.

125. Morgenthau, *Political Parties in French-Speaking West Africa*, 85.

126. ANS, 17G573, Guinée Française, Services de Police, Conakry, "Renseignements *Objet:* Constitution de Nouveaux Groupements Politiques," 10 March 1947.

127. CRDA, "Statuts de la Section de Guinée du R.D.A.," adoptés à Conakry, 14 June 1947; Secrétaire Général, P.D.G., "Circulaire," Conakry, 15 June 1947; AG, 5B49, Guinée Française, Inspecteur des Affaires Administratives, pour le Gouverneur, Conakry, à Consul de France au Liberia, l'Agent Consulaire à Bissao, l'Agent Consulaire à Freetown, 5 July 1948, #383/APA; Kéïta, *P.D.G.,* 1:194.

128. ANS, 17G573, Section Locale du R.D.A. . . . , 9 July 1947; 17G573, Guinée Française, Chef du Service de la Sûreté, Conakry, à Inspecteur Général de la Sûreté en AOF, Dakar, 5 Nov. 1948, #11762/64 PS; Kéïta, *P.D.G.,* 1:194–96.

129. ANS, 17G573, Section Locale du R.D.A. . . . , 9 July 1947; 17G573, Sûreté, Conakry, à Sûreté, Dakar, 5 Nov. 1948; Kéïta, *P.D.G.,* 1:194–96.

African teachers (*instituteurs africains*), doctors (*médecins africains*), pharmacists (*pharmaciens africains*), and veterinarians (*vétérinaires africains*) constituted the elite among African civil servants. However, their diplomas had no equivalence outside French West Africa. Their training deemed inferior, their licenses were not recognized and they could not practice in France. Suret-Canale, *République de Guinée*, 142, 147; Suret-Canale, *French Colonialism in Tropical Africa*, 373–74, 377–78, 388; Morgenthau, *Political Parties in French-Speaking West Africa*, 11–15; Mortimer, *France and the Africans*, 68, 68n3; Peggy R. Sabatier, "'Elite' Education in French West Africa: The Era of Limits, 1903–1945," *International Journal of African Historical Studies* 11, no. 2 (1978): 247–66; e-mail communication from Martin Klein, 6 Feb. 2006.

130. ANS, 17G573, Guinée Française, Services de Police, Conakry, "Renseignements *Objet:* Groupements Politiques en Guinée," 13 July 1947. See also 17G573, Guinée Française, Services de Police, Conakry, "Renseignements A/S Député Yacine Diallo et Association Gilbert Vieillard," 15 March 1947; 17G573, Guinée Française, Services de Police, Conakry, "Renseignements A/S Section R.D.A. Kindia," 1 July 1947, 504 A. #575 G.

For overlapping GEC/RDA memberships, see ANS, 17G573, Police, " . . . Constitution de Nouveaux Groupements Politiques," 10 March 1947; 17G573, Section Locale du R.D.A. . . . , 9 July 1947.

131. CRDA, "Statuts de la Section de Guinée du R.D.A.," 14 June 1947. See also AG, 1E41, Madéïra Kéïta, Secrétaire Général, R.D.A., Section de Guinée, à Gouverner,

Guinée Française, "Declaration d'Association," Conakry, 30 June 1947; 1E41, Secrétaire Général, R.D.A., S/Section de Macenta, à Commandant de Cercle, Macenta, 5
Aug. 1947; Kéïta, *P.D.G.,* 1:197.

132. Interviews in Conakry with Bocar Biro Barry, 21 and 29 Jan. 1991; Aissa-
tou N'Diaye, 8 April 1991; Ibrahima Fofana, 5 May 1991; Victor D. Du Bois, *Guinea's
Prelude to Independence: Political Activity, 1945–58,* West Africa Series 5, no. 6 (New
York: American Universities Field Staff, 1962), 7–8. See also Schmidt, *Mobilizing the
Masses,* chap. 4.

133. CRDA, Doudou Guèye, "Notre Volonté d'Union," *Le Phare de Guinée,* 15 Oct.
1947, 1; ANS, 17G573, Sûreté, Conakry, à Sûreté, Dakar, 5 Nov. 1948.

134. Kéïta, *P.D.G.,* 1:197.

Gabriel d'Arboussier epitomized RDA internationalism. A native of the French
Soudan, he had represented the Congo and Gabon in the first Constituent Assembly.
From 1947–52, he represented the Ivory Coast in the Assembly of the French Union.
In 1957, he was elected to Niger's Territorial Assembly and represented Niger in the
Grand Council in Dakar, where he served first as vice president and then as president.
He remained in Senegal after the September 1958 referendum. ANS, 21G91, "Assem-
blée de l'Union Française, Liste des Conseillers Élus," after 13 January 1947; Morgen-
thau, *Political Parties in French-Speaking West Africa,* 22, 81n2; Thompson and Adloff,
French West Africa, 96; Chaffard, *Carnets Secrets de la Décolonisation,* 1:103–4; Georges
Chaffard, *Les Carnets Secrets de la Décolonisation* (Paris: Calmann-Lévy, 1967),
2:290–91.

A police report noted the registration of the Guinean section of the RDA "after a
long stay in Conakry" by Gabriel d'Arboussier. ANS, 17G573, Police, " . . . Groupements Politiques en Guinée," 13 July 1947. See also, 17G573, Guinée Française, Assistant de Police Sidibé Soulé, Kankan, à Commissaire de Police, Kankan, 24 June 1947;
17G573, "Revue Trimestrielle de la Guinée, 4ème Trimestre 1947"; 17G573, "Rapport Général d'Activité 1947–1950," présenté par Mamadou Madéïra Kéïta, Secrétaire
Général du P.D.G. au Premier Congrès Territorial du Parti Démocratique de Guinée
(Section Guinéenne du Rassemblement Démocratique Africain), Conakry, 15–18
Oct. 1950; CRDA, P.D.G., "Circulaire," 15 June 1947.

135. AG, 1E41, Guinée Française, Services de Police, "Renseignements A/S Divers
Intérieur Guinée," 20 July 1947, 504 A., #672/C.

136. ANS, 17G573, Police, Sidibé Soulé, à Commissaire de Police, Kankan, 24
June 1947. The ethnic diversity of the gatherings is also noted in: 17G573, Guinée Française, Service de la Sûreté, "Extraits du Rapport #487—Police Kankan du 22 Juillet
1947 concernant Partis Politiques Haute Guinée"; 17G573, Guinée Française, Service de
la Sûreté, Kankan, "Compte-Rendu de Réunion," 1 Dec. 1947, #1454/240 C.

137. ANS, 17G573, Sûreté, Kankan, "Compte-Rendu de Réunion," 1 Dec. 1947.

138. ANS, 17G573, Guinée Française, Services de Police, "Renseignements *Objet:*
Activité du Parti R.D.A.," 14 Dec. 1947; Kéïta, *P.D.G.,* 1:191, 196. For similar re-
marks, see AG, 1E41, Secrétaire Général, R.D.A., Macenta, à Commandant de Cercle,
Macenta, 5 Aug. 1947.

139. ANS, 17G573, "Revue Trimestrielle de la Guinée, 4ème Trimestre 1947";
Kéïta, *P.D.G.,* 1:198.

140. ANS, 17G573, "Revue Trimestrielle de la Guinée, 4ème Trimestre 1947"; 17G573, Guinée Française, Services de Police, Conakry, "Renseignements A/S Nouveaux Groupements Politiques," 10 Nov. 1947.

141. AG, 1E37, Guinée Française, Cercle de Labé, "Rapport Politique Annuel, 1947"; 1E39, Guinée Française, Cercle de Labé, "Rapport Politique Annuel, 1949."

142. AG, 1E38, Guinée Française, Cercle de Labé, Subdivision de Tougué, "Rapport Politique Annuel, 1948."

143. AG, 1E39, Guinée Française, Cercle de Mamou, "Rapport Politique Annuel, 1949"; ANS, 21G9, Guinée Française, Service de la Sûreté, "Rapport Mensuel de Mars 1949," #364 PS/C.

144. Mortimer, *France and the Africans*, 26, 85, 120.

145. *Le Phare de Guinée* was published from 1947–49. CRDA, *Le Phare de Guinée*, no. 1, 27 Sept. 1947; ANS, 17G573, Côte d'Ivoire, Service de la Sûreté, "Renseignement," 13 Oct. 1947; 2G47/121, "Revues Trimestrielles des Événements, 3ème Trimestre 1947," 5 Dec. 1947; 2G47/121, Guinée Française, Affaires Politiques et Administratives, "Revues Trimestrielles des Événements, 4ème Trimestre 1947," 17 Feb. 1948, #35 APA; Kéïta, *P.D.G.,* 1:198.

146. Kéïta, *P.D.G.,* 2:184.

147. ANS, 17G573, Côte d'Ivoire, Sûreté, "Renseignement," 13 Oct. 1947; 2G47/121, "Revues Trimestrielles des Événements, 4ème Trimestre 1947," 17 Feb. 1948.

148. CRDA, *Réveil,* 17 Nov. 1947; ANS, 2G47/121, "Revues Trimestrielles des Événements, 4ème Trimestre 1947," 17 Feb. 1948; AG, 1E39, Labé, "Rapport Politique Annuel, 1949."

149. Marshall, *French Colonial Myth and Constitution-Making*, 147, 150–51, 260–62, 284–85, 294, 314; Mortimer, *France and the Africans*, 88–89, 100; Rioux, *Fourth Republic*, 99–106, 110; Morgenthau, *Political Parties in French-Speaking West Africa*, 59, 86; de Gaulle, *War Memoirs of Charles de Gaulle: Salvation*, 328; de Gaulle, *Memoirs of Hope*, 15–16, 30–31.

150. Young, *France, the Cold War and the Western Alliance*, 146–47; Wall, *United States and the Making of Postwar France*, 68–69; Hitchcock, *France Restored*, 72–73; Costigliola, *France and the United States*, 53, 59–60, 64–67; Mortimer, *France and the Africans*, 117–18; Morgenthau, *Political Parties in French-Speaking West Africa*, 59; Rioux, *Fourth Republic*, 125; Georgette Elgey, *La République des Illusions, 1945–1951* (Paris: Fayard, 1965), 246–93.

151. Marshall, *French Colonial Myth and Constitution-Making*, 245.

152. Wall, *United States and the Making of Postwar France*, 63–64, 85–86, 93; Hitchcock, *France Restored*, 85; Young, *France, the Cold War and the Western Alliance*, 167; Rioux, *Fourth Republic*, 127–30; Tiersky, *French Communism*, 160.

153. Wall, *United States and the Making of Postwar France*, 85–86, 93; Hitchcock, *France Restored*, 85; Young, *France, the Cold War and the Western Alliance*, 167.

154. Interview with Mamadou Bela Doumbouya, 26 Jan. 1991.

155. Ibid.; Morgenthau, *Political Parties in French-Speaking West Africa*, 90–91; Kéïta, *P.D.G.,* 1:233.

156. Chafer, *End of Empire in French West Africa*, 91–92, 105.

157. Ibid., 105; Mortimer, *France and the Africans*, 117, 119.

158. Morgenthau, *Political Parties in French-Speaking West Africa,* 90, 98, 241–43, 307; Mortimer, *France and the Africans,* 143, 247; Cooper, *Decolonization and African Society,* 407–8, 604n29; Chaffard, *Carnets Secrets de la Décolonisation,* 2:181.

159. Morgenthau, *Political Parties in French-Speaking West Africa,* 198, 305; Mortimer, *France and the Africans,* 128, 131, 214, 217; Thompson and Adloff, *French West Africa,* 143–44; Richard A. Joseph, *Radical Nationalism in Cameroun: Social Origins of the U.P.C. Rebellion* (Oxford: Oxford University Press, 1977), 181; Patrick Manning, *Slavery, Colonialism and Economic Growth in Dahomey, 1640–1960* (New York: Cambridge University Press, 1982), 277.

160. CAOM, Carton 2143, dos. 8, "Informations Politiques et Sociales . . . La Situation Politique en Guinée Française," *Interafrique Presse,* ca. Oct. 1955; CRDA, Bureau Exécutif, P.D.G., Conakry, aux S/Sections et Comités du R.D.A., 6 Oct. 1955, in *P.D.G.-R.D.A., Parti Démocratique de Guinée, 1947–1959: Activités—Répression—Élections;* Sékou Touré, Dakar, à Ministre, FOM, Paris, 6 Oct. 1955, in *P.D.G.-R.D.A.;* Sékou Touré, Dakar, à Haut Commissaire, Dakar, 7 Oct. 1955, in *P.D.G.-R.D.A.;* interview with Mamadou Bela Doumbouya, 26 Jan. 1991; Morgenthau, *Political Parties in French-Speaking West Africa,* 60–61, 63, 90–94, 97, 100–101, 106; Kéïta, *P.D.G.,* 1:129, 298–301.

161. ANS, 17G271, Guinée Française, Services de Police, "Renseignements A/S Activités du R.D.A.," 23 June 1949, #579, C/PS. The RDA faced similar obstacles in Kankan. See 17G573, Gouvernement Général de l'AOF, Cabinet, Bureau Technique de Liaison et de Coordination, "Note de Renseignements *Objet:* Activité de la Sous-Section R.D.A. de Kankan," 25 Nov. 1949, #738, CAB/LC/DK.

162. ANS, 17G573, Guinée Française, Services de Police, Conakry, "Renseignements A/S Meeting R.D.A.," 29 April 1949, #387, C/PS; 17G573, Guinée Française, Services de Police, "Renseignements A/S Activités Traoré Mamadou, dit 'Ray Autra' et R.D.A.," 29 Aug. 1949, #776, C/PS; 17G573, Guinée Française, Services de Police, Conakry, "Renseignements A/S Réunion Publique Organisée par le R.D.A.," 4 Oct. 1949, #1055, C/PS; 17G573, Guinée Française, Services de Police, "Renseignements A/S Condamnation Traoré Mamadou dit Ray Autra et Cissé Ibrahima," 31 March 1950 #289/161, C/PS; 17G573, "La Semaine Politique et Sociale en Guinée," Extrait du Rapport Hebdomadaire, 13–20 Nov. 1950; 17G573, "La Semaine Politique et Sociale en Guinée," Extrait du Rapport Hebdomadaire, 20–27 Nov. 1950.

163. ANS, "Rapport Général d'Activité 1947–1950," Section Guinéenne du RDA, 15–18 Oct. 1950; 17G573, Karamoko Diafodé Kéïta, Prison Civile de Kankan, à Groupe Parlementaire R.D.A., Paris, 3 Jan. 1951.

164. ANS, 17G573, Guinée Française, Services de Police, "Renseignements A/S Activités R.D.A.," 19 May 1949, #470, C/PS; 17G573, Guinée Française, Services de Police, Kankan, "Compte-Rendu de la Réunion Publique Organisée par la Sous-Section du R.D.A. de Kankan, le 26 janvier 1950," 27 Jan. 1950; 17G573, Guinée Française, Services de Police, "Renseignements A/S Mutations à Youkounkoun de Traoré Mamady," 2 June 1950, #571/291, C/PS/BM; 17G573, Guinée Française, Services de Police, "Renseignements A/S Baba Camara R.D.A.," 31 July 1950, #912/511, C/PS.2; 17G573, "Évolution et Activité des Partis Politiques et Aperçu des Principaux Événements Politiques en 1950"; 17G573, Gouverneur à Haut Com-

missaire, 7 Oct. 1952; interviews in Conakry with: Mamadou Bela Doumbouya, 26 Jan. 1991; Léon Maka, 20 Feb. 1991; Mira Balde (Mme. Maka), 25 Feb. 1991; Joseph Montlouis, 28 Feb. and 3 March 1991.

165. ANS, 17G573, Police, " . . . Activités R.D.A.," 19 May 1949.

166. Interviews with Joseph Montlouis, 28 Feb. and 3 March 1991. See also AG, 5B47, Gouverneur à Joseph Montlouis, 13 June 1947.

167. AG, 1E41, Guinée Française, Services de Police, "Renseignements A/S R.D.A. et Montlouis, Joseph," 12 April 1952, #703/405/C/PS.2.

168. ANS, 17G573, Comité Directeur, P.D.G., Conakry, "Rapport à la Délégation du Comité de Coordination et Groupe Parlementaire R.D.A., Assemblée Nationale, Paris," 14 Jan. 1952, #1.

169. AG, 5B47, Guinée Française, Gouverneur, Conakry, à Président de l'Amicale G. Vieillard et Président de l'Union Mandé, Conakry, et Secrétaire Général de la S/Section du R.D.A., Mamou, 23 Sept. 1947, #645; 5B47, Guinée Française, Gouverneur, Conakry, à Secrétaire Général de la Section R.D.A. de Guinée, Conakry, 24 Sept. 1947, #651; ANS, 17G573, Police, " . . . Réunion Publique Organisée par le R.D.A.," 4 Oct. 1949; 17G573, Guinée Française, Services de Police, Conakry, "Renseignements A/S Attitude de Certains Éléments du R.D.A. face au Désapparentement," 27 Feb. 1951, #257/114, C/PS.2; ANS, 17G573, P.D.G., "Rapport à . . . Comité de Coordination et Groupe Parlementaire R.D.A. . . . ," 14 Jan. 1952; interview with Léon Maka, 20 Feb. 1991; interview with Mira Baldé, 25 Feb. 1991.

170. ANS, 17G573, P.D.G., "Rapport à . . . Comité de Coordination et Groupe Parlementaire R.D.A. . . . ," 14 Jan, 1952; AG, 5B47, Gouverneur à l'Amicale G. Vieillard, l'Union Mandé, et S/Section du R.D.A., Mamou, 23 Sept. 1947; Kéïta, P.D.G., 1:205.

171. ANS, 17G573, P.D.G., "Rapport à . . . Comité de Coordination et Groupe Parlementaire R.D.A. . . . ," 14 Jan, 1952.

172. ANS, 17G573, Guinée Française, Services de Police, "Renseignements A/S Réunion R.D.A. à Kankan," 13 Aug. 1951, #1226/612, C/PS.2.

173. ANS, 17G573, Police, " . . . Mutations à Youkounkoun de Traoré Mamady," 2 June 1950.

174. ANS, 17G573, Police, Kankan, " . . . Réunion Publique Organisée par la Sous-Section du R.D.A. de Kankan . . . ," 27 Jan. 1950; 17G573, Guinée Française, Services de Police, "Renseignements," 4 Feb. 1950, #115/61, C/PS.2.

175. ANS, 17G573, Guinée Française, Services de Police, Kankan, "Compte-Rendu, Réunion de la Section du R.D.A. de Kankan, le 10 Décembre 1949 a 18 h.," 11 Dec. 1949, #154 C.

The journalist Mamadou Diallo claimed that shopkeepers sympathetic to the RDA were forced to pay taxes incommensurate with their commerce. 17G573, Guinée Française, Services de Police, "Renseignements A/S Réunion Publique Organisée à Kindia le 1er Février par le R.D.A.," 2 Feb. 1948, #159/55 C.

176. ANS, 17G573, Police, Kankan, " . . . Réunion Publique Organisée par la Sous-Section du R.D.A. de Kankan . . . ," 27 Jan. 1950.

177. ANS, 17G573, Guinée Française, Services de Police, "Renseignements A/S R.D.A.," 7 Nov. 1950, #1294/742, C/PS.2.

178. Interview with Mamadou Bela Doumbouya, 26 Jan. 1991.

179. Ibid.

180. Mamadou Traoré generally was known by his alias, "Ray Autra." Morgenthau notes that when the syllables are pronounced in reverse order, "Traoré" becomes "Ray-Au-tra." Morgenthau, *Political Parties in French-Speaking West Africa,* 281n1.

181. AG, 5B47, Guinée Française, Gouverneur, Conakry, à Ministre, FOM, Paris, 27 Nov. 1947, #778; ANS, 2G47/121, "Revues Trimestrielles des Événements, 4ème Trimestre 1947," 17 Feb. 1948; Kéïta, *P.D.G.,* 1:219.

182. ANS, 17G573, Gouverneur à Haut Commissaire, 7 Oct. 1952.

183. CRDA, Guinée Française, Gouverneur, Conakry, à Haut Commissaire, Dakar, 26 Sept. 1952, #411/CP.

184. Ibid.

185. ANS, 17G573, Police, " . . . Activités R.D.A.," 19 May 1949.

186. ANS, 17G573, Police, " . . . Baba Camara R.D.A.," 31 July 1950; 17G573, "Évolution et Activité des Partis Politiques . . . en 1950."

187. ANS, 17G573, Guinée Française, Services de Police, "Renseignements A/S Presse Locale et Syndicalisme à Mamou," 17 Oct. 1950, #1217/706, C/PS.2.

188. Suret-Canale, *République de Guinée,* 146; Kéïta, *P.D.G.,* 1:308; Sidiki Kobélé Kéïta, *Ahmed Sékou Touré: L'Homme du 28 Septembre 1958,* 2nd ed. (Conakry: I.N.R.D.G., Bibliothèque Nationale, 1977), 52; Sidiki Kobélé Kéïta, *Ahmed Sékou Touré: L'Homme et son Combat Anti-Colonial* (1922–1958) (Conakry: Éditions S.K.K., 1998), 117–18.

189. ANS, 17G573, Police, " . . . Presse Locale et Syndicalisme à Mamou," 17 Oct. 1950; AG, 1F21, Guinée Française, Services de Police, "Rapport Hebdomadaire, 29 Janvier-4 Février 1951," 6 Feb. 1951, #167/63, C/PS/I; Kéïta, *Ahmed Sékou Touré: 28 Septembre,* 44.

190. ANS, 17G573, Police, " . . . Meeting R.D.A.," 29 April 1949; 17G573, Police, " . . . Réunion Publique Organisée par le R.D.A.," 4 Oct. 1949.

191. ANS, 17G573, Côte d'Ivoire, Sûreté, "Renseignement," 13 Oct. 1947; 2G47/121, "Revues Trimestrielles des Événements, 4ème Trimestre 1947," 17 Feb. 1948; 21G9, Guinée Française, Service de la Sûreté, "Renseignements A/S Amicale Gilbert Vieillard," 21 April 1949, #361 PS/C; 17G573, Police, " . . . Meeting R.D.A.," 29 April 1949.

192. ANS, 17G573, Police, " . . . Activités Traoré Mamadou, dit 'Ray Autra' . . . ," 29 Aug. 1949; Kéïta, *P.D.G.,* 1:206. See also 17G573, Sûreté, Conakry, à Sûreté, Dakar, 5 Nov. 1948.

193. *Coup de Bambou* was published in 1950 only. CRDA, *Coup de Bambou,* no. 1, 5 April 1950; ANS, 17G573, Guinée Française, Services de Police, "Renseignements A/S R.D.A. et 'Coup de Bambou,'" 22 Aug. 1950, #989/562, C/PS.2; 17G573, "Rapport Général d'Activité 1947–1950," Section Guinéenne du RDA, 15–18 Oct. 1950; 17G573, Guinée Française, Services de Police, "Renseignements A/S Activités Actuelles R.D.A. et C.G.T.," 2 Oct. 1951, #1730/940, C/PS.2. See also Hodgkin, *African Political Parties,* 139.

194. ANS, 17G573, "Rapport Général d'Activité 1947–1950," Section Guinéenne du RDA, 15–18 Oct. 1950; 17G573, "La Semaine Politique et Sociale en Guinée," 13–20 Nov. 1950; 17G573, "Évolution et Activité des Partis Politiques . . . en 1950"; Kéïta, *P.D.G.,* 1:206–7; Suret-Canale, "Fin de la Chefferie en Guinée," 479.

195. CRDA, *Coup de Bambou*, 5 April 1950; ANS, 17G573, "La Semaine Politique et Sociale en Guinée," 13–20 Nov. 1950; 17G573, "La Semaine Politique et Sociale en Guinée," 20–27 Nov. 1950.

196. ANS, 17G573, Police, " . . . Activités Traoré Mamadou, dit 'Ray Autra' . . . ," 29 Aug. 1949.

197. ANS, 17G573, Police, " . . . Condamnation Traoré Mamadou dit Ray Autra et Cissé Ibrahima," 31 March 1950. See also 17G573, Guinée Française, Services de Police, "Renseignements A/S Situation R.D.A. N'Zérékoré," 16 Dec. 1949, #2576/102, C/PS.2; 17G573, "Évolution et Activité des Partis Politiques . . . en 1950."

198. ANS, 17G271, Police, " . . . Activités du R.D.A.," 23 June 1949. See also 17G573, AOF, " . . . Activité de la Sous-Section R.D.A. de Kankan," 25 Nov. 1949.

199. ANS, 2G47/121, "Revues Trimestrielles des Événements, 3ème Trimestre 1947," 5 Dec. 1947; 17G573, Police, " . . . Réunion Publique Organisée par le R.D.A.," 4 Oct. 1949. See also AG, 5B47, Guinée Française, Gouverneur, Conakry, à Administrateur de Cercle, Macenta, 5 Sept. 1947, #599/APA.

200. ANS, 17G573, Police, " . . . Réunion Publique Organisée par le R.D.A.," 4 Oct. 1949.

In February 1949, eight of the Ivory Coast's most important RDA leaders were imprisoned at Grand-Bassam and not freed until the end of the repression. This marked the beginning of a brutal crackdown on the RDA in its home territory. Morgenthau, *Political Parties in French-Speaking West Africa*, 190, 194; Mortimer, *France and the Africans*, 146–47.

201. ANS, 17G573, Guinée Française, Services de Police, "Renseignements A/S Activités R.D.A.," 1 June 1949, #517, C/PS; 17G573, Gouvernement Général de l'AOF, Cabinet, Bureau Technique de Liaison et de Coordination, "Note de Renseignements *Objet:* Activité Politique et Sociale en Guinée pendant le Mois de Décembre 1949," 15 Jan. 1950, #141, CAB/LC/DK; 17G573, Guinée Française, Services de Police, "Renseignements A/S Activités R.D.A.," 12 Feb. 1950, #149/76, C/PS.2; 17G573, "Évolution et Activité des Partis Politiques . . . en 1950"; AG, AM-1339, Idiatou Camara, "La Contribution de la Femme de Guinée à la Lutte de Libération Nationale (1945–1958)," Mémoire de Fin d'Études Supérieures, Conakry, IPGAN, 1979, 52–65, 111; interview with Aissatou N'Diaye, 8 April 1991; interview with Néné Diallo, Conakry, 11 April 1991; Milcent, *A.O.F. Entre en Scène*, 51, 53; Chaffard, *Carnets Secrets de la Décolonisation*, 1:117; Kéïta, *P.D.G.*, 1:208, 223.

202. Kéïta, *P.D.G.*, 1:209–10.

203. ANS, 17G573, Guinée Française, Services de Police, Kissidougou, "Renseignements *Objet:* Activité du R.D.A.," 15 Sept. 1948; 17G573, Guinée Française, Services de Police, "Renseignements A/S Assemblée Générale, Union du Mandé, Section de Kankan," 23 Sept. 1948, #KE/1018/12; 17G573, Sûreté, Conakry, à Sûreté, Dakar, 5 Nov. 1948; 17G573, Guinée Française, Services de Police, Kankan, "Compte-Rendu A/S Réunion Publique Organisée par S/Section R.D.A. de Kankan," 11 Sept. 1950, #208 C; AG, 1E42, Guinée Française, "Note de Renseignement: A.O.F., Les Établissements KABA KOUROU à Kankan, Liaison avec l'Étranger," 19 Oct. 1949, #776; Kéïta, *P.D.G.*, 1:209–10.

204. AG, 1E38, Guinée Française, Cercle de N'Zérékoré, "Rapport Politique Annuel, 1948"; ANS, 17G573, Sûreté, Conakry, à Sûreté, Dakar, 5 Nov. 1948. See also

21G102, Guinée Française, Service de la Sûreté, "Renseignements A/S R.D.A., Union du Mandé et Montrat," 4 June 1948, #648/217 C; Suret-Canale, *République de Guinée,* 144.

205. ANS 17G573, Police, "... Député Yacine Diallo et Association Gilbert Vieillard," 15 March 1947; 17G573, Section Locale du R.D.A...., 9 July 1947; 17G573, Sûreté, Conakry, à Sûreté, Dakar, 5 Nov. 1948; Kéïta, *P.D.G.,* 1:194–96.

206. ANS, 17G573, Guinée Française, Services de Police, "Renseignements A/S Passage Kankan Parlementaires Guinéens," 3 Feb. 1951, #171/65, C/PS.2. See also AG, 5B43, Guinée Française, Services de Police, "Renseignements A/S Élections Conseil Général, Guinée," 26 Dec. 1947, #14/C.

207. AG, 2Z16, "... Declaration d'Associations," 18 Oct. 1946; 5B49, Guinée Française, Inspecteur des Affaires Administratives, pour le Gouverneur, Conakry, à Commandant de Cercle, Beyla, 24 June 1948, #364/APA; 5B49, Guinée Française, Inspecteur des Affaires Administratives, pour le Gouverneur, Conakry, à l'Agent Consulaire de France, Bathurst (Gambie), 5 July 1948, #382/APA; 5B49, Gouverneur à Consul de France au Liberia, l'Agent Consulaire à Bissao, l'Agent Consulaire à Freetown, 5 July 1948; 1E38, Guinée Française, Cercle de Gaoual, Subdivision Centrale, "Rapport Politique Annuel, 1948"; 1E42, Guinée Française, Services de Police, "Renseignements A/S Retour Almamy de Mamou et Attitude A.G.V.," 27 Oct. 1949, #2137/C/PS.2; Morgenthau, *Political Parties in French-Speaking West Africa,* 19, 221–24; Kéïta, *P.D.G.,* 1:171.

208. AG, 1E38, N'Zérékoré, "Rapport Politique Annuel, 1948." Férébory Camara had represented the Union Forestière on the Guinean RDA's first board of directors. Kéïta, *P.D.G.,* 1:195.

209. AG, 1E41, Guinée Française, Services de Police, "Renseignements A/S Comité de Renovation de Basse Guinée et Opposition R.D.A.," 17 Aug. 1949, #796/C/PS.

210. ANS, 2G47/121, Guinée Française, Affaires Politiques et Administratives, "Revues Trimestrielles des Événements, 2ème Trimestre 1947," 11 Oct. 1947, #273 APA; 17G573, "Revue Trimestrielle de la Guinée, 4ème Trimestre 1947"; 21G13,"État d'Esprit de la Population," 1–15 Dec. 1950; AG, 1E38, Tougué, "Rapport Politique Annuel, 1948"; Morgenthau, *Political Parties in French-Speaking West Africa,* 224–25, 418; Kéïta, *P.D.G.,* 1:170.

211. AG, 1E38, Gaoual, "Rapport Politique Annuel, 1948."

212. AG, 1E41, Police, "... Comité de Renovation de Basse Guinée et Opposition R.D.A.," 17 Aug. 1949; Rivière, *Guinea,* 47, 66–67; Kéïta, *P.D.G.,* 1:210–11; Morgenthau, *Political Parties in French-Speaking West Africa,* 225. See also Hodgkin, *African Political Parties,* 72.

213. ANS, 17G573, Police, "... Réunion Publique Organisée par le R.D.A.," 4 Oct. 1949. See also 17G573, Guinée Française, Services de Police, "Renseignements A/S Réunion des Membres du R.D.A. réunis en Assemblée Générale tenue au Cinéma 'Rialto' le 12 Septembre 1948," 13 Sept. 1948, #KE/978/3; Morgenthau, *Political Parties in French-Speaking West Africa,* 90; Hodgkin, *Nationalism in Colonial Africa,* 156.

214. ANS, 17G573, AOF, "... Activité de la Sous-Section R.D.A. de Kankan," 25 Nov. 1949.

215. AG, 1E39, Guinée Française, Cercle de Kankan, "Rapport Politique Annuel, 1949"; ANS, 17G573, AOF, "... Activité de la Sous-Section R.D.A. de Kankan," 25

Nov. 1949; 17G573, AOF, " . . . Activité Politique et Sociale en Guinée . . . Décembre 1949," 15 Jan. 1950; 17G573, Guinée Française, Services de Police, "Renseignements," 4 Feb. 1950, #114/60, C/PS.2; Morgenthau, *Political Parties in French-Speaking West Africa,* 235–36, 324.

216. AG, 1E42, " . . . A.O.F., Les Établissements KABA KOUROU à Kankan . . . ," 19 Oct. 1949; 1E42, Guinée Française, Services de Police, "Renseignements," 8 Dec. 1949, #2488/82/C/PS/I; 1E39, Kankan, "Rapport Politique Annuel, 1949"; ANS, 17G573, AOF, " . . . Activité de la Sous-Section R.D.A. de Kankan," 25 Nov. 1949; 17G573, AOF, " . . . Activité Politique et Sociale en Guinée . . . Décembre 1949," 15 Jan. 1950; 17G573, Police, "Renseignements," 4 Feb. 1950; 17G586, Guinée Française, Services de Police, Kankan, "Renseignements A/S Section RDA de Kankan—Assemblée Extraordinaire des Notables et des Délégués RDA chez le Chef de Canton, Alpha Amadou Kaba, 24-10-54," 3 Nov. 1954, #2884/1112, C/PS.2.

217. ANS, 17G573, "La Semaine Politique et Sociale en Guinée," 13–20 Nov. 1950; 17G573, "La Semaine Politique et Sociale en Guinée," 20–27 Nov. 1950.

218. For further discussion of rural resistance to the colonial chieftaincy—and RDA support for this campaign—see Schmidt, *Mobilizing the Masses,* chap. 4.

219. ANS, 2G47/121, "Revues Trimestrielles des Événements, 1er Trimestre 1947," 17 June 1947; AG, 1E39, Guinée Française, Cercle de Macenta, "Rapport Politique Annuel, 1949"; Suret-Canale, *French Colonialism in Tropical Africa,* 79, 323–24; Suret-Canale, "Fin de la Chefferie en Guinée," 470–71; Suret-Canale, *République de Guinée,* 138.

220. ANS, 2G46/22, "Rapport Politique Annuel, 1946"; 2G47/121, "Revues Trimestrielles des Événements, 1er Trimestre 1947," 17 June 1947; 2G47/121, "Revues Trimestrielles des Événements, 2ème Trimestre 1947," 11 Oct. 1947; 2G47/22, Guinée Française, Gouverneur, "Rapport Politique Annuel, 1947"; AG, 1E37, Guinée Française, Cercle de Gaoual, Subdivision Centrale, "Rapport Politique Annuel, 1947"; MO-33, Sékou Mara, "La Lutte de Libération Nationale et la Chefferie dite Coutumière en Guinée Forestière," Mémoire de Fin d'Études Supérieures, Kankan, IPJN, 1975–76, 47; CRDA, Léon Maka, "Le R.D.A. et Certaines Pratiques Coutumières," *La Liberté,* no. 48, 1 March 1955, 2; Sékou Touré, "Contre Tout Travail Forcé," *La Liberté,* no. 48, 1 March 1955, 3. See also Schmidt, *Mobilizing the Masses,* chap. 4.

221. For examples of pro-RDA chiefs, see ANS, 17G573, Télégramme Arrivée, Haut Commissaire, Dakar. Envoyé par Gouverneur, Guinée Française, Conakry, 19 Oct. 1949, #448; 17G573, Guinée Française, Inspecteur des Affaires Administratives, Conakry, "Rapport sur la Manifestation R.D.A. au 18 Octobre 1949 à N'Zérékoré," 8 Nov. 1949; AG, 1E39, Guinée Française, Cercle de N'Zérékoré, "Rapport Politique Annuel, 1949."

222. AG, 1E41, Guinée Française, Services de Police, Kankan, "Renseignements A/S Caba, Tiranke Madi, Membre Influent R.D.A., Kankan," 16 Nov. 1949, #2264/39/C/PS/I; 1E39, N'Zérékoré, "Rapport Politique Annuel, 1949"; ANS, 17G573, Police, " . . . Situation R.D.A. N'Zérékoré," 16 Dec. 1949; 17G573, "Rapport Général d'Activité 1947–1950," Section Guinéenne du RDA, 15–18 Oct. 1950; 17G573, "Évolution et Activité des Partis Politiques . . . en 1950"; Kéïta, *P.D.G.,* 1:223–25.

223. ANS, 17G573, Procureur Général, Dakar, à Directeur Général de l'Intérieur, Service des Affaires Politiques, Dakar, 19 Nov. 1949, #2658 PJ.

224. AG, 1E39, N'Zérékoré, "Rapport Politique Annuel, 1949."

225. ANS, 17G573, "Rapport sur la Manifestation R.D.A. . . . à N'Zérékoré," 8 Nov. 1949.

226. ANS, 17G573, Télégramme Arrivée, Haut Commissaire. Envoyé par Gouverneur, Guinée Française, 19 Oct. 1949; 17G573, "Rapport sur la Manifestation R.D.A. . . . à N'Zérékoré," 8 Nov. 1949; AG, 1E39, N'Zérékoré, "Rapport Politique Annuel, 1949."

227. ANS, 17G573, "Rapport sur la Manifestation R.D.A. . . . à N'Zérékoré," 8 Nov. 1949.

228. ANS, 17G573, Police, " . . . Situation R.D.A. N'Zérékoré," 16 Dec. 1949.

229. AG, 1E39, N'Zérékoré, "Rapport Politique Annuel, 1949."

230. ANS, 17G573, AOF, " . . . Activité Politique et Sociale en Guinée . . . Décembre 1949," 15 Jan. 1950; AG, 1E39, N'Zérékoré, "Rapport Politique Annuel, 1949."

231. ANS, 17G573, Police, " . . . Situation R.D.A. N'Zérékoré," 16 Dec. 1949; 17G573, AOF, " . . . Activité Politique et Sociale en Guinée . . . Décembre 1949," 15 Jan. 1950; AG, 1E39, N'Zérékoré, "Rapport Politique Annuel, 1949."

232. ANS, 17G573, "Rapport Général d'Activité 1947–1950," Section Guinéenne du RDA, 15–18 Oct. 1950.

233. AG, 1E42, Guinée Française, Commissariat de Police, Kankan, "Rapport Mensuel, Mois de Mai 1950," #95/C.

Chapter Two

1. Ruth Schachter Morgenthau, *Political Parties in French-Speaking West Africa* (Oxford: Clarendon Press, 1964), 93–94, 97–98; Ernest Milcent, *L'A.O.F. Entre en Scène* (Paris: Bibliothèque de l'Homme d'Action, 1958), 46; Edward Mortimer, *France and the Africans, 1944–1960: A Political History* (New York: Walker and Co., 1969), 149; Tony Chafer, *The End of Empire in French West Africa: France's Successful Decoloniziation?* (New York: Berg, 2002), 106; Elizabeth Schmidt, "Cold War in Guinea: The Rassemblement Démocratique Africain and the Struggle over Communism, 1950–1958," *Journal of African History* 48, no. 1 (March 2007): 101–5.

2. AG, 1E41, Guinée Française, Services de Police, "Renseignements A/S Réunion Publique du R.D.A., tenue à Kankan, le 8 Avril 1952," 10 April 1952, #693/400/C/PS.2; interview with Mamadou Bela Doumbouya, Conakry, 26 Jan. 1991; Morgenthau, *Political Parties in French-Speaking West Africa,* 27, 90–91, 97–98; Chafer, *End of Empire in French West Africa,* 106–7, 118; Sidiki Kobélé Kéïta, *Le P.D.G.: Artisan de l'Indépendance Nationale en Guinée (1947–1958)* (Conakry: I.N.R.D.G., Bibliothèque Nationale, 1978), 1:232, 234, 237. For an analysis of d'Arboussier's political thought, see Siba N. Grovogui, *Beyond Eurocentrism and Anarchy: Memories of International Order and Institutions* (New York: Palgrave Macmillan, 2006), chap. 4.

3. Chafer, *End of Empire in French West Africa,* 109, 118, 127, 132, 149–50.

In Guinea, as elsewhere in Africa, the term "youth" was broadly defined, including both schoolboys and young, but mature, men. See Thomas Hodgkin, *African Political Parties: An Introductory Guide* (Gloucester, MA: Peter Smith, 1971), 122–23.

4. Morgenthau, *Political Parties in French-Speaking West Africa*, 166, 169–72, 177; Chafer, *End of Empire in French West Africa*, 91–92, 105.

5. Quoted in Morgenthau, *Political Parties in French-Speaking West Africa*, 90–91. See also Mortimer, *France and the Africans*, 123; Kéïta, *P.D.G.*, 1:127.

6. Morgenthau, *Political Parties in French-Speaking West Africa*, 97, 188–202; Milcent, *A.O.F. Entre en Scène*, 49–52; Georges Chaffard, *Les Carnets Secrets de la Décolonisation* (Paris: Calmann-Lévy, 1965), 1:105–21; Aristide R. Zolberg, *One-Party Government in the Ivory Coast* (Princeton: Princeton University Press, 1964), 131–39.

7. Interview with Bocar Biro Barry, Conakry, 21 Jan. 1991.

8. Morgenthau, *Political Parties in French-Speaking West Africa*, 166, 169–72, 177.

9. Ibid., 98; Milcent, *A.O.F. Entre en Scène*, 47–48; Mortimer, *France and the Africans*, 144; Kéïta, *P.D.G.*, 1:234.

10. ANS, 17G573, Guinée Française, Services de Police, "Renseignements A/S Visite de D'Arboussier à Conakry," 8 Dec. 1949, #2485/80, C/PS.2. See also Mortimer, *France and the Africans*, 153; Chafer, *End of Empire in French West Africa*, 118.

11. Milcent, *A.O.F. Entre en Scène*, 78–87; Mortimer, *France and the Africans*, 137, 153–54, 156, 177–78, 199; Zolberg, *One-Party Government in the Ivory Coast*, 157, 157n29; Morgenthau, *Political Parties in French-Speaking West Africa*, 98. As "the supreme directing organ" of the RDA, the coordinating committee was superior in authority to the parliamentarians' ad hoc group. Thus, all binding decisions had to be approved by it. See the political resolution of the 1949 RDA Congress in Abidjan, quoted in Morgenthau, *Political Parties in French-Speaking West Africa*, 98, 303–4. See also ANS, 17G573, Guinée Française, Services de Police, Conakry, "Rapport Hebdomadaire, Semaine du 23 au 30 Septembre 1951, Semaine du 1er au 7 Octobre 1951," #1794/984, C/PS.2; Kéïta, *P.D.G.*, 1:236.

12. Technically, disaffiliation meant that the RDA parliamentarians severed their links to the URR, and through it, their ties to the PCF. ANS, 17G573, Police, "Rapport Hebdomadaire, Semaine du 23 au 30 Septembre 1951, Semaine du 1er au 7 Octobre 1951"; Morgenthau, *Political Parties in French-Speaking West Africa*, 79–80, 98–99, 99n1; Mortimer, *France and the Africans*, 156; Kéïta, *P.D.G.*, 1:236; Chafer, *End of Empire in French West Africa*, 106.

13. Mortimer, *France and the Africans*, 146, 156.

14. Morgenthau, *Political Parties in French-Speaking West Africa*, 99–100, 303–4, 309, 317; Chaffard, *Carnets Secrets de la Décolonisation*, 1:127–28; Milcent, *A.O.F. Entre en Scène*, 54; Mortimer, *France and the Africans*, 156, 161; Kéïta, *P.D.G.*, 1:237–38.

15. ANS, 21G13, Guinée Française, Service de la Sûreté, "État d'Esprit de la Population," 1–15 Dec. 1950.

16. Specifically, Sékou Touré opposed the RDA's affiliation to the Indépendants d'Outre-Mer (IOM), an MRP-sponsored parliamentary group charged with undermining RDA influence in the African territories. ANS, 17G573, Guinée Française, Services de Police, "Renseignements A/S Position de Sékou Touré face au 'Désapparentement du R.D.A.,'" 24 Oct. 1950, #1249/722, C/PS.2; Morgenthau, *Political Parties in French-Speaking West Africa*, 93–94.

17. AG, 1E41, Guinée Française, Services de Police, "Renseignements A/S Autour des Activités Politiques Actuelles," 27 June 1951, #934/432/C/PS.

18. Morgenthau, *Political Parties in French-Speaking West Africa,* 99.

19. Ibid., 101; Chaffard, *Carnets Secrets de la Décolonisation,* 1:105, 123–24; Mortimer, *France and the Africans,* 157, 163, 165; Kéïta, *P.D.G.,* 1:127–28; Jean-Pierre Rioux, *The Fourth Republic, 1944–1958,* trans. Godfrey Rogers (New York: Cambridge University Press, 1987), 146; Denis MacShane, *François Mitterrand: A Political Odyssey* (New York: Universe Books, 1982), 55; interview with Bocar Biro Barry, 21 Jan. 1991; interview with Mamadou Bela Doumbouya, 26 Jan. 1991.

20. Morgenthau, *Political Parties in French-Speaking West Africa,* 59; Mortimer, *France and the Africans,* 157; "Rassemblement du Peuple Français," http://fr.wikipedia.org/wiki/Rassemblement_du_peuple_fran%C3%A7ais.

21. Chaffard, *Carnets Secrets de la Décolonisation,* 1:121–27; Mortimer, *France and the Africans,* 157, 163, 173; Rioux, *Fourth Republic,* 144, 146; MacShane, *François Mitterrand,* 55; Finn Fuglestad, *A History of Niger, 1850–1960* (New York: Cambridge University Press, 1983), 164.

René Pleven was prime minister from July 12, 1950, to February 28, 1951, and from August 10, 1951, to January 7, 1952. Morgenthau, *Political Parties in French-Speaking West Africa,* 378.

22. Morgenthau, *Political Parties in French-Speaking West Africa,* 61, 63, 101, 378; Mortimer, *France and the Africans,* 157, 163, 172–73; Kéïta, *P.D.G.,* 1:128–29, 228; MacShane, *François Mitterrand,* 55; Chafer, *End of Empire in French West Africa,* 106.

23. Morgenthau, *Political Parties in French-Speaking West Africa,* 104, 378; Milcent, *A.O.F. Entre en Scène,* 65; Mortimer, *France and the Africans,* 173; Rioux, *Fourth Republic,* 462; Claude Rivière, *Guinea: The Mobilization of a People,* trans. Virginia Thompson and Richard Adloff (Ithaca: Cornell University Press, 1977), 68; interview with Bocar Biro Barry, 21 Jan. 1991.

24. Rioux, *Fourth Republic,* 164–65; Mortimer, *France and the Africans,* 163.

25. Rioux, *Fourth Republic,* 165–66; Morgenthau, *Political Parties in French-Speaking West Africa,* 59; Mortimer, *France and the Africans,* 172.

26. Rioux, *Fourth Republic,* 166; Mortimer, *France and the Africans,* 172.

27. Rioux, *Fourth Republic,* 110, 165–66.

28. Kéïta, *P.D.G.,* 1:292.

29. Ibid., 1:293; Morgenthau, *Political Parties in French-Speaking West Africa,* 30, 55–56; Virginia Thompson and Richard Adloff, *French West Africa* (New York: Greenwood Press, 1969), 45, 58–60; Victor D. Du Bois, *Guinea's Prelude to Independence: Political Activity, 1945–58,* West Africa Series 5, no. 6 (New York: American Universities Field Staff, 1962), 3; e-mail communications from Pierre Gouhier, 15 and 27 March 2006.

For the impact of the expanded rural franchise in Dahomey, see Martin Staniland, "The Three-Party System in Dahomey: I, 1946–56," *Journal of African History* 14, no. 2 (1973): 291, 296–97, 301–3, 312; Martin Staniland, "The Three-Party System in Dahomey: II, 1956–1957," *Journal of African History* 14, no. 3 (1973): 496, 500–504.

30. Morgenthau, *Political Parties in French-Speaking West Africa,* 397; Mortimer, *France and the Africans,* 168.

31. Morgenthau, *Political Parties in French-Speaking West Africa,* 55–56, 56n1; Kéïta, *P.D.G.,* 1:124; Thomas Hodgkin, *Nationalism in Colonial Africa* (New York: New York University Press, 1957), 149; Kenneth Robinson, "Political Development in

French West Africa," in *Africa in the Modern World,* ed. Calvin W. Stillman (Chicago: University of Chicago Press, 1955), 163; Patrick Manning, *Francophone Sub-Saharan Africa, 1880–1985* (New York: Cambridge University Press, 1988), 143.

32. Thompson and Adloff, *French West Africa,* 60; Odile Goerg, "Femmes Africaines et Politique: Les Colonisées au Féminin en Afrique Occidentale," *Clio,* no. 6 (1997), http://clio.revues.org/document378.html?format=print; e-mail communications from Pierre Gouhier, 15 and 27 March 2006. I am grateful to Pierre Gouhier for his precise explication of the May 23, 1951, franchise law.

33. Morgenthau, *Political Parties in French-Speaking West Africa,* 396–97; Thompson and Adloff, *French West Africa,* 47, 58–59.

Other figures differ slightly from those cited above. Kéïta claims that 95,563 Guinean voters (49 percent of those registered) had cast their ballots in the 1946 legislative elections. In contrast, 282,287 Guineans (73 percent of those registered) voted in the 1951 legislative elections. The governor of Guinea reports that 221,256 Guineans (56 percent of those registered) cast their ballots in 1951. See Kéïta, *P.D.G.,* 1:296; ANS, 2G55/152, Guinée Française, Gouverneur, "Rapport Politique Annuel, 1955," #281/APA.

34. Kéïta, *P.D.G.,* 1:301; Rivière, *Guinea,* 67.

35. Morgenthau, *Political Parties in French-Speaking West Africa,* 222, 224–25, 418; Rivière, *Guinea,* 67.

36. Morgenthau, *Political Parties in French-Speaking West Africa,* 418; Rivière, *Guinea,* 66–67.

37. Interview with Léon Maka, Conakry, 20 Feb. 1991; Kéïta, *P.D.G.,* 1:301.

38. ANS, 17G573, Haut Commissaire, Dakar, à Gouverneur, Guinée Française, Conakry, 25 June 1951, #591, AP.2; 17G573, Haut Commissaire, Dakar, à Ministre, FOM, Paris, 28 April 1952, #471, INT/AP.2. See also CRDA, Claude Gérard, "Incidents en Guinée Française, 1954–1955," *Afrique Informations,* no. 34, 15 March–1 April 1955, 3–4; Morgenthau, *Political Parties in French-Speaking West Africa,* 246; Rivière, *Guinea,* 67.

39. ANS, 20G136, "Note sur les Bureaux de Vote," n.d. (after 24 May 1951).

40. CRDA, Sékou Touré, "Les Candidats de la Liste d'Union Démocratique des Travailleurs et Anciens Combattants aux Élections Législatives du 17 Juin 1951—Circonscription Guinée," à M. le Président de l'Assemblée Nationale, Paris, in *P.D.G.-R.D.A., Parti Démocratique de Guinée, 1947–1959: Activités—Répression—Élections.* See also CRDA, Gérard, "Incidents en Guinée Française, 1954–1955," 3; Morgenthau, *Political Parties in French-Speaking West Africa,* 102–3; Mortimer, *France and the Africans,* 166–67; Kéïta, *P.D.G.,* 1:298–301.

For similar irregularities in Dahomey, see Staniland, "Three-Party System in Dahomey: I," 296–97.

41. Kéïta, *P.D.G.,* 1:298–301; Morgenthau, *Political Parties in French-Speaking West Africa,* 61.

42. CRDA, Gérard, "Incidents en Guinée Française, 1954–1955," 3.

43. AG, 1E41, Police, " . . . des Activités Politiques Actuelles," 27 June 1951.

44. CRDA, Touré, "Candidats de la Liste d'Union . . . aux Élections Législatives du 17 Juin 1951 . . . ," in *P.D.G.-R.D.A.;* Morgenthau, *Political Parties in French-Speaking*

West Africa, 102–3; Kéïta, *P.D.G.,* 1:303; Rivière, *Guinea,* 67; Manning, *Francophone Sub-Saharan Africa,* 144; Rioux, *Fourth Republic,* 166.

In 1951, both Barry Diawadou and Sékou Touré failed to win seats in the National Assembly elections. Although both candidacies had gone down in defeat, Sékou Touré received 11,648 more votes than his rival. Barry Diawadou's support was concentrated almost exclusively among the Peul in the Futa Jallon. Of the 20,423 votes cast for Barry Diawadou in 1951, 18,515 had come from the Futa region. Most of Sékou Touré's 32,071 votes had come from the forest region and Upper-Guinea, where he won 15,564 and 9,153 votes respectively.

In 1951, there were 393,628 registered voters in Guinea. By 1954, that figure had grown to 476,503, an increase of 82,875. Of the newly registered voters, 72,056 resided in the Futa Jallon. In areas of RDA strength—N'Zérékoré, Guéckédou, Forécariah, Kankan, Siguiri—a diminution of 10,627 registered voters was recorded between 1951 and 1954. Most of these had been declared ineligible and officially struck from the electoral lists.

Despite the decrease in registered voters in RDA strongholds, official records indicate that Sékou Touré gained nearly 54,000 votes in the 1954 legislative elections. Claude Gérard, a French journalist, militant Christian, and former regional leader in the French Resistance movement, claimed that these disparate results supported the RDA's charges of electoral fraud during the 1951 legislative elections. Given severe government repression against the RDA during the intervening period, the RDA's increased strength was even more remarkable.

CRDA, "Élections de Guinée," *Afrique Nouvelle,* no. 385, 22 Dec. 1954; Gérard, "Incidents en Guinée Française, 1954–1955," 3–5; IFAN, Claude Gérard, "Lettre Ouverte à Sékou Touré," *La Liberté,* 15 March 1955; Morgenthau, *Political Parties in French-Speaking West Africa,* 240, 397; Thompson and Adloff, *French West Africa,* 59.

45. Morgenthau, *Political Parties in French-Speaking West Africa,* 30–31, 223–24; Mortimer, *France and the Africans,* 166, 176; Thompson and Adloff, *French West Africa,* 60; Kéïta, *P.D.G.,* 1:240.

46. ANS, 17G573, Guinée Française, Services de Police, Conakry, "Compte-Rendu de la Réunion Publique du Parti Démocratique de Guinée Française (P.D.G.)—Ex-R.D.A.—tenue au Domicile d'Amara Soumah le 24 Octobre 1950 de 18h30 à 20 heures," 25 Oct. 1950, #1248/221, C/PS/BM; AG, AM-1339, Idiatou Camara, "La Contribution de la Femme de Guinée à la Lutte de Libération Nationale (1945–1958)," Mémoire de Fin d'Études Supérieures, Conakry, IPGAN, 1979, 33; Kéïta, *P.D.G.,* 1:238–39.

In 1991, informants in Guinea invariably referred to the preindependence political party as the "RDA." It was only after independence in 1958, and Guinea's disaffiliation from the interterritorial RDA, that the appellation "PDG" took root.

47. ANS, 17G573, "Les Partis Politiques en Guinée, 1er Semestre 1951"; 17G573, Gendarmerie, AOF, "En Guinée Française," 12 Sept. 1951, #174/4; 17G573, Guinée Française, Services de Police, Conakry, "Rapport de Quinzaine du 1er au 15 Octobre 1951," #1847/1019, C/PS.2; 17G573, Guinée Française, Services de Police, "Revue Trimestrielle, 3ème Trimestre," 24 Nov. 1951; 17G573, Comité Directeur, P.D.G., "Analyse de la Situation Politique en Afrique Noire et des Méthodes du R.D.A. en Vue de Dégager un Programme d'Action," ca. 14 Jan. 1952; Kéïta, *P.D.G.,* 1:238, 241–42;

Morgenthau, *Political Parties in French-Speaking West Africa,* 26, 98; Hodgkin, *Nationalism in Colonial Africa,* 147.

48. ANS, 17G573, Police, ". . . Réunion Publique du Parti Démocratique de Guinée Française . . . ," 25 Oct. 1950; Kéïta, *P.D.G.,* 1:242, 339, 2:113; Jean Suret-Canale, "La Fin de la Chefferie en Guinée," *Journal of African History* 7, no. 3 (1966): 481.

49. In the mid-1950s, the RDA began to disband its ethnic and regional committees in order to promote national rather than ethnic identity. By 1956, most local committees were organized exclusively on neighborhood or village, rather than ethnic or regional, bases. However, some ethnic committees survived through 1957. ANS, 17G622, Guinée Française, Services de Police, "Renseignements A/S Conférence Publique d'Information, tenue à Conakry, Salle du Cinéma 'VOX,' le Vendredi 18 Octobre 1957, sur les Travaux du Congrès de Bamako et les Prochaines Élections aux Bureaux-Directeurs des S/Sections P.D.G.," 19 Oct. 1957, #2350/875, C/PS.2; Kéïta, *P.D.G.,* 1:241; 2:113, 178–79; Morgenthau, *Political Parties in French-Speaking West Africa,* 249; B. Ameillon, *La Guinée: Bilan d'une Indépendance* (Paris: François Maspero, 1964), 21; R. W. Johnson, "The Parti Démocratique de Guinée and the Mamou 'Deviation,'" in *African Perspectives: Papers in the History, Politics and Economics of Africa Presented to Thomas Hodgkin,* ed. Christopher Allen and R. W. Johnson (New York: Cambridge University Press, 1970), 355.

50. ANS, 17G573, "Partis Politiques en Guinée, 1er Semestre 1951."

51. ANS, 17G573, Police, "Rapport de Quinzaine du 1er au 15 Octobre 1951."

52. ANS, 17G573, Police, "Revue Trimestrielle, 3ème Trimestre," 24 Nov. 1951.

53. Morgenthau, *Political Parties in French-Speaking West Africa,* 231; Kéïta, *P.D.G.,* 1:240; Jean Suret-Canale, *La République de Guinée* (Paris: Éditions Sociales, 1970), 146; Elizabeth Schmidt, "Top Down or Bottom Up? Nationalist Mobilization Reconsidered, with Special Reference to Guinea (French West Africa)," *American Historical Review* 110, no. 4 (Oct. 2005): 993–95.

54. *La Liberté,* 28 Dec. 1954, quoted in Morgenthau, *Political Parties in French-Speaking West Africa,* 235. *La Liberté* was the official party newspaper from 1951 through independence.

55. ANS, 17G586, Guinée Française, Services de Police, "Renseignements *Objet:* Réunion Publique R.D.A. à Conakry et ses Suites," 8 Sept. 1954, #2606/942, C/PS.2; 17G586, Guinée Française, Services de Police, "Renseignements *Objet:* Fêtes Musulmanes à Conakry," 26 May 1955, #1054/439, C/PS.2; Morgenthau, *Political Parties in French-Speaking West Africa,* 236–37; Camara, "Contribution de la Femme," 61; Hodgkin, *African Political Parties,* 136.

56. Kéïta, *P.D.G.,* 1:242.

57. ANS, 17G573, P.D.G., "Analyse de la Situation Politique . . . et des Méthodes du R.D.A. . . . ," ca. 14 Jan. 1952; 17G573, Guinée Française, Services de Police, "Renseignements *Objet:* Section R.D.A. du Kankan," 21 Oct. 1954, #2842/1090, C/PS.2; Suret-Canale, "Fin de la Chefferie en Guinée," 481.

58. ANS, 17G586, Guinée Française, Services de Police, Kankan, "Renseignements A/S Entretien à Kankan de Sékou Touré (Sily) avec Magassouba Moriba et Touré Sékou (Chavanel) sur Cas Lamine Kaba et Instructions sur Organisation Intérieure Sections R.D.A.," 17 Nov. 1954, #2955/1158, C/PS.2; Kéïta, *P.D.G.,* 1:242.

59. CRDA, Madéïra Kéïta, "Instructions pour les Camarades de N'Zérékoré," Conakry, 9 Dec. 1949, in *P.D.G.-R.D.A.*

60. ANS, 17G573, Guinée Française, Services de Police, "Renseignements A/S Plan de Travail Élaboré par le Comité Directeur de la Section Guinéenne du R.D.A.," 4 April 1950, #315/173, C/PS/BM; Morgenthau, *Political Parties in French-Speaking West Africa,* 231.

61. ANS, 17G573, "Partis Politiques en Guinée, 1er Semestre 1951."

62. ANS, 17G573, Gendarmerie, "En Guinée Française," 12 Sept. 1951. See also interview with Léon Maka, 25 Feb. 1991; Hodgkin, *African Political Parties,* 125, 145–46; Ameillon, *Guinée,* 22; Elizabeth Schmidt, *Mobilizing the Masses: Gender, Ethnicity, and Class in the Nationalist Movement in Guinea, 1939–1958* (Portsmouth, NH: Heinemann, 2005), 52, 102–3, 106.

63. ANS, 17G573, Guinée Française, Services de Police, "Renseignements A/S Activité du R.D.A. à N'Zérékoré," 10 Oct. 1951, #1820/1003, C/PS.2.

64. ANS, 17G573, Direction Générale de l'Intérieur, Service des Affaires Politiques, Dakar, à Gouverneur, Guinée Française, Conakry, 19 Oct. 1951, #906, INT/AP.2.

65. Although the Guinean section of the RDA had been officially registered in 1947, in the early 1950s the government claimed that each new subsection also had to be registered with the government. Until the government recognized the subsection through a notice in the *Journal Officiel,* the activities of that body were deemed illegal. ANS, 17G573, Comité Directeur, P.D.G., Conakry, "Rapport à la Délégation du Comité de Coordination et Groupe Parlementaire R.D.A., Assemblée Nationale, Paris," 14 Jan. 1952, #1.

66. ANS, 17G573, Guinée Française, Services de Police, "Renseignements A/S Activité R.D.A.," 12 Jan. 1952, #88/51, C/PS.2. See also 17G573, P.D.G., "Rapport à . . . Comité de Coordination et Groupe Parlementaire R.D.A. . . . ," 14 Jan. 1952.

67. ANS, 17G573, Ray Autra, Comité Directeur, P.D.G., "Rapport sur la Situation Politique du Cercle de N'Zérékoré," N'Zérékoré, 1 March 1951; Suret-Canale, "Fin de la Chefferie en Guinée," 481.

68. ANS, 17G573, Gouvernement Général de l'AOF, Cabinet, Bureau Technique de Liaison et de Coordination, "Note de Renseignements *Objet:* Activité Politique et Sociale en Guinée pendant le Mois de Décembre 1949," 15 Jan. 1950 #141, CAB/LC/DK; 17G573, Guinée Française, Services de Police, Conakry, "Rapport Hebdomadaire, Semaine du 17 au 23 Septembre 1951," #1676/898, C/PS.2; 17G573, Guinée Française, Services de Police, "Renseignements A/S Parti Démocratique Guinéen (R.D.A.)," 20 Sept. 1951, #1649/881, C/PS.2.

69. ANS, 17G573, Guinée Française, Services de Police, "Renseignements A/S les Démissions du R.D.A.," 3 Oct. 1951, #1747/954, C/PS.2; 17G573, Guinée Française, Services de Police, "Renseignements A/S Propagande R.D.A. à N'Zérékoré," 24 Oct. 1951, #1934/1071, C/PS.2; 17G573, Gouverneur, Guinée Française, Conakry, à Haut Commissaire, Dakar, 21 Dec. 1951, #503/APA. For military veterans' varying attitudes toward the RDA, see Schmidt, *Mobilizing the Masses,* chap. 2.

70. AG, 1E42, Guinée Française, Services de Police, "Renseignements A/S le R.D.A. à Guéckédou," 2 Nov. 1951, #1994/1109/C/PS.2.

71. ANS, 17G573, Guinée Française, Services de Police, 6 Aug. 1951.

72. ANS, 17G573, Police, "Rapport de Quinzaine du 1er au 15 Octobre 1951"; AG, 1E41, Guinée Française, Services de Police, "Renseignements A/S Politique Actuelle du R.D.A.," 19 Oct. 1951, #1890/1048/C/PS.2; 1E41, Guinée Française, Services de Police, "Renseignements A/S Attitude Comité Directeur du R.D.A. Locale," 2 Nov. 1951, #1999/C/PS.2.

73. ANS, 17G573, Guinée Française, Administrateur du Cercle de Labé, Labé, à Gouverneur, Guinée Française, Conakry, 9 Oct. 1950, #167 C; 17G573, Guinée Française, Services de Police, "Renseignements A/S Activité Politique," 18 July 1951, #1040/490, C/PS.2; 17G573, Police, "Rapport Hebdomadaire, Semaine du 23 au 30 Septembre 1951, Semaine du 1er au 7 Octobre 1951"; 17G573, Guinée Française, Services de Police, Conakry, "Rapport Hebdomadaire, Semaine du 29 Octobre au 4 Novembre 1951," #2008/1118, C/PS.2; 17G271, Gouverneur, Guinée Française, Conakry, à Haut Commissaire, Dakar, "A/S Activité Syndicale," 25 Feb. 1952, #85/APA; 17G573, Haut Commissaire à Ministre, FOM, 28 April 1952; CRDA, Ministre, FOM, Paris, à Haut Commissaire, Dakar, 21 March 1952.

74. ANS, 17G573, Guinée Française, Services de Police, Conakry, "Rapport Hebdomadaire, Semaine du 10 au 16 Septembre 1951," 18 Sept. 1951, #1622/870, C/PS; 17G573, Police, "Rapport de Quinzaine du 1er au 15 Octobre 1951."

75. ANS, 17G271, Gouverneur à Haut Commissaire, "A/S Activité Syndicale," 25 Feb. 1952; CRDA, Ministre, FOM à Haut Commissaire, 21 March 1952.
At its August 1953 congress in Labé, the African teachers' union adopted a principle of autonomy, thus ending its affiliation with the CGT. See ANS, 2G53/187, Guinée Française, Governor, "Revues Trimestrielles des Événements, 3ème Trimestre 1953," 12 Sept. 1953, #862/APA.

76. ANS 17G573, Haut Commissaire à Ministre, FOM, 28 April 1952. See also ANS, 17G573, Guinée Française, Services de Police, "Renseignements A/S Propagande R.D.A. à l'Hôpital Ballay (Conakry)," 30 Aug. 1951, #1395/723, C/PS.2.

77. ANS, 17G573, Police, "Rapport Hebdomadaire, Semaine du 29 Octobre au 4 Novembre 1951"; Aimé Césaire, *Volcans Coloniaux* (Paris, 1951); Robin D. G. Kelley, "A Poetics of Anticolonialism," Introduction to *Discourse on Colonialism,* by Aimé Césaire (New York: Monthly Review Press, 2000), 23; Maurice Thorez, *Fils du Peuple* (Paris: Éditions Sociales, 1937).
PCF secretary-general Maurice Thorez was dubbed the "fils du peuple." This was also the title of his autobiography, first published in 1937 and reprinted in 1949. See George Ross, *Workers and Communists in France: From Popular Front to Eurocommunism* (Berkeley: University of California Press, 1982), 13; "Maurice Thorez 'Fils du Peuple.'" http://www.thefileroom.org/documents/dyn/DisplayCase.cfm/id/219.

78. ANS, 17G573, Guinée Française, Services de Police, 6 Aug. 1951.

79. ANS, 17G573, Guinée Française, Services de Police, Conakry, "Rapport Hebdomadaire, Semaine du 27 Août au 2 Septembre 1951," #1435/745, C/PS.2.

80. ANS, 17G573, "Partis Politiques en Guinée, 1er Semestre 1951."

81. ANS, 17G573, Guinée Française, Services de Police, "Renseignements A/S Correspondance R.D.A.," 27 Sept. 1951.

82. ANS, 17G573, Guinée Française, Services de Police, 16 Oct. 1951, #1863, C/PS.2; 17G573, Guinée Française, Services de Police, Conakry, "Rapport Hebdomadaire,

Semaine du 15 au 21 Octobre 1951," #1907/1053, C/PS.2; 17G573, "Partis Politiques en Guinée, 1er Semestre 1951." See also Morgenthau, *Political Parties in French-
Speaking West Africa,* 98.

83. ANS, 17G573, Police, "Rapport Hebdomadaire, Semaine du 29 Octobre au 4
Novembre 1951." See also 17G573, Haut Commissaire à Ministre, FOM, 28 April 1952.

84. ANS, 17G573, Police, "Rapport Hebdomadaire, Semaine du 15 au 21 Octobre 1951."

85. ANS, 17G573, Police, "Rapport Hebdomadaire, Semaine du 29 Octobre au 4
Novembre 1951." See also 17G573, Haut Commissaire à Ministre, FOM, 28 April
1952.

86. ANS, 17G573, "Partis Politiques en Guinée, 1er Semestre 1951"; 17G573,
Police, "Rapport de Quinzaine du 1er au 15 Octobre 1951."

87. Mortimer, *France and the Africans,* 180; Kéïta, *P.D.G.,* 1:257; Frank Costigliola, *France and the United States: The Cold Alliance since World War II* (New York: Twayne,
1992), 66–67; Frederick Cooper, *Decolonization and African Society: The Labor Question
in French and British Africa* (New York: Cambridge University Press, 1996), 285, 409;
James A. Jones, *Industrial Labor in the Colonial World: Workers of the Chemin de Fer Dakar-
Niger, 1881–1963* (Portsmouth, NH: Heinemann, 2002), 66.

88. Hodgkin, *Nationalism in Colonial Africa,* 129; Rivière, *Guinea,* 53–55; Cooper,
Decolonization and African Society, 285, 409.

89. Cooper, *Decolonization and African Society,* 409.

90. ANS, 21G13, Sûreté, "État d'Esprit de la Population," 1–15 Dec. 1950; 17G573,
Haut Commissaire à Ministre, FOM, 28 April 1952; CRDA, Ministre, FOM, Paris, à
Haut Commissaire, Dakar, 21 March 1952; AG, 1E41, Guinée Française, Services de Po-
lice, "Fiche de Renseignements Biographiques Relative à M. Sékou Touré," 2 Jan. 1956;
Mortimer, *France and the Africans,* 200; Cooper, *Decolonization and African Society,* 409.

91. Cooper, *Decolonization and African Society,* 410, 414; Chafer, *End of Empire in
French West Africa,* 123.

92. ANS, 17G573, "Partis Politiques en Guinée, 1er Semestre 1951." See also
Cooper, *Decolonization and African Society,* 409–10.

93. ANS, 17G573, Haut Commissaire à Ministre, FOM, 28 April 1952.

94. Georges Chaffard, *Les Carnets Secrets de la Décolonisation* (Paris: Calmann-
Lévy, 1967), 2:181; Cooper, *Decolonization and African Society,* 604n29. See also Morgenthau, *Political Parties in French-Speaking West Africa,* 243.

95. Cooper, *Decolonization and African Society,* 410.

96. AG, 1E41, Côte d'Ivoire, Services de Police, Abidjan, "Renseignements A/S
Position du R.D.A. Après le Congrès Cégétiste de Bamako," 5 Nov. 1951, #5446/757/
PS/BM/C. See also Cooper, *Decolonization and African Society,* 410; Chafer, *End of Em-
pire in French West Africa,* 123.

97. ANS, 17G573, Police, "Rapport Hebdomadaire, Semaine du 29 Octobre au 4
Novembre 1951." See also 17G573, Haut Commissaire à Ministre, FOM, 28 April
1952. Cooper, *Decolonization and African Society,* 410.

98. See, e.g., ANS, 17G573, Guinée Française, Services de Police, "Renseignements A/S Diagne Ibrahima, Secrétaire de la Section R.D.A. de N'Zérékoré," 8 Nov.
1951, #2033/1137, C/PS.2; 17G573, Guinée Française, Services de Police, "Rensei-

gnements A/S Démission du R.D.A. de Savané Morikandian," 14 Nov. 1951, #2093/1167, C/PS.2; AG, 1E41, Guinée Française, Services de Police, "Renseignements A/S Réunion R.D.A.," 5 Dec. 1951, #2282/1293/C/PS.2; 1E41, Guinée Française, Services de Police, "Renseignements A/S Réunion R.D.A.," 19 Dec. 1951, #2394/1350/C/PS.2.

99. ANS, 17G573, Police, " . . . Diagne Ibrahima, Secrétaire de la Section R.D.A. de N'Zérékoré," 8 Nov. 1951.

100. ANS, 17G573, Police, " . . . Démission du R.D.A. de Savané Morikandian," 14 Nov. 1951.

101. AG, 1E41, Guinée Française, Services de Police, "Renseignements A/S Démissions du R.D.A.," 4 Dec. 1951, #2261/1279/C/PS.2. See also 1E41, Guinée Française, Services de Police, "Renseignements A/S Lettre Bandja, Richard à Félix Houphouët (copie)," 24 June 1952, #1129/627/C/PS.2; ANS, 17G573, Haut Commissaire à Ministre, FOM, 28 April 1952.

102. AG, 1E41, Police, " . . . Réunion R.D.A.," 5 Dec. 1951.

103. AG, 1E41, Police, " . . . Réunion R.D.A.," 19 Dec. 1951.

104. ANS, 17G573, Police, "Rapport Hebdomadaire, Semaine du 29 Octobre au 4 Novembre 1951"; AG, 1E41, Guinée Française, Services de Police, "Renseignements A/S Position de Madéïra Kéïta, Secrétaire Général du P.D.G.," 19 Nov. 1951, #2123/1187/C/PS.2; 1E41, Guinée Française, Services de Police, "Renseignements A/S Réunion R.D.A.," 21 Nov. 1951, #2149/1300/C/PS.2; 1E41, Police, " . . . Réunion R.D.A.," 19 Dec. 1951.

A member of the French parliament could not be arrested for crimes or misdemeanors unless caught committing an infraction, or unless the National Assembly had suspended the parliamentarian's immunity for "inciting rebellion." In contrast, parliamentarians' followers could be—and were—imprisoned. Morgenthau, *Political Parties in French-Speaking West Africa,* 78, 97, 123, 188, 190, 193, 241; Mortimer, *France and the Africans,* 146.

105. AG, 1E41, Police, " . . . Réunion R.D.A.," 19 Dec. 1951.

Houphouët-Boigny's fears were not unfounded. In 1947, the National Assembly revoked the immunity of three Malagasy deputies whose followers were engaged in acts of rebellion. The deputies subsequently were arrested. In January 1950, Ivory Coast authorities had attempted, but failed, to arrest Houphouët-Boigny, despite his parliamentary immunity. Morgenthau, *Political Parties in French-Speaking West Africa,* 78, 97, 193–95; Chaffard, *Carnets Secrets de la Décolonisation,* 1:112–16; Mortimer, *France and the Africans,* 117, 147; Milcent, *A.O.F. Entre en Scène,* 50.

106. AG, 1E41, Police, " . . . Réunion R.D.A.," 19 Dec. 1951. See also 1E41, Police, " . . . Réunion R.D.A.," 5 Dec. 1951.

107. A law of February 6, 1952, renamed the African general councils "territorial assemblies." Morgenthau, *Political Parties in French-Speaking West Africa,* 56–57; Mortimer, *France and the Africans,* 173, 174n1.

108. ANS, 17G573, Guinée Française, Services de Police, "Renseignements A/S Soumah Amara, Conseiller R.D.A.," 26 April 1949, #378, C/PS; 17G573, Police, " . . . Activité R.D.A.," 12 Jan. 1952; 17G573, Guinée Française, Services de Police, "Renseignements A/S Passage Député Houphouët-Boigny, Aérodrome, Conakry, le

25/2/1952," ca. 26 Feb. 1952, #369/231, C/PS.2; 17G573, Haut Commissaire à Ministre, FOM, 28 April 1952; Kéïta, *P.D.G.,* 1:93, 306.

109. Amara Soumah defeated the clergy's candidate, Louis David Soumah, 6,106 to 344. ANS, 17G573, Police, ". . . Soumah Amara, Conseiller R.D.A.," 26 April 1949; 17G573, Haut Commissaire à Ministre, FOM, 28 April 1952; AG, 1E41, Police, " . . . Réunion Publique du R.D.A., . . . Kankan, le 8 Avril 1952," 10 April 1952; 1E41, Guinée Française, Services de Police, "Renseignements A/S R.D.A. et Mont-louis, Joseph," 12 April 1952, #703/405/C/PS.2; Morgenthau, *Political Parties in French-Speaking West Africa,* 61; Mortimer, *France and the Africans,* 174; Suret-Canale, *République de Guinée,* 145; Rivière, *Guinea,* 67; Kéïta, *P.D.G.,* 1:306–8; Sidiki Kobélé Kéïta, *Ahmed Sékou Touré: L'Homme et son Combat Anti-Colonial (1922–1958)* (Conakry: Éditions S.K.K., 1998), 113–14.

110. ANS, 17G573, Police, " . . . Soumah Amara, Conseiller R.D.A.," 26 April 1949; 17G573, Guinée Française, Services de Police, "Renseignements A/S Activités R.D.A.," 19 May 1949, #470, C/PS; Kéïta, *P.D.G.,* 1:195.

111. ANS, 17G573, Niger, Services de Police, "Renseignements A/S Copie Document P.D.G.," 3 July 1952, #530/C/355/PS.

112. Mortimer, *France and the Africans,* 156, 161, 177–78.

113. Ibid., 178; Milcent, *A.O.F. Entre en Scène,* 82–83; Morgenthau, *Political Parties in French-Speaking West Africa,* 98; Thompson and Adloff, *French West Africa,* 90; Immanuel Wallerstein, *The Road to Independence: Ghana and the Ivory Coast* (Paris: Mouton and Co., 1964), 49.

As a result of his ouster from the party, d'Arboussier also lost his seat in the Assembly of the French Union because the RDA refused to support his candidacy. D'Arboussier and the RDA were reconciled in 1956, when he was allowed to rejoin the party. In 1957, he was elected to the Grand Council in Dakar, where he served first as vice president and later as president. He also was elected one of four secretaries of the interterritorial RDA. Morgenthau, *Political Parties in French-Speaking West Africa,* 98, 159, 303–4, 309; Mortimer, *France and the Africans,* 156, 161, 177–78, 219–20, 251, 255, 266, 279–80, 293; Milcent, *A.O.F. Entre en Scène,* 88–89; Hodgkin, *African Political Parties,* 71; Chaffard, *Carnets Secrets de la Décolonisation,* 1:127, 2:290; Thompson and Adloff, *French West Africa,* 96; Kéïta, *P.D.G.,* 1:236; Zolberg, *One-Party Government in the Ivory Coast,* 222n10; Chafer, *End of Empire in French West Africa,* 138n2; André Blanchet, *L'Itinéraire des Partis Africains depuis Bamako* (Paris: Librarie Plon, 1958), 41.

114. ANS, 17G573, Gouverneur, Guinée Française, Conakry, à Haut Commissaire, Dakar, 7 Oct. 1952, #444/APA.

115. AG, 1E41, Guinée Française, Services de Police, "Renseignements A/S P.C.F. et R.D.A.," 18 Sept. 1952, #1776/873/C/PS.2.

116. ANS, 17G573, Gouverneur à Haut Commissaire, 7 Oct. 1952.

Diallo previously had been transferred from one territory to another due to his political activities. See ANS, 17G573, Police, " . . . Propagande R.D.A. a l'Hôpital Ballay . . . ," 30 Aug. 1951; 17G573, Police, "Rapport Hebdomadaire, Semaine du 27 Août au 2 Septembre 1951."

117. ANS, 17G573, Gouverneur à Haut Commissaire, 7 Oct. 1952. See also 17G573, Police, "Rapport Hebdomadaire, Semaine du 27 Août au 2 Septembre 1951";

17G573, Guinée Française, Services de Police, "Renseignements A/S Activités Actuelles R.D.A. et C.G.T.," 2 Oct. 1951, #1730/940, C/PS.2; 17G573, Police, " . . . Activité R.D.A.," 12 Jan. 1952.

118. ANS, 17G573, Gouverneur à Haut Commissaire, 7 Oct. 1952. For further discussion of military veterans' role in the RDA, see Schmidt, *Mobilizing the Masses,* chap. 2.

119. The forest region's isolation vis-à-vis the capital gradually diminished after the opening of the Conakry-Monrovia road in 1952. Suret-Canale, "Fin de la Chefferie en Guinée," 482.

120. ANS, 17G573, Gouverneur à Haut Commissaire, 7 Oct. 1952.

121. Kéïta, *Ahmed Sékou Touré: Combat Anti-Colonial,* 117–18.

122. Kéïta, *P.D.G.,* 1:309.

Peasants were required to contribute to the Société Indigène de Prévoyance, a government-run insurance fund in which they had no voice. The mandatory payments were the focus of considerable discontent. AG, 1E38, Guinée Française, Cercle de Macenta, "Rapport Politique Annuel, 1948"; 1E38, Guinée Française, Cercle de Kankan, "Rapport Politique Annuel, 1948"; Kéïta, *P.D.G.* 1:116; Suret-Canale, "Fin de la Chefferie en Guinée," 475; Jacques Richard-Molard, *Afrique Occidentale Française* (Paris: Éditions Berger-Levrault, 1952), 156.

123. ANS, 2G53/187, "Revues Trimestrielles des Événements, 3ème Trimestre 1953," 12 Sept. 1953; Kéïta, *P.D.G.,* 1:309, 311; Suret-Canale, "Fin de la Chefferie en Guinée," 482.

124. ANS, 2G53/187, "Revues Trimestrielles des Événements, 3ème Trimestre 1953," 12 Sept. 1953.

125. ANS, 2G53/187, "Revues Trimestrielles des Événements, 3ème Trimestre 1953," 12 Sept. 1953.

126. Morgenthau, *Political Parties in French-Speaking West Africa,* 61; Kéïta, *P.D.G.,* 1:320–21; Suret-Canale, "Fin de la Chefferie en Guinée," 481.

127. ANS, 17G573, Police, "Rapport de Quinzaine du 1er au 15 Octobre 1951."

CHAPTER 3

1. See, e.g., ANS, 1K44, Haut Commissaire, Dakar, à FOM, Paris, 16 June 1950, #300–301; 1K44, Inspecteur Général du Travail, Dakar, "Rapport: Fixation du Salaire Minimum en Guinée et Grève des 9 et 10 Juin 1950," 19 June 1950, #113/C IGT/AOF; 2G55/152, Guinée Française, Gouverneur, "Rapport Politique Annuel, 1955," #281/APA. For further discussion of the RDA and the Guinean trade union movement, see Elizabeth Schmidt, *Mobilizing the Masses: Gender, Ethnicity, and Class in the Nationalist Movement in Guinea, 1939–1958* (Portsmouth, NH: Heinemann, 2005), chap. 3.

2. Ruth Schachter Morgenthau, *Political Parties in French-Speaking West Africa* (Oxford: Clarendon Press, 1964), 229; Sidiki Kobélé Kéïta, *Le P.D.G.: Artisan de l'Indépendance Nationale en Guinée (1947–1958)* (Conakry: I.N.R.D.G., Bibliothèque Nationale, 1978), 1:308; R. W. Johnson, "The Parti Démocratique de Guinée and the Mamou 'Deviation,'" in *African Perspectives: Papers in History, Politics and Economics of*

Africa Presented to Thomas Hodgkin, ed. Christopher Allen and R. W. Johnson (New York: Cambridge University Press, 1970), 354.

3. Interview with Mamadou Bela Doumbouya, Conakry, 26 Jan. 1991; Schmidt, *Mobilizing the Masses,* chap. 3.

4. Kéïta, *P.D.G.,* 1:285.

5. Morgenthau, *Political Parties in French-Speaking West Africa,* 229, 414. See also Edward Mortimer, *France and the Africans, 1944–1960: A Political History* (New York: Walker and Co., 1969), 200.

6. Sidiki Kobélé Kéïta, *Ahmed Sékou Touré: L'Homme et son Combat Anti-Colonial (1922–1958)* (Conakry: Éditions S.K.K., 1998), 87; Ruth Schachter and Immanuel Wallerstein, "French Africa's Road to Independence: 1," *West Africa* 1, no. 2140 (19 April 1958): 372; Ruth Schachter and Immanuel Wallerstein, "French Africa's Road to Independence: 2," *West Africa* 2, no. 2141 (26 April 1958): 395.

7. Morgenthau, *Political Parties in French-Speaking West Africa,* 229; Frederick Cooper, *Decolonization and African Society: The Labor Question in French and British Africa* (New York: Cambridge University Press, 1996), 310–11.

8. Kéïta, *P.D.G.,* 1:301, 306, 309, 311; Kéïta, *Ahmed Sékou Touré: Combat Anti-Colonial,* 113–14.

9. Morgenthau, *Political Parties in French-Speaking West Africa,* 106; Kéïta, *P.D.G.,* 1:312.

10. The RPF was the cornerstone of the Républicains Sociaux, a Gaullist parliamentary group. After his electoral victory, Barry Diawadou affiliated with the Républicains Sociaux in parliament. CRDA, "Élections de Guinée," *Afrique Nouvelle,* no. 385, 22 Dec. 1954; Claude Gérard, "Incidents en Guinée Française, 1954–1955," *Afrique Informations,* no. 34, 15 March-1 April 1955, 3; Morgenthau, *Political Parties in French-Speaking West Africa,* 222, 233, 240; Mortimer, *France and the Africans,* 11, 205–6, 228; Kéïta, *P.D.G.,* 1:312–13, 315, 318; Victor D. Du Bois, *Guinea's Prelude to Independence: Political Activity, 1945–58,* West Africa Series 5, no. 6 (New York: American Universities Field Staff, 1962), 7, 15n11.

11. Morgenthau, *Political Parties in French-Speaking West Africa,* 233.

12. Ibid.

13. Ibid.; Mortimer, *France and the Africans,* 205; Thomas E. O'Toole, *Historical Dictionary of Guinea (Republic of Guinea/Conakry),* 2nd ed. (Metuchen, NJ: Scarecrow Press, 1987), 26.

The Amicale Gilbert Vieillard president Abdoulaye Diallo was not the same individual as the CGT trade union leader Abdoulaye Diallo, who was based in the French Soudan. For the latter, see chap. 4.

14. For further discussion of ethnicity and class as determinants of voters' choice, see Schmidt, *Mobilizing the Masses,* chaps. 3 and 6.

15. ANS, 17G586, Guinée Française, Services de Police, "Renseignements *Objet:* R.D.A. Guinée et Madéïra Kéïta," 2 March 1955, #491/195, C/PS.2; interview with Mamadou Bela Doumbouya, 26 Jan. 1991; Morgenthau, *Political Parties in French-Speaking West Africa,* 233; Schmidt, *Mobilizing the Masses,* chaps. 3 and 6; Elizabeth Schmidt, "Top Down or Bottom Up? Nationalist Mobilization Reconsidered, with Special Reference to Guinea (French West Africa)," *American Historical Review* 110, no. 4 (Oct. 2005): 990, 1002–4.

16. ANS, 17G586, Police, " . . . R.D.A. Guinée et Madéïra Kéïta," 2 March 1955; interview with Bocar Biro Barry, Conakry, 21 Jan. 1991.

17. Morgenthau, *Political Parties in French-Speaking West Africa*, 12, 20, 251; Jean Suret-Canale, *La République de Guinée* (Paris: Éditions Sociales, 1970), 142–43. For further discussion of the hierarchical educational system in French West Africa, see Schmidt, "Top Down or Bottom Up?" 998–1001; Peggy R. Sabatier, "'Elite' Education in French West Africa: The Era of Limits, 1903–1945," *International Journal of African Historical Studies* 11, no. 2 (1978): 247–66.

18. ANS, 17G573, "Rapport Général d'Activité 1947–1950," présenté par Mamadou Madéïra Kéïta, Secrétaire Général, P.D.G., au Premier Congrès Territorial du Parti Démocratique de Guinée (Section Guinéenne du Rassemblement Démocratique Africain), Conakry, 15–18 Oct. 1950; Morgenthau, *Political Parties in French-Speaking West Africa*, 20, 251; Suret-Canale, *République de Guinée*, 142–43. For a more general discussion of this phenomenon, see John Breuilly, *Nationalism and the State*, 2nd ed. (Chicago: University of Chicago Press, 1994), 48.

Notable RDA adversaries among Ponty alumni in Guinea included several members of the French parliament: National Assembly Deputies Yacine Diallo, Mamba Sano, and Barry Diawadou, and Council of the Republic Senator Fodé Mamadou Touré. Another Ponty graduate was Framoï Bérété, president of the anti-RDA ethnic association the Union du Mandé and a member of the equally hostile Comité d'Entente Guinéenne. Koumandian Kéïta, secretary-general of the African teachers' union, was a graduate of École Normale de Katibougou, the Ponty equivalent in the French Soudan. Morgenthau, *Political Parties in French-Speaking West Africa*, 222, 224–25; Johnson, "Parti Démocratique de Guinée," 358, 368; interviews in Conakry with Bocar Biro Barry, 21 Jan. 1991; Léon Maka, 20 Feb. 1991; Fodé Mamdou Touré, 13 March 1991.

19. Morgenthau, *Political Parties in French-Speaking West Africa*, 20–21.

20. Interview with Bocar Biro Barry, 21 Jan. 1991; Kéïta, *Ahmed Sékou Touré: Combat Anti-Colonial*, 10–11, 30; Suret-Canale, *République de Guinée*, 142.

Morgenthau contends that strains between the more and less educated Guinean elites were comparable to those that existed in colonial Ghana. Basil Davidson writes that militants who mobilized for the Convention People's Party, which ultimately became the ruling party of independent Ghana, were derisively referred to by more educated opponents as "Standard VII Boys" or, in reference to homeless youths who organized for the party by night and slept on porches, "verandah boys, hooligans, flotsam and jetsam, town rabble." Morgenthau, *Political Parties in French-Speaking West Africa*, 20–21; Basil Davidson, *Black Star: A View of the Life and Times of Kwame Nkrumah*, 2nd ed. (Boulder: Westview Press, 1989), 68, 70. See also David Apter, *Ghana in Transition* (Princeton: Princeton University Press, 1963), 167, 207–8; Thomas Hodgkin, *African Political Parties: An Introductory Guide* (Gloucester, MA: Peter Smith, 1971), 30–31.

21. AG, 1E41, Guinée Française, Services de Police, "Fiche de Renseignements Biographiques Relative à M. Sékou Touré," 2 Jan. 1956; Morgenthau, *Political Parties in French-Speaking West Africa*, 12, 20, 251; Suret-Canale, *République de Guinée*, 142–43, 147; Kéïta, *Ahmed Sékou Touré: Combat Anti-Colonial*, 24, 29, 32, 36; Sidiki Kobélé Kéïta, *Ahmed Sékou Touré: L'Homme du 28 Septembre 1958*, 2nd ed. (Conakry: I.N.R.D.G.,

Bibliothèque Nationale, 1977), 29, 31; B. Ameillon, *La Guinée: Bilan d'une Indépendance* (Paris: François Maspero, 1964), 49.

22. ANS, 17G586, Guinée Française, Services de Police, Labé, "Renseignements *Objet:* Les A.C. et le R.D.A. dans le Cercle de Labé," 17 Feb. 1955, #374/150, C/PS.2; 17G586, Guinée Française, Services de Police, Kankan, "Renseignements A/S P.D.G. et Congrès de Dabola," 24 Sept. 1956, #1965/682, C/PS.2; 17G622, Guinée Française, Services de Police, "Renseignements A/S Rebondissement du Conflit des Enseignants Africains," 8 Nov. 1957, #2485/919, C/PS.2; interview with Bocar Biro Barry, Conakry, 29 Jan. 1991; Johnson, "Parti Démocratique de Guinée," 358. For the political role of Ponty-educated teachers prior to the establishment of the RDA, see Jean-Hervé Jézéquel, "Les Enseignants Comme Élite Politique en AOF (1930–1945): Des 'Meneurs de Galopins' dans l'Arène Politique," *Cahiers d'Études Africaines* 45, no. 2 (2005): 519–43.

23. Interview with Bocar Biro Barry, 21 Jan. 1991.

24. See chaps. 1 and 2.

25. Jean Suret-Canale, *French Colonialism in Tropical Africa, 1900–1945,* trans. Till Gottheiner (New York: Pica Press, 1971), 341, 374–75, 377, 381, 384, 388, 393n30, 393n31; Suret-Canale, *République de Guinée,* 136–37; Kéïta, *P.D.G.,* 1:73. For enrollment statistics, see ANS, 2G41/21, Guinée Française, Gouverneur, "Rapport Politique Annuel, 1941"; 2G42/22, Guinée Française, Gouverneur, "Rapport Politique Annuel, 1942"; 2G43/19, Guinée Française, Gouverneur, "Rapport Politique Annuel, 1943."

26. Suret-Canale, *French Colonialism in Tropical Africa,* 341, 374–75, 377, 381, 384, 388, 393n30, 393n31; Suret-Canale, *République de Guinée,* 136–37; Kéïta, *P.D.G.,* 1:73; Martin Klein, *Slavery and Colonial Rule in French West Africa* (New York: Cambridge University Press, 1998), 251; communication from Siba N. Grovogui, 24 Oct. 1991.

27. Suret-Canale, *French Colonialism in Tropical Africa,* 374–75, 377, 384, 388; Suret-Canale, *République de Guinée,* 136–37; Klein, *Slavery and Colonial Rule,* 251; interview with Léon Maka, 25 Feb. 1991; interview with Ibrahima Fofana, Conakry, 5 May 1991.

28. Kéïta, *P.D.G.,* 2:99; interview with Bocar Biro Barry, 21 Jan. 1991;

29. ANS, 2G53/187, Guinée Française, Governor, "Revues Trimestrielles des Événements, 3ème Trimestre 1953," 12 Sept. 1953, #862/APA; 2G55/150, Guinée Française, Gouverneur, "Rapport Politique Mensuel, Août 1955," 28 Sept. 1955, #487/APAS/CAB; 2G57/128, Guinée Française, Police et Sûreté, "Synthèse Mensuelle de Renseignements, Novembre 1957," 25 Nov. 1957, #2593/C/PS.2; 17G622, Guinée Française, Services de Police, "Renseignements A/S 6ème Congrès des Enseignants Africains qui s'est Ouvert à Mamou, le 6 Août Dernier," 10 Aug. 1957, #1800/692, C/PS.2; 17G622, Guinée Française, Services de Police, "Renseignements A/S Conférence Publique tenue dans la Salle du Cinéma de Mamou, par les Enseignants, le Samedi 10 Août Dernier," 16 Aug. 1957, #1837/709, C/PS.2; AG, 2D297, Guinée Française, Secrétaire Général du Comité de Coordination des Syndicats de l'Enseignement Primaire Public de l'AOF, Conakry, à Gouverneur, Conakry, 11 Oct. 1954, #1/CCE; interview with Bocar Biro Barry, 21 Jan. 1991; Johnson, "Parti Démocratique de Guinée," 358, 364.

30. ANS, 17G622, Guinée Française, Services de Police, "Renseignements A/S Répercussions à Mamou, de l'Article Intitulé 'Communiqué du P.D.G.' Publié dans le Dernier Numéro du Journal *La Liberté,* Organe de ce Parti," 6 Sept. 1957, #2029/773,

C/PS.2; 17G622, Guinée Française, Services de Police, "Renseignements A/S Exclusion du P.D.G./R.D.A. de Plusieurs Dirigeants de la S/Section de Mamou," 15 Nov. 1957, #25__/941, C/PS.2; interview with Bocar Biro Barry, 21 Jan. 1991; Johnson, "Parti Démocratique de Guinée," 358.

31. ANS, 2G54/160, Guinée Française, Gendarmerie Nationale, Détachement de l'AOF-Togo, Compagnie de la Guinée, "Fiche sur la Situation du Territoire de la Guinée au Cours du 2ème Trimestre 1954," Conakry, 9 July 1954, #89/4.

32. Quoted in CAOM, Carton 2144, dos. 1, Ministre, FOM, "Rapport Pruvost," 31 March 1955.

33. Morgenthau, *Political Parties in French-Speaking West Africa*, 233.

34. Ibid., 241–42; Mortimer, *France and the Africans*, 201–2; Jean-Pierre Rioux, *The Fourth Republic, 1944–1958*, trans. Godfrey Rogers (New York: Cambridge University Press, 1987), 216–18, 224–26, 465.

35. ANS, 2G55/152, "Rapport Politique Annuel, 1955." See also Kéïta, *P.D.G.*, 2:21.

Other sources provide slightly different figures: Out of 257,602 ballots cast, 147,701 (57.3 percent) were for Barry Diawadou; 85,906 (33.3 percent) were for Sékou Touré (RDA); 7,995 (3.1 percent) were for Barry III (DSG); and 16,005 (6.2 percent) were for various independents. Note that the figures for the DSG and independent parties are reversed. See CRDA, Gérard, "Incidents en Guinée Française, 1954–1955," 3; Morgenthau, *Political Parties in French-Speaking West Africa*, 233, 240; Mortimer, *France and the Africans*, 206.

36. Morgenthau, *Political Parties in French-Speaking West Africa*, 240.

37. Ibid., 103, 106, 240; Kéïta, *P.D.G.*, 1:316–18, 347; interview with Mamadou Bela Doumbouya, 26 Jan. 1991.

38. Morgenthau, *Political Parties in French-Speaking West Africa*, 241; Kéïta, *P.D.G.*, 1:129.

39. CRDA, Gérard, "Incidents en Guinée Française, 1954–1955," 5; "Élections Législatives Partielles de Guinée," 17 June 1954, in *P.D.G.-R.D.A., Parti Démocratique de Guinée, 1947–1959: Activités—Répression—Élections*; AG, AM-1339, Idiatou Camara, "La Contribution de la Femme de Guinée à la Lutte de Libération Nationale (1945–1958)," Mémoire de Fin d'Études Supérieures, Conakry, IPGAN, 1979, 77; Morgenthau, *Political Parties in French-Speaking West Africa*, 241; Kéïta, *P.D.G.*, 1:315.

40. CRDA, Gérard, "Incidents en Guinée Française, 1954–1955," 6; "Élections Législatives Partielles de Guinée," 17 June 1954, in *P.D.G.-R.D.A. . . . Activités—Répression—Élections*; Camara, "Contribution de la Femme," 77; Morgenthau, *Political Parties in French-Speaking West Africa*, 106, 240.

41. CRDA, "Élections Législatives Partielles de Guinée," 17 June 1954, in *P.D.G.-R.D.A. . . . Activités—Répression—Élections*; Morgenthau, *Political Parties in French-Speaking West Africa*, 240.

42. CRDA, Gérard, "Incidents en Guinée Française, 1954–1955," 7; "Élections Législatives Partielles de Guinée," 17 June 1954, in *P.D.G.-R.D.A. . . . Activités—Répression—Élections*; ANS, 20G136, Haut Commissaire, Dakar, à tous Gouverneurs, AOF, ca. November 1956; Morgenthau, *Political Parties in French-Speaking West Africa*, 240; Kenneth Robinson, "Senegal: The Elections to the Territorial Assembly, March

1957," in *Five Elections in Africa,* ed. W. J. M. MacKenzie and Kenneth Robinson (Oxford: Oxford University Press, 1960), 303.

43. CRDA, Gérard, "Incidents en Guinée Française, 1954–1955," 6–7; Morgenthau, *Political Parties in French-Speaking West Africa,* 240; Kéïta, *P.D.G.,* 1:317.

44. CRDA, Gérard, "Incidents en Guinée Française, 1954–1955," 7; "Élections Législatives Partielles de Guinée," 17 June 1954, in *P.D.G.-R.D.A. . . . Activités—Répression—Élections;* Morgenthau, *Political Parties in French-Speaking West Africa,* 240.

45. CRDA, Gérard, "Incidents en Guinée Française, 1954–1955," 5–7; Morgenthau, *Political Parties in French-Speaking West Africa,* 103, 106, 240.

46. Interview with Aissatou N'Diaye, Conakry, 8 April 1991.

47. For the RDA's use of song, see Schmidt, *Mobilizing the Masses,* chap. 5; Schmidt, "Top Down or Bottom Up?" 976, 980, 985, 995, 1006–7, 1009–13; Elizabeth Schmidt, "'Emancipate Your Husbands!': Women and Nationalism in Guinea, 1953–1958," in *Women in African Colonial Histories,* ed. Jean Allman, Susan Geiger, and Nakanyike Musisi (Bloomington: Indiana University Press, 2002), 287–89, 294–95.

48. Interview with Fatou Diarra, Conakry, 17 March 1991. See also Camara, "Contribution de la Femme," 80. The party symbol, syli or elephant, often was used to denote the person of Sékou Touré, as well as the party as a whole.

49. Interview with Aissatou N'Diaye, 8 April 1991.

50. Ibid. See also interviews with Fatou Kéïta, Conakry, 7 April and 24 May 1991.

51. CRDA, Gérard, "Incidents en Guinée Française, 1954–1955," 9; Camara, "Contribution de la Femme," 78. See also interview with Fatou Kéïta, 24 May 1991.

52. Camara, "Contribution de la Femme," 79.

53. Ibid., 80. See also interviews with Fatou Diarra, 17 March 1991 and Fatou Kéïta, 24 May 1991.

For information about Saliou Diallo see ANS, 17G586, Guinée Française, Services de Police, Conakry, "Renseignements A/S Petit Incident entre Femmes Bagistes et R.D.A., au Marché de Madina (Banlieue)," 7 Sept. 1956, #1813/631, C/PS.2; 17G586, Guinée Française, Services de Police, P. Humbert, Commissaire Divisionnaire, Conakry, à Gouverneur, Guinée Française, Conakry, 19 Sept. 1956, #1924, C/PS.2.

54. Quoted in Morgenthau, *Political Parties in French-Speaking West Africa,* 240–41.

55. ANS, 17G586, Guinée Française, Commissaire Central de la Ville de Conakry, "Manifestation sur la Voie Publique," 13 Sept. 1954, #1317/SP.

56. CRDA, Gérard, "Incidents en Guinée Française, 1954–1955," 9, 11, 13; Morgenthau, *Political Parties in French-Speaking West Africa,* 240–41.

57. ANS, 17G586, Guinée Française, Services de Police, "Renseignements *Objet:* Incidents à Conakry," 7 Oct. 1954, #2768/1036, C/PS.2; 17G586, Guinée Française, Services de Police, "Renseignements *Objet:* Incidents à Conakry," 11 Oct. 1954, #2785/1045, C/PS.2.

For further discussion of mass parties and political violence—and tensions between the party leadership and the rank and file over this issue—see Hodgkin, *African Political Parties,* 125–33; Schmidt, *Mobilizing the Masses,* chap. 6.

58. ANS, 17G586, Commissaire Central, "Manifestation sur la Voie Publique," 13 Sept. 1954; 17G573, Guinée Française, Services de Police, "Renseignements *Objet:* Incidents à Conakry," 26 Oct. 1954, #2850/1094, C/PS.2.

59. CRDA, Gérard, "Incidents en Guinée Française, 1954–1955," 9, 11, 13; Morgenthau, *Political Parties in French-Speaking West Africa*, 240–41.

60. ANS, 17G586, Guinée Française, Services de Police, "Renseignements *Objet:* Passage de Touré Sékou à Kindia," 18 Aug. 1954, #2471/888, C/PS.2; 17G586, Guinée Française, Services de Police, "Renseignements *Objet:* Passage de Sékou Touré à Mamou," 21 Aug. 1954, #2506/905, C/PS.2; 17G586, Guinée Française, Services de Police, "Renseignements A/S Lettre-Circulaire de Sékou Touré," 7 Oct. 1954, #2766/1034, C/PS.2.

61. ANS, 17G586, Police, " . . . Passage de Sékou Touré à Mamou," 21 Aug. 1954; interview with Mamdou Bela Doumbouya, 26 Jan. 1991.

62. ANS, 17G586, Guinée Française, Services de Police, Kindia, "Renseignements A/S Réunion Privée par Touré Sékou (Sily) à Kindia," 25 Nov. 1954, #3017/1196, C/PS.2; Morgenthau, *Political Parties in French-Speaking West Africa*, 19.

63. ANS, 17G586, Police, " . . . Passage de Touré Sékou à Kindia," 18 Aug. 1954.

64. Morgenthau, *Political Parties in French-Speaking West Africa*, 241–42; Rioux, *Fourth Republic*, 227–28; Mortimer, *France and the Africans*, 201–2; Kéïta, *P.D.G.*, 1:127.

65. Morgenthau, *Political Parties in French-Speaking West Africa*, 106; Kéïta, *P.D.G.*, 1:318.

66. ANS, 17G586, Guinée Française, Services de Police, "Renseignements Réunion Privée des Femmes R.D.A. à Conakry," 7 Oct. 1954, #2765/1033, C/PS.2; Morgenthau, *Political Parties in French-Speaking West Africa*, 242. For party usurpation of state functions, see interview with Léon Maka, 25 Feb. 1991; Hodgkin, *African Political Parties*, 125, 145–46; Schmidt, *Mobilizing the Masses*, 52, 102–3, 106; Ameillon, *Guinée*, 22.

67. Morgenthau, *Political Parties in French-Speaking West Africa*, 242.

68. Ibid., 242–43.

69. Quoted in Kéïta, *P.D.G.*, 1:318 and Suret-Canale, *République de Guinée*, 161n1. See also Morgenthau, *Political Parties in French-Speaking West Africa*, 106.

70. Interview with Mamadou Bela Doumbouya, 26 Jan. 1991. See also ANS, 2G54/159, Guinée Française, Gouverneur, Conakry, à Haut Commissaire, Dakar, "Revues Trimestrielles des Événements, 3ème Trimestre 1954," 22 Jan. 1955, #40 CAB/APA.

71. ANS, 2G54/159, "Revues Trimestrielles des Événements, 3ème Trimestre 1954," 22 Jan. 1955.

72. ANS, 17G586, Guinée Française, Services de Police, Kankan, "Renseignements *Objet:* Conférence Publique R.D.A. à Kankan," 27 Jan. 1955, #212/83, C/PS.2.

73. ANS, 2G54/159, "Revues Trimestrielles des Événements, 3ème Trimestre 1954," 22 Jan. 1955; 2G55/152, "Rapport Politique Annuel, 1955."

74. ANS, 2G55/152, "Rapport Politique Annuel, 1955."

75. CAOM, Carton 2143, dos. 9, Gouverneur, Guinée Française, Conakry, à Haut Commissaire, Dakar, 16 Dec. 1954, #1 CAB/AP; ANS, 2G54/159, "Revues Trimestrielles des Événements, 3ème Trimestre 1954," 22 Jan. 1955.

76. CAOM, Carton 2143, dos. 8, "Informations Politiques et Sociales . . . La Situation Politique en Guinée Française, " *Interafrique Presse,* ca. Oct. 1955; Morgenthau, *Political Parties in French-Speaking West Africa*, 247.

77. ANS, 2G54/159, "Revues Trimestrielles des Événements, 3ème Trimestre 1954," 22 Jan. 1955; 2G55/152, "Rapport Politique Annuel, 1955." See also Hodgkin, *African Political Parties*, 37.

78. ANS, 17G586, Guinée Française, Services de Police, Kankan, "Renseignements A/S Arrivé Kankan, Sékou Touré et Conférence Publique du 9 Novembre 1954," 13 Nov. 1954, #2936/1142, C/PS.2.

For the significance of party uniforms, see Schmidt, "Top Down or Bottom Up?" 976, 985, 1006–9.

79. Interview with Mamadou Bela Doumbouya, 26 Jan. 1991. See also interview with Léon Maka, 25 Feb. 1991; Hodgkin, *African Political Parties*, 125, 145–46; Ameillon, *Guinée*, 22; Schmidt, *Mobilizing the Masses*, 52, 102–3, 106.

80. ANS, 2G54/159, "Revues Trimestrielles des Événements, 3ème Trimestre 1954," 22 Jan. 1955. See also 2G55/151, Guinée Française, Gouverneur, Conakry, à Haut Commissaire, Dakar, "Revues Trimestrielles des Événements, 4ème Trimestre 1955," 15 March 1956, #131/APA; CAOM, Carton 2143, dos. 9, Gouverneur à Haut Commissaire, 16 Dec. 1954; interview with Léon Maka, 25 Feb. 1991; Schmidt, *Mobilizing the Masses*, 52, 102–3, 106; Hodgkin, *African Political Parties*, 125, 145–46; Ameillon, *Guinée*, 22.

81. ANS, 17G586, Guinée Française, Services de Police, N'Zérékoré, "Renseignements A/S Plaintes contre les Agissements des Militants R.D.A.," 6 Dec. 1956, #2500/892, C/PS.2.

82. ANS, 17G586, Guinée Française, Services de Police, Dubréka, "Renseignements *Objet:* Incidents à Dubréka," 10 Dec. 1954, #3132/1241, C/PS.2.

83. CAOM, Carton 2143, dos. 9, H. Bernard, Procureur Général près la Cour d'Appel de Dakar, à Ministre, FOM, Paris, 23 Feb. 1955, #1779.

84. ANS, 17G586, Guinée Française, Services de Police, Conakry, "Renseignements A/S Réunion Publique d'Informations tenue le Jeudi 30 Août 1956, par le Député *Diallo* Saïfoulaye, à Conakry, Salle de Cinéma 'VOX,'" 31 Aug. 1956, #1761/619, C/PS.2.

85. ANS, 2G55/152, "Rapport Politique Annuel, 1955"; CAOM, Carton 2143, dos. 8., Gouverneur, Guinée Française, Conakry, à Haut Commissaire, Dakar, 22 Oct. 1955, #520/CAB/APA; Kéïta, *P.D.G.*, 1:129.

86. CAOM, Carton 2143, dos. 9, Gouverneur à Haut Commissaire, 16 Dec. 1954. See also ANS, 17G586, Guinée Française, Services de Police, Labé, "Renseignements *Objet:* Situation Politique à Labé dans la Première Quinzaine de Novembre 1954," 23 Nov. 1954, #2999/1180, C/PS.2; Morgenthau, *Political Parties in French-Speaking West Africa*, 241–43.

87. ANS, 2G54/159, "Revues Trimestrielles des Événements, 3ème Trimestre 1954," 22 Jan. 1955; CAOM, Carton 2143, dos. 9, Gouverneur à Haut Commissaire, 16 Dec. 1954. See also Carton 2143, dos. 9, Télégramme Arrivée, Haut Commissaire, Paris et Dakar. Envoyé par Gouverneur, Guinée Française, Conakry, 3 Feb. 1955, #47–50.

88. CAOM, Carton 2143, dos. 9, Gouverneur à Haut Commissaire, 16 Dec. 1954; Johnson, "Parti Démocratique de Guinée," 349.

89. ANS, 2G54/159, "Revues Trimestrielles des Événements, 3ème Trimestre 1954," 22 Jan. 1955. See also CAOM, Carton 2143, dos. 9, Gouverneur à Haut Commissaire, 16 Dec. 1954.

90. CAOM, Carton 2143, dos. 9, Gouverneur à Haut Commissaire, 16 Dec. 1954.

91. ANS, 2G55/152, "Rapport Politique Annuel, 1955"; Morgenthau, *Political Parties in French-Speaking West Africa,* 232–33.

92. ANS, 17G586, Guinée Française, Services de Police, Conakry, "Renseignements *Objet:* Comité de Coordination des Groupements Regionaux de Guinée," 20 Nov. 1954, #2985/1172, C/PS.2.

93. ANS, 17G586, Guinée Française, Services de Police, Kankan, "Renseignements *Objet:* Réunion de la Section de l'Union du Mandé de Kankan," 13 Jan. 1955, #84/29, C/PS.2.

94. ANS, 2G54/159, "Revues Trimestrielles des Événements, 3ème Trimestre 1954," 22 Jan. 1955. See also CAOM, Carton 2143, dos. 9, Gouverneur à Haut Commissaire, 16 Dec. 1954.

95. CAOM, Carton 2143, dos. 9, Gouverneur à Haut Commissaire, 16 Dec. 1954; Carton 2143, dos. 7, Claude Gérard, "Le 'B.A.G.' en Guinée," *Interafrique Presse,* no. 43, 8 Sept. 1955; ANS, 2G55/150, "Rapport Politique Mensuel, Août 1955"; 2G55/150, Guinée Française, Gouverneur, "Rapport Politique Mensuel, Octobre 1955," 21 Nov. 1955, #549/APA/CAB; 2G55/152, "Rapport Politique Annuel, 1955"; interviews in Conakry with: Bocar Biro Barry, 21 and 29 Jan. 1991; Aissatou N'Diaye, 8 April 1991; Sidiki Kobélé Kéïta, 9 April 1991; Ibrahima Fofana, 5 May 1991; interview with Tourou Sylla, Mamou, 30 May 1991; Morgenthau, *Political Parties in French-Speaking West Africa,* 232–33. See also 2G56/138, Guinée Française, Gouverneur, "Rapport Politique Mensuel, Mars 1956," 19 April 1956, #185/APA; Hodgkin, *African Political Parties,* 69.

The BAG consciously chose the term *bloc,* which was favored by the socialists and which distinguished it from the communist-inspired *rassemblement* of the RDA. Morgenthau, *Political Parties in French-Speaking West Africa,* 138, 225, 304–5; Mortimer, *France and the Africans,* 110, 142; Ernest Milcent, *L'A.O.F. Entre en Scène* (Paris: Bibliothèque de l'Homme d'Action, 1958), 44.

96. ANS, 2G55/150, Guinée Française, Gouverneur, "Rapport Politique Mensuel, Juin 1955," 10 Aug. 1955.

97. CAOM, Carton 2143, dos. 9, Gouverneur à Haut Commissaire, 16 Dec. 1954; Carton 2143, dos. 9, Haut Commissaire, Dakar, à Ministre, FOM, Paris, "*Objet:* Événements de Guinée," 14 March 1955; ANS, 17G586, Guinée Française, Services de Police, Conakry, "Renseignements *Objet:* Activités des Conseillers Territoriaux de la Basse Guinée," 17 Jan. 1955, #113/50, C/PS.2; Morgenthau, *Political Parties in French-Speaking West Africa,* 222, 225.

98. ANS, 17G586, Guinée Française, Services de Police, Conakry, "Renseignements *Objet:* Activité de l'Union du Mandé," 17 Jan. 1955, #109/46, C/PS.2.

99. ANS, 2G54/159, "Revues Trimestrielles des Événements, 3ème Trimestre 1954," 22 Jan. 1955; 17G586, Police, Kankan, " . . . P.D.G. et Congrès de Dabola," 24 Sept. 1956; AG, 2D297, Syndicats de l'Enseignement Primaire Public de l'AOF à Gouverneur, 11 Oct. 1954; CAOM, Carton 2143, dos. 9, Gouverneur à Haut Commissaire, 16 Dec. 1954; interview with Bocar Biro Barry, 21 Jan. 1991; Johnson, "Parti Démocratique de Guinée," 358.

100. ANS, 17G586, Guinée Française, Services de Police, Mamou, "Renseignements *Objet:* Réunion RDA à Mamou," 25 Jan. 1955, #202/78, C/PS.2.

101. ANS, 2G55/152, "Rapport Politique Annuel, 1955."

102. ANS, 17G586, Guinée Française, Services de Police, Conakry, "Renseignements *Objet:* Validation de *Barry* Diawadou," 19 Jan. 1955, #137/67, C/PS.2.

103. ANS, 17G586, Guinée Française, Services de Police, Conakry, "Renseignements *Objet:* La Validation de Barry Diawadou et l'Activité Politique à Conakry," 22 Jan. 1955, #197/76, C/PS.2; CRDA, Gérard, "Incidents en Guinée Française, 1954–1955," 8, 11–12.

104. Mortimer, *France and the Africans,* 206; Kéïta, *P.D.G.,* 1:318.

105. CRDA, Gérard, "Incidents en Guinée Française, 1954–1955," 11–12; Morgenthau, *Political Parties in French-Speaking West Africa,* 103–4, 106, 243; Mortimer, *France and the Africans,* 206.

106. CRDA, "Troubles en Guinée," Extrait de *Afrique Nouvelle,* 15 Feb. 1955, 1.

107. CRDA, Gérard, "Incidents en Guinée Française, 1954–1955," 13, 17; "Conakry," *Interafrique Presse,* 3 Feb. 1955; "Troubles en Guinée," 15 Feb. 1955, 1; Carton 2143, dos. 9, Télégramme Arrivée, Délégaof, Haut Commissaire, Paris. Envoyé par Gouverneur, Guinée Française, Conakry, 1 Feb. 1955, #41–42; Carton 2143, dos. 9, Télégramme Arrivée, Délégaof, Haut Commissaire, Paris. Envoyé par Gouverneur, Guinée Française, Conakry, 2 Feb. 1955, #45; Carton 2143, dos. 9, Télégramme Arrivée, Haut Commissaire. Envoyé par Gouverneur, Guinée Française, 3 Feb. 1955; Carton 2143, dos. 9, Télégramme Arrivée, Délégaof, Paris. Envoyé par Gouverneur, Guinée Française, Conakry, 4 Feb. 1955, #2–7; Morgenthau, *Political Parties in French-Speaking West Africa,* 106, 243.

108. CAOM, Carton 2143, dos. 9, Télégramme Arrivée, Délégaof, Haut Commissaire, Paris. Envoyé par Gouverneur, Guinée Française, Conakry, 2 Feb. 1955, #43–44. See also Carton 2143, dos. 9, Télégramme Arrivée, Haut Commissaire. Envoyé par Gouverneur, Guinée Française, 3 Feb. 1955.

109. CAOM, Carton 2143, dos. 9, Télégramme Arrivée, FOM, Paris. Envoyé par Mission d'Inspection (Pruvost), Conakry, 20 Feb. 1955, #2. See also Carton 2143, dos. 9, Télégramme Arrivée, Haut Commissaire. Envoyé par Gouverneur, Guinée Française, 3 Feb. 1955; Carton 2143, dos. 9, Télégramme Arrivée, Délégaof, Haut Commissaire, Paris et Dakar. Envoyé par Gouverneur, Guinée Française, Conakry, ca. 7 Feb. 1955, #58–60; ANS, 2G55/152, "Rapport Politique Annuel, 1955"; CRDA,"Troubles en Guinée," 15 Feb. 1955, 1. See also Hodgkin, *African Political Parties,* 125–33, 145–46.

110. CAOM, Carton 2143, dos. 9, Télégramme Arrivée, Délégaof. Envoyé par Gouverneur, Guinée Française, 4 Feb. 1955.

111. Interview with Néné Diallo, Conakry, 11 April 1991.

112. CAOM, Carton 2143, dos. 9, Télégramme Arrivée, Haut Commissaire. Envoyé par Gouverneur, Guinée Française, 3 Feb. 1955; Carton 2143, dos. 9, Télégramme Arrivée, Délégaof, Haut Commissaire. Envoyé par Gouverneur, Guinée Française, ca. 7 Feb. 1955.

RDA infiltration of the colonial administration was not uncommon. For instance, Abdoulaye Condé, a military veteran and RDA partisan, worked as an interpreter for the Mamou circle commandant. Having access to messages transmitted between the circle commandant and the territorial administration in Conakry, he regularly passed this information to the Mamou RDA subsection. Johnson, "Parti Démocratique de Guinée," 351–52.

113. CAOM, Carton 2143, dos. 9, Télégramme Arrivée, Délégaof, Haut Commissaire. Envoyé par Gouverneur, Guinée Française, ca. 7 Feb. 1955.

114. See, for instance, AG, 1E37, Guinée Française, Cercle de Macenta, "Rapport Politique Annuel, 1947"; 1E38, Guinée Française, Cercle de Macenta, "Rapport Politique Annuel, 1948"; 1E39, Guinée Française, Cercle de Beyla, "Rapport Politique Annuel, 1949."

For further discussion of chiefly abuses, popular resistance to the chieftaincy, and the RDA's role in the protests see Schmidt, *Mobilizing the Masses,* chap. 4.

115. Interview with Bocar Biro Barry, 29 Jan. 1991; CAOM, Carton 2143, dos. 9, Claude Gérard, "Dans l'Ouest Africain, Après les Incidents de . . . Conakry," *Interafrique Presse,* no. 17, 10 March 1955; Camara, "Contribution de la Femme," 94; Kéïta, *P.D.G.,* 1:343; Kéïta, *Ahmed Sékou Touré: 28 Septembre,* 60. See also Hodgkin, *African Political Parties,* 132.

116. Camara, "Contribution de la Femme," 94, 132; Kéïta, *P.D.G.,* 1:343; Kéïta, *Ahmed Sékou Touré: 28 Septembre,* 60.

117. CRDA, Gérard, "Incidents en Guinée Française, 1954–1955," 13; CAOM, Carton 2143, dos. 9, Procureur Général à Ministre, FOM, 23 Feb. 1955; Camara, "Contribution de la Femme," 95, 132; Kéïta, *P.D.G.,* 1:342–44; Kéïta, *Ahmed Sékou Touré: 28 Septembre,* 60.

118. See interview with Léon Maka, 25 Feb. 1991. See also ANS, 2G55/151, "Revues Trimestrielles des Événements, 4ème Trimestre 1955," 15 March 1956; Ameillon, *Guinée,* 22; Schmidt, *Mobilizing the Masses,* 52, 102–3, 106.

119. Suret-Canale, *République de Guinée,* 95; Suret-Canale, *French Colonialism in Tropical Africa,* 324, 346; Kéïta, *P.D.G.,* 1:88; Schmidt, *Mobilizing the Masses,* 92.

120. CAOM, Carton 2143, dos. 9, Télégramme Arrivée, FOM, Paris. Envoyé par Haut Commissaire, Dakar, 10 Feb. 1955, #94–98; Carton 2143, dos. 9, "Incidents dans le Cercle de Dubréka," *Agence France-Presse,* Special Outre Mer, no. 2567, 15 Feb. 1955; Carton 2143, dos. 9, Procureur Général à Ministre, FOM, 23 Feb. 1955; Carton 2143, dos. 9, Gérard, "Dans l'Ouest Africain . . . ," 10 March 1955; "Incidents Graves à Tondon, Canton de Labaya, Cercle de Dubréka," *La Liberté,* no. 47, 15 Feb. 1955, 3; Camara, "Contribution de la Femme," 94–95.

For a discussion of women's political activities and their relationship to precolonial protest forms, see Schmidt, "'Emancipate Your Husbands,'" 291–92; Schmidt, *Mobilizing the Masses,* 129–31, 133–36; Schmidt, "Top Down or Bottom Up?" 996, 1012–13.

121. CAOM, Carton 2143, dos. 9, Télégramme Arrivée, FOM. Envoyé par Haut Commissaire, 10 Feb; Carton 2143, dos. 9, "Incidents dans le Cercle de Dubréka," 15 Feb. 1955; Carton 2143, dos. 9, Procureur Général à Ministre, FOM, 23 Feb. 1955; Carton 2143, dos. 9, Gérard, "Dans l'Ouest Africain . . . ," 10 March 1955; CRDA, Gérard, "Incidents en Guinée Française, 1954–1955," 13–17; Camara, "Contribution de la Femme," 132; Kéïta, *P.D.G.,* 1:343; Kéïta, *Ahmed Sékou Touré: 28 Septembre,* 60.

122. CRDA, Moricandian Savané, "Les Grandioses Obsèques de Camara M'Ballia," *La Liberté,* 1 March 1955, 1; interview with Aissatou N'Diaye, 8 April 1991;

Camara, "Contribution de la Femme," 95, 132; Kéïta, *P.D.G.*, 1:342–44; Kéïta, *Ahmed Sékou Touré: 28 Septembre,* 60.

123. Interview with Aissatou N'Diaye, 8 April 1991.

124. Ibid.; ANS, 17G586, Guinée Française, Services de Police, "Renseignements *Objet:* Suite aux Incidents de Tondon," 18 Feb. 1955, #389/160, C/PS.2; CRDA, Savané, "Grandioses Obsèques de Camara M'Ballia," 1 March 1955; Camara, "Contribution de la Femme," 132; Kéïta, *P.D.G.*, 1:343–44; Kéïta, *Ahmed Sékou Touré: 28 Septembre,* 62.

125. ANS, 17G586, Police, " . . . Suite aux Incidents de Tondon," 18 Feb. 1955.

126. Interview with Aissatou N'Diaye, 8 April 1991.

127. ANS, 17G586, Police, " . . . Suite aux Incidents de Tondon," 18 Feb. 1955; CRDA, Savané, "Grandioses Obsèques de Camara M'Ballia," 1 March 1955; CAOM, Carton 2143, dos. 9, Gérard, "Dans l'Ouest Africain . . . ," 10 March 1955.

128. Interview with Mamady Kaba, Conakry, 15 Jan. 1991; interview with Bocar Biro Barry, 29 Jan. 1991; Kéïta, *P.D.G.*, 1:344; Kéïta, *Ahmed Sékou Touré: 28 Septembre,* 62. For a discussion of "heroic memories and the cult of martyrs," see Hodgkin, *African Political Parties,* 129.

129. Interview with Aissatou N'Diaye, 8 April 1991. See also interviews with Mamady Kaba, 15 Jan. 1991 and Bocar Biro Barry, 29 Jan. 1991; Camara, "Contribution de la Femme," 96.

130. Camara, "Contribution de la Femme," 96.

131. AG, 1E41, Guinée Française, Services de Police, "Renseignements *Objet:* R.D.A. et Religion à Conakry et à Kindia," 28 April 1955, #879/559/C/PS.2; 1E41, Télégramme Officiel Départ, Afcour, Bureau du Chiffre, Conakry, à Tous Cercles et Subdivisions, 28 April 1955, #365.

132. ANS, 2G55/150, Guinée Française, Gouverneur, "Rapport Politique Mensuel, Juillet 1955," #435/APAS/CAB; Morgenthau, *Political Parties in French-Speaking West Africa,* 241; Milcent, *A.O.F. Entre en Scène,* 88; Virginia Thompson and Richard Adloff, *French West Africa* (New York: Greenwood Press, 1969), 94.

133. Morgenthau, *Political Parties in French-Speaking West Africa,* 98, 241; Mortimer, *France and the Africans,* 156, 161, 177–78; Milcent, *A.O.F. Entre en Scène,* 44, 87–88; Thompson and Adloff, *French West Africa,* 94.

Milcent claims that the coordinating committee had not met since 1948, while Thompson and Adloff set the date at 1949. Thompson and Adloff may be confusing the coordinating committee meeting with the RDA's second interterritorial congress, held in Abidjan in February 1949. The RDA did not hold a third interterritorial congress until September 1957. See Aristide R. Zolberg, *One-Party Government in the Ivory Coast* (Princeton: Princeton University Press, 1964), 220–22; André Blanchet, *L'Itinéraire des Partis Africains depuis Bamako* (Paris: Librarie Plon, 1958), 39–40.

134. ANS, 17G573, Guinée Française, Services de Police, Conakry, "Rapport Hebdomadaire, Semaine du 23 au 30 Septembre 1951, Semaine du 1er au 7 Octobre 1951," #1794/984, C/PS.2; 2G55/150, "Rapport Politique Mensuel, Juillet 1955"; Morgenthau, *Political Parties in French-Speaking West Africa,* 98, 309.

135. Morgenthau, *Political Parties in French-Speaking West Africa,* 157, 159, 307–9, 317; Mortimer, *France and the Africans,* 162, 176, 178, 200, 213, 219–20, 250–51; Mil-

cent, *A.O.F. Entre en Scène,* 88–89; Thompson and Adloff, *French West Africa,* 94; Hodgkin, *African Political Parties,* 71; Schachter and Wallerstein, "French Africa's Road to Independence: 1," 372; Finn Fuglestad, "Djibo Bakary, the French, and the Referendum of 1958 in Niger," *Journal of African History* 14, no. 2 (1973): 315; Richard A. Joseph, *Radical Nationalism in Cameroun: Social Origins of the U.P.C. Rebellion* (Oxford: Oxford University Press, 1977), 172–73, 182, 290–92.

136. See examples in Morgenthau, *Political Parties in French-Speaking West Africa,* 238–39, 243–44.

137. Interview with Mamadou Bela Doumbouya, 26 Jan. 1991; Morgenthau, *Political Parties in French-Speaking West Africa,* 229; Cooper, *Decolonization and African Society,* 310–11; Schmidt, *Mobilizing the Masses,* chap. 3.

138. CAOM, Carton 2144, dos. 1, FOM, "Rapport Pruvost," 31 March 1955; Schmidt, "'Emancipate Your Husbands,'" 285–89, 293, 295–96; Schmidt, *Mobilizing the Masses,* chap. 5.

Women interviewed decades later frequently credited Sékou Touré personally for the party initiatives that benefitted women. See interviews with Aissatou N'Diaye, 8 April 1991; Néné Diallo, 11 April 1991; Fatou Kéïta, 28 April and 24 May 1991.

139. CAOM, Carton 2144, dos. 1, FOM, "Rapport Pruvost," 31 March 1955. See also Hodgkin, *African Political Parties,* 137.

140. ANS, 2G55/150, "Rapport Politique Mensuel," July 1955.

141. See chap. 2. See also ANS, 17G573, "Les Partis Politiques en Guinée, 1er Semestre 1951"; Cooper, *Decolonization and African Society,* 409–10.

142. See CAOM, Carton 2144, dos. 1, FOM, "Rapport Pruvost," 31 March 1955.

143. ANS, 17G573, Guinée Française, Services de Police, 16 Oct. 1951, #1863, C/PS.2; 17G573, Guinée Française, Services de Police, Conakry, "Rapport Hebdomadaire, Semaine du 15 au 21 Octobre 1951," #1907/1053, C/PS.2; 17G573, "Partis Politiques en Guinée, 1er Semestre 1951"; Morgenthau, *Political Parties in French-Speaking West Africa,* 98, 241–42, 307; Milcent, *A.O.F. Entre en Scène,* 136; Cooper, *Decolonization and African Society,* 407–8; Kéïta, *P.D.G.,* 2:119; Riviere, *Guinea,* 59; Johnson, "Parti Démocratique de Guinée," 347.

144. ANS, 21G13, Guinée Française, Service de la Sûreté, "État d'Esprit de la Population," 1–15 Dec. 1950; 17G573, Haut Commissaire, Dakar, à Ministre, FOM, Paris, 28 April 1952, #471, INT/AP.2; CRDA, Ministre, FOM, Paris, à Haut Commissaire, Dakar, 21 March 1952; Morgenthau, *Political Parties in French-Speaking West Africa,* 242; Mortimer, *France and the Africans,* 202; Cooper, *Decolonization and African Society,* 409.

145. ANS, 2G55/150, "Rapport Politique Mensuel, Juillet 1955."

146. Ibid.

147. Morgenthau, *Political Parties in French-Speaking West Africa,* 241; Thompson and Adloff, *French West Africa,* 94.

148. ANS, 2G55/150, "Rapport Politique Mensuel, Juillet 1955."

149. ANS, 2G55/152, "Rapport Politique Annuel, 1955."

150. ANS, 2G55/150, "Rapport Politique Mensuel, Juillet 1955."

151. CRDA, P.D.G., Bureau Directeur, Sous-Section de Mamou, au Comité Directeur du P.D.G., Conakry, 1 Aug. 1955, in *P.D.G.-R.D.A., Parti Démocratique de Guinée,*

1947–1960: Les Sections—Les Syndicats; interview with Ibrahima Fofana, Conakry, 24 May 1991.

Although his full name was Pléah Koniba Coulibaly, the Mamou activist generally was known as Pléah Koniba.

152. CRDA, P.D.G., Bureau Directeur, Sous-Section de Mamou, au Comité Directeur du P.D.G., Conakry, 19 Aug. 1955, #22, in *P.D.G.-R.D.A. . . . Sections . . . Syndicats.*

153. ANS, 17G622, Police, " . . . Exclusion du P.D.G./R.D.A. de Plusieurs Dirigeants de . . . Mamou," 15 Nov. 1957; 17G622, Guinée Française, Services de Police, "Renseignements A/S Conférence Publique tenue à Mamou, le 14 Novembre 1957, par l'Ex-Sous-Section du P.D.G./R.D.A.," 19 Nov. 1957, #2565/954, C/PS.2; 2G57/128, Police et Sûreté, "Synthèse Mensuelle de Renseignements, Novembre 1957"; interview with Fanta Diarra and Ibrahima Fofana, Conakry, 24 May 1991; Johnson, "Parti Démocratique de Guinée," 362, 365. For further elaboration, see chap. 5.

154. CRDA, Gérard, "Incidents en Guinée Française, 1954–1955," 17; Morgenthau, *Political Parties in French-Speaking West Africa,* 107.

155. CAOM, Carton 2143, dos. 7, Télégramme Arrivée, FOM, Paris. Envoyé par Haut Commissaire, Dakar, 7 Aug. 1955, #499; Carton 2143, dos. 7, Gouvernement Général AOF, Direction des Affaires Politiques, "Rapport Complet sur le Congrès du Bloc Africain de Guinée, tenu à Conakry du 4 au 7 Août 1955," 25 Aug. 1955, #11741; Carton 2143, dos. 7, "Clôture du Congrès du Bloc Africain de Guinée," *Agence France-Presse,* Special Outre Mer, no. 2712, 7–8 Aug. 1955; Carton 2143, dos. 7, Gérard, "'B.A.G.' en Guinée," 8 Sept. 1955; ANS, 2G55/150, "Rapport Politique Mensuel, Août 1955"; Du Bois, *Guinea's Prelude to Independence,* 15n11; Rioux, *Fourth Republic,* 240.

Faure was expelled from the Parti Radical Socialiste in December 1955. In the parliament of January 1956, the BAG affiliated with Faure's new right-wing splinter party, the Rassemblement des Gauches Républicains. Mortimer, *France and the Africans,* 228; Rioux, *Fourth Republic,* 257.

156. ANS, 2G54/159, "Revues Trimestrielles des Événements, 3ème Trimestre 1954," 22 Jan. 1955.

157. CAOM, Carton 2143, dos. 9, Haut Commissaire à Ministre, FOM, " . . . Événements de Guinée," 14 March 1955.

158. ANS, 17G586, Police, " . . . Activité de l'Union du Mandé," 17 Jan. 1955.

159. ANS, 17G586, Police, " . . . Activités des Conseillers Territoriaux de la Basse Guinée," 17 Jan. 1955.

160. ANS, 17G586, Guinée Française, Services de Police, "Renseignements *Objet:* Arrivée de *Barry* Diawadou à Conakry," 25 March 1955, #653/268, C/PS.2.

161. ANS, 17G586, Guinée Française, Services de Police, Kankan, "Renseignements A/S Passage à Kankan du Député *Barry* Diawadou," 2 June 1955, #1081/451, C/PS.2.

162. ANS, 17G586, Guinée Française, Services de Police, "Renseignements *Objet:* Réunion Publique du R.D.A., le 8/8/54 à Kankan," 18 Aug. 1954, #2480/894, C/PS.2; 17G586, Police, Kankan, " . . . Sékou Touré et Conférence Publique du 9 Novembre 1954," 13 Nov. 1954; CRDA, Gérard, "Incidents en Guinée Française, 1954–1955," 9; Kéïta, *P.D.G.,* 1:319.

163. ANS, 17G586, Police, Kankan, " . . . Passage à Kankan du Député *Barry* Diawadou," 2 June 1955.

164. CAOM, Carton 2143, dos. 9, Télégramme Arrivée, FOM, Paris. Envoyé par Afcour, Dakar, 31 May 1955, #306; CAOM, Carton 2143, dos. 9, Télégramme Arrivée, FOM, Paris. Envoyé par Afcour, Dakar, 1 June 1955, #307; ANS, 2G55/152, "Rapport Politique Annuel, 1955."

165. ANS, 2G55/152, "Rapport Politique Annuel, 1955"; CRDA, "Que de Tractations Autour des Incidents de Macenta," *La Liberté*, 23 Aug. 1955, 2; Kéïta, *P.D.G.*, 1:323.

166. CAOM, Carton 2143, dos. 9, Télégramme Arrivée, FOM, Paris. Envoyé par Afcour, Haut Commissaire, Dakar, 3 June 1955, #311–12; ANS, 2G55/152, "Rapport Politique Annuel, 1955."

167. CAOM, Carton 2143, dos. 9, Gouverneur, Guinée Française, sur le "Mangin," à Haut Commissaire, Dakar, 13 July 1955.

168. ANS, 2G55/152, "Rapport Politique Annuel, 1955." See also 2G55/150, "Rapport Politique Mensuel, Juillet 1955."

169. CAOM, Carton 2143, dos. 7, *Agence France-Presse,* Special Outre Mer, no. 2714, 10 Aug. 1955.

170. CAOM, Carton 2143, dos. 7, Gérard, "'B.A.G.' en Guinée," 8 Sept. 1955.

171. ANS, 2G55/151, "Revues Trimestrielles des Événements, 4ème Trimestre 1955," 15 March 1956; 2G55/150, "Rapport Politique Mensuel, Octobre 1955."

172. CAOM, Carton 2143, dos. 8., Gouverneur à Haut Commissaire, 22 Oct. 1955.

173. CAOM, Carton 2143, dos. 7, Ministre, FOM, "Incidents de Guinée," 20 Oct. 1955, #1294/SC/FOM; ANS, 2G55/152, "Rapport Politique Annuel, 1955."

174. ANS, 2G55/151, "Revues Trimestrielles des Événements, 4ème Trimestre 1955," 15 March 1956; 2G55/152," Rapport Politique Annuel, 1955"; CAOM, Carton 2143, dos. 8., Gouverneur à Haut Commissaire, 22 Oct. 1955.

175. ANS, 2G55/151, "Revues Trimestrielles des Événements, 4ème Trimestre 1955," 15 March 1956; 2G55/152, "Rapport Politique Annuel, 1955." See also Hodgkin, *African Political Parties,* 69, 71–72, 143.

176. ANS, 2G55/151, "Revues Trimestrielles des Événements, 4ème Trimestre 1955," 15 March 1956; 17G586, P. Humbert, Commissaire Divisionnaire, Police, Conakry, à Gouverneur, Guinée Française, Conakry, 18 Aug. 1956, #1633, C/PS.2; 17G586, Guinée Française, Services de Police, "Renseignements A/S Prochaines Élections Municipales," 9 Oct. 1956, #2072/722, C/PS.2; Morgenthau, *Political Parties in French-Speaking West Africa,* 233.

177. ANS, 2G55/152, "Rapport Politique Annuel, 1955." See also 2G55/150, "Rapport Politique Mensuel, Juillet 1955."

178. ANS, 2G55/151, "Revues Trimestrielles des Événements, 4ème Trimestre 1955," 15 March 1956.

179. ANS, 2G55/152, "Rapport Politique Annuel, 1955."

180. ANS, 20G122, Gouverneur, Guinée Française, Conakry, "Rapport Politique Mensuel, Decémbre 1955," 2 Feb. 1956, #50/APA; 2G55/151, "Revues Trimestrielles des Événements, 4ème Trimestre 1955," 15 March 1956. See also 17G573, Guinée Française, Services de Police, Conakry, "Compte-Rendu de la Réunion Publique du Parti Démocratique de Guinée Française (P.D.G.)—Ex-R.D.A.—tenue au Domicile d'Amara Soumah le 24 Octobre 1950 de 18h30 à 20 heures," 25 Oct. 1950,

#1248/221, C/PS/BM; Christopher Hayden, e-mail communication, 26 Oct. 2001; Hodgkin, *African Political Parties,* 69, 71–72, 143; Kéïta, *P.D.G.,* 1:245.

181. Kéïta, *P.D.G.,* 1:129. On numerous occasions, Sékou Touré publicly thanked Governor Parisot for his staunch opposition to the RDA, asserting that it was state-sponsored repression that had "allowed the [RDA] to become the organized champion of the people." Quoted in Morgenthau, *Political Parties in French-Speaking West Africa,* 243.

182. CAOM, Carton 2143, dos. 8, "Motion," R.D.A. Comités de Quartier, Conakry, 29 Sept. 1955; Carton 2143, dos. 8, " . . . La Situation Politique en Guinée Française, " *Interafrique Presse,* ca. Oct. 1955; CRDA, Bureau Exécutif, P.D.G., Conakry, aux S/Sections et Comités du R.D.A., 6 Oct. 1955, in *P.D.G.-R.D.A. . . . Activités—Répression—Élections;* Bureau Exécutif, P.D.G., Conakry, aux Sections Territoriales du R.D.A., ca. 6 Oct. 1955, in *P.D.G.-R.D.A. . . . Activités—Répression—Élections;* Sékou Touré, Dakar, à Ministre, FOM, Paris, 6 Oct. 1955, in *P.D.G.-R.D.A. . . . Activités—Répression—Élections;* Sékou Touré, Dakar, à Haut Commissaire, Dakar, 7 Oct. 1955, in *P.D.G.-R.D.A. . . . Activités—Répression—Élections;* interview with Fatou Diarra, 17 March 1991; Kéïta, *P.D.G.,* 1:325.

CHAPTER 4

1. Jean-Pierre Rioux, *The Fourth Republic, 1944–1958,* trans. Godfrey Rogers (New York: Cambridge University Press, 1987), 216–18, 227–28, 237–39, 244–45; Ivan Hrbek, "North Africa and the Horn," in *Africa since 1935,* ed. Ali A. Mazrui and C. Wondji, vol. 8 of *General History of Africa* (Berkeley: University of California Press, 1999), 127–37; Tony Chafer, *The End of Empire in French West Africa: France's Successful Decolonization?* (New York: Berg, 2002), 145.

2. Hrbek, "North Africa and the Horn," 129, 132–35; Ruth Schachter Morgenthau, *Political Parties in French-Speaking West Africa* (Oxford: Clarendon Press, 1964), 66, 71–72.

3. ANS, 20G136, Télégramme Départ, Afcours, à tous Gouverneurs, 4 July 1956, #80237; 20G136, Télégramme Départ, Haut Commissaire, Dakar, à tous Gouverneurs, 20 July 1956, #80266; 20G136, Gouverneur, Guinée Française, Conakry, à Haut Commissaire, Dakar, "*Objet:* Suffrage Universel dans les T.O.M.," 3 Aug. 1956, #2072, CB/SL.

4. Quoted in Morgenthau, *Political Parties in French-Speaking West Africa,* 66, 70.

5. Ibid., 71.

6. Ibid., 67; Edward Mortimer, *France and the Africans, 1944–1960: A Political History* (New York: Walker and Co., 1969), 259.

7. Mortimer, *France and the Africans,* 231–40; Rioux, *Fourth Republic,* 263; Georges Chaffard, *Les Carnets Secrets de la Décolonisation* (Paris: Calmann-Lévy, 1967), 2:174; Virginia Thompson and Richard Adloff, *French West Africa* (New York: Greenwood Press, 1969), 95; Kenneth Robinson, "Senegal: The Elections to the Territorial Assembly, March 1957," in *Five Elections in Africa,* ed. W. J. M. MacKenzie and Kenneth Robinson (Oxford: Oxford University Press, 1960), 332; Ruth Schachter and Im-

manuel Wallerstein, "French Africa's Road to Independence: 2," *West Africa* 2, no. 2141 (26 April 1958): 395.

The reasons for Houphouët-Boigny's antifederalist position are discussed more fully in chap. 5. The signatories to the law included the President of the Republic (René Coty), Prime Minister (Guy Mollet), Minister of Justice (François Mitterrand), Minister of Overseas France (Gaston Defferre), and Houphouët-Boigny (Minister without portfolio). Mortimer, *France and the Africans,* 234–35.

8. Sidiki Kobélé Kéïta, *Le P.D.G.: Artisan de l'Indépendance Nationale en Guinée (1947–1958)* (Conakry: I.N.R.D.G., Bibliothèque Nationale, 1978), 2:12; R. W. Johnson, "The Parti Démocratique de Guinée and the Mamou 'Deviation,'" in *African Perspectives: Papers in the History, Politics and Economics of Africa Presented to Thomas Hodgkin,* ed. Christopher Allen and R. W. Johnson (New York: Cambridge University Press, 1970), 349.

For nearly two centuries, the Almamy of Timbo was the most important political and religious leader of the Futa Jallon, ruling over a confederation of nine provinces. Two lineages, the Soriya and the Alfaya, alternately held the title. In 1896, a Soriya Almamy, Bokar Biro, died in battle while opposing French conquest. Subsequently, in an attempt to destroy Soriya power, French authorities moved Soriya lineage members from their capital in the central location of Timbo to Dabola, on the fringes of the Futa Jallon. Isolated and with little influence, the Almamy's status was reduced to that of canton chief—and collaborator with the colonial regime. In the 1950s, the Soriyas were represented by the Dabola canton chief, Almamy Barry Aguibou, father of the BAG deputy.

Meanwhile, the loyal Alfaya lineage was resettled in Mamou—close to Timbo—from which the Alfaya leader continued to exercise great influence. In 1950, the Mamou canton chief was designated paramount chief of the Futa Jallon by the colonial administration. In the 1950s, the Alfayas were represented by the Mamou canton chief, Almamy Ibrahima Sory Dara. Morgenthau, *Political Parties in French-Speaking West Africa,* 240; Johnson, "Parti Démocratique de Guinée," 349; Jean Suret-Canale, "La Fin de la Chefferie en Guinée," *Journal of African History* 7, no. 3 (1966): 464–68; William Derman, *Serfs, Peasants, and Socialists: A Former Serf Village in the Republic of Guinea* (Berkeley: University of California Press, 1973), 2, 12–14; Martin Klein, *Slavery and Colonial Rule in French West Africa* (New York: Cambridge University Press, 1998), 147–48.

9. Morgenthau, *Political Parties in French-Speaking West Africa,* 19, 243, 246, 345; Johnson, "Parti Démocratique de Guinée," 351; Thomas E. O'Toole, *Historical Dictionary of Guinea (Republic of Guinea/Conakry),* 2nd ed. (Metuchen, NJ: Scarecrow Press, 1987), 49; Aly Gilbert Iffono, *Lexique Historique de la Guinée-Conakry* (Paris: L'Harmattan, 1992), 48; interview with Bocar Biro Barry, Conakry, 29 Jan. 1991.

Aissatou N'Diaye claims that Saïfoulaye was also a grandson of Alfa Yaya Diallo, a chief of the Labé region, an early resister to colonial conquest, and a rival of Bokar Biro. Alfa Yaya eventually collaborated with the French in order to defeat Bokar Biro. In the end, his allies turned on him, and Alfa Yaya was arrested and deported. He died in exile in 1912. Suret-Canale, "Fin de la Chefferie en Guinée," 464–68; Klein, *Slavery and Colonial Rule,* 147–48; O'Toole, *Historical Dictionary of Guinea,* 16; Iffono,

Lexique Historique de la Guinée-Conakry, 19; interview with Aissatou N'Diaye, Conakry, 8 April 1991.

10. Kéïta, *P.D.G.,* 2:13, 21; Jean Suret-Canale, *La République de Guinée* (Paris: Éditions Sociales, 1970), 163.

11. ANS, 20G123, "Élections Législatives du 2 Janvier 1956, Liste du Rassemblement Démocratique Africain."

12. ANS, 2G55/152, Guinée Française, Gouverneur, "Rapport Politique Annuel, 1955," #281/APA; 2G55/151, Guinée Française, Gouverneur, Conakry, à Haut Commissaire, Dakar, "Revues Trimestrielles des Événements, 4ème Trimestre 1955," 15 March 1956, #131/APA. See also Thomas Hodgkin, *African Political Parties: An Introductory Guide* (Gloucester, MA: Peter Smith, 1971), 25–26.

13. ANS, 2G56/139, Guinée Française, Gouverneur, "Revues Trimestrielles des Événements, 1er Trimestre 1956," 11 May 1956, #223/APA.

14. ANS, 2G56/138, Guinée Française, Gouverneur, "Rapport Politique Mensuel, Février 1956."

15. ANS, 20G122, Gouverneur, Guinée Française, Conakry, "Rapport Politique Mensuel, Décembre 1955," 2 Feb. 1956, #50/APA; 2G55/152, "Rapport Politique Annuel, 1955." For popular resistance to the chieftaincy, see Elizabeth Schmidt, *Mobilizing the Masses: Gender, Ethnicity, and Class in the Nationalist Movement in Guinea, 1939–1958* (Portsmouth, NH: Heinemann, 2005), chap. 4.

16. ANS, 2G55/151, "Revues Trimestrielles des Événements, 4ème Trimestre 1955," 15 March 1956; 2G55/152, "Rapport Politique Annuel, 1955."

17. ANS, 20G123, Directeur des Services de Sécurité, Dakar, à tous Chefs de Sûreté, AOF, 12 Dec. 1955, Circulaire #07800/INT/S/DA.

18. ANS, 20G123, "Élections Législatives du 2 Janvier 1956, Liste du RDA."

19. From an unpublished speech by Sékou Touré, Dakar, 19 Feb. 1956, quoted in Morgenthau, *Political Parties in French-Speaking West Africa,* 65–66. See also ANS, 20G123, "Élections Législatives du 2 Janvier 1956, Liste du RDA."

20. ANS, 20G122, Gouverneur, Guinée Française, Conakry, à Haut Commissaire, Dakar, 6 Jan. 1956, #6/CAB. See also Hodgkin, *African Political Parties,* 69, 71–72, 143.

21. ANS, 2G55/152, "Rapport Politique Annuel, 1955." Hodgkin, *African Political Parties,* 69, 71.

22. ANS, 20G122, "Rapport Politique Mensuel, Décembre 1955"; 20G122, Gouverneur à Haut Commissaire, 6 Jan. 1956; 20G123, Guinée Française, Services de Police, Conakry, "Renseignements A/S Autocritique B.A.G. sur son Échec Partiel aux Élections Législatives du 2 Janvier Dernier," 19 Jan. 1956, #64/16, C/PS.2.

23. CRDA, "Élections de Guinée," *Afrique Nouvelle,* no. 385, 22 Dec. 1954; Claude Gérard, "Incidents en Guinée Française, 1954–1955," *Afrique Informations,* no. 34, 15 March-1 April 1955, 3–5; ANS, 2G55/152, "Rapport Politique Annuel, 1955." See also ANS, 20G123, Télégramme Départ, Haut Commissaire, Dakar, à FOM, Paris, 20 Dec. 1955, #769; Morgenthau, *Political Parties in French-Speaking West Africa,* 240, 397; Chafer, *End of Empire in French West Africa,* 147.

The governor's figures vary slightly. His report indicates that there were 472,837 registered voters in June 1954. See ANS, 2G55/152, "Rapport Politique Annuel, 1955."

24. Kéïta, *P.D.G.,* 2:11.

25. ANS, 20G122, Gouverneur à Haut Commissaire, 6 Jan. 1956. See also Hodgkin, *African Political Parties,* 35–36.

26. ANS, 2G55/152, "Rapport Politique Annuel, 1955."

27. ANS, 20G122, Gouverneur à Haut Commissaire, 6 Jan. 1956; Morgenthau, *Political Parties in French-Speaking West Africa,* 244.

28. ANS, 20G122, "Rapport Politique Mensuel, Décembre 1955."

29. Morgenthau, *Political Parties in French-Speaking West Africa,* 244. See also Hodgkin, *African Political Parties,* 71–72, 143.

30. Morgenthau, *Political Parties in French-Speaking West Africa,* 244; AG, AM-1339, Idiatou Camara, "La Contribution de la Femme de Guinée à la Lutte de Libération Nationale (1945–1958)," Mémoire de Fin d'Études Supérieures, Conakry, IPGAN, 1979, 99; interview with Fatou Diarra, Conakry, 17 March 1991.

31. Morgenthau, *Political Parties in French-Speaking West Africa,* 244.

32. ANS, 20G123, Sécurité, Dakar, à Chefs de Sûreté, AOF, 12 Dec. 1955.

33. ANS, 20G123, Télégramme Départ, Haut Commissaire, Dakar, à tous Gouverneurs, 12 Dec. 1955, #40.186–88.

34. ANS, 20G123, Télégramme Arrivée, Haut Commissaire, Dakar. Envoyé par Gouverneur, Guinée Française, Conakry, 13 Dec. 1955, #515; 20G123, Télégramme Arrivée, Haut Commissaire, Dakar. Envoyé par Gouverneur, Guinée Française, Conakry, 13 Dec. 1955, #516.

35. ANS, 20G123, Télégramme Départ, Haut Commissaire, Dakar, à tous Gouverneurs, 24 Dec. 1955, #40.193.

36. Quoted in Morgenthau, *Political Parties in French-Speaking West Africa,* 245.

For a discussion of government attempts to bribe CGT and RDA members, see Morgenthau, *Political Parties in French-Speaking West Africa,* 243, 245; Frederick Cooper, *Decolonization and African Society: The Labor Question in French and British Africa* (New York: Cambridge University Press, 1996), 604n29; Chaffard, *Carnets Secrets de la Décolonisation,* 2:181; ANS, 17G586, Guinée Française, Services de Police, Conakry, "Renseignements A/S Réunion Publique tenue le 8 Novembre 1956, à Conakry Cinéma 'VOX' par le P.D.G.-R.D.A., pour l'Ouverture de la Campagne Électorale," 9 Nov. 1956, #2301/804, C/PS.2; 17G586, Guinée Française, Services de Police, Kindia, "Renseignements A/S Conférence Publique tenue par la Section R.D.A. de Kindia, au Cinéma 'VOX' le 11 Nov. 1956," 13 Nov. 1956, #2325/817, C/PS.2; 17G613, Guinée Française, Services de Police, Conakry, "Renseignements A/S Conférence Publique d'Informations tenue à Conakry, Salle du Cinéma 'VOX,' le Lundi 11 Mars 1957, par le P.D.G.-R.D.A.," 12 March 1957, #565/249, C/PS.2.

37. The governor acknowledged that all previous elections had been conducted under the supervision of the canton chiefs, who had served as intermediaries for the administration. ANS, 20G122, "Rapport Politique Mensuel, Décembre 1955." See also 2G55/151, "Revues Trimestrielles des Événements, 4ème Trimestre 1955," 15 March 1956.

38. ANS, 20G122, "Rapport Politique Mensuel, Décembre 1955"; Kéïta, *P.D.G.,* 2:11; Camara, "Contribution de la Femme," 99.

39. Morgenthau compiled these stipulations from the RDA's mimeographed instructions, dated December 20, 1955 and drafted by Nfamara Kéïta, a clerk in the judiciary

and the second secretary of the Guinean RDA. Morgenthau, *Political Parties in French-Speaking West Africa*, 245–46.

40. ANS, 20G122, "Rapport Politique Mensuel, Décembre 1955."

41. Interview with Aissatou N'Diaye, 8 April 1991.

42. Camara, "Contribution de la Femme," 100.

43. ANS, 2G55/152, "Rapport Politique Annuel, 1955." See also Kéïta, *P.D.G.*, 2:9.

44. ANS, 20G122, Guinée Française, "Résultats, Élections Législatives, 2 Janvier 1956"; CAOM, Carton 2181, dos. 6, Télégramme Arrivée, FOM, Paris. Envoyé par Gouverneur, Guinée Française, Conakry, 17 Sept. 1958, #355–356; Sidiki Kobélé Kéïta, *Ahmed Sékou Touré: L'Homme du 28 Septembre 1958,* 2nd ed. (Conakry: I.N.R.D.G., Bibliothèque Nationale, 1977), 62.

45. ANS, 17G573, Haut Commissaire, Dakar, à Gouverneur, Guinée Française, Conakry, 25 June 1951, #591, AP.2; 20G122, "Rapport Politique Mensuel, Décembre 1955"; 2G55/152, "Rapport Politique Annuel, 1955"; 20G122, "Résultats, Élections Législatives, 2 Janvier 1956"; Morgenthau, *Political Parties in French-Speaking West Africa*, 246; Kéïta, *P.D.G.*, 2:21.

46. ANS, 2G55/152, "Rapport Politique Annuel, 1955."

47. Kéïta, *P.D.G.*, 1:309, 311, 2:9; Suret-Canale, *République de Guinée*, 164.

This calculation does not include Amara Soumah, who resigned from the RDA immediately after his re-election to the Territorial Assembly in March 1952. (See chap. 2.)

48. ANS, 20G122, Gouverneur à Haut Commissaire, 6 Jan. 1956. See also 2G55/152, "Rapport Politique Annuel, 1955."

49. ANS, 20G122, Gouverneur à Haut Commissaire, 6 Jan. 1956. See also Hodgkin, *African Political Parties*, 130.

50. Morgenthau, *Political Parties in French-Speaking West Africa*, 246.

51. ANS, 20G122, "Rapport Politique Mensuel, Décembre 1955."

52. ANS, 2G55/152, "Rapport Politique Annuel, 1955." See also Hodgkin, *African Political Parties*, 25–26, 125, 145–46.

53. ANS, 2G55/152, "Rapport Politique Annuel, 1955"; 2G56/138, Guinée Française, Gouverneur, "Rapport Politique Mensuel, Mai 1956," 11 June 1956, #260/APA.

54. ANS, 2G55/152, "Rapport Politique Annuel, 1955." See also Hodgkin, *African Political Parties*, 23–24, 135.

55. ANS, 20G122, "Rapport Politique Mensuel, Décembre 1955"; 2G55/152, "Rapport Politique Annuel, 1955"; 20G122, "Résultats, Élections Législatives, 2 Janvier 1956"; 20G122, Gouverneur à Haut Commissaire, 6 Jan. 1956.

56. ANS, 20G122, "Rapport Politique Mensuel, Décembre 1955"; 20G122, "Résultats, Élections Législatives, 2 Janvier 1956."

57. ANS, 2G55/150, Guinée Française, Gouverneur, "Rapport Politique Mensuel, Novembre 1955," 28 Dec. 1955, #587/APA.

58. ANS, 20G122, "Rapport Politique Mensuel, Décembre 1955"; 2G55/152, "Rapport Politique Annuel, 1955."

59. ANS, 20G122, "Rapport Politique Mensuel, Décembre 1955."

60. ANS, 2G56/139, "Revues Trimestrielles des Événements, 1er Trimestre 1956," 11 May 1956.

61. ANS, 2G55/152, "Rapport Politique Annuel, 1955."

62. ANS, 20G122, "Rapport Politique Mensuel, Décembre 1955"; 20G122, "Résultats, Élections Législatives, 2 Janvier 1956"; 20G122, Gouverneur à Haut Commissaire, 6 Jan. 1956; Kéïta, *P.D.G.*, 2:23; Suret-Canale, *République de Guinée,* 163.

63. ANS, 2G55/152, "Rapport Politique Annuel, 1955." For a comparison with 1954, see Morgenthau, *Political Parties in French-Speaking West Africa,* 233.

64. ANS, 20G122, Gouverneur à Haut Commissaire, 6 Jan. 1956.

65. ANS, 20G122, "Rapport Politique Mensuel, Décembre 1955."

66. Morgenthau, *Political Parties in French-Speaking West Africa,* 235. For further discussion of RDA mobilization of former slaves and their descendants, other low-status peoples, and ethnic outsiders in the Futa Jallon, see Schmidt, *Mobilizing the Masses,* chap. 6.

67. Klein, *Slavery and Colonial Rule,* 155, 253.

68. Ibid., 253; Suret-Canale, *République de Guinée,* 89.

69. Klein, *Slavery and Colonial Rule,* 45, 188; Suret-Canale, "Fin de la Chefferie en Guinée," 464–65; Derman, *Serfs, Peasants, and Socialists,* 12–13, 30; Walter Rodney, "Jihad and Social Revolution in Futa Djalon in the Eighteenth Century," *Journal of the Historical Society of Nigeria* 4, no. 2 (June 1968): 269–84; A. S. Kanya-Forstner, "Mali-Tukulor," in *West African Resistance: The Military Response to Colonial Occupation,* ed. Michael Crowder (New York: Africana, 1971), 53–79.

The term "Jallonke" or "men of the Jallon" refers to the people of a region, rather than an ethnic group. The Jallonke trace their roots to several populations. The Susu, part of the greater Mande group, settled in the Futa Jallon in the thirteenth century. They displaced or absorbed most of the original inhabitants, including the Limbas, Landumas, Bagas, and Bassaris. The resulting population is referred to collectively as the Jallonke. Rodney, "Jihad and Social Revolution," 270.

70. Suret-Canale, *République de Guinée,* 89.

71. Klein, *Slavery and Colonial Rule,* 155–56, 187, 192–93.

72. Ibid., 250–51.

73. ANS, 17G586, Guinée Française, Services de Police, Labé, "Renseignements *Objet:* Section R.D.A. de Labé," 29 Oct. 1954, #2870/1102, C/PS.2. See also interview with Bocar Biro Barry, 29 Jan. 1991; Klein, *Slavery and Colonial Rule,* 250–51.

74. Suret-Canale, "Fin de la Chefferie en Guinée," 464–65; Derman, *Serfs, Peasants, and Socialists,* 2, 16–17; Rodney, "Jihad and Social Revolution," 278; interview with Bocar Biro Barry, 29 Jan. 1991.

75. Andrew F. Clark, *From Frontier to Backwater: Economy and Society in the Upper Senegal Valley (West Africa), 1850–1920* (Lanham, MD: University Press of America, 1999), 47; interview with Bocar Biro Barry, 29 Jan. 1991.

76. Klein, *Slavery and Colonial Rule,* 194, 227, 250; Rodney, "Jihad and Social Revolution," 274, 278; Derman, *Serfs, Peasants, and Socialists,* 17, 37–39; Suret-Canale, *République de Guinée,* 88; Clark, *Frontier to Backwater,* 47; communication from Siba N. Grovogui, 1991.

77. Klein, *Slavery and Colonial Rule,* 238; Derman, *Serfs, Peasants, and Socialists,* 8, 15; Suret-Canale, *République de Guinée,* 92; interview with Bocar Biro Barry, 29 Jan. 1991.

78. Informant quoted in Morgenthau, *Political Parties in French-Speaking West Africa*, 234–35. See also Klein, *Slavery and Colonial Rule*, 238.

The late-nineteenth-century empire of the Malinke leader Samori Touré brought together a vast expanse of territory that included Upper-Guinea and the forest region and extended eastward to modern Ghana. Although Samori Touré was revered during the nationalist period for his seventeen-year conflict with the French, which staved off colonial rule for nearly two decades, inhabitants of the region he conquered were devastated by war and enslavement. Morgenthau, *Political Parties in French-Speaking West Africa*, 234–35; Yves Person, "Guinea-Samori," trans. Joan White, in Crowder, ed., *West African Resistance*, 111–43; Daniel R. Headrick, *The Tools of Empire: Technology and European Imperialism in the Nineteenth Century* (New York: Oxford University Press, 1981), 119–20; interview with Bocar Biro Barry, 29 Jan. 1991. See also papers presented at the panel "Samori Touré One Hundred Years On: Exploring the Ambiguities," Annual Meeting of the African Studies Association, Philadelphia, PA, 13 Nov. 1999: David C. Conrad, "Victims, Warriors, and Power Sources: Portrayals of Women in Guinean Narratives of Samori Touré"; Saidou Mohamed N'Daou, "Almamy Samory Touré: Politics of Memories in Post-Colonial Guinea (1958–1984)"; Emily Osborn, "Samori Touré in Upper Guinea: Hero or Tyrant?"; Jeanne M. Toungara, "Kabasarana and the Samorian Conquest of Northwestern Cote d'Ivoire."

79. ANS, 20G122, "Rapport Politique Mensuel, Décembre 1955"; 2G55/152, "Rapport Politique Annuel, 1955"; 2G56/139, "Revues Trimestrielles des Événements, 1er Trimestre 1956," 11 May 1956.

80. ANS, 2G55/152, "Rapport Politique Annuel, 1955"; 2G56/139, "Revues Trimestrielles des Événements, 1er Trimestre 1956," 11 May 1956.

81. ANS, 20G122, "Rapport Politique Mensuel, Décembre 1955."

82. ANS, 2G55/152, "Rapport Politique Annuel, 1955"; 20G122, Gouverneur à Haut Commissaire, 6 Jan. 1956.

83. ANS, 20G122, Gouverneur à Haut Commissaire, 6 Jan. 1956.

84. ANS, 2G55/152, "Rapport Politique Annuel, 1955."

85. ANS, 20G122, Gouverneur à Haut Commissaire, 6 Jan. 1956.

86. ANS, 20G122, "Rapport Politique Mensuel, Décembre 1955."

87. ANS, 2G55/152, "Rapport Politique Annuel, 1955."

88. ANS, 2G56/139, "Revues Trimestrielles des Événements, 1er Trimestre 1956," 11 May 1956.

89. ANS, 20G122, Gouverneur à Haut Commissaire, 6 Jan. 1956.

90. ANS, 20G122, "Rapport Politique Mensuel, Décembre 1955"; 20G123, Police, " . . . Autocritique B.A.G. sur son Échec Partiel . . . ," 19 Jan. 1956.

91. Morgenthau, *Political Parties in French-Speaking West Africa*, 108–9.

92. Mortimer, *France and the Africans*, 247; Cooper, *Decolonization and African Society*, 418–19.

93. Mortimer, *France and the Africans*, 231; Rioux, *Fourth Republic*, 263; Chaffard, *Carnets Secrets de la Décolonisation*, 2:174; Thompson and Adloff, *French West Africa*, 95.

94. Morgenthau, *Political Parties in French-Speaking West Africa*, 241–42, 307; Kéïta, *P.D.G.*, 2:119; Cooper, *Decolonization and African Society*, 407–8; Claude Rivière,

Guinea: The Mobilization of a People, trans. Virginia Thompson and Richard Adloff (Ithaca: Cornell University Press, 1977), 59.

95. ANS, 21G215, Union des Syndicats Sénégal-Mauritanie, Confédération Générale des Travailleurs Africains (C.G.T.A.), Kaolack, "Appel à tous les Travailleurs Africains," 12 Nov. 1955; 21G215, Sûreté, Sénégal, "Renseignements sur la Scission au Sein de l'Union Territoriale des Syndicats C.G.T.K. Sénégal-Mauritanie," 15 Nov. 1955, #1916 C/Su; 2G55/152, "Rapport Politique Annuel, 1955"; 2G56/138, "Rapport Politique Mensuel, Février 1956"; Cooper, *Decolonization and African Society,* 414; Rivière, *Guinea,* 59; Kéïta, *P.D.G.,* 2:119; Sidiki Kobélé Kéïta, *Ahmed Sékou Touré: L'Homme et son Combat Anti-Colonial (1922–1958)* (Conakry: Éditions S.K.K., 1998), 86; Ernest Milcent, *L'A.O.F. Entre en Scène* (Paris: Bibliothèque de l'Homme d'Action, 1958), 133–34; Elliot Berg, "French West Africa," in *Labor and Economic Development,* ed. Walter Galenson (New York: John Wiley and Sons, 1959), 213; Jean Meynaud and Anisse Salah Bey, *Trade Unionism in Africa: A Study of its Growth and Orientation,* trans. Angela Brench (London: Methuen and Co., 1967), 58.

96. ANS, 2G55/152, "Rapport Politique Annuel, 1955."

97. Ibid.; 2G56/138, Guinée Française, Gouverneur, "Rapport Politique Mensuel, Mars 1956," 19 April 1956, #185/APA; Mortimer, *France and the Africans,* 247; Meynaud and Bey, *Trade Unionism in Africa,* 58–59; Kéïta, *P.D.G.,* 2:119; Kéïta, *Ahmed Sékou Touré: Combat Anti-Colonial,* 87.

98. ANS, 2G56/138, "Rapport Politique Mensuel, Mars 1956"; 17G271, Guinée Française, Services de Police, "Renseignements A/S Réunion Intersyndicale tenue le 28 Avril 1956 au Cinema 'Rialto' à Conakry, par Touré Sékou en vue de la Constitution de la C.G.T.-A.," 29 April 1956, #781/258, C/PS; 179K432, Sékou Touré, Secrétaire Général, et Mamady Kaba, 1er Secrétaire, Union des Syndicats Confédérés de Guinée, Conakry, à Inspecteur Général du Travail, Conakry, 9 May 1956; 179K432, Abdoulaye N'Diaye, Secrétaire Général, C.G.T., Conakry, à Inspecteur Territorial du Travail, Conakry, 10 May 1956, #1/US/CGT/G; 17G271, Guinée Française, Services de Police, "Renseignements d'Activités Nationalistes, *Objet:* AOF-'C.G.T.A.' Activités de Sékou Touré," 11 May 1956, #65/68, ex./10; 179K432, Guinée Française, Inspecteur Territorial du Travail, Conakry, à Inspecteur Général du Travail, Dakar, 19 May 1956, #67T; 2G56/138, "Rapport Politique Mensuel, Mai 1956"; Kéïta, *P.D.G.,* 2:120; Kéïta, *Ahmed Sékou Touré: Combat Anti-Colonial,* 88–89; Cooper, *Decolonization and African Society,* 414; Johnson, "Parti Démocratique de Guinée," 347.

99. Bakary Djibo and his party, the Union Démocratique Nigérienne, had been expelled from the RDA after refusing to accept its decision to break from the PCF. Abdoulaye Diallo, a prominent trade unionist of Guinean origin who had emerged from the GEC milieu, was based in the French Soudan. When the schism occurred, he was secretary-general of the Soudanese CGT unions, a member of the French West African CGT's coordinating committee, and vice president of the World Federation of Trade Unions. AG, 1E41, Bakary Djibo, Niger, à Sékou Touré, 18 Dec. 1951; 1E41, Guinée Française, Services de Police, "Renseignementas A/S Réunion Comité Directeur du R.D.A. le 21 Janvier 1952," 22 Jan. 1952, #133/79/C/PS.2; ANS, 21G226, Service de la Sûreté, Délégation de Dakar, "Notice de Renseignements Concernant Diallo Abdoulaye," 1 March 1955, #324/C/Su; 2G56/138, "Rapport Politique Mensuel, Mars 1956"; 21G226,

---

Guinée Française, Service de la Sûreté, "Renseignements A/S un Rapprochement Possible des Centrales Syndicales C.G.T. (A & K)," 22 Sept. 1956, #1573; 21G226, Directeur Général de la Sûreté Nationale à Directeur des Services de Sécurité de l'AOF, Dakar, "Re. Déplacements de Syndicalistes," 2 Feb. 1957, SN.RG/10.s, #912; Berg, "French West Africa," 213; Morgenthau, *Political Parties in French-Speaking West Africa*, 309; Mortimer, *France and the Africans*, 255; Kéïta, *Ahmed Sékou Touré: Combat Anti-Colonial*, 86–87; Finn Fuglestad, *A History of Niger, 1850–1960* (New York: Cambridge University Press, 1983), 164; Pierre Kipré, *Le Congrès de Bamako: Ou la Naissance du RDA en 1946* (Paris: Collection Afrique Contemporaine, 1989), 103.

100. ANS, 17G613, Guinée Française, Services de Police, Conakry, "Renseignements A/S Retour en Guinée des Délégués à la Conférence de Cotonou," 23 Jan. 1957, #188/86, C/PS.2; Milcent, *A.O.F. Entre en Scène*, 135–37; Meynaud and Bey, *Trade Unionism in Africa*, 58–61; Kéïta, *P.D.G.*, 2:122–24; Robinson, "Senegal," 331; Cooper, *Decolonization and African Society*, 414–15; Ruth Schachter and Immanuel Wallerstein, "French Africa's Road to Independence: 3," *West Africa* 3, no. 2142 (3 May 1958): 419.

101. ANS, 20G136, Télégramme Départ, Afcours, à tous Gouverneurs, 4 July 1956; 20G136, Télégramme Départ, Haut Commissaire, à tous Gouverneurs, 20 July 1956; 20G136, Gouverneur à Haut Commissaire, "*Objet:* Suffrage Universel dans les T.O.M.," 3 Aug. 1956.

102. Morgenthau, *Political Parties in French-Speaking West Africa*, 70; Cooper, *Decolonization and African Society*, 407–8.

103. Morgenthau, *Political Parties in French-Speaking West Africa*, 67.

104. ANS, 17G613, Guinée Française, Services de Police, N'Zérékoré, "Renseignements A/S Passage à N'Zérékoré du Député-Maire Touré Sékou," 26 March 1957, #722/311, C/PS; Morgenthau, *Political Parties in French-Speaking West Africa*, 66–68, 246; Mortimer, *France and the Africans*, 258–61; Suret-Canale, *République de Guinée*, 164.

105. ANS, 20G122, "Rapport Politique Mensuel, Décembre 1955"; 20G136, Gouverneur à Haut Commissaire, "*Objet:* Suffrage Universel dans les T.O.M.," 3 Aug. 1956; Thompson and Adloff, *French West Africa*, 45–46, 54–56; Morgenthau, *Political Parties in French-Speaking West Africa*, 50, 56, 66; Kéïta, *P.D.G.*, 2:39, 71–72.

106. ANS, 20G136, Télégramme Départ, Haut Commissaire, Dakar, à tous Gouverneurs, 10 Nov. 1956, #80.394; 20G136, Haut Commissaire, Dakar, à tous Gouverneurs, Chefs de Territoire, AOF, 12 Feb. 1957, #140.AP.1.

107. Morgenthau, *Political Parties in French-Speaking West Africa*, 68.

108. Ibid., 69.

109. Ibid., 68–70; Mortimer, *France and the Africans*, 258, 260.

110. Morgenthau, *Political Parties in French-Speaking West Africa*, 68; Mortimer, *France and the Africans*, 260.

111. Morgenthau, *Political Parties in French-Speaking West Africa*, 66, 72–73; Mortimer, *France and the Africans*, 258.

112. ANS, 20G136, Télégramme Départ, Afcours, à tous Gouverneurs, 4 July 1956; 20G136, Télégramme Départ, Haut Commissaire, à tous Gouverneurs, 20 July 1956; 20G136, Gouverneur à Haut Commissaire, "*Objet:* Suffrage Universel dans les T.O.M.," 3 Aug. 1956.

There were some exceptions to the general franchise regulations. Some convicted criminals were not eligible to vote. Soldiers and civil servants were not bound by the residence obligations. ANS, 20G136, Gouverneur à Haut Commissaire, "*Objet:* Suffrage Universel dans les T.O.M.," 3 Aug. 1956.

113. ANS, 20G136, Gouverneur à Haut Commissaire, "*Objet:* Suffrage Universel dans les T.O.M.," 3 Aug. 1956; 20G136, Ministre, FOM, Paris à Haut Commissaires, Dakar, Brazzaville, Tananarive, Yaoundé, Lomé; Chefs de Territoires de l'AOF et AEF, 5 Nov. 1956, #1451/CAM; Morgenthau, *Political Parties in French-Speaking West Africa,* 425; Chafer, *End of Empire in French West Africa,* 147.

114. ANS, 20G136, Gouverneur à Haut Commissaire, "*Objet:* Suffrage Universel dans les T.O.M.," 3 Aug. 1956; 17G586, Police, Kindia, " . . . Conférence Publique . . . Section R.D.A. de Kindia . . . 11 Nov. 1956," 13 Nov. 1956; Camara, "Contribution de la Femme," 100; Chafer, *End of Empire in French West Africa,* 143, 147.

115. Kéïta, *P.D.G.,* 2:38–39.

Before the enactment of this law, Senegal was the only French West African territory with fully self-governing municipalities. ANS, 17G586, Guinée Française, Services de Police, Conakry, "Renseignements Conférence du R.D.A. sur les Prochaines Élections Municipales," 29 Oct. 1956, #2224/773, C/PS.2.

116. ANS, 20G132, Gouverneur, Guinée Française, Conakry à Ministre, FOM, Paris, 26 Nov. 1956, #341/APAS; Kéïta, *P.D.G.,* 2:40.

117. ANS, 17G586, Guinée Française, Services de Police, Kankan, "Renseignements A/S Conférence Publique R.D.A. le 31 Octobre 1956 à Kankan," 6 Nov. 1956, #2288/799, C/PS.2; Kéïta, *P.D.G.,* 2:39.

118. ANS, 17G586, Guinée Française, Services de Police, Conakry, "Renseignements A/S Commentaires sur les Élections Municipales du 18 Novembre Dernier à Conakry," 21 Nov. 1956, #2391/845, C/PS.2; 20G132, Gouverneur à Ministre, FOM, 26 Nov. 1956.

119. Morgenthau, *Political Parties in French-Speaking West Africa,* 397; Mortimer, *France and the Africans,* 58, 166, 168.

120. ANS, 20G132, Gouverneur à Ministre, FOM, 26 Nov. 1956. See also 20G132, "Élections Municipales 1956, Communes de Plein Exercice, Résultats"; 20G132, Télégramme Arrivée, Haut Commissaire, Dakar. Envoyé de Gouverneur, Guinée Française, Conakry, 19–22 Nov. 1956, #50.689-#50.696, #50.713.

121. Morgenthau, *Political Parties in French-Speaking West Africa,* 246; Camara, "Contribution de la Femme," 101; Kéïta, *Ahmed Sékou Touré: 28 Septembre,* 64–65.

122. ANS, 20G132, "Élections Municipales 1956 . . . Résultats"; 17G613, Guinée Française, Services de Police, "Renseignements A/S Seconde Conférence Territoriale du P.D.G.- R.D.A. tenue à Labé, les 23 et 24 Février 1957," 28 Feb. 1957, #478/210, C/PS.2; interview with Aissatou N'Diaye, 8 April 1991.

123. Johnson, "Parti Démocratique de Guinée," 349, 355.

124. ANS, 20G132, "Élections Municipales 1956 . . . Résultats"; Johnson, "Parti Démocratique de Guinée," 355.

125. ANS, 17G586, Police, " . . . Commentaires sur les Élections Municipales du 18 Novembre Dernier à Conakry," 21 Nov. 1956.

126. ANS, 17G613, Police, " . . . Seconde Conférence Territoriale du P.D.G.-R.D.A. . . . 23 et 24 Février 1957," 28 Feb. 1957.

127. ANS, 17G586, Police, " . . . Commentaires sur les Élections Municipales du 18 Novembre Dernier à Conakry," 21 Nov. 1956.

128. ANS, 20G132, Gouverneur à Ministre, FOM, 26 Nov. 1956; 20G132, "Élections Municipales 1956 . . . Résultats." No data were available for N'Zérékoré and Mamou.

129. ANS, 17G586, Guinée Française, Services de Police, Kankan, "Renseignements Copie d'une Lettre Adressée par le Député Barry Diawadou à un Ami de Kankan," 6 Nov. 1956, #2285/797, C/PS.2.

130. ANS, 17G586, Guinée Française, Services de Police, Mamou, "Renseignements A/S Conférence tenue le 28 Octobre 1956 à Mamou par le Bloc Africain de Guinée," 30 Oct. 1956, #2249/736, C/PS.2.

131. Interview with Néné Diallo, Conakry, 11 April 1991.

132. ANS, 17G586, Guinée Française, Services de Police, Conakry, "Renseignements A/S Meeting Public tenu le Samedi 1er Décembre 1956, à Conakry, Stade Cornut-Gentille, par le P.D.G.-R.D.A.," 3 Dec. 1956, #2468/881, C/PS.2.

133. Morgenthau, *Political Parties in French-Speaking West Africa,* 15.

134. ANS, 17G586, Guinée Française, Services de Police, Conakry, "Renseignements A/S Conférence Publique d'Information, tenue le 16 Septembre 1956 par le P.D.G.-R.D.A. au Cinéma 'VOX' à Conakry," 17 Sept. 1956, #1907/658, C/PS.2; 17G586, Guinée Française, Services de Police, P. Humbert, Commissaire Divisionnaire, Conakry, à Gouverneur, Guinée Française, Conakry, 19 Sept. 1956, #1924, C/PS.2. See also Hodgkin, *African Political Parties,* 122–23.

135. ANS, 17G586, Police, " . . . Meeting Public tenu le Samedi 1er Décembre 1956 . . . par le P.D.G.-R.D.A.," 3 Dec. 1956.

136. Morgenthau, *Political Parties in French-Speaking West Africa,* 109–11.

137. ANS, 21G215, Union des Syndicats Sénégal-Mauritanie (C.G.T.A.), "Appel à tous les Travailleurs Africains," 12 Nov. 1955; 21G215, Sûreté, Sénégal, " . . . Scission . . . Syndicats C.G.T.K. Sénégal-Mauritanie," 15 Nov. 1955; 2G55/152, "Rapport Politique Annuel, 1955"; 2G56/138, "Rapport Politique Mensuel, Février 1956"; 179K432, Sékou Touré et Mamady Kaba à Inspecteur Général du Travail, 9 May 1956; Meynaud and Bey, *Trade Unionism in Africa,* 58; Kéïta, *P.D.G.,* 2:119.

138. Milcent, *A.O.F. Entre en Scène,* 132–33; Meynaud and Bey, *Trade Unionism in Africa,* 59–60; Kéïta, *P.D.G.,* 2:120–21; Rivière, *Guinea,* 54n2, 59.

139. ANS, 17G271, Police, " . . . Réunion Intersyndicale tenue le 28 Avril 1956 . . . en vue de la Constitution de la C.G.T.-A.," 29 April 1956; 179K432, Sékou Touré et Mamady Kaba à Inspecteur Général du Travail, 9 May 1956; 2G56/138, "Rapport Politique Mensuel, Mai 1956"; Meynaud and Bey, *Trade Unionism in Africa,* 58.

140. ANS, 17G586, Guinée Française, Services de Police, "Renseignements d'Activités Communistes et Apparentés, la Réunion de Conakry," 11 Oct. 1956, #1160/Y (or 67/68 ex./9); 17G613, Police, " . . . Retour en Guinée des Délégués à la Conférence de Cotonou," 23 Jan. 1957; Morgenthau, *Political Parties in French-Speaking West Africa,* 111–12; Milcent, *A.O.F. Entre en Scène,* 135–37; Kéïta, *P.D.G.,* 2:122–24; Kéïta, *Ahmed Sékou Touré: Combat Anti-Colonial,* 89–90; Rivière, *Guinea,* 59; Meynaud

and Bey, *Trade Unionism in Africa,* 59–61; Cooper, *Decolonization and African Society,* 414–15.

141. ANS, 17G613, Guinée Française, Services de Police, Conakry, "Renseignements A/S Commemoration de la Fête du Travail du 1er Mai 1957 à Conakry," 2 May 1957, #979/395, C/PS.2; Kéïta, *P.D.G.,* 2:124; Kéïta, *Ahmed Sékou Touré: Combat Anti-Colonial,* 91.

142. Kéïta, *Ahmed Sékou Touré: Combat Anti-Colonial,* 92; Chafer, *End of Empire in French West Africa,* 124–25.

143. Mortimer, *France and the Africans,* 248; Berg, "French West Africa," 249–50n62; Immanuel Wallerstein, "How Seven States Were Born in Former French West Africa," *Africa Report* (March 1961): 4.

144. CRDA, "Autour du Procès David Sylla: Motion," *La Liberté,* 29 April 1956, 2; ANS, 17G573, Guinée Française, Services de Police, "Renseignements A/S Manifestation sur la Voie Publique Organisée par le R.D.A. à Kindia," 4 May 1956, #800/267, C/PS.2.

145. ANS, 17G613, Guinée Française, Services de Police, Gendarmerie, Conakry, "Renseignements A/S Vie Politique à l'Intérieur du Pays," 22 March 1957, #669/290, C/PS.2.

Only one year earlier, El-Hadj Abdoulaye Touré had chastised Kankan RDA leader Lamine Ibrahima Kaba for his insolent attitude toward the French. ANS, 2G56/138, "Rapport Politique Mensuel, Mars 1956."

146. ANS, 17G613, Police, Gendarmerie, " . . . Vie Politique à l'Intérieur du Pays," 22 March 1957.

147. Ibid. "Daba" is the Maninka term for a short-handled hoe.

148. ANS, 17G613, Guinée Française, Services de Police, "Renseignements A/S Vie Politique dans le Territoire," 11 March 1957, #557/248, C/PS.2; 17G613, Guinée Française, Services de Police, Gendarmerie, Conakry, "Renseignements A/S Vie Politique à l'Intérieur du Territoire," 28 March 1957, #734/316, C/PS.2.

149. ANS, 17G613, Guinée Française, Services de Police, Conakry, "Renseignements A/S Conférence Publique d'Informations Électorales tenue à Conakry, Salle du Cinéma 'VOX,' le Mercredi 27 Mars 1957, par le P.D.G.-R.D.A.," 28 March 1957, #731/315, C/PS.2. See also Morgenthau, *Political Parties in French-Speaking West Africa,* 247.

150. ANS, 20G136, "Suffrage Universel," unidentified press clipping, before 31 March 1957.

151. Morgenthau, *Political Parties in French-Speaking West Africa,* 246; Kéïta, *P.D.G.,* 2:51.

152. ANS, 17G613, Guinée Française, Services de Police, Conakry, "Renseignements A/S Commentaires sur la Récente Répartition des Sièges de l'Assemblée Territoriale Guinéenne," 23 Jan. 1957, #187/85, C/PS.2; Thompson and Adloff, *French West Africa,* 56; Kéïta, *P.D.G.,* 1:191.

153. CAOM, Carton 2181, dos. 6, "Note sur la Guinée," 6 May 1958; Morgenthau, *Political Parties in French-Speaking West Africa,* 400, 412; Thompson and Adloff, *French West Africa,* 555; Kéïta, *P.D.G.,* 1:191.

154. ANS, 17G586, Guinée Française, Services de Police, Conakry, "Renseignements A/S Réunion Publique Électorale tenue par le B.A.G. au Cinéma 'VOX' à Conakry,

le Mercredi 14 Novembre 1956," 15 Nov. 1956, #2345/822, C/PS.2; 17G613, Police, " . . . Répartition des Sièges de l'Assemblée Territoriale Guinéenne," 23 Jan. 1957.

155. ANS, 17G613, Police, " . . . Répartition des Sièges de l'Assemblée Territoriale Guinéenne," 23 Jan. 1957.

156. Ibid.; Morgenthau, *Political Parties in French-Speaking West Africa,* 412–13; Suret-Canale, *République de Guinée,* 150.

157. ANS, 17G613, Police, " . . . Répartition des Sièges de l'Assemblée Territoriale Guinéenne," 23 Jan. 1957; 17G613, Police, " . . . Seconde Conférence Territoriale du P.D.G.-R.D.A. . . . 23 et 24 Février 1957," 28 Feb. 1957; 17G613, Guinée Française, Services de Police, "Conférence Territoriale du P.D.G. tenue à Labé le 23 et 24 Février 1957"; Derman, *Serfs, Peasants, and Socialists,* 8, 14.

158. ANS, 17G613, Police, N'Zérékoré, " . . . Passage à N'Zérékoré du Député-Maire Touré Sékou," 26 March 1957; Kéïta, *P.D.G.,* 2:58–60; Suret-Canale, *République de Guinée,* 165.

159. ANS, 17G613, Police, Gendarmerie, " . . . Vie Politique à l'Intérieur du Territoire," 28 March 1957.

160. Ibid.

161. ANS, 17G586, Guinée Française, Services de Police, Kankan, "Renseignements A/S B.A.G. et Élections Municipales," 24 Oct. 1956, #2200/763, C/PS.2.

162. ANS, 17G613, Police, " . . . Conférence Publique d'Informations . . . 11 Mars 1957, par le P.D.G.-R.D.A.," 12 March 1957.

163. ANS, 17G613, Police, " . . . Conférence Publique d'Informations Électorales . . . 27 Mars 1957, par le P.D.G.-R.D.A., " 28 March 1957.

164. ANS, 17G613, Guinée Française, Services de Police, Conakry, "Renseignements A/S Réunions de Comités de Quartier R.D.A. tenues à Conakry le Vendredi 29 Mars 1957," 30 March 1957, #745/320, C/PS.2.

165. Suret-Canale, *République de Guinée,* 145, 164; Kéïta, *P.D.G.,* 2:55.

166. CAOM, Carton 2181, dos. 6, Télégramme Arrivée, FOM. Envoyé par Gouverneur, Guinée Française, 17 Sept. 1958; Morgenthau, *Political Parties in French-Speaking West Africa,* 246; Suret-Canale, *République de Guinée,* 164; Kéïta, *P.D.G.,* 2:55.

167. Morgenthau, *Political Parties in French-Speaking West Africa,* 246; Suret-Canale, *République de Guinée,* 164; Kéïta, *P.D.G.,* 2:60.

168. Quoted in Camara, "Contribution de la Femme," 104.

Noël Ballay, the first governor of Guinea (1890–1900), symbolized colonial rule more broadly. O'Toole, *Historical Dictionary of Guinea,* 23; Iffono, *Lexique Historique de la Guinée-Conakry,* 24–25; Rivière, *Guinea,* 42.

169. ANS, 17G613, Guinée Française, Services de Police, Conakry, "Renseignements A/S Démissions de la D.S.G.-M.S.A.," 7 May 1957, #1019/412, C/PS.2; 17G613, Guinée Française, Services de Police, Conakry, "Renseignements A/S Activité R.D.A. et Construction Projetée d'une École de Cadre," 15 May 1957, #1085/433, C/PS.2; Johnson, "Parti Démocratique de Guinée," 355.

170. Morgenthau, *Political Parties in French-Speaking West Africa,* 246, 425; Suret-Canale, *République de Guinée,* 164; Johnson, "Parti Démocratique de Guinée," 349.

171. Morgenthau, *Political Parties in French-Speaking West Africa,* 246; Suret-Canale, *République de Guinée,* 164; Kéïta, *Ahmed Sékou Touré: 28 Septembre,* 64–65; Camara, "Contribution de la Femme," 101, 107; Thompson and Adloff, *French West Africa,* 69.

172. For further discussion of tensions between RDA leaders and the rank and file over the use of political violence, see Schmidt, *Mobilizing the Masses,* chap. 6.

173. ANS, 17G613, Guinée Française, Services de Police, Gendarmerie, Conakry, "Vie Politique dans le Territoire," 11 April 1957, #840/357. See also 17G613, Guinée Française, Services de Police, Conakry, "Renseignements A/S Vie Politique à l'Intérieur du Territoire," 18 April 1957, #892/371, C/PS.2.

174. ANS, 17G613, Police, ". . . Vie Politique à l'Intérieur du Territoire," 18 April 1957.

175. ANS, 17G613, Guinée Française, Services de Police, Gendarmerie, Conakry, "Renseignements A/S Vie Politique dans le Territoire," 23 April 1957, #915/376, C/PS.2.

176. ANS, 17G613, Guinée Française, Services de Police, N'Zérékoré, "Renseignements A/S Vie Politique à N'Zérékoré," 3 May 1957, #998/401, C/PS.2.

177. ANS, 17G613, Guinée Française, Services de Police, N'Zérékoré, "Renseignements A/S *Doré* Jean-Marie," 3 May 1957, #1002/404, C/PS.2; 17G613, Guinée Française, Services de Police, N'Zérékoré, "Renseignements A/S Réunion du Bureau Directeur du Comité R.J.D.A. de N'Zérékoré, tenue le 28 Avril 1957," 6 May 1957, #1009/406, C/PS.2.

178. ANS, 17G613, Guinée Française, Services de Police, Conakry, "Renseignements A/S Appel au Calme Lancé par le R.D.A. le Vendredi 26 Avril 1957," 26 April 1957, #951/387, C/PS.2. For the RDA's use of religion in political mobilization, see Elizabeth Schmidt, "Top Down or Bottom Up? Nationalist Mobilization Reconsidered, with Special Reference to Guinea (French West Africa)," *American Historical Review* 110, no. 4 (Oct. 2005): 993–96.

179. ANS, 17G613, Guinée Française, Services de Police, Conakry, "Renseignements A/S Réunion des Jeunes du R.D.A., tenue Hier, Mercredi 17 Avril à Conakry, Quartier Boulbinet," 18 April 1957, #882/366, C/PS.2. For elaboration on these conflicts, see Schmidt, *Mobilizing the Masses,* chap. 7.

180. ANS, 17G613, Guinée Française, Services de Police, Conakry, "Renseignements A/S Réunion de Jeunes Militants R.D.A. du Quartier Boulbinet, tenue le Jeudi 2 Mai 1957 à Conakry," 3 May 1957, #996/400, C/PS.2; Johnson, "Parti Démocratique de Guinée," 355.
The youths' charges against the BAG echoed earlier claims by Governor Bonfils. In his year-end report for 1955, the governor wrote that RDA members filled the prisons and that many were there because BAG members had laid charges against them. The governor worried that BAG actions had backfired, because the RDA had quickly exposed the BAG's role in its plight. BAG members were now considered by the populace to be unabashed collaborators of the colonial administration. ANS, 2G55/152, "Rapport Politique Annuel, 1955."

181. ANS, 17G613, Police, ". . . Activité R.D.A. et Construction . . . École de Cadre," 15 May 1957. See also Hodgkin, *African Political Parties,* 122.

182. ANS, 17G622, Guinée Française, Services de Police, "Renseignements A/S Organisation de Cours Politiques R.D.A.," 21 Oct. 1957, #2357/879, C/PS.2. For the use of political violence by RDA women and youths, see Schmidt, *Mobilizing the Masses,* 133–36, 155–56.

CHAPTER 5

1. Jean Suret-Canale, *La République de Guinée* (Paris: Éditions Sociales, 1970), 164.

2. CAOM, Carton 2181, dos. 6, Gouverneur, Guinée Française, Conakry, à Ministre, FOM, Paris, "Discours Prononcé par le Président Sékou Touré, le 14 Septembre 1958," 15 Sept. 1958, #0191/CAB. See also "Unanimement le 28 Septembre la Guinée Votera Non," *La Liberté,* 23 Sept. 1958, 1–2; CRDA, Fodéba Kéïta, "Rapport du IVème Congrès sur les Réformes Administratives et les Nouvelles Structures," *La Liberté,* 25 July 1958, 3; Ruth Schachter Morgenthau, *Political Parties in French-Speaking West Africa* (Oxford: Clarendon Press, 1964), 250; Sidiki Kobélé Kéïta, *Le P.D.G.: Artisan de l'Indépendance Nationale en Guinée (1947–1958)* (Conakry: I.N.R.D.G., Bibliothèque Nationale, 1978), 2:69–76; Martin Klein, *Slavery and Colonial Rule in French West Africa* (New York: Cambridge University Press, 1998), 238.

3. Kéïta, *P.D.G.,* 2:66–67; Suret-Canale, *République de Guinée,* 164; Jean Suret-Canale, "La Fin de la Chefferie en Guinée," *Journal of African History* 7, no. 3 (1966): 459, 490; AG, MO-33, Sékou Mara, "La Lutte de Libération Nationale et la Chefferie dite Coutumière en Guinée Forestière," Mémoire de Fin d'Études Supérieures, Kankan, IPJN, 1975–76, 66. For a related discussion of chiefs and the nationalist movement in colonial Ghana, see Richard Rathbone, *Nkrumah and the Chiefs: The Politics of Chieftaincy in Ghana, 1951–1960* (Athens: Ohio University Press, 2000).

The abolition of the canton chieftaincy in Guinea was preceded by a high-level conference in July 1957, during which the Council of Government and the circle commandants discussed the pros and cons of the institution. The text of the conference proceedings is reproduced in *Guinée: Prélude à l'Indépendance* (Paris: Présence Africaine, 1958).

4. Suret-Canale, "Fin de la Chefferie en Guinée," 460, 490, 493.

5. Ibid., 459–60, 492; Kéïta, *P.D.G.,* 2:69–76, 147; Klein, *Slavery and Colonial Rule,* 238; Claude Rivière, *Guinea: The Mobilization of a People,* trans. Virginia Thompson and Richard Adloff (Ithaca: Cornell University Press, 1977), 77–78; interview with Mamadou Bela Doumbouya, Conakry, 26 Jan. 1991. For a discussion of Guinean chiefs and their opposition to the RDA, see Elizabeth Schmidt, *Mobilizing the Masses: Gender, Ethnicity, and Class in the Nationalist Movement in Guinea, 1939–1958* (Portsmouth, NH: Heinemann, 2005), chap. 4.

6. ANS, 17G613, Guinée Française, Services de Police, Conakry, "Renseignements A/S Mécontentement Regnant Chez les Évolués Guinéens, Après la Parution des Décrets d'Application de la Loi-Cadre Modifiés par le Conseil de la République," 30 April 1957, #966/393, C/PS.2; 17G622, Guinée Française, Services de Police, "Renseignements A/S Exclusion du P.D.G./R.D.A. de Plusieurs Dirigeants de la S/

Section de Mamou," 15 Nov. 1957, #25___/941, C/PS.2; 17G622, Guinée Française, Services de Police, "Renseignements A/S Conférence Publique tenue à Mamou, le 14 Novembre 1957, par l'Ex-Sous-Section du P.D.G./R.D.A.," 19 Nov. 1957, #2565/954, C/PS.2; 2G57/128, Guinée Française, Police et Sûreté, "Synthèse Mensuelle de Renseignements, Novembre 1957," Conakry, 25 Nov. 1957, #2593/C/PS.2; interview with Fanta Diarra and Ibrahima Fofana, Conakry, 24 May 1991; R. W. Johnson, "The Parti Démocratique de Guinée and the Mamou 'Deviation,'" in *African Perspectives: Papers in the History, Politics and Economics of Africa Presented to Thomas Hodgkin,* ed. Christopher Allen and R. W. Johnson (New York: Cambridge University Press, 1970), 347–48, 352, 354, 358, 362; Thomas Hodgkin, *African Political Parties: An Introductory Guide* (Gloucester, MA: Peter Smith, 1971), 122–23; Virginia Thompson and Richard Adloff, *French West Africa* (New York: Greenwood Press, 1969), 95; Tony Chafer, *The End of Empire in French West Africa: France's Successful Decoloniziation?* (New York: Berg, 2002), 193–217.

7. Chafer, *End of Empire in French West Africa,* 109, 118, 128, 145–50; Charles Diané, *La F.E.A.N.F. et Les Grandes Heures du Mouvement Syndical Étudiant Noir* (Paris: Éditions Chaka, 1990), 44.

8. ANS, 17G622, Police, " . . . Exclusion du P.D.G./R.D.A. de Plusieurs Dirigeants de . . . Mamou," 15 Nov. 1957; 17G622, Police, " . . . Conférence Publique . . . à Mamou . . . par l'Ex-Sous-Section du P.D.G./R.D.A.," 19 Nov. 1957; 2G57/128, Police et Sûreté, "Synthèse Mensuelle de Renseignements, Novembre 1957," 25 Nov. 1957; interview with Fanta Diarra and Ibrahima Fofana, 24 May 1991; Johnson, "Parti Démocratique de Guinée," 347, 352, 362; Hodgkin, *African Political Parties,* 122–23; Thompson and Adloff, *French West Africa,* 95.

9. ANS, 2G53/187, Guinée Française, Secrétaire Général, "Revues Trimestrielles des Événements, 3ème Trimestre 1953," 12 Sept. 1953, #862/APA; 17G613, Police, " . . . Mécontentement Regnant Chez les Évolués . . . ," 30 April 1957; Johnson, "Parti Démocratique de Guinée," 347–48, 354, 358; Hodgkin, *African Political Parties,* 122–23; Thompson and Adloff, *French West Africa,* 95; Kéïta, *P.D.G.,* 2:101; Chafer, *End of Empire in French West Africa,* 193–217; Edward Mortimer, *France and the Africans, 1944–1960: A Political History* (New York: Walker and Co., 1969), 232, 270.

For similar challenges by Asante "youngmen" in colonial Ghana, see Richard Rathbone, "Businessmen in Politics: Party Struggle in Ghana, 1949–57," *Journal of Development Studies* 9, no. 3 (1973): 398–99; Jean Marie Allman, "The Youngmen and the Porcupine: Class, Nationalism and Asante's Struggle for Self-Determination, 1954–57," *Journal of African History* 31, no. 2 (1990): 263–79; Jean Marie Allman, *The Quills of the Porcupine: Asante Nationalism in an Emergent Ghana* (Madison: University of Wisconsin Press, 1993), 8, 28–36; Pashington Obeng, "Gendered Nationalism: Forms of Masculinity in Modern Asante of Ghana," in *Men and Masculinities in Modern Africa,* ed. Lisa A. Lindsay and Stephan F. Miescher (Portsmouth, NH: Heinemann, 2003), 192, 202, 205.

10. Mortimer, *France and the Africans,* 224, 248, 271, 281; Morgenthau, *Political Parties in French-Speaking West Africa,* 112; Suret-Canale, *République de Guinée,* 169; Kéïta, *P.D.G.,* 2:108, 131; Chafer, *End of Empire in French West Africa,* 132, 137, 197, 205–6.

At its founding congress in January 1957, UGTAN condemned loi-cadre for balkanizing French West Africa. Mortimer, *France and the Africans,* 248, 271; Chafer, *End of Empire in French West Africa,* 197.

11. Morgenthau, *Political Parties in French-Speaking West Africa,* 116–17.

12. ANS, 17G586, Guinée Française, Services de Police, P. Humbert, Commissaire Divisionnaire, Conakry, à Gouverneur, Guinée Française, Conakry, 19 Sept. 1956, #1924, C/PS.2; 17G622, Guinée Française, Services de Police, "Renseignements A/S Entrevue ayant eu lieu 17 Juillet Dernier, à l'Assemblée Territoriale à Conakry, entre le Comité Directeur du P.D.G. et le Bureau de l'Union Générale des Étudiants et Élèves de Guinée (U.G.E.E.G.)," 23 July 1957, #1624/634, C/PS.2; 17G622, Guinée Française, Services de Police, "Renseignements A/S Réunion tenue le Lundi 22 Juillet 1957, à Conakry par la S/Section R.D.A. du Quartier Almamya (Prise de Position contre les Étudiants Africains)," 23 July 1957, #1627/636, C/PS.2; 17G622, Guinée Française, Services de Police, "Renseignements A/S Commentaires sur le Congrès Fédéral R.D.A. de Bamako," 9 Oct. 1957, #2257/838, C/PS.2. See also Chafer, *End of Empire in French West Africa,* 109, 125–37, 143, 145, 149–50, 157–58, 193–94, 202–7, 217.

13. ANS, 21G13, Guinée Française, Service de la Sûreté, "État d'Esprit de la Population," 1–15 Dec. 1950; Chafer, *End of Empire in French West Africa,* 145–47; Diané, *F.E.A.N.F.,* 38; Kéïta, *P.D.G.,* 1:233.

14. See below.

15. Chafer, *End of Empire in French West Africa,* 109, 118, 127–28, 136, 149–50.

16. Diané, *F.E.A.N.F.,* 40–41, 43–44; Mortimer, *France and the Africans,* 252.

17. Chafer, *End of Empire in French West Africa,* 150, 157, 202; Mortimer, *France and the Africans,* 252.

18. Diané, *F.E.A.N.F.,* 44; Chafer, *End of Empire in French West Africa,* 128.

19. Chafer, *End of Empire in French West Africa,* 157, 202; Mortimer, *France and the Africans,* 252.

20. ANS, 17G586, Guinée Française, Services de Police, Kankan, "Renseignements A/S P.D.G. et Congrès de Dabola," 24 Sept. 1956, #1965/682, C/PS.2; Diané, *F.E.A.N.F.,* 46–47. See also Mortimer, *France and the Africans,* 252; Chafer, *End of Empire in French West Africa,* 109.

21. See the FEANF cartoon in *L'Étudiant d'Afrique Noire* (June-September 1956), p. 16, described in Morgenthau, *Political Parties in French-Speaking West Africa,* 114.

22. Chafer, *End of Empire in French West Africa,* 136, 202–5.

23. A number of FEANF leaders emerged from the UGEAO milieu. At the FEANF's December 1956 congress, for instance, Charles Diané, a former president of the UGEAO, was elected third vice president. Diané, *F.E.A.N.F.,* 38–39, 46–47.

24. Immanuel Wallerstein, "How Seven States Were Born in Former French West Africa," *Africa Report* (March 1961): 3.

25. Chafer, *End of Empire in French West Africa,* 205.

26. ANS, 17G586, Police, Commissaire Divisionnaire, Conakry, à Gouverneur, 19 Sept. 1956. See also Hodgkin, *African Political Parties,* 122–23, 151.

27. ANS, 17G586, Guinée Française, Services de Police, Gendarmerie, "Renseignements A/S Conférence tenue à Dabola par le Député B.A.G. Barry Diawadou," 14 Sept. 1956, #1890/653, C/PS.2.

The deputy's younger brother is variously referred to as "Barry Bassamba" and "Barry Bassirou." See ANS, 17G622, Police, " . . . Entrevue . . . entre le Comité Directeur du P.D.G. et le Bureau de l' . . . U.G.E.E.G.," 23 July 1957.

28. Chafer, *End of Empire in French West Africa,* 132–33, 137, 143, 149–50, 158, 194, 205–6; Mortimer, *France and the Africans,* 281, 292.

29. AG, 2Z16, "Rassemblement de la Jeunesse Démocratique Africaine," Récépissé de Déclaration d'Association, 1 March 1955, #263; Morgenthau, *Political Parties in French-Speaking West Africa,* 248; Chafer, *End of Empire in French West Africa,* 118, 131.

30. Morgenthau, *Political Parties in French-Speaking West Africa,* 112; Mortimer, *France and the Africans,* 224, 281; Chafer, *End of Empire in French West Africa,* 132, 206; Wallerstein, "How Seven States Were Born," 3.

31. ANS, 17G586, Police, Kankan, " . . . P.D.G. et Congrès de Dabola," 24 Sept. 1956; Johnson, "Parti Démocratique de Guinée," 358.

The RDA's interterritorial congress, initially scheduled for October 1956, was ultimately postponed until September 1957. Aristide R. Zolberg, *One-Party Government in the Ivory Coast* (Princeton: Princeton University Press, 1964), 221–22.

32. ANS, 17G586, Police, Kankan, " . . . P.D.G. et Congrès de Dabola," 24 Sept. 1956.

33. Ibid.; 17G622, Guinée Française, Services de Police, "Renseignements A/S Réunion Publique Organisée, le 8 Décembre 1957, par la Sous-Section R.D.A. de Kankan," 13 Dec. 1957, #2765/1008, C/PS.2.

34. ANS, 17G613, Police, " . . . Mécontentement Regnant Chez les Évolués . . . ," 30 April 1957; 17G622, Guinée Française, Services de Police, "Renseignements A/S 6ème Congrès des Enseignants Africains qui s'est Ouvert à Mamou, le 6 Août Dernier," 10 Aug. 1957, #1800/692, C/PS.2; 17G622, Guinée Française, Services de Police, "Renseignements A/S Conférence Publique tenue dans la Salle du Cinéma de Mamou, par les Enseignants, le Samedi 10 Août Dernier," 16 Aug. 1957, #1837/709, C/PS.2; 17G622, Guinée Française, Services de Police, "Renseignements A/S Conférence Publique tenue le Samedi 17 Août Dernier, par la S/Section P.D.G.-R.D.A. de Kindia," 28 Aug. 1957, #1920/734, C/PS.2; 17G622, Police, " . . . Exclusion du P.D.G./ R.D.A. de Plusieurs Dirigeants de . . . Mamou," 15 Nov. 1957; 2G57/128, Police et Sûreté, "Synthèse Mensuelle de Renseignements, Novembre 1957," 25 Nov. 1957; Personal archives of Bocar Biro Barry, "Travaux du Congrès de Mamou (6–10 Août 1957): Motion sur la Loi-Cadre," *L'École Guinéenne,* no. 1 (1957–58): 1; Johnson, "Parti Démocratique de Guinée," 358, 364; Chafer, *End of Empire in French West Africa,* 203–4; Kéïta, *P.D.G.,* 2:101.

35. ANS, 17G622, Guinée Française, Services de Police, "Renseignements A/S Syndicat Autonome des Cheminots Africains du C.F.C.N.," 23 July 1957, #1623/633, C/PS.2; 17G622, Guinée Française, Services de Police, "Renseignements A/S Activité du Syndicat Autonome des Cheminots Africains," 27 July 1957, #1671/651, C/PS.2; 17G622, Guinée Française, Services de Police, "Renseignements A/S Activités du Syndicat Autonome des Cheminots Africains du Conakry-Niger, Assemblée Générale tenue le Samedi 27 Juillet 1957 à Conakry, devant le Local de ce Syndicat," 30 July 1957, #1690/658, C/PS.2; 17G622, Guinée Française, Services de Police, "Renseignements A/S Exclusion du R.D.A. de KOUYATÉ Diéli Bakar et Répercussions en

Ville," 31 July 1957, #1701/662, C/PS.2; 17G622, Guinée Française, Services de Police, "Renseignements A/S Répercussions à Mamou, de l'Article Intitulé 'Communiqué du P.D.G.' Publié dans le Dernier Numéro du Journal *La Liberté,* Organe de ce Parti," 6 Sept. 1957, #2029/773, C/PS.2; 17G622, Guinée Française, Services de Police, "Renseignements A/S Rebondissement du Conflit des Enseignants Africains," 8 Nov. 1957, #2485/919, C/PS.2; 17G622, Guinée Française, Services de Police, "Renseignements A/S Conflit des Enseignants Guinéens," 12 Nov. 1957, #2500/929, C/PS.2; 17G622, Guinée Française, Services de Police, "Copie du Communiqué du Comité Directeur du *P.D.G.,*" Conakry, 12 Nov. 1957, C/PS.2; 17G622, Police, " . . . Exclusion du P.D.G./R.D.A. de Plusieurs Dirigeants de . . . Mamou," 15 Nov. 1957; 2G57/128, Police et Sûreté, "Synthèse Mensuelle de Renseignements, Novembre 1957," 25 Nov. 1957; Johnson, "Parti Démocratique de Guinée," 347–69; Rivière, *Guinea,* 60; Frederick Cooper, *Decolonization and African Society: The Labor Question in French and British Africa* (New York: Cambridge University Press, 1996), 410–12, 422–24; Sidiki Kobélé Kéïta, *Ahmed Sékou Touré: L'Homme et son Combat Anti-Colonial (1922–1958)* (Conakry: Éditions S.K.K., 1998), 92.

36. ANS, 17G622, Police, " . . . Entrevue . . . entre le Comité Directeur du P.D.G. et le Bureau de l' . . . U.G.E.E.G.," 23 July 1957.

37. ANS, 17G586, Police, Gendarmerie, " . . . A/S Conférence tenue à Dabola par . . . Barry Diawadou," 14 Sept. 1956.

38. ANS, 17G622, Police, " . . . Entrevue . . . entre le Comité Directeur du P.D.G. et le Bureau de l' . . . U.G.E.E.G.," 23 July 1957.

39. Chafer, *End of Empire in French West Africa,* 204–5, 214–17.

40. ANS, 17G622, Police, " . . . Réunion . . . à Conakry par la S/Section R.D.A. du Quartier Almamya (Prise de Position contre les Étudiants Africains)," 23 July 1957.

41. ANS, 17G622, Police, " . . . 6ème Congrès des Enseignants Africains . . . ," 10 Aug. 1957; 17G622, Police, " . . . Conférence Publique . . . par les Enseignants . . . ," 16 Aug. 1957; 2G57/128, Police et Sûreté, "Synthèse Mensuelle de Renseignements, Novembre 1957," 25 Nov. 1957; Johnson, "Parti Démocratique de Guinée," 358, 364.

42. Personal archives of Bocar Biro Barry, " . . . Congrès de Mamou . . . Motion sur la Loi-Cadre."

43. ANS, 17G622, Police, " . . . Conférence Publique . . . S/Section P.D.G.-R.D.A. de Kindia," 28 Aug. 1957; 2G57/128, Police et Sûreté, "Synthèse Mensuelle de Renseignements, Novembre 1957," 25 Nov. 1957; Kéïta, *P.D.G.,* 2:101, 103.

44. See "Communiqué du P.D.G.—Le Congrès des Enseignants à Mamou Lié à la Nouvelle Situation Politique," *La Liberté,* no. 127, 27 Aug. 1957, quoted in ANS, 17G622, Police, " . . . Répercussions à Mamou, de l'Article Intitulé 'Communiqué du P.D.G.' . . . ," 6 Sept. 1957; 17G622, Police, " . . . Conflit des Enseignants Guinéens," 12 Nov. 1957; 17G622, Police, " . . . Exclusion du P.D.G./R.D.A. de Plusieurs Dirigeants de . . . Mamou," 15 Nov. 1957; Personal archives of Bocar Biro Barry, "Nouveau Bureau Directeur [Syndicat du Personnel Enseignant Africain de Guinée]," *L'École Guinéenne,* no. 1 (1957–58).

45. Subsequent arbitration by UGTAN resulted in the cancellation of the November strike. Although Autra was forced to return to his post in Boffa, the RDA

government did not carry out its threat to transfer him out of Guinea as punishment for his insubordination. ANS, 17G622, Police, " . . . Rebondissement du Conflit des Enseignants Africains," 8 Nov. 1957; 17G622, Guinée Française, Services de Police, "Renseignements A/S Conférence d'Information Syndicale tenue le 7 Novembre Dernier, à Mamou, Salle du Cinéma 'REX,' par les Enseignants Africains de cette Ville," 12 Nov. 1957, #2503/932, C/PS.2; 17G622, Guinée Française, Services de Police, "Copie du Communiqué du Bureau Directeur, Syndicat des Enseignants," ca. 12 Nov. 1957, C/PS.2; 17G622, Télégramme Arrivée, Haut Commissaire, Dakar. Envoyé par Gouverneur, Guinée Française, Conakry, 15 Nov. 1957, #329; 2G57/128, Police et Sûreté, "Synthèse Mensuelle de Renseignements, Novembre 1957," 25 Nov. 1957; Kéïta, *P.D.G.*, 2:101, 103; Johnson, "Parti Démocratique de Guinée," 358–60.

46. ANS, 17G622, Police, " . . . Rebondissement du Conflit des Enseignants Africains," 8 Nov. 1957; 17G622, Police, " . . . Conférence d'Information Syndicale . . . Mamou . . . par les Enseignants Africains . . . ," 12 Nov. 1957; 2G57/128, Police et Sûreté, "Synthèse Mensuelle de Renseignements, Novembre 1957," 25 Nov. 1957.

47. ANS, 17G622, Guinée Française, Services de Police, "Renseignements A/S Réunion du Comité Directeur du Syndicat des Cheminots Africains," 14 Nov. 1957, #__531/118, C/PCF; 2G57/128, Police et Sûreté, "Synthèse Mensuelle de Renseignements, Novembre 1957," 25 Nov. 1957.

48. ANS, 17G622, Police, " . . . Exclusion du R.D.A. de KOUYATÉ Diéli Bakar . . . ," 31 July 1957; 17G622, Guinée Française, Services de Police, "Renseignements A/S des Répercussions Causées par la Radiation du R.D.A. du Secrétaire Général du Syndicat Autonome des Cheminots du C.F.C.N. KOUYATÉ Diéli Bakar," 5 Aug. 1957, #1746/675, C/PS.2; 2G57/128, Police et Sûreté, "Synthèse Mensuelle de Renseignements, Novembre 1957," 25 Nov. 1957.

49. ANS, 17G622, Police, " . . . Conflit des Enseignants Guinéens," 12 Nov. 1957; 17G622, Police, " . . . Réunion . . . Syndicat des Cheminots Africains," 14 Nov. 1957; 2G57/128, Police et Sûreté, "Synthèse Mensuelle de Renseignements, Novembre 1957," 25 Nov. 1957.

50. ANS, 17G622, Police, " . . . Commentaires sur le Congrès Fédéral R.D.A. de Bamako," 9 Oct. 1957; 2G57/128, Police et Sûreté, "Synthèse Mensuelle de Renseignements, Novembre 1957," 25 Nov. 1957; Mortimer, *France and the Africans*, 271.

51. Morgenthau, *Political Parties in French-Speaking West Africa*, 81n2, 115, 311; Mortimer, *France and the Africans*, 238–39, 271, 274; Thompson and Adloff, *French West Africa*, 96, 117; Zolberg, *One-Party Government in the Ivory Coast*, 222, 222n10.

D'Arboussier was permitted to rejoin the RDA in 1956. In 1957, he represented Niger in the Grand Council in Dakar, where he served first as vice president and then as president. Morgenthau, *Political Parties in French-Speaking West Africa*, 22, 81n2; Mortimer, *France and the Africans*, 251; Thompson and Adloff, *French West Africa*, 96; Georges Chaffard, *Les Carnets Secrets de la Décolonisation* (Paris: Calmann-Lévy, 1967), 2:290–91; André Blanchet, *L'Itinéraire des Partis Africains depuis Bamako* (Paris: Librarie Plon, 1958), 41.

52. CAOM, Carton 2181, dos. 6, "S.T. Presse Communiqué," *Agence France-Press*, Conakry, 29 Aug. 1958; Morgenthau, *Political Parties in French-Speaking West Africa*, 72, 114–15; Mortimer, *France and the Africans*, 103, 238–39, 274–75; Thompson and Adloff, *French West Africa*, 64–65, 67, 105, 107.

Although each French West African territory was represented in the Grand Council by five councillors, Senegal's influence was disproportionate. Not only did Senegalese councillors hold the presidency for many years, they tended to be better educated than their counterparts from other territories, and thus more persuasive advocates for their positions. Moreover, given their comparatively easy access to Dakar, they were less likely to be absent from council sessions for professional or financial reasons. See Thompson and Adloff, *French West Africa,* 64–65, 67, 69, 75–76.

53. Morgenthau, *Political Parties in French-Speaking West Africa,* 115, 311, 321; Mortimer, *France and the Africans,* 103–4, 231–40, 271, 276–77; Elliot J. Berg, "The Economic Basis of Political Choice in French West Africa," *American Political Science Review* 54, no. 2 (June 1960): 402–5; Pierre Messmer, *Après Tant de Batailles: Mémoires* (Paris: Albin Michel, 1992), 239.

54. ANS, 17G613, Police, " . . . Mécontentement Regnant Chez les Évolués . . . ," 30 April 1957; 17G622, Police, " . . . Commentaires sur le Congrès Fédéral R.D.A. de Bamako," 9 Oct. 1957; Morgenthau, *Political Parties in French-Speaking West Africa,* 110, 310; Hodgkin, *African Political Parties,* 122–23; Zolberg, *One-Party Government in the Ivory Coast,* 220–22; Blanchet, *Itinéraire des Partis Africains depuis Bamako,* 85–86; Ernest Milcent, *L'A.O.F. Entre en Scène* (Paris: Bibliothèque de l'Homme d'Action, 1958), 144.

The RDA's second interterritorial congress had been held in Abidjan in February 1949. There would not be another interterritorial congress for nearly nine years. The third interterritorial congress, originally scheduled for October 1956, was postponed numerous times as a result of the serious divisions within the movement. It finally was held in September 1957. Morgenthau, *Political Parties in French-Speaking West Africa,* 98; Thompson and Adloff, *French West Africa,* 96; Zolberg, *One-Party Government in the Ivory Coast,* 221–22, 222n9; Ruth Schachter and Immanuel Wallerstein, "French Africa's Road to Independence: 3," *West Africa* 3, no. 2142 (3 May 1958): 419; Kenneth Robinson, "Senegal: The Elections to the Territorial Assembly, March 1957," in *Five Elections in Africa,* ed. W. J. M. MacKenzie and Kenneth Robinson (Oxford: Oxford University Press, 1960), 332–33.

55. Mortimer, *France and the Africans,* 271; Morgenthau, *Political Parties in French-Speaking West Africa,* 309–10; Schachter and Wallerstein, "French Africa's Road to Independence: 3," 419; Wallerstein, "How Seven States Were Born," 3, 7; Zolberg, *One-Party Government in the Ivory Coast,* 222–24; Sylvain Soriba Camara, *La Guinée sans la France* (Paris: Presses de la Fondation Nationale des Sciences Politiques, 1976), 61.

56. Quoted in Mortimer, *France and the Africans,* 273.

57. Morgenthau, *Political Parties in French-Speaking West Africa,* 309–10; Mortimer, *France and the Africans,* 271, 278; Zolberg, *One-Party Government in the Ivory Coast,* 222–24; Wallerstein, "How Seven States Were Born," 3, 7.

58. Quoted in ANS, 17G622, Police, " . . . Commentaires sur le Congrès Fédéral R.D.A. de Bamako," 9 Oct. 1957; Morgenthau, *Political Parties in French-Speaking West Africa,* 110–11, 117, 309–10.

59. Johnson, "Parti Démocratique de Guinée," 349–50.

60. ANS, 17G622, Police, " . . . Exclusion du P.D.G./R.D.A. de Plusieurs Dirigeants de . . . Mamou," 15 Nov. 1957; interview with Fanta Diarra and Ibrahima Fofana,

24 May 1991; Johnson, "Parti Démocratique de Guinée," 351, 363–64; Morgenthau, *Political Parties in French-Speaking West Africa,* 244.

The Malinke and Soninke peoples are part of the greater Mande group. The Soninke are sometimes called "Saracolet" or "Marka." Andrew F. Clark, *From Frontier to Backwater: Economy and Society in the Upper Senegal Valley (West Africa), 1850–1920* (Lanham, MD: University Press of America, 1999), 43.

61. Johnson, "Parti Démocratique de Guinée," 351; interview with Kadiatou Meunier (pseudonym), Conakry, 5 March 1991.

62. ANS, 17G622, Police, " . . . Exclusion du P.D.G./R.D.A. de Plusieurs Dirigeants de . . . Mamou," 15 Nov. 1957; 17G622, Police, " . . . Conférence Publique . . . à Mamou . . . par l'Ex-Sous-Section du P.D.G./R.D.A.," 19 Nov. 1957; 2G57/128, Police et Sûreté, "Synthèse Mensuelle de Renseignements, Novembre 1957," 25 Nov. 1957; interview with Fanta Diarra and Ibrahima Fofana, 24 May 1991; Johnson, "Parti Démocratique de Guinée," 347–48, 352, 354, 358, 362; Kéïta, *P.D.G.,* 2:101. See also Hodgkin, *African Political Parties,* 71.

63. ANS, 17G622, Police, " . . . Exclusion du P.D.G./R.D.A. de Plusieurs Dirigeants de . . . Mamou," 15 Nov. 1957; 2G57/128, Police et Sûreté, "Synthèse Mensuelle de Renseignements, Novembre 1957," 25 Nov. 1957; 17G622, Guinée Française, Services de Police, "Renseignements A/S Activité de l'Ex-S/Section R.D.A. de Mamou," 20 Dec. 1957, #2798/1018, C/PS; interview with Mamdou Bela Doumbouya, 26 Jan.1991; interview with Kadiatou Meunier, 5 March 1991; Johnson, "Parti Démocratique de Guinée," 355, 362, 365.

64. ANS, 17G622, Police, " . . . Rebondissement du Conflit des Enseignants Africains," 8 Nov. 1957; 17G622, Police, " . . . Conflit des Enseignants Guinéens," 12 Nov. 1957; 17G622, Police, " . . . Conférence d'Information Syndicale . . . Mamou . . . par les Enseignants Africains . . . ," 12 Nov. 1957; 17G622, Police, " . . . Communiqué du Comité Directeur du P.D.G.," Conakry, 12 Nov. 1957; 17G622, Police, " . . . Exclusion du P.D.G./R.D.A. de Plusieurs Dirigeants de . . . Mamou," 15 Nov. 1957; 2G57/128, Police et Sûreté, "Synthèse Mensuelle de Renseignements, Novembre 1957," 25 Nov. 1957; 17G622, Police, " . . . Activité de l'Ex-S/Section R.D.A. de Mamou," 20 Dec. 1957; Kéïta, *P.D.G.,* 2:103; Johnson, "Parti Démocratique de Guinée," 358–60, 362, 365.

65. Suret-Canale, *République de Guinée,* 169; Kéïta, *P.D.G.,* 2:108, 131; Camara, *Guinée sans la France,* 63–64.

66. Suret-Canale, *République de Guinée,* 170; Camara, *Guinée sans la France,* 63–64.

67. ANS, 17G573, Guinée Française, Services de Police, "Renseignements A/S Diagne Ibrahima, Secrétaire de la Section R.D.A. de N'Zérékoré," 8 Nov. 1951, #2033/1137, C/PS.2; Kéïta, *P.D.G.,* 1:238, 308; Johnson, "Parti Démocratique de Guinée," 354.

68. Kéïta, *P.D.G.,* 2:108–10; Morgenthau, *Political Parties in French-Speaking West Africa,* 248.

69. Kéïta, *P.D.G.,* 2:112; AG, AM-1339, Idiatou Camara, "La Contribution de la Femme de Guinée à la Lutte de Libération Nationale (1945–1958)," Mémoire de Fin d'Études Supérieures, Conakry, IPGAN, 1979, 47–48.

70. Kéïta, *P.D.G.*, 2:112.

71. Rivière, *Guinea*, 60; Kéïta, *Ahmed Sékou Touré: Combat Anti-Colonial*, 92.

72. Morgenthau, *Political Parties in French-Speaking West Africa*, 109, 111, 309, 317, 426; Mortimer, *France and the Africans*, 254–55; Hodgkin, *African Political Parties*, 71; Kéïta, *P.D.G.*, 2:51; Chafer, *End of Empire in French West Africa*, 209; Finn Fuglestad, "Djibo Bakary, the French, and the Referendum of 1958 in Niger," *Journal of African History* 14, no. 2 (1973): 139; Finn Fuglestad, *A History of Niger, 1850–1960* (New York: Cambridge University Press, 1983), 164, 182–84.

73. Morgenthau, *Political Parties in French-Speaking West Africa*, 252–53; Diané, *F.E.A.N.F.*, 118–19; Chafer, *End of Empire in French West Africa*, 210; "La Résolution," *La Liberté*, 23 Sept. 1958, 2.

74. CAOM, Carton 2194, dos. 4, Ministre, FOM, Paris, "Bulletin de Renseignements," 19 April 1958, #1012/Be; ANS, 17G622, Guinée Française, Services de Police, "Renseignements A/S Réunion Privée tenue à Conakry, le 26 Avril 1958, par les Militantes du P.R.A.," 29 April 1958, #832/285, C/PS.2.

75. Morgenthau, *Political Parties in French-Speaking West Africa*, 310–11.

76. ANS, 17G622, Guinée Française, Services de Police, "Renseignements A/S Diffusion d'une Circulaire du P.R.A.," 25 April 1958, #808/280, C/PS.2; CAOM, Carton 2194, dos. 4, Haut Commissaire, Dakar, à Ministre, FOM, Paris, "Incidents de Mai," 10 Sept. 1958, #10238; Carton 2194, dos. 4, "Annexe: Incidents de Conakry (22 Avril au 5 Mai 1958)"; Carton 2181, dos. 6, "L'U.P.G.-P.R.A. se Prononce pour le 'Non' au Référendum," *Agence France-Presse*, 16 Sept. 1958; Kéïta, *P.D.G.*, 2:51–52; Morgenthau, *Political Parties in French-Speaking West Africa*, 253.

77. CAOM, Carton 2194, dos. 4, FOM, "Bulletin de Renseignements," 19 April 1958; ANS, 17G622, Police, " . . . Diffusion d'une Circulaire du P.R.A.," 25 April 1958; 17G622, Police, " . . . Réunion Privée . . . par les Militantes du P.R.A.," 29 April 1958.

78. Morgenthau, *Political Parties in French-Speaking West Africa*, 82; Jean-Pierre Rioux, *The Fourth Republic, 1944–1958*, trans. Godfrey Rogers (New York: Cambridge University Press, 1987), 266, 271, 282–83.

79. Rioux, *Fourth Republic*, 283, 296.

80. Ibid., 297.

81. Ibid., 281, 285–300.

82. Ibid., 286, 289, 295, 298, 301, 467; Morgenthau, *Political Parties in French-Speaking West Africa*, 102; Charles de Gaulle, *Memoirs of Hope: Renewal and Endeavor*, trans. Terence Kilmartin (New York: Simon and Schuster, 1971), 17, 21.

83. Rioux, *Fourth Republic*, 264, 291; Nancy Ellen Lawler, *Soldiers of Misfortune: Ivoirien Tirailleurs of World War II* (Athens: Ohio University Press, 1992), 157, 167.

84. Rioux, *Fourth Republic*, 303; Mortimer, *France and the Africans*, 305n1; de Gaulle, *Memoirs of Hope*, 20.

85. Before assuming military command in Algeria, General Salan had overseen the French Expeditionary Corps in Indochina (May 1951–May 1953). He was succeeded in that position by General Henri-Eugène Navarre, who commanded the French troops during their final defeat at Dien Bien Phu. Rioux, *Fourth Republic*, 216–18, 304; de Gaulle, *Memoirs of Hope*, 18, 23; Chaffard, *Carnets Secrets de la Décolonisa-*

tion, 2:175; James J. Schneider, "T. E. Lawrence and the Mind of an Insurgent," *Army* (July 2005): 31–32.

86. Rioux, *Fourth Republic,* 289, 301, 467; de Gaulle, *Memoirs of Hope,* 21; Mortimer, *France and the Africans,* 305n1.

87. Rioux, *Fourth Republic,* 301.

88. Ibid., 299–303, 305; Messmer, *Après Tant de Batailles,* 231–32.

89. De Gaulle, *Memoirs of Hope,* 21. See also Rioux, *Fourth Republic,* 305.

90. Rioux, *Fourth Republic,* 306–7; de Gaulle, *Memoirs of Hope,* 24.

91. Rioux, *Fourth Republic,* 308–9; de Gaulle, *Memoirs of Hope,* 26, Mortimer, *France and the Africans,* 305n1.

92. De Gaulle, *Memoirs of Hope,* 18.

93. Rioux, *Fourth Republic,* 309, 468; de Gaulle, *Memoirs of Hope,* 28; Kéïta, *P.D.G.,* 2:129.

No African deputies voted against de Gaulle's election. Houphouët-Boigny, Hamani Diori, and Modibo Kéïta—all RDA—voted for him, as did PRA deputies Sourou Migan Apithy, Jean-Félix Tchicaya, Hubert Maga, Fily Dabo Sissoko, Hammadoun Dicko, and Jules Ninine. The remaining African deputies did not vote; most of them were absent from Paris at the time. Mortimer, *France and the Africans,* 303.

94. Rioux, *Fourth Republic,* 309; de Gaulle, *Memoirs of Hope,* 28–30, 60; Morgenthau, *Political Parties in French-Speaking West Africa,* 61; Kéïta, *P.D.G.,* 1:127–28; Jacques Foccart, *Foccart Parle: Entretiens avec Philippe Gaillard* (Paris: Fayard/Jeune Afrique, 1995), 1:163; Rulers, "Senegal," http://rulers.org/ruls2.html.

95. De Gaulle, *Memoirs of Hope,* 18.

96. Rioux, *Fourth Republic,* 309, 468; de Gaulle, *Memoirs of Hope,* 27–30, 60.

97. Kéïta, *P.D.G.,* 2:129.

98. The so-called Bayeux Constitution was merely a brief sketch proposed by de Gaulle in that city on June 16, 1946, the anniversary of its liberation from German occupation. Rioux, *Fourth Republic,* 104–5; Mortimer, *France and the Africans,* 88–89; de Gaulle, *Memoirs of Hope,* 15–16, 30–31; Charles de Gaulle, *The War Memoirs of Charles de Gaulle: Salvation, 1944–1946* (New York: Simon and Schuster, 1960), 328; D. Bruce Marshall, *The French Colonial Myth and Constitution-Making in the Fourth Republic* (New Haven: Yale University Press, 1973), 147, 150–51, 260–62.

99. Morgenthau, *Political Parties in French-Speaking West Africa,* 73, 388–90; Kéïta, *P.D.G.,* 2:132–33; de Gaulle, *Memoirs of Hope,* 66.

For the definitive text of the 1958 Constitution, see Morgenthau, *Political Parties in French-Speaking West Africa,* 385–92.

100. Morgenthau, *Political Parties in French-Speaking West Africa,* 73.

101. Kéïta, *P.D.G.,* 2:134–35.

102. Morgenthau, *Political Parties in French-Speaking West Africa,* 71, 75, 77.

103. Ibid., 72, 113–14; Mortimer, *France and the Africans,* 238–39.

104. Internal SFIO document, quoted in Morgenthau, *Political Parties in French-Speaking West Africa,* 109.

105. Morgenthau, *Political Parties in French-Speaking West Africa,* 109; Ruth Schachter and Immanuel Wallerstein, "French Africa's Road to Independence: 2," *West Africa* 2, no. 2141 (26 April 1958): 395.

106. Morgenthau, *Political Parties in French-Speaking West Africa,* 109; Rioux, *Fourth Republic,* 309.

107. Mortimer, *France and the Africans,* 268, 305–6, 309–10; Chaffard, *Carnets Secrets de la Décolonisation,* 2:177–78, 181; Kéïta, *P.D.G.,* 2:129–30; Rioux, *Fourth Republic,* 309; Morgenthau, *Political Parties in French-Speaking West Africa,* 426; Elikia M'Bokolo, "Equatorial West Africa," in *Africa since 1935,* ed. Ali A. Mazrui and C. Wondji, vol. 8 of *General History of Africa* (Berkeley: University of California Press, 1999), 210.

108. Chaffard, *Carnets Secrets de la Décolonisation,* 2:178–79, 181–82; Foccart, *Foccart Parle,* 1:158–59; Messmer, *Après Tant de Batailles,* 232.

109. Mortimer, *France and the Africans,* 310.

110. Kéïta, *P.D.G.,* 2:137.

111. Morgenthau, *Political Parties in French-Speaking West Africa,* 71, 311; Mortimer, *France and the Africans,* 307–12; Kéïta, *P.D.G.,* 2:132–33.

112. Mortimer, *France and the Africans,* 303–6; Kéïta, *P.D.G.,* 2:108, 131.

113. Morgenthau, *Political Parties in French-Speaking West Africa,* 155, 157n3, 163, 309, 311, 317; Mortimer, *France and the Africans,* 118, 142, 251–52, 295–96, 306–9; Chaffard, *Carnets Secrets de la Décolonisation,* 2:182, 269; Chafer, *End of Empire in French West Africa,* 211; Fuglestad, "Djibo Bakary," 321; Virginia Thompson, "Niger," in *National Unity and Regionalism in Eight African States,* ed. Gwendolen M. Carter (Ithaca: Cornell University Press, 1966), 162.

114. Chaffard, *Carnets Secrets de la Décolonisation,* 2:176, 182; Foccart, *Foccart Parle,* 1:158–59; Morgenthau, *Political Parties in French-Speaking West Africa,* 253; Suret-Canale, *République de Guinée,* 172.

115. Morgenthau, *Political Parties in French-Speaking West Africa,* 116–17, 311. See also de Gaulle, *Memoirs of Hope,* 43.

116. Diané, *F.E.A.N.F.,* 107, 113–14; Chafer, *End of Empire in French West Africa,* 107–8, 197; Morgenthau, *Political Parties in French-Speaking West Africa,* 116; Wallerstein, "How Seven States Were Born," 4.

117. Chafer, *End of Empire in French West Africa,* 206.

118. Diané, *F.E.A.N.F.,* 49, 105–10, 115, 118–19. See also interview with Bocar Biro Barry, Conakry, 21 Jan. 1991; Thompson and Adloff, *French West Africa,* 95, 106; Mortimer, *France and the Africans,* 287.

119. Diané, *F.E.A.N.F.,* 107, 113–14; Wallerstein, "How Seven States Were Born," 4.

120. Kéïta, *P.D.G.,* 2:145.

121. Diané, *F.E.A.N.F.,* 126, 129.

122. Chaffard, *Carnets Secrets de la Décolonisation,* 2:178–79.

123. CRDA, "Notre Position sur la Réforme Consitutionnelle," *La Liberté,* 25 July 1958, 2.

124. Morgenthau, *Political Parties in French-Speaking West Africa,* 116, 321; Thomas E. O'Toole, *Historical Dictionary of Guinea (Republic of Guinea/Conakry),* 2nd ed. (Metuchen, NJ: Scarecrow Press, 1987), 114; "Félix Houphouët-Boigny," http://people.africadatabase.org/en/person/2617.html.

125. CRDA, Sékou Touré, "L'Afrique et le Référendum," *La Liberté,* 25 July 1958, 1.

126. Morgenthau, *Political Parties in French-Speaking West Africa,* 98, 312.

127. Chaffard, *Carnets Secrets de la Décolonisation,* 2:186–87; Kéïta, *P.D.G.,* 2:131.

128. Chaffard, *Carnets Secrets de la Décolonisation,* 2:187–88.

129. Mortimer, *France and the Africans,* 248; Wallerstein, "How Seven States Were Born," 4; Elliot Berg, "French West Africa," *Labor and Economic Development,* ed. Walter Galenson (New York: John Wiley and Sons, 1959), 215–16, 249–250n62.

130. Kéïta, *P.D.G.,* 2:131.

131. Quoted in Chaffard, *Carnets Secrets de la Décolonisation,* 2:189; Foccart, *Foccart Parle,* 1:159, 166; Mortimer, *France and the Africans,* 311–12.

132. Quoted in Chaffard, *Carnets Secrets de la Décolonisation,* 2:190.

133. Morgenthau, *Political Parties in French-Speaking West Africa,* 68.

134. CAOM, Carton 2181, dos. 6, Gouverneur, Guinée Française, Conakry, à Haut Commissaire, Dakar, 18 Aug. 1958, #0140/CAB; Kéïta, *P.D.G.,* 1:129.

135. Chaffard, *Carnets Secrets de la Décolonisation,* 2:176–77; Messmer, *Après Tant de Batailles,* 233.

136. Interview with Bocar Biro Barry, 21 Jan. 1991.

Pierre Messmer, high commissioner of French West Africa in 1958, presents an alternative explanation. He contends that the original plan had called for stops in the federal capitals, Brazzaville and Dakar, as well as in Tananarive, the capital of Madagascar. There had been no plans to stop in any of the territorial capitals except Abidjan, which was included in the itinerary to honor de Gaulle's close collaborator Houphouët-Boigny, and Fort-Lamy (Chad), for servicing en route to Madagascar. Thus, the bypassing of Conakry was the rule, rather than the exception. It was the decision to visit Conakry that was anomalous, not the decision to avoid it. See Messmer, *Après Tant de Batailles,* 233.

137. Chaffard, *Carnets Secrets de la Décolonisation,* 2:190–91; Kéïta, *P.D.G.,* 1:128; de Gaulle, *Memoirs of Hope,* 28; interview with Bocar Biro Barry, 21 Jan. 1991.

138. Chaffard, *Carnets Secrets de la Décolonisation,* 2:176–79, 181, 190–91; Foccart, *Foccart Parle,* 1:163; Messmer, *Après Tant de Batailles,* 233; Lansiné Kaba, *Le "Non" de la Guinée à de Gaulle* (Paris: Éditions Chaka, 1989), 88; interview with Bocar Biro Barry, 21 Jan. 1991.

As French West African high commissioner, Cornut-Gentille had had extensive dealings with Sékou Touré, most notably in 1955–56, when he had encouraged the Guinean leader to break from the CGT and to form an independent African trade union federation. Mortimer, *France and the Africans,* 247; Cooper, *Decolonization and African Society,* 418–19.

139. Chaffard, *Carnets Secrets de la Décolonisation,* 2:193. For a discussion of that day's events in Conakry, see Kaba, *"Non" de la Guinée,* 73–117.

140. Morgenthau, *Political Parties in French-Speaking West Africa,* 73, 387–88, 390; Chaffard, *Carnets Secrets de la Décolonisation,* 2:191–93; Kéïta, *P.D.G.,* 2:131; Foccart, *Foccart Parle,* 1:161; Kaba, *"Non" de la Guinée,* 76; Victor D. Du Bois, *The Guinean Vote for Independence: The Maneuvering before the Referendum of September 28, 1958,* West Africa Series 5, no. 7 (New York: American Universities Field Staff, 1962), 3.

See Constitutional Articles 72, 76, and 86, in Morgenthau, *Political Parties in French-Speaking West Africa,* 387–88, 390.

141. Chaffard, *Carnets Secrets de la Décolonisation,* 2:177, 193–94; Morgenthau, *Political Parties in French-Speaking West Africa,* 253; Kéïta, *P.D.G.,* 2:138; Messmer, *Après Tant de Batailles,* 234; Kaba, *"Non" de la Guinée,* 80.

The *Croix de Lorraine* was the symbol of the Free French, and as a corollary, of General de Gaulle personally.

142. Interview with Bocar Biro Barry, 21 Jan. 1991.

143. Chaffard, *Carnets Secrets de la Décolonisation,* 2:177, 193–94, 196; Kaba, *"Non" de la Guinée,* 80–86; Du Bois, *Guinean Vote for Independence,* 4; Camara, "Contribution de la Femme," 108; Messmer, *Après Tant de Batailles,* 234; interview with Aissatou N'Diaye, Conakry, 8 April 1991.

144. De Gaulle, *Memoirs of Hope,* 55.

145. Chaffard, *Carnets Secrets de la Décolonisation,* 2:193–94; Kaba, *"Non" de la Guinée,* 80–81; Kéïta, *P.D.G.,* 2:138; Messmer, *Après Tant de Batailles,* 234.

146. Kaba, *"Non" de la Guinée,* 86.

147. Interview with Aissatou N'Diaye, 8 April 1991.

148. Chaffard, *Carnets Secrets de la Décolonisation,* 2:194–96; Messmer, *Après Tant de Batailles,* 234–35; Foccart, *Foccart Parle,* 1:162; Kaba, *"Non" de la Guinée,* 86; Suret-Canale, *République de Guinée,* 170.

Houphouët-Boigny resigned from the presidency of the Grand Council in March-April 1958. He was replaced by Gabriel d'Arboussier, a strong federalist. Mortimer, *France and the Africans,* 293; Morgenthau, *Political Parties in French-Speaking West Africa,* 81n2.

149. Suret-Canale, *République de Guinée,* 170. See also Victor D. Du Bois, *Guinea's Prelude to Independence: Political Activity, 1945–58,* West Africa Series 5, no. 6 (New York: American Universities Field Staff, 1962), 14.

150. Quoted in Chaffard, *Carnets Secrets de la Décolonisation,* 2:197–98. See also CRDA, Sékou Touré, "Les Conditions de Notre Vote," *La Liberté,* 25 Aug. 1958, 1–2; Kaba, *"Non" de la Guinée,* 98–99.

151. CAOM, Carton 2181, dos. 6, Télégramme Arrivée, FOM, Paris. Envoyé par Gouverneur, Guinée Française, Conakry, 27 Aug. 1958, #239–241; Chaffard, *Carnets Secrets de la Décolonisation,* 2:196–98; Foccart, *Foccart Parle,* 1:162–63; Messmer, *Après Tant de Batailles,* 235.

152. Quoted in Suret-Canale, *République de Guinée,* 170; Chaffard, *Carnets Secrets de la Décolonisation,* 2:198–99; Mortimer, *France and the Africans,* 315–16; Kaba, *"Non" de la Guinée,* 109. See also CAOM, Carton 2181, dos. 6, Gouverneur, Guinée Française, Conakry, à Ministre, FOM, Paris, "Motion du Parti Démocratique de la Guinée en date du 14 Septembre 1958," 15 Sept. 1958, #0191/CAB. See retrospective view in de Gaulle, *Memoirs of Hope,* 55.

153. Chaffard, *Carnets Secrets de la Décolonisation,* 2:199.

154. Quoted in Chaffard, *Carnets Secrets de la Décolonisation,* 2:198–99; Foccart, *Foccart Parle,* 1:375; Messmer, *Après Tant de Batailles,* 235; Mortimer, *France and the Africans,* 316; Du Bois, *Guinean Vote for Independence,* 2–3; Kaba, *"Non" de la Guinée,* 114; interview with Bocar Biro Barry, 21 Jan. 1991.

155. Chaffard, *Carnets Secrets de la Décolonisation,* 2:195, 206; Foccart, *Foccart Parle,* 1:165; Messmer, *Après Tant de Batailles,* 235; Du Bois, *Guinea's Prelude to Independence,* 14.

156. De Gaulle, *Memoirs of Hope,* 56. See also Messmer, *Après Tant de Batailles,* 235–36.

157. Quoted in Chaffard, *Carnets Secrets de la Décolonisation,* 2:200; de Gaulle, *Memoirs of Hope,* 56; Kaba, *"Non" de la Guinée,* 117.

158. CAOM, Carton 2181, dos. 6, Gouverneur, Guinée Française, Conakry, à Haut Commissaire, Dakar, 27 Aug. 1958, #1960/CAB.

159. CAOM, Carton 2181, dos. 6, Gouverneur à Haut Commissaire, 27 Aug. 1958, #1960/CAB; Carton 2181, dos. 6, "S.T. Presse Communiqué," 29 Aug. 1958; Chaffard, *Carnets Secrets de la Décolonisation,* 2:202; Mortimer, *France and the Africans,* 318; Morgenthau, *Political Parties in French-Speaking West Africa,* 253; Rivière, *Guinea,* 60.

On September 11, UGTAN's cadre conference in Bamako ratified the board's call for a "No" vote. Mortimer, *France and the Africans,* 318, 320.

160. Chaffard, *Carnets Secrets de la Décolonisation,* 2:194, 199; Foccart, *Foccart Parle,* 1:166; Mortimer, *France and the Africans,* 316.

161. Chaffard, *Carnets Secrets de la Décolonisation,* 2:202; Foccart, *Foccart Parle,* 1:166.

162. CRDA, Touré, "Conditions de Notre Vote"; Chaffard, *Carnets Secrets de la Décolonisation,* 2:202–3.

163. CAOM, Carton 2181, dos. 6, "S.T. Presse Communiqué," 29 Aug. 1958; Chaffard, *Carnets Secrets de la Décolonisation,* 2:203; Suret-Canale, *République de Guinée,* 172. See also CRDA, Touré, "Conditions de Notre Vote."

164. Chaffard, *Carnets Secrets de la Décolonisation,* 2:203; Foccart, *Foccart Parle,* 1:168.

165. CAOM, Carton 2181, dos. 6, Télégramme Arrivée, FOM, Paris. Envoyé par Gouverneur, Guinée Française, Conakry, 29 Aug. 1958, #242–244.

166. CAOM, Carton 2181, dos. 6, Télégramme Arrivée, FOM, Paris. Envoyé par Gouverneur, Guinée Française, Conakry, 31 Aug. 1958, #251–257. See also Carton 2181, dos. 6, Télégramme Arrivée, FOM, Paris. Envoyé par Gouverneur, Guinée Française, Conakry, 18 Sept. 1958, #371.

167. Chaffard, *Carnets Secrets de la Décolonisation,* 2:203.

168. CAOM, Carton 2181, dos. 6, Télégramme Arrivée, FOM. Envoyé par Gouverneur, Guinée Française, 31 Aug. 1958; Carton 2181, dos. 6, Télégramme Arrivée, FOM, Paris. Envoyé par Gouverneur, Guinée Française, Conakry, 2 Sept. 1958, #266–267; Carton 2181, dos. 6, Gouverneur, Guinée Française, Conakry, à Ministre, FOM, Paris, 2 Sept. 1958, #8/B.E; Carton 2181, dos. 6, "Discours Prononcé par M. le Président Sékou Touré à la Chambre de Commerce de Conakry, le 1er Septembre 1958."

169. CAOM, Carton 2181, dos. 6, "Discours . . . par . . . Sékou Touré à la Chambre de Commerce . . . 1er Septembre 1958"; Carton 2181, dos. 6, Télégramme Arrivée, FOM. Envoyé par Gouverneur, Guinée Française, 2 Sept. 1958. See also Wallerstein, "How Seven States Were Born," 4.

170. CAOM, Carton 2181, dos. 6, "Discours . . . par . . . Sékou Touré à la Chambre de Commerce . . . 1er Septembre 1958"; Kéïta, *P.D.G.,* 2:132.

171. CAOM, Carton 2181, dos. 6, Bordereau du Ministre, FOM, Paris, 29 Sept. 1958, #1997/BE: "Bulletin de Renseignements A/S Prise de Position de Sékou Touré," 25 Sept. 1958, #11369/A; Chaffard, *Carnets Secrets de la Décolonisation,* 2:210.

172. CAOM, Carton 2181, dos. 6, Télégramme Arrivée, FOM. Envoyé par Gouverneur, Guinée Française, 31 Aug. 1958; Chaffard, *Carnets Secrets de la Décolonisation,* 2:204.

173. CAOM, Carton 2181, dos. 6, Télégramme Arrivée, FOM, Paris. Envoyé par Gouverneur, Guinée Française, Conakry, 1 Sept. 1958, #259–260.

174. Chaffard, *Carnets Secrets de la Décolonisation,* 2:176, 182; Foccart, *Foccart Parle,* 1:158–59; Morgenthau, *Political Parties in French-Speaking West Africa,* 253; Suret-Canale, *République de Guinée,* 172.

175. Mortimer, *France and the Africans,* 320; Suret-Canale, *République de Guinée,* 172.

176. CAOM, Carton 2181, dos. 6, Bordereau à Ministre, FOM, Paris, de G. Gilbert (pour le Gouverneur, Guinée Française), "Nouvelles Locales Reçues de l'A.F.P. en date du 19 Septembre 1958," 19 Sept. 1958, #2276/CAB; Chaffard, *Carnets Secrets de la Décolonisation,* 2:204.

177. Chaffard, *Carnets Secrets de la Décolonisation,* 2:204–5; Mortimer, *France and the Africans,* 318–20; Morgenthau, *Political Parties in French-Speaking West Africa,* 312.

178. CAOM, Carton 2181, dos. 6, Bordereau à Ministre, FOM, Paris, de M. Remondière, Chef du Cabinet Militaire, Conakry, "Extraits du Bulletin de l'Agence France-Presse du 18 Septembre," 19 Sept. 1958, #1244/CAB; Mortimer, *France and the Africans,* 313–14. The text of the October 4, 1958, Constitution can be found in Morgenthau, *Political Parties in French- Speaking West Africa,* 385–92.

CHAPTER 6

1. CAOM, Carton 2181, dos. 6, Télégramme Arrivée, FOM, Paris. Envoyé par Gouverneur, Guinée Française, Conakry, 29 Aug. 1958, #242–244; Carton 2181, dos. 6, Bordereau à Ministre, FOM, Paris, de M. Remondière, Chef du Cabinet Militaire, Conakry, "Extraits du Bulletin de l'Agence France-Presse du 18 Septembre," 19 Sept. 1958, #1244/CAB; Sidiki Kobélé Kéïta, *Le P.D.G.: Artisan de l'Indépendance Nationale en Guinée (1947–1958)* (Conakry: I.N.R.D.G., Bibliothèque Nationale, 1978), 2:142; Charles Diané, *La F.E.A.N.F. et Les Grandes Heures du Mouvement Syndical Étudiant Noir* (Paris: Éditions Chaka, 1990), 126; Tony Chafer, *The End of Empire in French West Africa: France's Successful Decolonization?* (New York: Berg, 2002), 205.

2. CAOM, Carton 2181, dos. 6, "Discours Prononcé par M. le Président Sékou Touré à la Chambre de Commerce de Conakry, le 1er Septembre 1958."

3. Diané, *F.E.A.N.F.,* 127–28. See also Immanuel Wallerstein, "How Seven States Were Born in Former French West Africa," *Africa Report* (March 1961): 4.

4. Edward Mortimer, *France and the Africans, 1944–1960: A Political History* (New York: Walker and Co., 1969), 320; Jean Suret-Canale, *La République de Guinée* (Paris: Éditions Sociales, 1970), 172.

5. Kéïta, *P.D.G.,* 2:142.

6. CAOM, Carton 2181, dos. 6, "S.T. Presse Communiqué," *Agence France-Press,* Conakry, 29 Aug. 1958; Mortimer, *France and the Africans,* 295, 318, 320–21; Wallerstein, "How Seven States Were Born," 4, 12; Ruth Schachter Morgenthau, *Political Parties in French-Speaking West Africa* (Oxford: Clarendon Press, 1964), 253; Georges Chaffard, *Les Carnets Secrets de la Décolonisation* (Paris: Calmann-Lévy, 1967), 2:202; Finn Fuglestad, "Djibo Bakary, the French, and the Referendum of 1958 in Niger," *Journal of African History* 14, no. 2 (1973): 323.

7. CAOM, Carton 2181, dos. 6, Télégramme Arrivée, FOM, Paris. Envoyé par Gouverneur, Guinée Française, Conakry, 6 Sept. 1958, #276–277; Carton 2181, dos. 6, Cabinet Militaire, "Extraits du Bulletin de l'Agence France-Presse . . . ," 19 Sept. 1958; Mortimer, *France and the Africans,* 321.

8. Mortimer, *France and the Africans,* 321; Chaffard, *Carnets Secrets de la Décolonisation,* 2:285.

9. Mortimer, *France and the Africans,* 321–23; Chaffard, *Carnets Secrets de la Décolonisation,* 2:285; Victor D. Du Bois, *The Guinean Vote for Independence: The Maneuvering before the Referendum of September 28, 1958,* West Africa Series 5, no. 7 (New York: American Universities Field Staff, 1962), 2–3, 5, 12n11.

10. Mortimer, *France and the Africans,* 319; Chaffard, *Carnets Secrets de la Décolonisation,* 2:206.

11. Mortimer, *France and the Africans,* 320; Chaffard, *Carnets Secrets de la Décolonisation,* 2:206.

12. CAOM, Carton 2181, dos. 6, Gouverneur, Guinée Française, Conakry, à Ministre, FOM, Paris, "Motion du Parti Démocratique de la Guinée en date du 14 Septembre 1958," 15 Sept. 1958, #0191/CAB; Carton 2181, dos. 6, Bordereau à Ministre, FOM, Paris, de G. Gilbert (pour le Gouverneur, Guinée Française), "Nouvelles Locales Reçues de l'A.F.P. en date du 19 Septembre 1958," 19 Sept. 1958, #2276/CAB; Chaffard, *Carnets Secrets de la Décolonisation,* 2:204, 206; Morgenthau, *Political Parties in French-Speaking West Africa,* 219.

13. Interview with Bocar Biro Barry, Conakry, 21 Jan. 1991. See also interview with Aissatou N'Diaye, Conakry, 8 April 1991.

FEANF leader Charles Diané also claims that Sékou Touré opted for the "No" vote in the eleventh hour—pushed by the student movement. See Diané, *F.E.A.N.F.,* 128–29.

14. Interview with Bocar Biro Barry, 21 Jan. 1991. See also Mortimer, *France and the Africans,* 318; Chafer, *End of Empire in French West Africa,* 217, 225–26.

15. CAOM, Carton 2181, dos. 6, Gouverneur, Guinée Française, Conakry, à Ministre, FOM, Paris, "Discours Prononcé par le Président Sékou Touré, le 14 Septembre 1958," 15 Sept. 1958, #0191/CAB. See also "Unanimement le 28 Septembre la Guinée Votera Non," *La Liberté,* 23 Sept. 1958, 1–2; Wallerstein, "How Seven States Were Born," 4.

16. CAOM, Carton 2181, dos. 6, "Discours . . . par . . . Sékou Touré, le 14 Septembre 1958." See also "Unanimement le 28 Septembre la Guinée Votera Non," 1–2; Chaffard, *Carnets Secrets de la Décolonisation,* 2:206.

17. CAOM, Carton 2181, dos. 6, "Discours . . . par . . . Sékou Touré, le 14 Septembre 1958." See also "Unanimement le 28 Septembre la Guinée Votera Non," 2.

18. CAOM, Carton 2181, dos. 6, "Motion du Parti Démocratique de la Guinée . . . du 14 Septembre 1958"; "Unanimement le 28 Septembre la Guinée Votera Non," 2; "La Résolution," *La Liberté,* 23 Sept. 1958, 2; Morgenthau, *Political Parties in French-Speaking West Africa,* 219; Chaffard, *Carnets Secrets de la Décolonisation,* 2:206.

19. CAOM, Carton 2181, dos. 6, "Communiqué du Conseil de Gouvernement," *Agence France-Presse,* 16 Sept. 1958.

20. CAOM, Carton 2181, dos. 6, Télégramme Arrivée, FOM, Paris. Envoyé par Gouverneur, Guinée Française, Conakry, 18 Sept. 1958, #375; Carton 2181, dos. 6,

"Nouvelles Locales Reçues de l'A.F.P. . . . ," 19 Sept. 1958; Du Bois, *Guinean Vote for Independence*, 6.

21. Kéïta, *P.D.G.*, 2:166, 190–91; Suret-Canale, *République de Guinée*, 172; Du Bois, *Guinean Vote for Independence*, 6.

The Guinean PRA officially disbanded on November 29, 1958, when PRA leaders Barry III and Barry Diawadou instructed their followers to join the PDG (Guinean RDA). Du Bois, *Guinean Vote for Independence*, 8.

22. CAOM, Carton 2181, dos. 6, Télégramme Arrivée, Ministre, FOM, Bureau du Cabinet. Envoyé par Genesuper, Dakar, "*Objet*: Situation en Guinée au 21 Septembre," 22 Sept. 1958, #3.100/GCS/AOF/2.

23. Kéïta, *P.D.G.*, 2:146; Suret-Canale, *République de Guinée*, 172.

RDA fears were not far-fetched. Immediately after the September 14 territorial congress, the high commissioner ordered a company of paratroopers to Guinea "to assure the security of the French on the day of the referendum" and to remove French assets from the territory. Plans were laid for naval maneuvers off the coast of Conakry and the possible intervention of mobile military units from the French Soudan, Upper Volta, or Senegal. In Niger, the situation was far more serious. France moved troops into Niger to intimidate Djibo's supporters; on September 28, Niamey was virtually in a state of siege. Quoted in Pierre Messmer, *Après Tant de Batailles: Mémoires* (Paris: Albin Michel, 1992), 241. See also CAOM, Carton 2181, dos. 6, Télégramme Arrivée, FOM, Paris. Envoyé par Gouverneur, Guinée Française, Conakry, 15 Sept. 1958, #343–345; Carton 2181, dos. 6, Télégramme Arrivée, FOM, Paris. Envoyé par Gouverneur, Guinée Française, Conakry, 16 Sept. 1958, #351–352; Carton 2181, dos. 6, Télégramme Arrivée, FOM, Paris. Envoyé par Haut Commissaire, Dakar, 16 Sept. 1958, #725; Carton 2181, dos. 6, Télégramme Arrivée, FOM, Paris. Envoyé par Haut Commissaire, Dakar, 17 Sept. 1958, #730–731; Carton 2181, dos. 6, Télégramme Arrivée, Ministre, FOM, " . . . Situation en Guinée au 21 Septembre," 22 Sept. 1958; Chaffard, *Carnets Secrets de la Décolonisation*, 2:211, 293; Mortimer, *France and the Africans*, 322; Wallerstein, "How Seven States Were Born," 4, 7; Fuglestad, "Djibo Bakary," 328; Virginia Thompson, "Niger," in *National Unity and Regionalism in Eight African States*, ed. Gwendolen M. Carter (Ithaca: Cornell University Press, 1966), 162–63.

24. Kéïta, *P.D.G.*, 2:146; AG, AM-1339, Idiatou Camara, "La Contribution de la Femme de Guinée à la Lutte de Libération Nationale (1945–1958)," Mémoire de Fin d'Études Supérieures, Conakry, IPGAN, 1979, 110.

25. Interview with Aissatou N'Diaye, 8 April 1991.

Contradicting N'Diaye's personal recollections, Morgenthau maintains that there was no campaigning in the two weeks preceding the referendum—so certain were the RDA leaders of their members' loyalty. Suret-Canale also claims that there was no pre-referendum campaign. However, he attributes this anomaly not to complacency, but to fear that provocations by opponents could serve as a pretext for military intervention. Kéïta, in contrast, asserts that there were no large public meetings, but that mobilization did take place through local party cells. His eyewitness assessment is compatible with N'Diaye's recollections and conforms to the RDA's past practices. Morgenthau, *Political Parties in French-Speaking West Africa*, 219; Suret-Canale, *Répub-*

lique de Guinée, 172; Kéïta, *P.D.G.,* 2:146; interview with Aissatou N'Diaye, 8 April 1991. See also Mortimer, *France and the Africans,* 320; L. Gray Cowan, "Guinea," in *African One-Party States,* ed. Gwendolen M. Carter (Ithaca: Cornell University Press, 1962), 169.

26. Interview with Aissatou N'Diaye, 8 April 1991.

27. Camara, "Contribution de la Femme," 111.

28. CAOM, Carton 2181, dos. 6, Télégramme Arrivée, FOM, Paris. Envoyé par Afcour, Dakar, 15 Sept. 1958, #722; Carton 2181, dos. 6, Télégramme Arrivée, FOM, Paris. Envoyé par Gouverneur, Guinée Française, Conakry, 23 Sept. 1958, #401–402.

29. CAOM, Carton 2181, dos. 6, Télégramme Arrivée, FOM. Envoyé par Gouverneur, Guinée Française, 29 Aug. 1958; Carton 2181, dos. 6, Télégramme Arrivée, FOM. Envoyé par Afcour, 15 Sept. 1958; Carton 2181, dos. 6, Télégramme Arrivée, FOM, Paris. Envoyé par Gouverneur, Guinée Française, Conakry, 17 Sept. 1958, #357–360; Chaffard, *Carnets Secrets de la Décolonisation,* 2:207–8.

30. CAOM, Carton 2181, dos. 6, Télégramme Arrivée, FOM, Paris. Envoyé par Gouverneur, Guinée Française, Conakry, 17 Sept. 1958, #366–368.

31. Chaffard, *Carnets Secrets de la Décolonisation,* 2:210; Messmer, *Après Tant de Batailles,* 242.

32. CAOM, Carton 2181, dos. 6, Télégramme Arrivée, FOM, Paris. Envoyé par Gouverneur, Guinée Française, Conakry, 17 Sept. 1958, #366–368. See also Morgenthau, *Political Parties in French-Speaking West Africa,* 57, 118; Messmer, *Après Tant de Batailles,* 242.

33. Chaffard, *Carnets Secrets de la Décolonisation,* 2:212–13, 218; Mortimer, *France and the Africans,* 329–33; Suret-Canale, *République de Guinée,* 172–73; Messmer, *Après Tant de Batailles,* 241–42; Morgenthau, *Political Parties in French-Speaking West Africa,* 253; Kéïta, *P.D.G.,* 2:149; Claude Rivière, *Guinea: The Mobilization of a People,* trans. Virginia Thompson and Richard Adloff (Ithaca: Cornell University Press, 1977), 83; Charles de Gaulle, *Memoirs of Hope: Renewal and Endeavor,* trans. Terence Kilmartin (New York: Simon and Schuster, 1971), 56.

34. CAOM, Carton 2181, dos. 6, Télégramme Arrivée, FOM, Paris. Envoyé par Gouverneur, Guinée Française, Conakry, 20 Sept. 1958, #363–364.

35. CAOM, Carton 2181, dos. 6, Télégramme Arrivée, FOM, Paris. Envoyé par Gouverneur, Guinée Française, Conakry, 18 Sept. 1958, #372–373; Messmer, *Après Tant de Batailles,* 240–41. The bank in question was most likely the Banque de l'Afrique Occidentale.

36. CAOM, Carton 2181, dos. 6, Télégramme Arrivée, FOM. Envoyé par Haut Commissaire, 16 Sept. 1958; Carton 2181, dos. 6, Télégramme Arrivée, FOM. Envoyé par Haut Commissaire, 17 Sept. 1958; Carton 2181, dos. 6, Télégramme Arrivée, Ministre, FOM, " . . . Situation en Guinée au 21 Septembre," 22 Sept. 1958; Chaffard, *Carnets Secrets de la Décolonisation,* 2:211; Messmer, *Après Tant de Batailles,* 241; Jacques Foccart, *Foccart Parle: Entretiens avec Philippe Gaillard* (Paris: Fayard/Jeune Afrique, 1995), 1:172.

37. CAOM, Carton 2181, dos. 6, Télégramme Arrivée, FOM. Envoyé par Gouverneur, Guinée Française, 15 Sept. 1958; Carton 2181, dos. 6, Télégramme Arrivée,

FOM. Envoyé par Gouverneur, Guinée Française, 16 Sept. 1958; Carton 2181, dos. 6, Télégramme Arrivée, FOM, Paris. Envoyé par Gouverneur, Guinée Française, Conakry, 22 Sept. 1958, #397–398.

38. Quoted in Chaffard, *Carnets Secrets de la Décolonisation,* 2:208.

39. CAOM, Carton 2181, dos. 6, Télégramme Arrivée, FOM. Envoyé par Gouverneur, Guinée Française, 20 Sept. 1958. For a description of the semiautonomous railway administration, see Jean Suret-Canale, "The French West African Railway Workers' Strike, 1947–1948," in *African Labor History,* ed. Peter C. W. Gutkind, Robin Cohen, and Jean Copans (Beverly Hills: Sage, 1978), 131–32; Frederick Cooper, "'Our Strike': Equality, Anticolonial Politics and the 1947–48 Railway Strike in French West Africa," *Journal of African History* 37, no. 1 (1996): 89.

40. Chaffard, *Carnets Secrets de la Décolonisation,* 2:210–11; Foccart, *Foccart Parle,* 1:171–72; Mortimer, *France and the Africans,* 329.

Article 88 reads: "The Republic or the Community may make agreements with States that wish to associate themselves with the Community in order to develop their own civilizations." See Morgenthau, *Political Parties in French-Speaking West Africa,* 390.

41. Chaffard, *Carnets Secrets de la Décolonisation,* 2:210.

42. Jean-Pierre Rioux, *The Fourth Republic, 1944–1958,* trans. Godfrey Rogers (New York: Cambridge University Press, 1987), 312.

43. Chaffard, *Carnets Secrets de la Décolonisation,* 2:204–6, 285; Mortimer, *France and the Africans,* 318–25; Morgenthau, *Political Parties in French-Speaking West Africa,* 312.

44. Kéïta, *P.D.G.,* 2:147; Jean Suret-Canale, "La Fin de la Chefferie en Guinée," *Journal of African History* 7, no. 3 (1966): 459–60, 492; interview with Mamadou Bela Doumbouya, Conakry, 26 Jan. 1991.

45. "Les Résultats du Scrutin," *La Liberté,* 4 Oct. 1958, 5; Kéïta, *P.D.G.,* 2:147–48; Morgenthau, *Political Parties in French-Speaking West Africa,* 219, 399; Suret-Canale, *République de Guinée,* 172.

46. Morgenthau, *Political Parties in French-Speaking West Africa,* 312, 399; Mortimer, *France and the Africans,* 324; Chaffard, *Carnets Secrets de la Décolonisation,* 2:212; Kéïta, *P.D.G.,* 2:148; Fuglestad, "Djibo Bakary," 313; Thompson, "Niger," 162.

The French government exerted enormous pressure on the Nigerien population, using money, political influence, and military intervention to sway the vote. Most damaging to opponents of the constitution, the colonial administration instigated a split in Djibo's party, encouraging powerful chiefs to secede from it and to campaign in favor of the constitution. Chaffard, *Carnets Secrets de la Décolonisation,* 2:275, 279, 284–87, 289–90, 292–95, 298; Morgenthau, *Political Parties in French-Speaking West Africa,* 311–12, 317–18, 399; Thompson, "Niger," 162–63, 165; Mortimer, *France and the Africans,* 322; Wallerstein, "How Seven States Were Born," 4, 7; Fuglestad, "Djibo Bakary," 324–28; Finn Fuglestad, *A History of Niger, 1850–1960* (New York: Cambridge University Press, 1983), 184–86.

47. Morgenthau, *Political Parties in French-Speaking West Africa,* 17, 22, 84, 89, 100, 271–72, 275, 279, 281, 299, 316, 335; Mortimer, *France and the Africans,* 39, 41, 64–66, 128–29; Chaffard, *Carnets Secrets de la Décolonisation,* 2:272; Thompson,

"Niger," 161; Fuglestad, "Djibo Bakary," 318; Fuglestad, *History of Niger,* 154, 181–82; Virginia Thompson and Richard Adloff, *French West Africa* (New York: Greenwood Press, 1969), 142–44, 534–35; Ernest Milcent, *L'A.O.F. Entre en Scène* (Paris: Bibliothèque de l'Homme d'Action, 1958), 130; Kenneth Robinson, "Senegal: The Elections to the Territorial Assembly, March 1957," in *Five Elections in Africa: A Group of Electoral Studies,* ed. W. J. M. Mackenzie and Kenneth Robinson (New York: Oxford University Press, 1960), 320, 335; Aristide R. Zolberg, "The Ivory Coast," in *Political Parties and National Integration in Tropical Africa,* ed. James S. Coleman and Carl G. Rosberg Jr. (Berkeley: University of California Press, 1964), 73; Aristide R. Zolberg, *Creating Political Order: The Party-States of West Africa* (Chicago: Rand McNally, 1966), 31; Martin Staniland, "The Three-Party System in Dahomey: I, 1946–56," *Journal of African History* 14, no. 2 (1973): 294–95, 301, 306–7, 309; Martin Staniland, "The Three-Party System in Dahomey: II, 1956–1957," *Journal of African History* 14, no. 3 (1973): 491, 500, 503; Patrick Manning, *Slavery, Colonialism and Economic Growth in Dahomey, 1640–1960* (New York: Cambridge University Press, 1982), 276–77; Frank Gregory Snyder, *One-Party Government in Mali: Transition Toward Control* (New Haven: Yale University Press, 1965), 19, 47; Alfred G. Gerteiny, *Mauritania* (New York: Frederick A. Praeger, 1967), 126.

48. Morgenthau, *Political Parties in French-Speaking West Africa,* 256–57, 285–86, 311–12, 317–18; Chaffard, *Carnets Secrets de la Décolonisation,* 2:272, 275, 279, 284–90, 293; Mortimer, *France and the Africans,* 107, 322; Snyder, *One-Party Government in Mali,* 19, 43, 47–48, 58, 73; Fuglestad, "Djibo Bakary," 315, 318, 320–21, 324–28; Fuglestad, *History of Niger,* 154, 171–72, 181–85; Thompson, "Niger," 161–63, 165, 185–86; Zolberg, *Creating Political Order,* 31; Wallerstein, "How Seven States Were Born," 4, 7; Rivière, *Guinea,* 51–61; Frederick Cooper, *Decolonization and African Society: The Labor Question in French and British Africa* (New York: Cambridge University Press, 1996), 605n39; Elliot J. Berg and Jeffrey Butler, "Trade Unions," in Coleman and Rosberg, eds., *Political Parties and National Integration in Tropical Africa,* 343, 347–48, 358, 366, 373; Jean Meynaud and Anisse Salah Bey, *Trade Unionism in Africa: A Study of Its Growth and Orientation,* trans. Angela Brench (London: Methuen and Co., 1967), 58; Elizabeth Schmidt, *Mobilizing the Masses: Gender, Ethnicity, and Class in the Nationalist Movement in Guinea, 1939–1958* (Portsmouth, NH: Heinemann, 2005), chap. 3.

49. For Guinea, see ANS, 17G586, Guinée Française, Services de Police, "Renseignements *Objet:* Création de Sections R.D.A. à Kindia," 7 Aug. 1954, #2417/864, C/PS.2; 17G586, Guinée Française, Services de Police, "Renseignements *Objet:* Réception de Sékou Touré à Kankan le 9/8/1954," 19 Aug. 1954, #2481/895, C/PS.2; 17G586, Guinée Française, Services de Police, "Renseignements *Objet:* Réunion Publique R.D.A. à Kankan le 10/8/54," 19 Aug. 1954, #2483/896, C/PS.2; 17G586, Guinée Française, Services de Police, "Renseignements *Objet:* Réunion Publique R.D.A. à Conakry et ses Suites," 8 Sept. 1954, #2606/942, C/PS.2; Kéïta, *P.D.G.,* 1:326, 340; Camara, "Contribution de la Femme," 44; Schmidt, *Mobilizing the Masses,* chaps. 3 and 5; Elizabeth Schmidt, "'Emancipate Your Husbands!': Women and Nationalism in Guinea, 1953–1958," in *Women in African Colonial Histories,* ed. Jean Allman, Susan Geiger, and Nakanyike Musisi (Bloomington: Indiana University Press, 2002), 282–304; interviews in Conakry with: Mamadou Bela Doumbouya, 26 Jan.

1991; Léon Maka and Mira Baldé (Mme. Maka), 25 Feb. 1991; Fatou Kéïta, 7 April 1991; Néné Diallo, 11 April 1991.

In 1954, Abdoulaye Diallo, a Guinean trade unionist based in the French Soudan, remarked that while the RDA was strong in the French Soudan, "the women were not as well organized as in Guinea." Jane Turrittin notes that "[i]n the French Soudan, militant activity by women in support of the independence movement rarely extended beyond the actions of a small number of elite women, such as Aoua Kéita, and wives of Union Soudanaise party leaders." ANS, 17G586, Police, " . . . Réunion Publique R.D.A. à Conakry . . . ," 8 Sept. 1954; Jane Turrittin, "Aoua Kéita and the Nascent Women's Movement in the French Soudan," *African Studies Review* 36, no. 1 (April 1993): 77. See also Morgenthau, *Political Parties in French-Speaking West Africa,* 287; Zolberg, *Creating Political Order,* 33; Turrittin, "Aoua Kéita," 59-89.

50. Fuglestad, "Djibo Bakary," 329.

51. Staniland, "Three-Party System in Dahomey: I," 291, 303, 305-6, 312; Staniland, "Three-Party System in Dahomey: II," 495-97; Morgenthau, *Political Parties in French-Speaking West Africa,* 291; Zolberg, *Creating Political Order,* 28, 32-34.

52. Staniland, "Three-Party System in Dahomey: I," 291, 301, 303, 305-6, 312; Staniland, "Three-Party System in Dahomey: II," 495-99, 503; Morgenthau, *Political Parties in French-Speaking West Africa,* 291-93, 295-96, 339; Thomas Hodgkin and Ruth Schachter Morgenthau, "Mali," in Coleman and Rosberg, eds., *Political Parties and National Integration in Tropical Africa,* 223-25, 237.

53. See chap. 5.

54. Morgenthau, *Political Parties in French-Speaking West Africa,* 257, 284, 314, 316-18, 422; Mortimer, *France and the Africans,* 111n1, 132, 140-41, 322; Thompson and Adloff, *French West Africa,* 119, 145, 153, 155-61, 175; Thompson, "Niger," 157-58, 167, 174; Fuglestad, "Djibo Bakary," 314-15, 318, 320-21, 324-26; Fuglestad, *History of Niger,* 161-62, 183-85; Chaffard, *Carnets Secrets de la Décolonisation,* 2:284; Kéïta, *P.D.G.,* 2:67, 69, 147; Manning, *Slavery, Colonialism and Economic Growth,* 279; Hodgkin and Morgenthau, "Mali," 235, 237-38, 240-41; Snyder, *One-Party Government in Mali,* 57; Suret-Canale, "Fin de la Chefferie en Guinée," 459-60, 490, 492-93; Schmidt, *Mobilizing the Masses,* 175-76; Zolberg, "Ivory Coast," 83; Aristide R. Zolberg, *One-Party Government in the Ivory Coast* (Princeton: Princeton University Press, 1964), 286-87, 289, 289n9; Martin Staniland, "Single-Party Regimes and Political Change: The P.D.C.I. and Ivory Coast Politics," in *Politics and Change in Developing Countries: Studies in the Theory and Practice of Development,* ed. Colin Leys (New York: Cambridge University Press, 1969), 149, 152, 161; Martin Klein, *Slavery and Colonial Rule in French West Africa* (New York: Cambridge University Press, 1998), 238.

55. Morgenthau, *Political Parties in French-Speaking West Africa,* 312; Mortimer, *France and the Africans,* 324; Chaffard, *Carnets Secrets de la Décolonisation,* 2:212; Kéïta, *P.D.G.,* 2:148.

56. Chaffard, *Carnets Secrets de la Décolonisation,* 2:211-13; Mortimer, *France and the Africans,* 329-33; Kéïta, *P.D.G.,* 2:149; Messmer, *Après Tant de Batailles,* 241.

57. Chaffard, *Carnets Secrets de la Décolonisation,* 2:218; Mortimer, *France and the Africans,* 329, 333; Suret-Canale, *République de Guinée,* 172-73; Kéïta, *P.D.G.,* 2:149; Morgenthau, *Political Parties in French-Speaking West Africa,* 253; de Gaulle, *Memoirs of*

Hope, 56; Messmer, *Après Tant de Batailles,* 242; "African Frontier," *Look* 26, no. 15 (17 July 1962): 80, 86.

58. The 110 teachers who remained at their posts constituted about one-third of the teaching force. Suret-Canale, *République de Guinée,* 172–73; Chaffard, *Carnets Secrets de la Décolonisation,* 2:218; Mortimer, *France and the Africans,* 333; Rivière, *Guinea,* 83.

59. Interview with Léon Maka, 25 Feb. 1991. See also Du Bois, *Guinean Vote for Independence,* 10–11, 13n22.

60. Camara, "Contribution de la Femme," 112.

61. Suret-Canale, *République de Guinée,* 122–32, 172–73; Chaffard, *Carnets Secrets de la Décolonisation,* 2:218, 220; Mortimer, *France and the Africans,* 329–30; Du Bois, *Guinean Vote for Independence,* 10–11; de Gaulle, *Memoirs of Hope,* 56; Foccart, *Foccart Parle,* 1:172; Rivière, *Guinea,* 84.

The American company Olin Mathieson Chemical Corporation controlled 48.5 percent of Société Fria's capital, while the French concern Péchiney-Ugine controlled 26.5 percent. British, Swiss, and West German firms controlled the remainder.

From its source in the Futa Jallon, the Konkouré River flows near the large bauxite deposits of Fria, Kindia, and Boké and includes many waterfalls over a 300 km stretch. The building of a dam would have permitted the construction of an irrigation network, increasing the amount of arable land, and provided a significant source of hydroelectric power for the mining of bauxite and its processing first into aluminium oxide (alumina), and subsequently, aluminum.

In late 1951, a feasibility study was conducted to determine whether such a dam could provide energy cheap enough to make an aluminum industry in Guinea profitable. The dam project was to cost approximately 300 billion metropolitan francs and was expected to generate four to five billion kilowatt hours of power per year. In November 1955, Société Fria, the French Bauxites du Midi, and an Italian company agreed to finance and build two aluminum plants. These were to be powered by the hydroelectric energy supplied by the Konkouré River. Independence brought a halt to all of these plans. Suret-Canale, *République de Guinée,* 122–32, 172–73; Foccart, *Foccart Parle,* 1:172; Thompson and Adloff, *French West Africa,* 382–83.

62. Morgenthau, *Political Parties in French-Speaking West Africa,* 74; Mortimer, *France and the Africans,* 333; Suret-Canale, *Republique de Guinée,* 172; Kéïta, *P.D.G.,* 2:149; Rivière, *Guinea,* 83; John H. Morrow, *First American Ambassador to Guinea* (New Brunswick: Rutgers University Press, 1968), 37.

63. Chaffard, *Carnets Secrets de la Décolonisation,* 2:218, 218n1; Messmer, *Après Tant de Batailles,* 242.

64. Chaffard, *Carnets Secrets de la Décolonisation,* 2:218, 220; Kéïta, *P.D.G.,* 2:149; Messmer, *Après Tant de Batailles,* 242.

65. Roger Faligot and Pascal Krop, *La Piscine: Les Services Secrets Français, 1944–1984* (Paris: Éditions du Seuil, 1985), 246–47.

66. Suret-Canale, *République de Guinée,* 172; Chaffard, *Carnets Secrets de la Décolonisation,* 2:218.

67. Suret-Canale, *République de Guinée,* 172; Chaffard, *Carnets Secrets de la Décolonisation,* 2:218, 220; Mortimer, *France and the Africans,* 333; Kéïta, *P.D.G.,* 2:149.

68. Chaffard, *Carnets Secrets de la Décolonisation,* 2:214. See also Messmer, *Après Tant de Batailles,* 242.

69. Kéïta, *P.D.G.,* 2:151–52; Suret-Canale, *République de Guinée,* 172; Chaffard, *Carnets Secrets de la Décolonisation,* 2:215; Faligot and Krop, *La Piscine,* 245.

70. Kéïta, *P.D.G.,* 2:149.

71. CAOM, Carton 2181, dos. 6, Bordereau du Ministre, FOM, Paris, 29 Sept. 1958, #1997/BE: Service de Documentation Extérieure et de Contre-Espionnage (SDECE), "Bulletin de Renseignements A/S Inquiétudes aux États Unis sur le Sort de la Guinée Française et du Niger," 26 Sept. 1958, #11424/A; Carton 2181, dos. 6, Directeur, Direction des Affaires Politiques, "Note pour Monsieur le Ministre, *Objet:* Attitude des États-Unis à l'Égard de la Guinée," 27 Sept. 1958; Foccart, *Foccart Parle,* 1:176; Mortimer, *France and the Africans,* 332.

72. Morrow, *First American Ambassador to Guinea,* 36, 68–69, 248–51; Suret-Canale, *République de Guinée,* 175.

73. Morrow, *First American Ambassador to Guinea,* 36–38, 61–62, 67–68, 79–80, 130–31; Chaffard, *Carnets Secrets de la Décolonisation,* 2:215; Faligot and Krop, *La Piscine,* 245; "African Frontier," 80, 86.

74. Chaffard, *Carnets Secrets de la Décolonisation,* 2:215–17, 220; Messmer, *Après Tant de Batailles,* 242–43; Kéïta, *P.D.G.,* 2:153; Suret-Canale, *République de Guinée,* 173. For the text of Article 88, see Morgenthau, *Political Parties in French-Speaking West Africa,* 390.

75. Quoted in Chaffard, *Carnets Secrets de la Décolonisation,* 2:221–22.

French citizens who refused to leave Guinea were, in fact, targeted for retribution. See the case of Jean Suret-Canale, below.

76. Chaffard, *Carnets Secrets de la Décolonisation,* 2:219; Suret-Canale, *République de Guinée,* 122–32.

77. Chaffard, *Carnets Secrets de la Décolonisation,* 2:219

78. Morrow, *First American Ambassador to Guinea,* 131; "African Frontier," 80, 86.

79. Morrow, *First American Ambassador to Guinea,* 37–38, 61–62, 71–72, 79–80, 127–28, 130–32; Chaffard, *Carnets Secrets de la Décolonisation,* 2:234–35; Suret-Canale, *République de Guinée,* 174, 178; Mortimer, *France and the Africans,* 333, 335; Rivière, *Guinea,* 101; Cowan, "Guinea," 212; "African Frontier," 80, 86; personal communication from Siba N. Grovogui, 1991.

Jean Suret-Canale, a French communist and a teacher in Dakar, was among those who went to Guinea after independence. In contrast to de Gaulle's official statement, Suret-Canale claimed that the French government threatened to revoke his citizenship if he refused to leave Guinea. Morgenthau, *Political Parties in French-Speaking West Africa,* 23n1; Chaffard, *Carnets Secrets de la Décolonisation,* 2:221–22; e-mail communication from Martin Klein, 6 Feb. 2006.

80. Chaffard, *Carnets Secrets de la Décolonisation,* 2:218–19, 236–51, 259–61; Faligot and Krop, *La Piscine,* 217, 226, 245–49, 252, 335–37; Foccart, *Foccart Parle,* 1:166, 175; Foccart, *Foccart Parle,* 2:193–94; Rivière, *Guinea,* 121–40; Mortimer, *France and the Africans,* 335; Cowan, "Guinea," 229; R. W. Johnson, "Sekou Touré and the Guinean Revolution," *African Affairs* 69, no. 277 (Oct. 1970): 357–58; Bernard Charles, *La République de Guinée* (Paris: Éditions Berger-Levrault, 1972), 32; Lansiné

Kaba, "Guinean Politics: A Critical Historical Overview," *Journal of Modern African Studies* 15, no. 1 (1977): 33.

81. CAOM, Carton 2181, dos. 7, Haut Commissaire de l'AOF, Bobo-Diolasso, à Ministre, FOM, Paris, "Référendum du 28 Septembre," 17 Sept. 1958, T/0 #3987/3986/3988; Mortimer, *France and the Africans,* 331–32; Messmer, *Après Tant de Batailles,* 242; Wallerstein, "How Seven States Were Born," 4.

82. Kéïta, *P.D.G.,* 2:154.

83. Chaffard, *Carnets Secrets de la Décolonisation,* 2:217, 234–35; Mortimer, *France and the Africans,* 331; Messmer, *Après Tant de Batailles,* 242; Wallerstein, "How Seven States Were Born," 4.

These sentiments were echoed by Jacques Foccart, Prime Minister de Gaulle's chief Africa adviser, who supervised the Africa-related activities of the French secret services (Service de Documentation Extérieure et de Contre-Espionnage or SDECE) during this period. See Foccart, *Foccart Parle,* 1:172; Faligot and Krop, *La Piscine,* 27, 225–26.

84. Kéïta, *P.D.G.,* 2:158.

As noted in chap. 2, the Guinean RDA officially had been renamed the Parti Démocratique de Guinée at its second party congress in October 1950. However, Guineans generally continued to refer to their local branch as the "RDA" until after independence. See Kéïta, *P.D.G.,* 1:238–39; interviews conducted in Guinea in 1991.

85. Kéïta, *P.D.G.,* 2:159; Aly Gilbert Iffono, *Lexique Historique de la Guinée-Conakry* (Paris: L'Harmattan, 1992), 168; Sylvain Soriba Camara, *La Guinée sans la France* (Paris: Presses de la Fondation Nationale des Sciences Politiques, 1976), 115–16; Kwame Nkrumah, *I Speak of Freedom: A Statement of African Ideology* (New York: Frederick A. Praeger, 1961), 176–77, 232; Ali A. Mazrui, "Seek Ye First the Political Kingdom," in *Africa since 1935,* ed. Ali A. Mazrui and C. Wondji, vol. 8 of *General History of Africa* (Berkeley: University of California Press, 1999), 108.

86. Chaffard, *Carnets Secrets de la Décolonisation,* 2:228–29; Mortimer, *France and the Africans,* 332–33; Kéïta, *P.D.G.,* 2:159.

87. Chaffard, *Carnets Secrets de la Décolonisation,* 2:228–29; Mortimer, *France and the Africans,* 333; Kéïta, *P.D.G.,* 2:159; Suret-Canale, *République de Guinée,* 173; Foccart, *Foccart Parle,* 1:176–77.

88. Kéïta, *P.D.G.,* 2:161; Suret-Canale, *République de Guinée,* 173; Faligot and Krop, *La Piscine,* 245.

89. For a discussion of France's postcolonial economic and military arrangements, see Samir Amin, *Neo-colonialism in West Africa,* trans. Francis McDonagh (Baltimore: Penguin, 1973).

90. Mazrui, "Seek Ye First the Political Kingdom," 109.

91. Kéïta, *P.D.G.,* 2:161; Morgenthau, *Political Parties in French-Speaking West Africa,* 73–74, 390. For the original text of Article 86 and its revision, see Morgenthau, *Political Parties in French-Speaking West Africa,* 390.

92. Morgenthau, *Political Parties in French-Speaking West Africa,* xxi, 74; Kéïta, *P.D.G.,* 2:162; Foccart, *Foccart Parle,* 1:169–70, 198–99, 223; Faligot and Krop, *La Piscine,* 222; Mazrui, "Seek Ye First the Political Kingdom," 108–11; Sidiki Kobélé Kéïta, *Ahmed Sékou Touré: L'Homme du 28 Septembre 1958,* 2nd ed. (Conakry: I.N.R.D.G., Bibliothèque Nationale, 1977), 75.

93. Morgenthau, *Political Parties in French-Speaking West Africa,* 119.

94. In February 1960, British Prime Minister Harold Macmillan told a South African audience that "the wind of change is blowing through this continent, and, whether we like it or not, this growth of national consciousness is a political fact." Independent nations were bound to emerge, and European powers needed to accept this fact and adapt their policies accordingly. Quoted in Frank Myers, "Harold Macmillan's 'Winds of Change' Speech: A Case Study in the Rhetoric of Policy Change," *Rhetoric and Public Affairs* 3, no. 4 (Winter 2000): 556, 559, 564–65.

Conclusion

1. This calculation excludes Amara Soumah's victory in the territorial elections of March 1952, since Soumah resigned from the RDA immediately after his election. (See chap. 2.)

2. L. Gray Cowan, "Guinea," in *African One-Party States,* ed. Gwendolen M. Carter (Ithaca: Cornell University Press, 1962), 149–236; Victor D. Du Bois, *The Problems of Independence: The Decolonization of Guinea,* West Africa Series 5, no. 8 (New York: American Universities Field Staff, 1962), 1–18; Victor D. Du Bois, *Reorganization of the Guinean Economy: The Attempt to Remove the Economic Vestiges of Colonialism,* West Africa Series 6, no. 1 (New York: American Universities Field Staff, 1963): 1–22; Victor D. Du Bois, *The Decline of the Guinean Revolution,* West Africa Series, 8, nos. 7–9 (New York: American Universities Field Staff, 1965); Victor D. Du Bois, *The Rise of an Opposition to Sékou Touré,* West Africa Series 9, nos. 1–5, 7 (New York: American Universities Field Staff, 1966); B. Ameillon, *La Guinée: Bilan d'une Indépendance,* Cahiers Libres, nos. 58–59 (Paris: François Maspero, 1964); Bernard Charles, *Guinée* (Lausanne: Éditions Recontre, 1963); Bernard Charles, *Guinée et son Régime Politique* (Paris: Fondation Nationale des Sciences Politiques, 1963); Bernard Charles, *La République de Guinée* (Paris: Éditions Berger-Levrault, 1972); Sylvain Soriba Camara, *La Guinée sans la France* (Paris: Presses de la Fondation Nationale des Sciences Politiques, 1976); 'Ladipo Adamolekun, *Sékou Touré's Guinea: An Experiment in Nation Building* (London: Methuen, 1976); Claude Rivière, *Guinea: The Mobilization of a People,* trans. Virginia Thompson and Richard Adloff (Ithaca: Cornell University Press, 1977); Lansiné Kaba, "Guinean Politics: A Critical Historical Overview," *Journal of Modern African Studies* 15, no. 1 (1977): 25–45.

3. See, e.g., Rivière, *Guinea;* Yves Person, "French West Africa and Decolonization," in *The Transfer of Power in Africa: Decolonization, 1940–1960,* ed. Prosser Gifford and William Roger Louis (New Haven: Yale University Press, 1982), 141–72; Victor D. Du Bois, "Guinea," in *Political Parties and National Integration in Tropical Africa,* ed. James S. Coleman and Carl G. Rosberg Jr. (Berkeley: University of California Press, 1970), 186–215.

4. AG, 1E41, Guinée Française, Services de Police, "Renseignements A/S Réunion R.D.A.," 5 Dec. 1951, #2282/1293/C/PS.2; 1E41, Guinée Française, Services de Police, "Renseignements A/S Réunion R.D.A.," 19 Dec. 1951, #2394/1350/C/PS.2; CAOM, Carton 2144, dos. 1, Ministre, FOM, "Rapport Pruvost," 31 March 1955; ANS, 2G55/150, Guinée Française, Gouverneur, "Rapport Politique Mensuel,

Juillet 1955," #435/APAS/CAB; CRDA, P.D.G., Bureau Directeur, Sous-Section de Mamou, au Comité Directeur du P.D.G., Conakry, 1 Aug. 1955, in *P.D.G.-R.D.A., Parti Démocratique de Guinée, 1947–1960: Les Sections—Les Syndicats;* interviews in Conakry with Aissatou N'Diaye, 8 April 1991; Néné Diallo, 11 April 1991; Fatou Kéïta, 28 April and 24 May 1991; Ibrahima Fofana, 24 May 1991.

5. Rivière, *Guinea,* 60, 86–87; Adamolekun, *Sékou Touré's Guinea,* 11; Sidiki Kobélé Kéïta, *Le P.D.G.: Artisan de l'Indépendance Nationale en Guinée (1947–1958)* (Conakry: I.N.R.D.G., Bibliothèque Nationale, 1978), 1:180, 186, 308–9, 311; Sidiki Kobélé Kéïta, *Ahmed Sékou Touré: L'Homme et son Combat Anti-Colonial (1922–1958)* (Conakry: Éditions S.K.K., 1998), 88–94; Ruth Schachter Morgenthau, *Political Parties in French-Speaking West Africa* (Oxford: Clarendon Press, 1964), 229, 246, 394; Jean Suret-Canale, "La Fin de la Chefferie en Guinée," *Journal of African History* 7, no. 3 (1966): 482; Jean Suret-Canale, *La République de Guinée* (Paris: Éditions Sociales, 1970), 164; R. W. Johnson, "The Parti Démocratique de Guinée and the Mamou 'Deviation,'" in *African Perspectives: Papers in the History, Politics and Economics of Africa Presented to Thomas Hodgkin,* ed. Christopher Allen and R. W. Johnson (New York: Cambridge University Press, 1970), 349.

6. See chap. 5.

7. For the postindependence crackdown on intellectuals, see Rivière, *Guinea,* 127–28; Ameillon, *Guinée,* 179–81; Cowan, "Guinea," 203–4; Camara, *Guinée sans la France,* 175–76; Charles, *République de Guinée,* 31; Kaba, "Guinean Politics," 30; R. W. Johnson, "Sekou Touré and the Guinean Revolution," *African Affairs* 69, no. 277 (Oct. 1970): 357–58.

8. Kéïta, *P.D.G.,* 2:166, 190–91; Suret-Canale, *République de Guinée,* 172; Victor D. Du Bois, *The Guinean Vote for Independence: The Maneuvering before the Referendum of September 28, 1958,* West Africa Series 5, no. 7 (New York: American Universities Field Staff, 1962): 6, 8.

9. See chap. 6.

Bibliography

INTERVIEWS CONDUCTED BY ELIZABETH SCHMIDT AND SIBA N. GROVOGUI

Baldé, Mira (Mme. Maka). Sangoyah, Conakry, 25 Feb., 19 May 1991.
Barry, Bocar Biro. Camayenne, Conakry, 21 and 29 Jan. 1991.
Diallo, Néné. Conakry, 11 April 1991.
Diarra, Fanta. Lansanaya, Conakry, 24 May 1991.
Diarra, Fatou. Lansanaya, Conakry, 17 March 1991.
Doumbouya, Mamadou Bela. Camayenne, Conakry, 26 Jan. 1991.
Fofana, Ibrahima. Lansanaya, Conakry, 17 March, 5 and 24 May 1991.
Kaba, Mamady. Donka, Conakry, 15 Jan. 1991.
Kéïta, Fatou. Km 43, Conakry, 7 and 28 April, 24 May 1991.
Kéïta, Sidiki Kobélé. Donka, Conakry, 20 Oct. 1990, 9 April 1991.
Maka, Léon. Sangoyah, Conakry, 20 and 25 Feb. 1991.
Meunier, Kadiatou (pseudonym). Minière, Conakry, 18 Jan., 19 Feb., 5 March 1991.
Montlouis, Joseph. Coléah, Conakry, 28 Feb., 3 and 6 March 1991.
N'Diaye, Aissatou. Kaloum, Sandervalia, Conakry, 8 April 1991.
Sylla, Tourou. Kimbely, Mamou, 30 May 1991.
Touré, Fodé Mamadou. Ratoma, Conakry, 13 March 1991.

ARCHIVES

In Guinea

Archives de Guinée (AG), Conakry
Personal archives of Bocar Biro Barry, Conakry
Personal archives of Joseph Montlouis, Conakry

In Senegal

Archives Nationales du Sénégal (ANS), Dakar
Institut Fondamental d'Afrique Noire (IFAN), Dakar

In France

Centre d'Accueil et de Recherche des Archives Nationales de France (CARAN), Paris
Centre des Archives d'Outre-Mer, Archives Nationales de France (CAOM), Aix-en-
    Provence
Centre de Recherche et de Documentation Africaine (CRDA), Paris

Published Primary Sources

Periodicals housed at IFAN and CRDA:
    Coup de Bambou, 1950.
    La Liberté, 1951–60.
    Le Phare de Guinée, 1947–49.
    Réveil, 1946–50.
Act of March 11, 1941 (Lend-Lease Act). Public Law 11, 77th Congress. http://www.
    history.navy.mil/faqs/faq59-23.htm.
"The Atlantic Charter, Joint Declaration by the President and the Prime Minister,
    Declaration of Principles, Known as the Atlantic Charter." 14 August 1941.
    U.S.-U.K. 55 Stat. App. 1603. http://www1.umn.edu/humanrts/education/
    FDRjointdec.html.
"Charter of the United Nations." San Francisco, 26 June 1945. 59 Stat. 1031, *Treaty
    Ser.* 993. http://www.un.org/aboutun/charter.
"Declaration by United Nations." 1 January 1942. *FRUS* I, 25–26. http://www.ibiblio.
    org/pha/policy/1942/420101a.html.
Guinée: Prélude à l'Indépendance. Paris: Présence Africaine, 1958.
"Nouveau Bureau Directeur [Syndicat du Personnel Enseignant Africain de Guinée]."
    L'École Guinéenne, no. 1 (1957–58). Personal archives of Bocar Biro Barry.
"Recommendations Adopted by the Brazzaville Conference." In *Colonial Rule in Africa:
    Readings from Primary Sources,* edited by Bruce Fetter, 168–73. Madison: Uni-
    versity of Wisconsin Press, 1979.
"Travaux du Congres de Mamou (6–10 Août 1957): Motion sur la Loi-Cadre." *L'École
    Guinéenne,* no. 1 (1957–58): 1. Personal archives of Bocar Biro Barry.

Secondary Sources

Adamolekun, 'Ladipo. "The Road to Independence in French Tropical Africa." In *Afri-
    can Nationalism and Independence,* edited by Timothy K. Welliver, 66–79. New
    York: Garland, 1993.
———. *Sékou Touré's Guinea: An Experiment in Nation Building.* London: Methuen,
    1976.
"African Frontier." *Look* 26, no. 15 (17 July 1962): 78–68.
Allman, Jean Marie. *The Quills of the Porcupine: Asante Nationalism in an Emergent Ghana.*
    Madison: University of Wisconsin Press, 1993.

————. "The Youngmen and the Porcupine: Class, Nationalism and Asante's Struggle for Self-Determination, 1954–57." *Journal of African History* 31, no. 2 (1990): 263–79.

Ameillon, B. *La Guinée: Bilan d'une Indépendance.* Cahiers Libres, nos. 58–59. Paris: François Maspero, 1964.

Amin, Samir. *Neo-colonialism in West Africa.* Translated by Francis McDonagh. Baltimore: Penguin, 1973.

Apter, David. *Ghana in Transition.* Princeton: Princeton University Press, 1963.

Azema, Jean-Pierre. *From Munich to the Liberation, 1938–1944.* Translated by Janet Lloyd. New York: Cambridge University Press, 1984.

Berg, Elliot J. "The Economic Basis of Political Choice in French West Africa." *American Political Science Review* 54, no. 2 (June 1960): 391–405.

————. "French West Africa." In *Labor and Economic Development,* edited by Walter Galenson, 186–259. New York: John Wiley and Sons, 1959.

Berg, Elliot J., and Jeffrey Butler. "Trade Unions." In *Political Parties and National Integration in Tropical Africa,* edited by James S. Coleman and Carl G. Rosberg Jr., 340–81. Berkeley: University of California Press, 1964.

Blanchet, André. *L'Itinéraire des Partis Africains depuis Bamako.* Paris: Librarie Plon, 1958.

Boahen, A. Adu. "Colonialism in Africa: Its Impact and Significance." In *Africa under Colonial Domination, 1880–1935,* edited by A. Adu Boahen, 782–809, vol. 7 of *General History of Africa.* Berkeley: University of California Press, 1985.

————. "Politics and Nationalism in West Africa, 1919–35." In *Africa under Colonial Domination, 1880–1935,* edited by A. Adu Boahen, 624–47, vol. 7 of *General History of Africa.* Berkeley: University of California Press, 1985.

Breuilly, John. *Nationalism and the State,* 2nd ed. Chicago: University of Chicago Press, 1994.

Camara, Sylvain Soriba. *La Guinée sans la France.* Paris: Presses de la Fondation Nationale des Sciences Politiques, 1976.

Césaire, Aimé. *Volcans Coloniaux.* Paris, 1951.

Chafer, Tony. *The End of Empire in French West Africa: France's Successful Decolonization?* New York: Berg, 2002.

Chaffard, Georges. *Les Carnets Secrets de la Décolonisation.* 2 vols. Paris: Calmann-Lévy, 1965–67.

Charles, Bernard. *Guinée.* Lausanne: Éditions Recontre, 1963.

————. *Guinée et son Régime Politique.* Paris: Fondation Nationale des Sciences Politiques, 1963.

————. *La République de Guinée.* Paris: Éditions Berger-Levrault, 1972.

Clark, Andrew F. *From Frontier to Backwater: Economy and Society in the Upper Senegal Valley (West Africa), 1850–1920.* Lanham, MD: University Press of America, 1999.

Coleman, James S. *Nigeria: Background to Nationalism.* Berkeley: University of California Press, 1958.

Cooper, Frederick. *Decolonization and African Society: The Labor Question in French and British Africa.* New York: Cambridge University Press, 1996.

————. "'Our Strike': Equality, Anticolonial Politics and the 1947–48 Railway Strike in French West Africa." *Journal of African History* 37, no. 1 (1996): 81–118.

Coquery-Vidrovitch, Catherine. "Nationalité et Citoyenneté en Afrique Occidentale Français[e]: Originaires et Citoyens dans le Sénégal Colonial." *Journal of African History* 42, no. 2 (2001): 285–305.

Costigliola, Frank. *France and the United States: The Cold Alliance since World War II.* New York: Twayne, 1992.

Cowan, L. Gray. "Guinea." In *African One-Party States,* edited by Gwendolen M. Carter, 149–236. Ithaca: Cornell University Press, 1962.

Davidson, Basil. *Black Star: A View of the Life and Times of Kwame Nkrumah,* 2nd ed. Boulder: Westview Press, 1989.

de Gaulle, Charles. *Memoirs of Hope: Renewal and Endeavor.* Translated by Terence Kilmartin. New York: Simon and Schuster, 1971.

————. *Salvation, 1944–1946.* Vol. 3 of *The War Memoirs of Charles de Gaulle.* New York: Simon and Schuster, 1960.

————. *Unity, 1942–1944.* Vol. 2 of *The War Memoirs of Charles de Gaulle.* New York: Simon and Schuster, 1959.

Derman, William. *Serfs, Peasants, and Socialists: A Former Serf Village in the Republic of Guinea.* Berkeley: University of California Press, 1973.

Diané, Charles. *La F.E.A.N.F. et Les Grandes Heures du Mouvement Syndical Étudiant Noir.* Afrique Contemporaine 5. Paris: Éditions Chaka, 1990.

Du Bois, Victor D. *The Decline of the Guinean Revolution.* West Africa Series 8, nos. 7–9. New York: American Universities Field Staff, 1965.

————. "Guinea." In *Political Parties and National Integration in Tropical Africa,* edited by James S. Coleman and Carl G. Rosberg Jr., 186–215. Berkeley: University of California Press, 1964.

————. *The Guinean Vote for Independence: The Maneuvering before the Referendum of September 28, 1958.* West Africa Series 5, no. 7. New York: American Universities Field Staff, 1962.

————. *Guinea's Prelude to Independence: Political Activity, 1945–58.* West Africa Series 5, no. 6. New York: American Universities Field Staff, 1962.

————. *The Problems of Independence: The Decolonization of Guinea.* West Africa Series 5, no. 8. New York: American Universities Field Staff, 1962.

————. *Reorganization of the Guinean Economy: The Attempt to Remove the Economic Vestiges of Colonialism.* West Africa Series 6, no. 1. New York: American Universities Field Staff, 1963.

————. *The Rise of an Opposition to Sékou Touré.* West Africa Series 9, nos. 1–5, 7. New York: American Universities Field Staff, 1966.

Echenberg, Myron. *Colonial Conscripts: The Tirailleurs Sénégalais in French West Africa, 1857–1960.* Social History of Africa Series. Portsmouth, NH: Heinemann, 1991.

Elgey, Georgette. *La République des Illusions, 1945–1951.* Paris: Fayard, 1965.

Faligot, Roger, and Pascal Krop. *La Piscine: Les Services Secrets Français, 1944–1984.* Paris: Éditions du Seuil, 1985.

Foccart, Jacques. *Foccart Parle: Entretiens avec Philippe Gaillard.* 2 vols. Paris: Fayard/ Jeune Afrique, 1995.

Fuglestad, Finn. "Djibo Bakary, the French, and the Referendum of 1958 in Niger." *Journal of African History* 14, no. 2 (1973): 313–30.

———. *A History of Niger, 1850–1960.* New York: Cambridge University Press, 1983.

Gerteiny, Alfred G. *Mauritania.* New York: Frederick A. Praeger, 1967.

Goerg, Odile. "Femmes Africaines et Politique: Les Colonisées au Féminin en Afrique Occidentale." *Clio,* no. 6 (1997). http://clio.revues.org/document378.html? format=print.

Grovogui, Siba N. *Beyond Eurocentrism and Anarchy: Memories of International Order and Institutions.* New York: Palgrave Macmillan, 2006.

Hargreaves, John D. *Decolonization in Africa.* 2nd ed. New York: Longman, 1996.

Headrick, Daniel R. *The Tools of Empire: Technology and European Imperialism in the Nineteenth Century.* New York: Oxford University Press, 1981.

Hitchcock, William I. *France Restored: Cold War Diplomacy and the Quest for Leadership in Europe, 1944–1954.* Chapel Hill: University of North Carolina Press, 1998.

Hodgkin, Thomas. *African Political Parties: An Introductory Guide.* Gloucester, MA: Peter Smith, 1971.

———. *Nationalism in Colonial Africa.* New York: New York University Press, 1957.

Hodgkin, Thomas, and Ruth Schachter Morgenthau. "Mali." In *Political Parties and National Integration in Tropical Africa,* edited by James S. Coleman and Carl G. Rosberg Jr., 216–58. Berkeley: University of California Press, 1964.

Hrbek, Ivan. "North Africa and the Horn." In *Africa since 1935,* edited by Ali A. Mazrui and C. Wondji, 127–60, vol. 8 of *General History of Africa.* Berkeley: University of California Press, 1999.

Iffono, Aly Gilbert. *Lexique Historique de la Guinée-Conakry.* Paris: L'Harmattan, 1992.

Jézéquel, Jean-Hervé. "Les Enseignants Comme Élite Politique en AOF (1930–1945): Des 'Meneurs de Galopins' dans l'Arène Politique." *Cahiers d'Études Africaines* 45, no. 2 (2005): 519–43.

Johnson, R. W. "The Parti Démocratique de Guinée and the Mamou 'Deviation.'" In *African Perspectives: Papers in the History, Politics and Economics of Africa Presented to Thomas Hodgkin,* edited by Christopher Allen and R. W. Johnson, 347–69. New York: Cambridge University Press, 1970.

———. "Sekou Touré and the Guinean Revolution." *African Affairs* 69, no. 277 (Oct. 1970): 350–65.

Jones, James A. *Industrial Labor in the Colonial World: Workers of the Chemin de Fer Dakar-Niger, 1881–1963.* Portsmouth, NH: Heinemann, 2002.

Joseph, Richard A. *Radical Nationalism in Cameroun: Social Origins of the U.P.C. Rebellion.* Oxford: Oxford University Press, 1977.

Kaba, Lansiné. "Guinean Politics: A Critical Historical Overview," *Journal of Modern African Studies* 15, no. 1 (1977): 25–45.

———. *Le "Non" de la Guinée à de Gaulle.* Afrique Contemporaine 1. Paris: Éditions Chaka, 1989.

Kaniki, M. H. Y. "The Colonial Economy: The Former British Zones." In *Africa under Colonial Domination, 1880–1935*, edited by A. Adu Boahen, 382–419, vol. 7 of *General History of Africa*. Berkeley: University of California Press, 1985.

Kanya-Forstner, A. S. "Mali-Tukulor." In *West African Resistance: The Military Response to Colonial Occupation*, edited by Michael Crowder, 53–79. New York: Africana, 1971.

Kéïta, Sidiki Kobélé. *Ahmed Sékou Touré: L'Homme du 28 Septembre 1958*. 2nd ed. Conakry: I.N.R.D.G., Bibliothèque Nationale, 1977.

————. *Ahmed Sékou Touré: L'Homme et son Combat Anti-Colonial (1922–1958)*. Conakry: Éditions S.K.K., 1998.

————. *Le P.D.G.: Artisan de l'Indépendance Nationale en Guinée (1947–1958)*. 2 vols. Conakry: I.N.R.D.G., Bibliothèque Nationale, 1978.

Kelley, Robin D. G. "A Poetics of Anticolonialism." Introduction to *Discourse on Colonialism*, by Aimé Césaire. New York: Monthly Review Press, 2000.

Kipré, Pierre. *Le Congrès de Bamako: Ou la Naissance du RDA en 1946*. Afrique Contemporaine 3. Paris: Collection Afrique Contemporaine, 1989.

Klein, Martin. *Slavery and Colonial Rule in French West Africa*. New York: Cambridge University Press, 1998.

————. "Slavery and the French Colonial State." http://scholar.google.com/scholar?hl=en&lr=&q=cache:9eTKZB09Y20J:www.tekrur.org/publications/AOFINTERNET.PDF/4S1CULTOK.PDF/04S1KLEIN.pdf+henri+d%27arboussier.

Lawler, Nancy Ellen. *Soldiers of Misfortune: Ivoirien Tirailleurs of World War II*. Athens: Ohio University Press, 1992.

Leffler, Melvyn P. "The Cold War: What Do 'We Now Know'?" *American Historical Review* 104, no. 2 (April 1999): 520–21.

Lonsdale, John. "The Emergence of African Nations: A Historiographical Analysis." *African Affairs* 67, no. 266 (1968): 11–28.

————. "Some Origins of Nationalism in East Africa." *Journal of African History* 9, no. 1 (1968): 119–46.

MacShane, Denis. *François Mitterrand: A Political Odyssey*. New York: Universe Books, 1982.

Mamdani, Mahmood. *Citizen and Subject: Contemporary Africa and the Legacy of Late Colonialism*. Princeton: Princeton University Press, 1996.

Manning, Patrick. *Francophone Sub-Saharan Africa, 1880–1985*. New York: Cambridge University Press, 1988.

Manning, Patrick. *Slavery, Colonialism and Economic Growth in Dahomey, 1640–1960*. New York: Cambridge University Press, 1982.

Marshall, D. Bruce. *The French Colonial Myth and Constitution-Making in the Fourth Republic*. New Haven: Yale University Press, 1973.

Mazrui, Ali A. "Seek Ye First the Political Kingdom." In *Africa since 1935*, edited by Ali A. Mazrui and C. Wondji, 105–26, vol. 8 of *General History of Africa*. Berkeley: University of California Press, 1999.

M'Bokolo, Elikia. "Equatorial West Africa." In *Africa since 1935*, edited by Ali A. Mazrui and C. Wondji, 192–220, vol. 8 of *General History of Africa*. Berkeley: University of California Press, 1999.

Messmer, Pierre. *Après Tant de Batailles: Mémoires.* Paris: Albin Michel, 1992.

Meynaud, Jean, and Anisse Salah Bey. *Trade Unionism in Africa: A Study of Its Growth and Orientation.* Translated by Angela Brench. London: Methuen and Co., 1967.

Milcent, Ernest. *L'A.O.F. Entre en Scène.* Paris: Bibliothèque de l'Homme d'Action, 1958.

Morgenthau, Ruth Schachter. *Political Parties in French-Speaking West Africa.* Oxford: Clarendon Press, 1964.

Morrow, John H. *First American Ambassador to Guinea.* New Brunswick: Rutgers University Press, 1968.

Mortimer, Edward. *France and the Africans, 1944–1960: A Political History.* New York: Walker and Co., 1969.

Myers, Frank. "Harold Macmillan's 'Winds of Change' Speech: A Case Study in the Rhetoric of Policy Change." *Rhetoric and Public Affairs* 3, no. 4 (Winter 2000): 555–75.

Nkrumah, Kwame. *I Speak of Freedom: A Statement of African Ideology.* New York: Frederick A. Praeger, 1961.

Obeng, Pashington. "Gendered Nationalism: Forms of Masculinity in Modern Asante of Ghana." In *Men and Masculinities in Modern Africa,* edited by Lisa A. Lindsay and Stephan F. Miescher, 192–208. Social History of Africa Series. Portsmouth, NH: Heinemann, 2003.

O'Toole, Thomas E. *Historical Dictionary of Guinea (Republic of Guinea/Conakry),* 2nd ed. Metuchen, NJ: Scarecrow Press, 1987.

Ousby, Ian. *Occupation: The Ordeal of France, 1940–1944.* New York: St. Martin's Press, 1997.

Person, Yves. "French West Africa and Decolonization." In *The Transfer of Power in Africa: Decolonization, 1940–1960,* edited by Prosser Gifford and William Roger Louis, 141–72. New Haven: Yale University Press, 1982.

———. "Guinea-Samori." Translated by Joan White. In *West African Resistance: The Military Response to Colonial Occupation,* edited by Michael Crowder, 111–43. New York: Africana, 1971.

Rathbone, Richard. "Businessmen in Politics: Party Struggle in Ghana, 1949–1957." *Journal of Development Studies* 9, no. 3 (1973): 391–401.

———. *Nkrumah and the Chiefs: The Politics of Chieftaincy in Ghana, 1951–1960.* Athens: Ohio University Press, 2000.

Rice-Maximin, Edward. "The United States and the French Left, 1945–1949: The View from the State Department." *Journal of Contemporary History* 19, no. 4 (Oct. 1984): 729–47.

Richard-Molard, Jacques. *Afrique Occidentale Française.* Paris: Éditions Berger-Levrault, 1952.

Rioux, Jean-Pierre. *The Fourth Republic, 1944–1958.* Translated by Godfrey Rogers. New York: Cambridge University Press, 1987.

Rivière, Claude. *Guinea: The Mobilization of a People.* Translated by Virginia Thompson and Richard Adloff. Ithaca: Cornell University Press, 1977.

Robinson, Kenneth. "Political Development in French West Africa." In *Africa in the Modern World,* edited by Calvin W. Stillman, 140–81. Chicago: University of Chicago Press, 1955.

————. "Senegal: The Elections to the Territorial Assembly, March 1957." In *Five Elections in Africa,* edited by W. J. M. MacKenzie and Kenneth Robinson, 281–390. Oxford: Oxford University Press, 1960.

Rodney, Walter. "The Colonial Economy." In *Africa under Colonial Domination, 1880–1935,* edited by A. Adu Boahen, 332–50, vol. 7 of *General History of Africa.* Berkeley: University of California Press, 1985.

————. "Jihad and Social Revolution in Futa Djalon in the Eighteenth Century." *Journal of the Historical Society of Nigeria* 4, no. 2 (June 1968): 269–84.

Ross, George. *Workers and Communists in France: From Popular Front to Eurocommunism.* Berkeley: University of California Press, 1982.

Rotberg, Robert I. *The Rise of Nationalism in Central Africa: The Making of Malawi and Zambia, 1873–1964.* Cambridge: Harvard University Press, 1965.

Sabatier, Peggy R. "'Elite' Education in French West Africa: The Era of Limits, 1903–1945." *International Journal of African Historical Studies* 11, no. 2 (1978): 247–66.

Schachter, Ruth, and Immanuel Wallerstein. "French Africa's Road to Independence." *West Africa* 1, no. 2140 (19 April 1958): 372; 2, no. 2141 (26 April 1958): 395; 3, no. 2142 (3 May 1958): 419.

Schmidt, Elizabeth. "Cold War in Guinea: The Rassemblement Démocratique Africain and the Struggle over Communism, 1950–1958." *Journal of African History* 48, no. 1 (March 2007): 95–121.

————. "'Emancipate Your Husbands!': Women and Nationalism in Guinea, 1953–1958." In *Women in African Colonial Histories,* edited by Jean Allman, Susan Geiger, and Nakanyike Musisi, 282–304. Bloomington: Indiana University Press, 2002.

————. *Mobilizing the Masses: Gender, Ethnicity, and Class in the Nationalist Movement in Guinea, 1939–1958.* Social History of Africa Series. Portsmouth, NH: Heinemann, 2005.

————. "Top Down or Bottom Up? Nationalist Mobilization Reconsidered, with Special Reference to Guinea (French West Africa)." *American Historical Review* 110, no. 4 (Oct. 2005): 975–1014.

Schneider, James J. "T. E. Lawrence and the Mind of an Insurgent." *Army* (July 2005): 31–37.

Smith, Anthony D. *State and Nation in the Third World: The Western State and African Nationalism.* New York: St. Martin's Press, 1983.

Snyder, Frank Gregory. *One-Party Government in Mali: Transition Toward Control.* New Haven: Yale University Press, 1965.

Staniland, Martin. "Single-Party Regimes and Political Change: The P.D.C.I. and Ivory Coast Politics." In *Politics and Change in Developing Countries: Studies in the Theory and Practice of Development,* edited by Colin Leys, 135–75. New York: Cambridge University Press, 1969.

————. "The Three-Party System in Dahomey." *Journal of African History* 14, no. 2 (1973): 291–312; 14, no. 3 (1973): 491–504.

Stryker, Richard E. "Political and Administrative Linkage in the Ivory Coast." In *Ghana and the Ivory Coast: Perspectives on Modernization,* edited by Philip Foster and Aristide R. Zolberg, 73–102. Chicago: University of Chicago Press, 1971.

Suret-Canale, Jean. "La Fin de la Chefferie en Guinée." *Journal of African History* 7, no. 3 (1966): 459–93.

———. *French Colonialism in Tropical Africa, 1900–1945.* Translated by Till Gottheiner. New York: Pica Press, 1971.

———. "The French West African Railway Workers' Strike, 1947–1948." In *African Labor History,* edited by Peter C. W. Gutkind, Robin Cohen, and Jean Copans, 129–54. Beverly Hills: Sage, 1978.

———. *La République de Guinée.* Paris: Éditions Sociales, 1970.

Thioub, Ibrahima. "Gabriel d'Arboussier et la Question de l'Unité Africaine, 1945–1965." http://scholar.google.com/scholar?hl=en&lr=&q=cache:UOIMw-gIYHcMJ:www.tekrur.org/publications/AOF/2POLBALK.PDF/09P4TIUBAR.pdf+henri+d%27arboussier.

Thompson, Virginia. "The Ivory Coast." In *African One-Party States,* edited by Gwendolen M. Carter, 237–324. Ithaca: Cornell University Press, 1962.

———. "Niger." In *National Unity and Regionalism in Eight African States,* edited by Gwendolen M. Carter, 151–230. Ithaca: Cornell University Press, 1966.

Thompson, Virginia, and Richard Adloff. *French West Africa.* New York: Greenwood Press, 1969.

Thorez, Maurice. *Fils du Peuple.* Paris: Éditions Sociales, 1937.

Tiersky, Ronald. *French Communism, 1920–1972.* New York: Columbia University Press, 1972.

Turrittin, Jane. "Aoua Kéita and the Nascent Women's Movement in the French Sudan." *African Studies Review* 36, no. 1 (April 1993): 59–89.

Wall, Irwin M. *The United States and the Making of Postwar France, 1945–1954.* New York: Cambridge University Press, 1991.

Wallerstein, Immanuel. "Elites in French-Speaking West Africa: The Social Basis of Ideas." *Journal of Modern African Studies* 3, no. 1 (1965): 1–33.

———. "How Seven States Were Born in Former French West Africa." *Africa Report* (March 1961): 3–4, 7, 12, 15.

———. *The Road to Independence: Ghana and the Ivory Coast.* Paris: Mouton and Co., 1964.

Wilder, Gary. *The French Imperial Nation-State: Negritude and Colonial Humanism between the Two World Wars.* Chicago: University of Chicago Press, 2005.

Wright, Gordon. *The Reshaping of French Democracy.* New York: Howard Fertig, 1970.

Young, John W. *France, the Cold War and the Western Alliance, 1944–49: French Foreign Policy and Post-war Europe.* New York: St. Martin's Press, 1990.

Zolberg, Aristide R. *Creating Political Order: The Party-States of West Africa.* Chicago: Rand McNally, 1966.

———. "The Ivory Coast." In *Political Parties and National Integration in Tropical Africa,* edited by James S. Coleman and Carl G. Rosberg Jr., 65–89. Berkeley: University of California Press, 1964.

———. *One-Party Government in the Ivory Coast.* Princeton: Princeton University Press, 1964.

———. "Political Development in the Ivory Coast since Independence." In *Ghana and the Ivory Coast: Perspectives on Modernization,* edited by Philip Foster and Aristide R. Zolberg, 9–31. Chicago: University of Chicago Press, 1971.

UNPUBLISHED THESES AND PAPERS

Camara, Idiatou. "La Contribution de la Femme de Guinée à la Lutte de Libération Nationale (1945–1958)." Mémoire de Fin d'Études Supérieures, Conakry, IPGAN, 1979. AG, AM-1339.

Conrad, David C. "Victims, Warriors, and Power Sources: Portrayals of Women in Guinean Narratives of Samori Touré." Paper presented to the Annual Meeting of the African Studies Association, Philadelphia, PA, 13 Nov. 1999.

Mara, Sékou. "La Lutte de Libération Nationale et la Chefferie dite Coutumière en Guinée Forestière." Mémoire de Fin d'Études Supérieures. Kankan, IPJN, 1975–76. AG, MO-33.

N'Daou, Saidou Mohamed. "Almamy Samory Touré: Politics of Memories in Post-Colonial Guinea (1958–1984)." Paper presented to the Annual Meeting of the African Studies Association, Philadelphia, PA, 13 Nov. 1999.

Osborn, Emily. "Samori Touré in Upper Guinea: Hero or Tyrant?" Paper presented to the Annual Meeting of the African Studies Association, Philadelphia, PA, 13 Nov. 1999.

Toungara, Jeanne M. "Kabasarana and the Samorian Conquest of Northwestern Cote d'Ivoire." Paper presented to the Annual Meeting of the African Studies Association, Philadelphia, PA, 13 Nov. 1999.

Index

Abidjan, 50, 61, 160, 168, 217n11, 238n133, 262n54, 267n136. *See also* Ivory Coast
Action (newspaper), 36
Adamolekun, 'Ladipo, 3
Adloff, Richard, 3, 238n133
Afrique Occidentale Française (AOF). *See* French West Africa
Agence France-Presse, 92, 162
Aguibou, Barry. *See* Barry, Aguibou
Alfaya line, 243n8
Algeria, 97, 128, 137–38, 177, 181, 204n93, 264n85. *See also* Front de Libération Nationale
Allah. *See* Rassemblement Démocratique Africain, Guinean Branch: and Islam
Almamy, 69, 73, 83, 85, 98, 115, 134, 171, 243n8
Almamya, 130
aluminum/alumina/bauxite, 171, 174, 277n61
Amicale Gilbert Vieillard, 30–31, 40, 66, 69–70, 137, 228n13. *See also* regional and ethnic associations
antifederalists. *See* territorialists
Apithy, Sourou Migan, 265n93
Aribot, Fatou, 134–35, 187
armed forces, French, 13, 138, 264–65n85. *See also* veterans, African military; World War II
artisans, 43, 96, 108, 138
Asante, 257n9
Asia, 5–6, 8–9, 14, 44, 143, 180
assimilation, 18
Association des Étudiants RDA (AERDA), 127, 143. *See also* students
Association des Parents d'Élèves, 131

Atlantic Charter, 9–10, 27
autonomy, African, 11, 18, 27, 33, 101, 110, 112, 116–18, 125, 127–28, 135, 142, 156, 182, 201n64, 223n75. *See also* federalists; government, federal; government, local; loi-cadre; territorialists
Autra, Ray, 37, 39, 49, 64, 131–32, 135, 212n180, 260–61n45

Baga, 63, 247n69
balafon, 32, 149
Baldé, Chaikhou, 70
Ballay, Noël (Governor), 121, 254n168
Ballay Hospital, 86
Bamako, 160; CGT Conference (1951), 60–61; RDA Congress (1946), 25–28, 59, 127; RDA Congress (1957), 133; UGTAN Cadre Conference (1958), 269n159. *See also* Soudan, French
Bambara, 134
Bangoura, Karim, 82, 91, 155
Bangoura, Mafory, 86
Bank of France, 172
Banque de l'Afrique Occidentale (Bank of French West Africa), 167, 273n35
Baro, Mamadi, 81
Barry, Aguibou, 69, 73, 83, 171, 243
Barry, Bassamba. *See* Barry, Bassirou
Barry, Bassirou, 128–30, 258–59n27
Barry, Bocar Biro, 46, 71, 146, 149, 160, 162
Barry, Diawadou: and the BAG, 81–82, 115–16, 118; as deputy, 90–94, 119–20, 128, 130, 228n10; elite status, 69–70, 72–73, 75, 81–82, 92–94, 137, 171, 229n18;